The Creative Suffering
of God

The Creative Suffering of God

PAUL S. FIDDES

CLARENDON PRESS · OXFORD

This book has been printed digitally and produced in a standard specification
in order to ensure its continuing availability

OXFORD
UNIVERSITY PRESS

Great Clarendon Street, Oxford OX2 6DP

Oxford University Press is a department of the University of Oxford.
It furthers the University's objective of excellence in research, scholarship,
and education by publishing worldwide in

Oxford New York

Auckland Bangkok Buenos Aires Cape Town Chennai
Dar es Salaam Delhi Hong Kong Istanbul Karachi Kolkata
Kuala Lumpur Madrid Melbourne Mexico City Mumbai Nairobi
São Paulo Shanghai Singapore Taipei Tokyo Toronto

with an associated company in Berlin

Oxford is a registered trade mark of Oxford University Press
in the UK and in certain other countries

Published in the United States
by Oxford University Press Inc., New York

© Paul S. Fiddes 1988

The moral rights of the author have been asserted
Database right Oxford University Press (maker)

Reprinted 2002

ISBN 0-19-826347-3

TO MARION

Preface

TEN years ago my interest in the theme of the suffering of God led me to spend a year at the University of Tübingen, to hear it expounded by two masters in the subject, Professors Jürgen Moltmann and Eberhard Jüngel. Though I have occasion to criticize aspects of their thought in the following study, I want to make clear my debt to their theological explorations, which they undertake not only with great learning but out of a deep passion for the truth of God in our world today. They are voices (not always speaking by any means in unison, as befits prophetic voices) from the German Church, to which our religious thinkers in Britain need to give heed, perhaps even more urgently at this time than before.

I was provided with the opportunity to develop the ideas in this book by the invitation to give the Whitley Lectures for 1979–80 (delivered that year in Spurgeon's College, London, and the Northern Baptist College, Manchester), and they have been further worked out through lectures given in the Faculty of Theology at Oxford.

The reader ought perhaps to be aware of the structure of this book. It contains a survey of thought about the suffering of God in the theology of the nineteenth and twentieth centuries, with a strong emphasis upon the most recent decades. This review is not, however, presented for the most part thinker by thinker, but in the course of considering various facets of the theme of the suffering of God. I am sure that the reader, no less than the author, will want to press on beyond recording the thought of others to developing his own thought about this central theme of Christian faith, and I hope that the thematic arrangement will prompt him to do so. The reader will find that I am also constructing my own argument, throughout each section of this study, about what it can mean to claim that God suffers. I am well aware of the cautious warnings often uttered against theological speculation in our pragmatic age, and I direct worriers to the conclusion which Karl Barth gave to the first volume of his *Church Dogmatics*, ostensibly writing about Augustine, but really about himself and all who dare to be theologians:

There are theologies whose authors have no need to be worried at the end, since for good reasons the 'fulness of visions' has been spared them. Augustine was not in this happy position. He had run the risk and the 'fulness of visions' had in fact come upon him. When this risk is run, one may come to grief.[1]

From Barth, and from others in recent times whose thought I review in this study, I hope that we may all learn to take the risk of talking about God.

Regent's Park College
Oxford, 1986   P.S.F.

----

[1] Barth, *CD* I/1, p. 489.

Contents

Abbreviations

CD Karl Barth, *Church Dogmatics*, English Translation, ed. G. W. Bromiley and T. F. Torrance (T. & T. Clark, Edinburgh, 1936–77). Cited by volume number, volume part number, and page: e.g. Barth, *CD* IV/1, p. 185. References to Vol. I/1 are to the Second Edition, trans. G. W. Bromiley, 1975.

NEB *New English Bible.*

S. Th. Thomas Aquinas, *Summa Theologiae*, Blackfriars Edition (Eyre & Spottiswoode, London, 1964–).

Where works are frequently cited, they appear in the footnotes under a short title only. Full details are to be found in the Bibliography.

I

Introduction: Questioning a Familiar Theme

'THERE, but for the grace of God, goes God.' Jokes often betray deep-laid feelings, and behind this witticism (attributed to Sir Winston Churchill, among others) lies a popular, but quite complex, view of what God must be like. It recognizes the hazards of our world and hints that God too might be exposed to them. But it also assumes that God uses his power to preserve himself from becoming a victim; it supposes that God must be a supreme potentate, guarding himself from every kind of pain and destruction that befalls his subjects in the world. The word 'grace' in this witty version of the traditional saying comes close to the imperial title 'His Grace'. Theological statements throughout the history of the Church have tended to support this view of God as a self-protecting monarch, unmoving, unchanging, unsuffering. We need recall only the warning pronounced by the Council of Chalcedon in AD 451: 'The synod deposes from the priesthood those who dare to say that the Godhead of the only-begotten is passible.'[1]

But the theological situation today has changed greatly. As early as 1926 when J. K. Mozley surveyed the history of the concept of the impassibility of God, he noted a growing reaction against this doctrine.[2] Today, whatever the popular view of God outside academic theological circles might be, inside them there is a strong conviction about the suffering of God. In many quarters the idea that God suffers hardly needs to be argued for any longer. But a careful examination is needed of what it *means* to talk about the suffering of God. On the one hand, many are happy to talk of it without facing up to its full implications; they invoke the theme of a suffering God but defuse it of its explosive effect upon the whole doctrine of God as they fail to follow it through into a theology that embraces divine weakness at the centre. They are puzzled as to why classical theism brought such a weight of argument against the idea of a suffering God because they have made of it

[1] Text in J. Stevenson (ed.), *Creeds, Councils and Controversies* (SPCK, London, 1966), p. 336.
[2] J. K. Mozley, *The Impassibility of God*, pp. 127–66.

something merely sentimental. On the other hand, some conclusions are often drawn from the idea which need cautious questioning. I have in mind two in particular, concerning the weakness of God and the universal scope of God's suffering.

I. BASIC ISSUES: THE SUPREME AND UNIVERSAL SUFFERING OF GOD

One conclusion which may be drawn too quickly from the idea of a suffering God is that this inevitably means a God who is helpless and inactive in the world. Dietrich Bonhoeffer's ringing phrases in his famous letter of 16 July 1944 from a Nazi prison are often incorrectly appealed to for support of this. Bonhoeffer says that:

God lets himself be pushed out of the world on to the cross. He is weak and powerless in the world, and that is precisely the way, the only way, in which he is with us and helps us . . . The Bible directs man to God's powerlessness and suffering; only the suffering God can help.[3]

This leads one theologian, Dorothee Sölle, to conclude that Bonhoeffer's secular theology is based upon 'the helplessness of God' in the world.[4] But we notice that Bonhoeffer does not speak of a helpless and absent God, but of a God who is without power in the sense of what the world— and all too often traditional theology—calls power. So he goes on to say:

[This] opens up a way of seeing the God of the Bible, who wins power and space in the world by his weakness.[5]

Thus we must attempt to think coherently about a God who is suffering and weak, and yet who remains recognizably God within the Christian tradition of strength through weakness. We must try to think of a God who can be the greatest sufferer of all and yet still be God. Someone might well ask why we should place such a premium upon coherence; might it not be better to have a fragmentary theology which recognizes the mystery in our experience of God? While accepting the limits of all human talk about God, we must I believe face the challenge of those who find the notion of a suffering God to be inadequate as a basis for religious belief. Such an objection need not only come from classical

---

[3] Dietrich Bonhoeffer, *Letters and Papers From Prison*, pp. 360–1.
[4] Dorothee Sölle, *Christ the Representative*, p. 150.
[5] Bonhoeffer, op. cit., p. 361.

theists. It can also come from a surprisingly different quarter, from those who find any notion of an objectively existing God to be a fatal blow against human freedom. Recently, for example, Don Cupitt has argued that human autonomy cannot be rescued by replacing belief in a cosmic monarch by belief in God as the fellow-sufferer with humanity, since this concept destroys the value of God as a religious ideal: 'The god of the modern patripassian believer is nothing but Humanity . . . He is merely the tears and fellow feeling of humanity. There is no salvation in him.'[6] We must then attempt to make coherent a notion of a God who suffers and yet remains a God who can fulfil his purposes.

A second conclusion often drawn from the idea of a suffering God is that if God suffers supremely and universally in this way, he cannot also suffer uniquely in the cross of Jesus. For example, Frances Young has recently argued that if God were present in the suffering of the cross in a way which was at all different from his presence in all men's sufferings, then 'On such a view the reality of God's involvement in other instances of profound tragedy may be overshadowed by the story of the cross rather than illuminated by it.' Rather, she urges, the cross must be taken simply as the 'classic case' of God's presence in the midst of human sin, suffering, and death.[7] But we must ask whether the conviction that God is present in the suffering and death of all human beings is in fact incompatible with the notion that God suffered uniquely and decisively in the death of Jesus. If we can coherently speak of a *particular* suffering of God in the context of a *universal* suffering, this itself might contribute some meaning to the traditional concept of an incarnation of God in Christ.

One obvious response to the challenge of reconciling a universal and a particular suffering of God would be to weaken the meaning of the suffering of God altogether.[8] But the task I hope to confront in this book is to speak consistently of *a God who suffers eminently and yet is still God, and a God who suffers universally and yet is still present uniquely and decisively in the sufferings of Christ.*

This double task might be summed up by critical reflection upon a story which has been often quoted and diversely used. A survivor from the Nazi concentration camp at Auschwitz, Elie Wiesel, relates in his

[6] Don Cupitt, *Taking Leave of God*, pp. 112–13.

[7] Frances Young, 'God Suffered and Died', in M. Goulder (ed.), *Incarnation and Myth: The Debate Continued* (SCM Press, London, 1979), pp. 102–3.

[8] See, for example, the response of B. Mitchell to the 'Myth of God Incarnate' debate, in *Incarnation and Myth*, p. 240.

book *Night* how one day the SS guards hanged two Jewish men and a young boy in front of the whole camp. The men died quickly, but the child did not:

'Where is God? Where is He? someone behind me asked. . . . But the third rope was still moving; being so light, the child was still alive.

For more than half an hour he stayed there, struggling between life and death, dying in slow agony under our eyes. And we had to look him full in the face. . . .

Behind me, I heard the same man asking: 'Where is God now?' And I heard a voice within me answer him: 'Where is He? here He is—He is hanging here on this gallows. . . .'[9]

This last phrase makes a fitting counterpoint to the epigram with which we began. There indeed 'goes God' *in* his grace; there goes God, as Barth says, 'into the far country'.[10] But in what sense is God there, hanging on the gallows? As related by J. Moltman in his book *The Crucified God*, this story means that 'God has made the suffering of the world his own in the cross of his son'.[11] It is because God suffered death in the cross of Jesus Christ that all the history of the suffering of the world is taken up into God, so that what the survivor said is true in a 'real, transferred sense'. Moltmann speaks of the cross of Jesus as the 'beginning' of the Trinitarian history of the suffering of God, which will end with the new creation and which includes such events as the gallows of Auschwitz. So it is clear that Moltmann does not want to speak of the cross as simply the classic case of this ongoing history. Somehow, he suggests, it is the beginning of God's history of universal suffering, so that 'the Trinitarian God-event on the cross *becomes* the history of God' (my italics).[12] Unfortunately, as well shall we see shortly, Moltmann does not altogether make clear how this might be so.

In complete contrast, when Dorothee Sölle relates this same story in

---

[9] Elie Wiesel, *Night*, trans. S. Rodway (Penguin Books, Harmondsworth, 1981), pp. 76–7. K. Surin, in his recent book *Theology and the Problem of Evil* (Basil Blackwell, Oxford, 1986), pp. 116–32, now also refers to this incident and comments on the use made of it by J. Moltmann and D. Sölle. Surin's book appeared while this present study was in the press, and I regret that I have not been able to take account of it here or elsewhere.   [10] Barth, *CD* IV/1, p. 185.

[11] Jürgen Moltmann, *The Crucified God*, pp. 277–8, cf. pp. 252, 255. Similarly, Ulrich Simon finds that 'God has entered history in the sacrifice of Jesus', and this made it possible to transform death at Auschwitz into sacrifice too: see U. Simon, *A Theology of Auschwitz* (1967, repr. SPCK, London, 1978), pp. 84–5.

[12] Moltmann, op. cit., p. 255.

her book *Suffering*, she concludes that it denies any unique suffering of Christ and that it also expresses the helplessness of the suffering God. The suffering of Christ, she asserts, cannot be claimed as either more intense or of a different kind from the suffering of the boy on the gallows. Indeed, in our own industrial society 'A fifty-year-old woman piece worker hangs on the cross no less than Jesus—only longer.'[13] We recall a similar comment from Samuel Beckett's tramps in his play *Waiting for Godot*, comparing themselves to Christ: 'But where he lived it was warm, it was dry! . . . Yes. And they crucified quick.'[14] Further, Sölle concludes that since (in her view) a suffering God has no power in the world, the only effective presence of God is in such human beings as the boy on the gallows; it is they who do God's work by affecting us and moving us towards true humanity. They are the representatives of the absent and hidden God, and they alone are the ones who can change us. They must be the hands of the helpless God; this is what it means to say, 'Here He is—He is hanging here on this gallows.'[15]

This profound application of the story is in accord with much recent Jewish reflection upon the suffering of the concentration camps, including that of the original narrator, Elie Wiesel, who speaks of his experience as having 'murdered my God and my soul, and turned my dreams to dust.[16] In the face of this, we must think very carefully if we want to claim that the suffering of Jesus in the cross was of such a unique kind that it is somehow the basis for a continuous suffering of God in the pain of the world, a suffering which is the mode of his presence rather than his absence. We should be able to identify some of the issues involved more clearly if we take as a test case the attempt of one theologian, Jürgen Moltmann, to make this sort of statement.

2. THE PROBLEM OF UNIQUENESS: AN ILLUSTRATION FROM RECENT THEOLOGY

Jürgen Moltmann intends to affirm that the universal suffering of God relies in some way upon the cross of Jesus, and his successive writings

[13] Dorothee Sölle, *Suffering*, p. 146.
[14] Samuel Beckett, *Waiting for Godot* (Faber and Faber, London, [2]1965), p. 52.
[15] Sölle, *Suffering*, pp. 148–9.
[16] Wiesel, op. cit., (n. 9 above), p. 45. A similar protest is made by Richard L. Rubenstein, *After Auschwitz: Radical Theology and Contemporary Judaism* (Bobbs-Merrill, Indianapolis, 1966).

display (though often, perhaps, unintentionally) a search for a theological vocabulary with which to express this belief. As we have already noticed, in his second major work *The Crucified God*, he speaks of the cross as the 'beginning' of the Trinitarian history of the suffering of God.[17] He expands this notion by claiming that by the death of Christ all human suffering is 'taken up' into God,[18] so that the suffering of Christ 'contains' the whole uproar of the history of human suffering:

There is no suffering which in this history of God is not God's suffering; no death which has not been God's death in the history on Golgotha.[18]

Moltmann evidently wants to declare that the particular death of Jesus was more than a *disclosure* of the continual love of God, though of course it was at least that.[20] In his view it was also the critical point in the contact of God with human suffering in general, and somehow even assists the participation of God in all human suffering now. I shall be attempting to state and justify these convictions too. But the question is whether they can be explained in an illuminating way by using such terms as a 'beginning' of a divine history of suffering, and a 'containing' of all human suffering, in the cross of Jesus.

When we ask how Moltmann thinks the cross could be this kind of event, we find his answer to be that in the cross God 'constitutes himself' as suffering love, a concept which Moltmann is still using in his later book *The Trinity and the Kingdom of God*.[21] That is, he believes that the historic event of the death of Christ creates a new situation for the being of the Trinitarian God, since in the forsakenness of Christ God encounters a suffering which is nothing less than a breach in the fellowship of divine life between Father and Son. Again we should enquire what Moltmann is really after in describing the event like this, and perhaps it amounts to the claim that the cross can only be of truly universal effect in human life if it has had some effect upon the being of God. If this is indeed Moltmann's point, I believe he is basically right; God himself is the objective link between the particular and the

---

[17] Moltmann, *The Crucified God*, p. 255; cf. id., 'The Trinitarian History of God', repr. in his collection *The Future of Creation*, p. 82.

[18] Moltmann, *The Crucified God*, pp. 246, 255, 277.   [19] Ibid., p. 246.

[20] Moltmann can, however, slip back and forth between talk of the cross as *determining* and *revealing* the divine suffering, as if these ideas were simply synonymous with each other: see Jürgen Moltmann, *The Trinity and the Kingdom of God*, p. 83, cf. pp. 118–19.

[21] Moltmann, *The Crucified God*, pp. 244, 245; *The Trinity and the Kingdom of God*, pp. 82–3.

universal in human experience because he is present in both. This was the strength of the traditional 'objective' theories of the Atonement, though their weakness lay in the *kind* of effect they envisaged the cross as creating upon the being of God, understanding it as a matter of satisfying his justice. In our present study, the clearer a concept we can achieve of what it means for human suffering to have an impact upon the being of God at all, the more we will be able to see the links between particular events of suffering and the universal human predicament. But to speak of the impact of the cross as 'constituting' God's being as suffering love is surely misleading; there is a perplexing impression being given—taken together with the former language of a 'beginning'—that constituting means instituting. Yet as Moltmann himself insists in the same breath, the eternal nature of God is self-emptying love: 'He is love. His very existence is love. He constitutes himself as love. That is what happens on the cross.'[22] How then shall we relate these last two phrases to each other?

Clearly, if God suffers universally, we cannot speak of the being of God as first becoming suffering love at the cross. God must always have been so. A familiarity with the old query as to what God was doing for mankind before the cross must not breed contempt for the question, since the last two millennia are, after all, only a piece of the total human story. In his earlier book *The Crucified God*, Moltmann himself appeals with enthusiasm to the Old Testament and later Jewish beliefs that God was already suffering in the humiliation of his covenant people Israel. In his more recent books *The Trinity and the Kingdom of God* and *God in Creation* he traces the story of the suffering of God back to the very act of creation *ex nihilo*. How then could we combine this with talk of God's constituting himself as love *in* the cross, and the cross as the beginning of the Trinitarian history of suffering? How shall we relate the particular history of God's Trinitarian suffering in the cross to the aeons of past history? At this point some theologians appeal to the notion of the timelessness of God to solve matters, as if a unique event at one moment in time could simply be understood as eternally contemporary in God. Hasty appeals are often made to the text of John of Patmos that he saw 'a lamb slain from the foundation of the world', and vague appeals are made to eternity as a kind of theological trump card. On the whole Moltmann resists this deceptively easy move, since his understanding of God as the God of promise in history requires some concept of

---

[22] *The Trinity and the Kingdom of God*, p. 82.

temporality in God, even if his time is not exactly like ours.[23] Here again I believe that Moltmann's basic instincts are right, and I shall be attempting to defend the idea of a God who suffers in time.

Though, curiously, Moltmann never directly draws attention to the problem of particularity, we notice that he has in fact been gradually moving away from describing the decisiveness of the cross in terms of a 'beginning' or 'constituting' of the being of God as suffering love. In the first place, he maintains that the Trinitarian God was 'opening himself' to the world from eternity in preparation for the cross; astonishingly, however, in a couple of places Moltmann can still blend this insight with reference to pain itself as a 'new experience' for God at the cross.[24] A second answer Moltmann gives seems much more satisfactory, though even less compatible with the language of a 'beginning'; he makes occasional mention of something like a 'completion' of God's self-humiliation in the cross of Jesus.[25] If he is affirming that God's perpetual suffering was intensified and deepened in the event of the cross (though the term 'completion' does not seem altogether apt), then he is surely pointing to the only valid way in which we can conceive of the death of Jesus as being a unique event of divine suffering.[26] This again is a claim I intend to explore in this study.

But this in turn raises a further question: in what sense is the suffering of God at the cross more intense than elsewhere or heretofore? Moltmann's earlier talk about a 'beginning' of a Trinitarian history of suffering at the cross has perhaps created a momentum in his thinking here, since he draws a rather sharp distinction between the suffering of God which results from dwelling with his people Israel, and the suffering involved in dwelling in his Son, Jesus Christ. The new thing

---

    23 Jürgen Moltmann, *God in Creation*, p. 117. But see his *Trinity and the Kingdom of God*, p. 81 (cf. p. 83), where he speaks of Golgotha as 'putting its impress upon the trinitarian life in eternity'.

    24 Jürgen Moltmann, *The Church in the Power of the Spirit*, pp. 62–3; also id., 'The Trinitarian History of God' (n. 17 above), p. 92. For the idea generally, see Moltmann, *The Trinity and the Kingdom of God*, pp. 74, 96, and *God in Creation*, pp. 90–1.

    25 Moltmann, *The Crucified God*, p. 276; *The Trinity and the Kingdom of God*, p. 118. Similar are references to the cross as a 'concentration' of God's self-revelation and as 'a consolidation of the universe': see *God in Creation*, pp. 59, 91.

    26 Cf. C. S. Song, *Third-Eye Theology: Theology in Formation in Asian Settings* (Lutterworth Press, 1980), p.74: 'In Jesus Christ we encounter God's love in its most intense concentration'; however, he also describes the suffering of God in the cross as 'the place where a new creation *begins*' (p. 54), and appeals to Wiesel's story of the hanged boy as witness that 'the cross is our suffering *become* God's suffering' (p. 166, my italics) without facing the question of uniqueness.

about the passion of God in the cross of Jesus, maintains Moltmann, was his entering into the human experience of death, in its most dreadful sense of God-forsakenness. This is why the cross represents such a deadly disturbance in the relations between the divine persons in the Trinity. While beforehand God had certainly participated in the stresses of suffering humanity, here he himself experienced the human death of abandonment by God that sin produces, and thereby opened a way into fellowship with himself for all the abandoned and rejected of the world.[27] There is a sequence here in God's suffering presence in the world which Moltmann also expresses as a contrast between the *kenosis* (self-emptying) of the Spirit universally, and the singular *kenosis* of the Logos.[28] In his most recent work, Moltmann describes God as only finally and at the cross exposing himself to that annihilating Nothingness against which he had affirmed the world at creation.[29] This is in line, however, with Moltmann's earlier hints that while the many dwellings of God in (Jewish) history can be called an 'entering' into human suffering, it is only at the cross that God actually 'adopts' human experience into his own being, so that he now suffers 'infinite pain'. Thus, in the cross:

God *becomes* the God who identifies himself with men and women to the point of death and beyond.[30]

So Moltmann searches, in these various and sometimes vague ways, for a vocabulary of uniqueness. Yet surely this account of the particular suffering of God in the cross will not do. If God has always been really dwelling with people in their suffering, then he must have been having the same *kind* of experience which Moltmann attributes to the cross, including the human predicament of death and forsakenness. If we profess a Trinitarian theology, then there must always be room for this experience in God, within the relationships of the Father and the Son. Anything less would indeed denigrate the presence of God in other occasions of human suffering. Rightly does J. Mackey protest that from the very first moment of creation God was encountering death.[31] While Moltmann has recently speculated that God enabled Nothingness to emerge as the 'primordial space' for creation by an act of divine self-

---

[27] Moltmann, *The Crucified God*, pp. 276–7; *The Trinity and the Kingdom of God*, pp. 118–19, 81, 83, 234 n. 34.

[28] Moltmann, *God in Creation*, p. 102.   [29] Ibid., pp. 90–3.

[30] Moltmann, *The Trinity and the Kingdom of God*, p. 119 (my italics) and p. 80.

[31] James P. Mackey, *The Christian Experience of God as Trinity*, p. 261.

limitation, he does not apparently conceive of God entering that void of Nothingness himself until the cross. However, our task must surely be to discover how to express a new *degree* of suffering within God at the cross, which is at the same time both a climax and a new stage in the relationship of God with his creation. We are to speak of a God whose eternal desire to share in the life of his world reaches a supreme expression at the cross, in a way which opens up yet still new depths of relationship. We must try to speak of God's new experience not as immersion into death and non-being for the first time, but of a deeper death leading to a richer life.

We have not yet come to the end of the questions usefully raised by Moltmann's insistence upon the critical place of the cross in the history of the suffering of God. If we grant that the cross is the most dense concentration of the suffering of God, it still remains to enquire what the causative link between this and all future events of divine suffering might be. Given a uniqueness about the suffering of God in this one historic event, how can it have an effect upon other, later events? I have already suggested that we must look, for an ultimate answer, towards the effect upon the being of God himself, and we shall be doing so in this study. The way that Moltmann puts the claim, in accord with his language of 'containment', is that all human sufferings can be said to be in God because they are 'in' the death of Christ. But what can this possibly mean? We might of course direct the same question at the Apostle Paul, with his preaching of our being 'in Christ', and it is the task of theology to ask such awkward questions of doxological statements. One kind of answer is the one which Moltmann supplies early on in his writings on the theme: people who suffer can voluntarily *take* their place within the being of God because God has suffered in the cross. They can respond to the love of God and find hope in God's future because they can recognize their own situation of suffering as belonging to God as well. In Moltmann's formulation, they can find themselves at home in the 'event' of relationships which is God: '. . . the Father delivers up his Son on the cross in order to be the Father of those who are delivered up'.[32] This certainly links the particular to the universal, but we should not miss the point that the universalizing feature here is subjective human response. Moreover, this sequence of thought in itself does not actually require God to suffer in all human suffering, but only for all who suffer to recognize *some* suffering in God.

---

[32] Moltmann, *The Crucified God*, p. 243, cf. pp. 246–8.

In his book *The Crucified God*, Moltmann does in fact seem to play down a universal suffering of God, in stressing the particular event of forsakenness in the cross. In later work, Moltmann speaks more clearly of being able to recognize God as suffering everywhere once we have seen him suffering in the cross of Jesus: 'Anyone who perceives God's presence and love in the God-forsakenness of the crucified Son, sees God in all things.'[33]

These answers are of course highly illuminating. Because God has suffered in the cross we can recognize our suffering as being akin to God's, and we can recognize his suffering elsewhere. But they do not seem to do full justice to the objective, consequential link between the one event of the cross and other human passion stories, which is implied in Moltmann's image of our sufferings being 'contained' in the cross of Jesus. Nor is the link adequately made by a further insight offered by Moltmann in his recent study *God in Creation*. Here he suggests that the resurrection of the crucified Jesus gives such an anticipation of the new creation that not only believers, but also the divine Spirit himself, are made the more conscious of present suffering. He now speaks of the Spirit who suffers immanently in creation as being 'awakened' to a (greater?) sighing and yearning in sympathy with unredeemed nature.[34] Such a scheme does depict one event in history as amplifying the continuing suffering of God in the world, but the effective event here is not the past suffering of the cross; it is the resurrection, with its protest against present reality from the perspective of the future. In this account, moreover, the universal divine suffering in the person of the Spirit is curiously dissociated from the particular suffering of the Son. (We have already noticed something similar with regard to Moltmann's idea of *kenosis*.) At this point, I suggest, we ought to admit straightaway that the imagery of the cross as 'containing' all suffering, or all suffering being 'taken up' into the cross, cannot be taken literally. However, the direction in which it points in a shorthand way is towards our participating in the life of God himself, and towards the cross as playing a decisive role in the way that God participates in our suffering. It is these affirmations, which Moltmann clearly wants to make, which are not satisfied by talk of recognizing suffering in God, and which cannot be bolstered by a merely emotive appeal to the cross as 'containing' all

[33] Moltmann, *The Trinity and the Kingdom of God*, p. 82.

[34] Moltmann, *God in Creation*, pp. 67–9. This adds a note of divine suffering to Moltmann's previous account of the resurrection as contradicting our present situation, as in his *Theology of Hope*, pp. 196–7.

human suffering. If perception were all, it could simply be an accident of
our culture and tradition that we happen to 'see' the suffering of God
uniquely in the cross.

Thus there is a curious blend of two elements in Moltmann's account:
on the one hand God is affirmed as suffering a very particular death
indeed on the cross, a disruption amounting to 'hell' in the divine life,
but on the other hand this apparently affects his suffering with *us* only in
terms of our noticing it. The difficulty Moltmann has in expressing the
link between Christ's Golgotha and ours today is of a piece with his
uneasiness about linking the cross to the suffering of God in earlier
history. The two questions with which we began this discussion, about
the uniqueness of the cross and the reality of God's presence in the
world, belong together: if we can begin to understand the way in which
God's suffering in one instance of history has an effect upon his suffering
in all others, then we shall be able to take seriously the suffering of the
God of the cross at all times and in all places. Moltmann himself seems to
realize this when he says that 'the Father who sends his Son through all
the abysses and hells of God-forsakenness . . . has become universally
present',[35] though we must add, 'present not for the first time but in a
new way'.

3.   FOUR MAJOR CONTRIBUTIONS TO THE PRESENT DEBATE

I have spent some time analysing Moltmann's approach to these questions, not only because it is regrettably easier to see the limits in
another's attempts to touch in the outlines of a mystery than to speak of
a mystery oneself. Moltmann has made some of the most profound
explorations into the meaning of divine suffering in contemporary
theology, and at many places in what follows we shall need to measure
our pace against his. But I am also referring to Moltmann as representing one strand of recent thought about the suffering of God, the *Kreuzestheologie* in Germany, which we can appropriately paraphrase as
'Theology *from* the Cross', and which has been expounded by both Protestant and Catholic theologians during the last two decades.[36]

---

[35] Moltman, *The Trinity and the Kingdom of God*, p. 82; cf. *God in Creation*, p. 91.

[36] We may perhaps find this way of thinking first identified as a distinct movement
by an ecumenical Conference held at Grafrath in October 1972, on the theme
'Kreuzestheologie'. This was reported, and significant papers printed, in *Evangelische
Theologie*, 33 (1973); see especially the review by H. G. Link, 'Zur Kreuzestheologie:
Gegenwärtige Probleme einer Kreuzestheologie. Ein Bericht', pp. 337–45. Major

The strength of this attempt to think through the nature of God as revealed by the cross of Jesus has been to take God's participation in human history with the utmost seriousness. Owing much to Luther's 'theology of the cross' and building upon Barth's theology of the humility of God, this modern version of *Kreuzestheologie* has also been constantly in dialogue with Hegel, blending criticism with a new admiration of his attempt to speak of God's encounter with nothingness and death in the midst of the worldly sphere. In fact, we might trace some of Moltmann's own problems to his ambiguous appraisal of Hegel. In his earliest work he had been concerned to defend a view of history as the place where God's promises are revealed, and so had opposed any notion of the divine passion as a dialectical process pervading all reality; the location of divine suffering was firmly outside the walls of Jerusalem in the first century.[37] Yet the more that Moltmann wants to speak of a universal suffering, the more he needs to have a view of process as well as particularity, and the more favourably he speaks of Hegel's dialectic of life.[38] This points to a weakness in the approach of *Kreuzestheologie* in general—a lack of a proper theology of creation, perhaps influenced by the long-standing worries over natural theology within Lutheran thought (even though Moltmann himself stands in the Reformed tradition). In struggling to find a vision of the whole process of creation, Hegel is not adequate as a theological sparring partner on his own. This

contributions have been made by H. Urs Von Balthasar and H. Mühlen in Catholic theology and in Protestant theology by E. Jüngel, H.-G. Geyer and J. Moltmann. See H. Urs Von Balthasar, 'Mysterium Paschale', in J. Feiner and M. Löhrer (eds.), *Mysterium Salutis: Grundriss heilsgeschichtlicher Dogmatik* III, 2 (Benziger Verlag, Einsideln, 1969), pp. 133–326; Heribert Mühlen, *Die abendländische Seinsfrage* and *Die Veränderlichkeit Gottes*; Eberhard Jüngel, 'Vom Tod des lebendigen Gottes. Ein Plakat', *Zeitschrift für Theologie und Kirche*, 65 (1968), pp. 93–116, repr. in *Unterwegs zur Sache*, Beiträge zur evangelischen Theologie, 61 (Chr. Kaiser, Munich, 1972), pp. 105–25 (page references henceforth to this edition), and *God as the Mystery of the World*; H.-G. Geyer, 'Atheismus und Christentum', *Evangelische Theologie*, 30 (1970), pp. 255–74; Jürgen Moltmann, *The Crucified God* and *The Trinity and the Kingdom of God*. All modern thought along these lines is heavily indebted to Karl Barth, e.g. *CD* IV/1, para. 59 and II/2, para. 33. A useful symposium of debate prompted by Moltmann's account of 'Kreuzestheologie' is *Diskussion über Jürgen Moltmanns Buch 'Der gekreuzigte Gott'*, herausg. Michael Welker (Chr. Kaiser, Munich, 1979).

[37] See Moltmann, *Theology of Hope*, pp. 171–2.

[38] See e.g. *The Future of Creation*, p. 82; *The Crucified God*, p. 246. Cf. *God in Creation*, p. 77: 'God wants in his work to recognize himself'. On this point, see the analysis of Christopher Morse, *The Logic of Promise in Moltmann's Theology* (Fortress Press, Philadelphia, 1979), pp. 117–26.

trend even continues in the latest major study by Moltmann, *God in Creation*, which is an unusual German Protestant venture upon a theology of nature. Moltmann now describes the divine Spirit as working through evolutionary development, opening up closed systems by offering new possibilities with a patience which is nothing less than suffering. But he still fails to recognize, as we shall see, that this process implies a situation of shared creativity between God and the world.[39]

This brings us to a second major strand of theological thought about the suffering of God in the contemporary scene, American 'process philosophy'. The strength of this system (which originated with the former Cambridge philosopher A. N. Whitehead, but which has failed to find much fertile ground in Britain) has been to form a theology of nature. Within a wide-ranging vision of a world in which each participant in life is bound in a network of mutual influences with all others, process theologians have been able to think of God as creating from inside the community of the world rather than from outside, so that divine suffering is central to divine action.[40] Since the lack in process thought is exactly the strength of *Kreuzestheologie*, namely a reflection upon the particularities of history, there is an evident need to bring together the insights from these two traditions.

A third thread of modern thought relevant to the idea of the suffering of God may by now seem to be too worn bare to be called contemporary any longer—that is, the 'death of God' theology that had its peak of popularity two decades ago.[41] But this movement is still of great significance for our discussion, taking up as it did the word of Hegel and Nietzsche that 'God is dead' which has also intrigued the advocates of *Kreuzestheologie*. Indeed, the German theologians were prompted by

---

[39] Moltmann, *God in Creation*, pp. 205–6, 210–12. He rejects the insights of Process thought as confusing creation with preservation (ibid., p. 76). For an expansion of my criticism, see below pp. 85–6, 137.

[40] For a summary of process thought, see below pp. 40–5. The seminal writings were those by Alfred North Whitehead and his erstwhile pupil Charles Hartshorne, and in this study I shall be giving particular attention to the following: A. N. Whitehead, *Religion in the Making*, *Process and Reality*, and *Adventures of Ideas*; Charles Hartshorne, *Man's Vision of God*, *The Divine Relativity*, and *A Natural Theology for our Time*. More recent contributions we shall be considering include writings by John B. Cobb, Daniel Day Williams, Schubert Ogden, Norman Pittenger, David R. Griffin, and Lewis S. Ford. Useful introductions to Process thought are: Peter Hamilton, *The Living God and the Modern World* (Hodder and Stoughton, London, 1967); N. Pittenger, *Process Thought and Christian Faith*; J. B. Cobb and D. R. Griffin, *Process Theology*. A history of the movement is provided by James R. Gray, *Modern Process Thought: A Brief Ideological History* (University Press of America, Washington, 1982), though Gray underplays the place of Charles Hartshorne.   [41] See Chapter 7 below, *passim*.

the challenge of the American movement to develop their cross-centred theology, giving the phrase 'death of God' a more Lutheran meaning, and coping with the assertion that God is dead by replying that the dictatorial God of much traditional theology was indeed dead, but that the God who experienced death in the cross is very much alive in our world. Process theology had already similarly criticized classical theism in the name of a suffering God. The 'death of God' movement itself is not without its heirs today, who have dropped the catchword but who have the same concern to face up to what they feel is the irrelevance to our modern culture of the notion of an objectively existing personal God. In this study we must ask how adequately we can meet that challenge with the concept of a suffering God, as well as seeing what insights about death and suffering came from the earlier discussion.

Meanwhile a fourth strand of contemporary thought remains constantly within the weave, though its colouring is at present a little subdued. There are the heirs of so-called classical theism, especially in English theology, who still have considerable objections to the notion of a suffering God, and feel that the present enthusiasm for this image of God has not taken the problems seriously enough. They are often offended by what they feel to be parodies of an apathetic and aloof God attributed to the Fathers and Scholastics of the Church. In this study we must give their protests a fair hearing, for their questions prevent a merely sentimental attachment to belief in a suffering God.

In taking the familiar theme of a suffering God seriously, we must review the contribution of these four modern movements of thought (among others), and see what fruitful interactions there are between them. In particular, I hope to show that the insights of process theology can be usefully modified by thoughts about the freedom of God expressed by a theologian who was a precursor and inspiration of the new movement for *Kreuzestheologie*—Karl Barth. While some recent discussion has presented Barth and process thinkers as exclusive alternatives for theology,[42] they are in fact closer fellows in thought than might appear from Barth's renunciation of natural theology. A theology of a suffering God needs to weave all four of these strands into a pattern, or to use another image, it must stand where four ways cross.

---

[42] See for example Colin E. Gunton, *Becoming and Being: The Doctrine of God in Charles Hartshorne and Karl Barth* (Oxford University Press, 1978), pp. 220 ff. However, John J. O'Donnell presents a more sympathetic view of common ground between successors of these two traditions, Ogden and Moltmann, in *Trinity and Temporality: The Christian Doctrine of God in the Light of Process Theology and the Theology of Hope* (Oxford University Press, 1983), pp. 167 ff.

2

Why Believe in a Suffering God?

THE belief that God is a suffering God has become compelling for recent theology. Centuries of traditional belief about the impassibility and the immutability of God have been overturned in our age, though a few pioneers signalled this revolution in our concept of God during the upheavals of nineteenth century thought.[1] We might detect four main reasons for this remarkable (though not universal) change in mind in Christendom, and although we shall be mainly occupied in this chapter with reviewing the ways in which recent theology has come to its convictions about a suffering God, these indicate four themes that will reappear throughout our study.

I.   THE MEANING OF THE LOVE OF GOD

Christian theologians have been required to reflect upon the meaning of God's love for the world in the light of a modern psychological understanding of what it means to be personal. Truly personal love, it has been emphasized, will involve the suffering of the one who loves; the world being what it is, love must be costly and sacrificial, if only in terms of mental pain. Sympathy must be taken in its literal sense of *sympatheia*—'suffering-with'. This is because love is the sharing of experience, so that 'concrete awareness of another's suffering can . . . only consist in participation in that suffering' (Charles Hartshorne).[2] This affirmation may by supported from another angle; love means at least a communication between persons, a self-expression of one to another in a way that creates true community, and this also will involve suffering. For we do not only communicate conceptually and verbally; suffering for and with another is a language which

---

[1] Notable pioneers were Horace Bushnell, *Vicarious Sacrifice* (Alexander Strahan, London, 1866), Ch. 2, and James Hinton (a medical doctor), *The Mystery of Pain* (London, 1866), Ch. 4.
[2] Hartshorne, *A Natural Theology for Our Time*, p. 105.

penetrates more deeply than words, and in a situation where community has broken down it is often the only kind of language that can restore communication. This idea of suffering love as the power for making relationships is widely expressed today in cultures of both East and West. The American process theologian, Daniel Day Williams, suggested that 'suffering's greatest work is to become the vehicle of human expression', and so 'God is revealed in Jesus' suffering because in him suffering is the authentic expression and communication of love'.[3] From the standpoint of Asian theology, C. S. Song berates some Western theologians for being too concerned for communication in rational speech, and for not paying enough heed to the intuitive levels of communication that are often expressed in terms of pain and suffering.[4]

Now, if God is not less than personal, and if the claim that 'God is love' is to have any recognizable continuity with our normal experience of love, the conclusion seems inescapable that a loving God must be a sympathetic and therefore suffering God. Traditional theology has nevertheless escaped that conclusion, by regarding love as an attitude and action of *goodwill* towards another person. True love, it has been argued, is to will and achieve the good of another, and has nothing to do with feelings. Augustine, for example, distinguished between emotions and moral actions as far as the perfect love of God is concerned: 'His pity is not the wretched heart of a fellow-sufferer . . . the pity of God is the goodness of his help . . . when God pities, he does not grieve and he liberates.'[5] The key thought here is that 'affects are effects' for God: he is not affected in his feelings by our sufferings, but he effects relief for us. Various refinements were added to this dictum in classical theism. Anselm suggested that while God's mercy is not actually compassionate (in the sense of suffering sorrow with us), it seems to us *as if* God were compassionate when we receive the effects of his mercy in our experience; in fact, confesses Anselm, 'if You are impassible, you do not have any compassion'.[6] Calvin in his later version of this argument is less subtle, though perhaps more comprehensible, in maintaining that when scripture speaks of God's grief and compassion for his people this

---

[3] Daniel Day Williams, *The Spirit and the Forms of Love*, pp. 183, 167. He aptly cites Rom. 5:8.

[4] Song, op. cit. (ch. 1, n. 26), pp. 41–8, 74–7.

[5] Augustine, *Contra Adversarium Legis et Prophetarum* 1. 40 (trans. Mozley, *The Impassibility of God*, pp. 106–7.)

[6] Anselm, *Proslogion*, Ch. 8 (trans. M. J. Charlesworth, Clarendon Press, Oxford, 1965, p. 125).

is a figure of speech which accommodates to our understanding, 'in order to move us more powerfully and draw us to himself'.[7] Aquinas made his contribution to the argument by asserting that love, like joy but unlike sadness or anger, can be simply an act of the will and the intellect. Love can be ascribed to God as a purely intellectual appetite.[8]

It may be seem to us that the classical theologians made a great deal of heavy weather of excluding feelings or emotions of compassion from God. But we must take due note of their insight that to be *affected* by others is to be *changed* by others; this is why they were so anxious to deny compassion in God, and if we are going to affirm it we must be prepared to accept the consequence from which they shrank. We shall be facing this in the next chapter. For the moment it might be sufficient riposte to observe that a doing of good without any fellow-feeling for the person being done good to, is precisely the attitude that is widely condemned today under the unlovely catch-word 'do-gooding'. An exclusive dwelling upon God's love as a 'doing good' without a 'feeling pain' also runs into the problem of restricting God's love for the world. For the scope of suffering in the world makes clear that God's equal love for all does not issue at present in all equally being done-good to. There does not then seem to be much meaning in the statement that God expresses his love towards all, if this love is to be restricted to creative beneficence. This problem has been sharpened by contemporary Black Theology, which observes that there are particular groups of people such as black people who as a whole group, and not just as random individuals, have been done less good to than others. Black theologians are often less concerned with the problem of suffering itself than the distribution of suffering so heavily among black people. This leads James Cone, for example, to conclude that only the fact that God *suffers* with black people makes the question 'Is God a white racist?' absurd.[9]

The importance of shared feelings within the nature of love is illustrated, contrary to the author's intention, in a recent study attacking this connection. R. E. Creel follows the classical theologians in

---

[7] Calvin, *Commentary on Isaiah* 63: 9, cf. 'Not that he can in any way endure anguish' (trans. W. Pringle for the Calvin Translation Society, Edinburgh, 1853, pp. 346–7).

[8] Thomas Aquinas, *S. Th.* 1a. 20, 1: 'Loving, enjoying and delighting are emotions when they signify activities of the sensitive appetite; not so, however, when they signify activities of intelligent appetite. It is in this last sense that they are attributed to God . . . he loves without passion.' Blackfriars Edition, Vol. 5, p. 57.

[9] James H. Cone, *God of the Oppressed* (SPCK, London, 1967), pp. 163, 166–7, 184–8. So the suffering of God in Christ is an active presence, making it possible to struggle for liberation (pp. 192–3).

recognizing that to suffer in one's feelings entails being changed by an outside force, and he therefore argues for an emotional impassibility in God.[10] Urging that perfect love for another need not involve sympathy, he invites us to agree that we admire a person who 'works diligently and intelligently against poverty, injustice and loneliness in his society, yet who is equally happy whether he meets success or defeat'. Further, he argues that there can be no logical connection between suffering and love, appealing to his own observation that a loving mother does not (in his view) participate emotionally in the distress of her child when she knows the child to be frightened by only an imagined danger. So, he maintains, 'we cannot rule out the possibility that God knows something about our destiny that renders it inappropriate for him to be disturbed by our suffering in this life'.[11] Although this is a philosophical case for suffering as being finally instrumental for good, we ought not to miss the point that Creel's arguments depend quite largely upon our being convinced by the way he observes and interprets the human experience of love. Such observations as those I have quoted above are, I suggest, simply inaccurate; the examples themselves show that he misses the whole dimension of suffering as a necessary form of communication between persons, whether between parent and and child or social worker and client. This also applies to his more fundamental premiss, that it is a sign of emotional maturity not to be distressed when one's love is rejected by another. He argues that by not grieving over being rejected, we allow the other person the freedom to be himself;[12] but the deeper observation would surely be that we only recognize the 'otherness' of someone when we allow his actions to make an impact upon our feelings.

This factor alerts us to the extent to which the Christian theologians of the past took lightly the Old Testament witness to a God who suffers because of his covenant-love (*ḥeseḏ*) for his people. The prophets, especially, speak of a God who grieves, is disappointed, and even labours under the burden of the plight of Israel. The classical theologians as exegetes of scripture seem to have been able to pass over references to the grief of God as being mere momentary accomodations to human

[10] Richard E. Creel, *Divine Impassibility*, pp. 11, 125–6. He argues for impassibility in God's nature, will, feeling, and knowledge of possibilities; in allowing for possibility in God's knowledge of actualities in the world he makes an interesting attempt to combine an insight of process theology with classical theism.

[11] Ibid., pp. 117, 119.   [12] Ibid, pp. 141–2, 146.

understanding, because they missed seeing a whole basic situation of
pain in the history of the relationship between Yahweh and his people.
The Old Testament speaks most acutely of the suffering of God, not in
using the word, but when it depicts the effect upon God of rejected love.
The sorrow of God because his people reject his loving care leads to a
unique kind of pain which is ascribed to God, a state of feeling which is
characterized by the prophets as *a blend of love and wrath*. This is
presented as a pathos which is God's own pathos. The prophet Jeremiah
above all penetrates to this anguish in the heart of God:

> Is Ephraim still my dear son,
> A child in whom I delight?
> As often as I turn my back on him
> I still remember him:
> and so my heart yearns for him,
> I am filled with tenderness towards him.
>
> (Jer. 31: 20, *NEB*)

Again God speaks of the pain and grief he himself feels when he has to
turn away his face from the people he loves:

> I have forsaken the house of Israel,
> I have cast off my own people.
> I have given my beloved into the power of her foes . . .
> Many shepherds have ravaged my vineyard
> and trampled down my field,
> They have made my pleasant field a desolate wilderness,
> made it a waste land, waste and waterless to my sorrow.
>
> (Jer. 12: 7–11, *NEB*)

The last phrase could also be translated 'On me the waste lies'.[13] This
Old Testament picture of the sorrowing heart of God offers two
significant points for a theological understanding of the idea of a
suffering God, though it also offers some hermeneutical problems for
today.

In the first place we notice that the prophet does not simply find that
God is sharing in the suffering of his people: he finds that he, the
prophet, is called to share in the suffering of *God* who is grieved for his

---

[13] So H. Wheeler Robinson, *The Cross of Jeremiah* (1925), repr. in *The Cross in the Old Testament* (SCM Press, London, 1955), p. 184.

people. That is, the prophet finds himself caught up into the situation of a God who is in pain, and only thus does he discover the true plight of his fellow men. This insight into the prophetic spirit has been emphasized by the Japanese theologian Kazoh Kitamori in his *Theology of the Pain of God*, written in the aftermath of war in 1945 and in the immediate shadow of the Hiroshima bombing. Kitamori speaks of God's own particular suffering (which he identifies from the Old Testament as a blend of love and wrath) as God's 'transcendent pain', to be distinguished from his 'immanent pain' of suffering in fellowship with the world. Man is called to make human pain 'serve the pain of God'.[14] Similarly the Jewish scholar Abraham Heschel in his study *The Prophets* speaks of the prophet as a man who is in sympathy with the pathos of God; it is as if God says, 'My pathos is not your pathos'.[15] Again it may be no accident that this scholar writes against a background of suffering—the persecution of Jews in his native Poland. But earlier, in 1925, H. Wheeler Robinson in his study *The Cross of Jeremiah* had written of the sorrow of God in similar terms, as the peculiar 'tragedy' of God to which the prophet must be recalled. Commenting on the oracle to Baruch in Jeremiah 45 he says:

Baruch is overwhelmed by the sense of failure of the prophet's work and of his own, and the prophet recalls him to the thought of *God's* failure. Is there room for his own complaint, in the presence of the tragedy of God's defeated purpose and all this means for God? . . . There is hardly a passage in the Old Testament which gives us a more impressive glimpse of the eternal cross in the heart of God, the bitterness of his disappointment with man.[16]

So man finds himself in the situation of God's suffering—God's 'transcendent pain' (Kitamori), or his 'own pathos' (Heschel), or his particular 'tragedy' (Wheeler Robinson). Man is being summoned to have a fellow-feeling for God who *already* feels for man. This Old Testament insight helps to establish the suffering of God as central to his love; it is only through the prophetic awareness of God's suffering that the prophet perceives his nation's neglect of God's love and understands the true meaning of *hesed*. Their religious experience takes the form not of projecting suffering onto God, but of having suffering disclosed to

[14] K. Kitamori, *Theology of the Pain of God*, pp. 50, 53 ff., 100–2.
[15] Abraham J. Heschel, *The Prophets*, pp. 276, 223 ff. Indeed, Heschel speaks not simply of the prophets' sympathy *with* the divine pathos, but *for* it, referring to 'emotional identity' and 'emotional nexus' with God (ibid., pp. 49, 115, 118–19).
[16] H. Wheeler Robinson, op. cit. (n. 13 above), p. 185.

them. Here too is a vivid example of suffering as the communication of love.

But the prophetic description of God's unique pathos as being a painful blend of love with wrath, in which the love-element triumphs, presents us with some hermeneutical problems. Kitamori does in fact make a conflict between the wrath and love of God the very basis of his theology of the pain of God:

An absolute being without wrath can have no real pain . . . The pain of God is his love—this love is based on the premise of his wrath, which is absolute, inflexible reality.[17]

According to this way of thinking, God's pain stems from his being torn between the urge to punish offenders justly, and the urge to forgive; salvation is understood in the tradition of Luther as being God's conquering of his wrath by his love in the interests of loving the unworthy.[18] The pain of God is his conflict with himself in our interest—God against God. Apart from other unsatisfactory aspects of this theology (such as the image of God it promotes), the result is certainly to ascribe a unique pathos to God, but one which is so unique that we are shut out from it. His pain is an internal transaction which does not involve us; the dissolution of the tension within God himself takes place over our heads like a celestial thunderstorm, and this can be no real participation in human pain and suffering. The transcendent pain in God in himself and his immanent pain in the world are driven too far apart by this theory.

A more subtle view of a conflict between love and wrath is offered by J. Y. Lee in his study *God Suffers for Us*. He suggests that we might think of the love of God as normally harmonizing the paradoxical elements of transcendent holiness and immanent mercy in God. But empathy with man's estranged state unbalances this harmony and causes tension, since one pole of God's being will be accepting sinful man while the other is rejecting him. The conflict in God is not then directly between his love and his wrath; 'wrath' is the name for the conflict which 'suspends' the normal harmonizing operation of love within God. Moreover, the aim

---

[17] K. Kitamori, *Theology of the Pain of God*, p. 27 and many times (e.g. pp. 35, 64, 83, 108–12).

[18] See Luther, *Lectures on Galatians* (1535), 3:13: 'The curse, which is divine wrath against the whole world, has the same conflict with the blessing, that is, with the eternal grace and mercy of God in Christ. Therefore the curse clashes with the blessing and wants to damn it and annihilate it. But it cannot.' American Edition of Luther's Works, General Editor H. T. Lehmann, Vol. 26 (Concordia, St. Louis, 1963), p. 281.

of this suspension of love is to urge us to participate in God's empathy with us.[19] But this picture still presents a struggle between God's acceptance and rejection of humanity, whatever terminology is used. It also contains a flaw of logic: since Lee has already rightly defined God's *agape* as empathy, or the passionate involvement of God in human life, it is impossible to see how divine love can be 'suspended' and active in empathy at the same time. Conversely, if love is empathy, it is hard to see how it could ever have maintained the harmony in the being of God which empathy is supposed to have disturbed. Lee's tangles are a vivid example of the way that any serious attempt to speak of God's loving sympathy with humanity will challenge the notion that God has an inner struggle with his wrath.

One response to such uses of Old Testament material would be to object that we should take the prophetic description of a blending of love and wrath in God simply as a way of depicting an intense emotional state. We do not do the prophets justice if we take this tension literally as a state of divine indecision and struggle; after all, they always insist that God's persistent searching love has the last word:

> How can I give you up, Ephraim?
> how surrender you, Israel? . . .
> My heart is changed within me,
> my remorse kindles already . . .
> For I am God and not man.
>
> (Hosea 11: 8–9, *NEB*)

The supposed conflict is nothing other than the torment of God's desire for his people, a longing which is suffused by a sense of failure and disappointment. 'Struggle' within God is the poet's way of evoking an emotion of pain.[20] While I agree with this insight as far as it goes, I think we can say more than this; we shall not be misled into building a theology upon a supposed internal conflict between love and wrath if we notice the manner in which the prophets speak of God's wrath

---

[19] Jung Young Lee, *God Suffers for Us*, pp. 15–16. Lee distinguishes between 'sympathy' as mere imaginative identity, and 'empathy' as an actual participation in feeling, in order to endorse God's empathy with the world (pp. 11–12). In this study I have generally used both terms indiscriminately, but with the meaning which Lee gives to empathy.

[20] Cf. James L. Mays, *Hosea: A Commentary* (Old Testament Library, SCM Press, London, 1969), pp. 156–7.

against his people. Though they do speak at times in a typically Hebraic manner of direct causation, with the Babylonian army, for instance, as the hammer of God directly punishing his people, they also speak characteristically in another way. They speak of the wrath of God as God's 'giving up' people to the natural consequences of their own actions. God 'hides his face', or 'turns away', or 'surrenders' his people.[21] That is, in his wrath God does not inflict a penalty, but he allows the self-destructiveness of people to work itself out in the social-political context of the time. He lets them go their own way, as for example a rotting society, deeply divided within, is no match for the Babylonian invader. God's wrath here is his active consent to the working out of human sin into its inevitable consequences. This is in line with the Priestly theology of an internal nexus between sin and disaster, the same term ('āwōn) expressing both sin and penalty. It is this Old Testament insight which the Apostle Paul takes up in Romans 1: 24–32, when he speaks of God's wrath against the wicked in terms of his 'giving them up' to the futility of their own desires.[22] It is God's consent to the reaction upon us of our own trespass against life, as Hegel defined 'fate' in his early writings.[23] It is God's sanctioning of consequences which Tillich identifies as belonging to 'the structure of being itself', so that justice is 'the structural form of love'.[24] Broken human relationships issue finally in utter alienation.

Within this biblical perspective, God's 'wrath' is not part of an internal conflict within the being of God, but is an aspect of the relative autonomy which he gives to mankind. It is the darker side of human freedom. Yet it is not a divine indifference, a detachment, a standing

---

[21] See Samuel E. Balentine, *The Hidden God: The Hiding of the Face of God in the Old Testament* (Oxford University Press, 1983), pp. 143–51: '. . . in some instances the language of the judgement is so poignantly compassionate as to suggest that God is actually the one who has grounds for lament and not Israel' (p. 151). Cf. Terence E. Fretheim, *The Suffering of God*, p. 126: 'God may finally be forced into a tearful withdrawal'.

[22] See C. H. Dodd on Rom. 1:18 ff., in *The Epistle of Paul to the Romans*, Moffat New Testament Commentary (Hodder and Stoughton, London, 1932), pp. 21–4, 29. However, since God as creator *consents* to the process of cause and effect ('sin is the cause, disaster the effect' op. cit., p. 23) and is intimately involved in his creation, Dodd misplaces the emphasis when he calls his own view of divine wrath 'impersonal'; it is a personal, but not an imposed judgement.

[23] G. W. F. Hegel, 'The Spirit of Christianity and its Fate', in *Early Theological Writings*, pp. 229–30: 'the disembodied spirit of the injured life comes on the scene against the trespass'.

[24] Paul Tillich, *Systematic Theology*, Vol. 2, p. 201.

back in non-involvement; according to the prophets, just because God is passionately concerned with the life of this world he cannot 'give up' people without feeling the pain of the consequences himself, and protesting against the situation which has been brought into being:

> How can I give you up, Ephraim?
> how surrender you, Israel?
> My heart is changed within me . . .

As God has given them up, so he continually woos them back to himself, and if they will only return then there can be no more 'wrath' since they will no longer be on their own headlong rush towards calamity. Neither wrath nor restoration are a mechanical process of causation, and both mean pain for God. We may then make the theological judgement that there is no conflict of love and wrath within God. There is an intricate double movement of pain, which is described poetically and anthropomorphically as struggle. The anthropopathism should therefore be taken seriously but not literally.

We must not, of course, infer from such Old Testament contexts that all human suffering is the result of man's trespass against life. The Old Testament itself does not suggest this either.[25] We have been concerned here to understand the way in which the Israelite prophets associate God's love with his suffering, and their identification of this pain of God as being peculiarly his own: they express this unique pain as a tension between divine love and wrath. Careful exegesis of this image of God should alert us to the dangers of building a theology upon 'struggle' in God, as well as offering us insights into the nature of God's suffering with his world which we shall build upon later. But we must not imagine that this particular image exhausts the meaning of either divine or human suffering.

2. THE CENTRAL PLACE OF THE CROSS

A further major reason for the theological conviction that God suffers is based on the central place of the cross of Jesus within Christian faith. If

---

[25] The Book of Job is the most obvious, though not the only, protest against the dogma of retributive suffering: see e.g. Psalm 73, Jer. 12, Ezek. 18, Malachi 3. The Wisdom movement of Ancient Israel both fostered and criticized this doctrine at different times; see Gerhard Von Rad, *Wisdom in Israel*, trans. J. D. Martin (SCM Press, London, 1972), pp. 195 ff., and J. Crenshaw, 'Popular Questioning of the Justice of God in Ancient Israel', *Zeitschrift für die alttestamentliche Wissenschaft*, 82 (1970), pp. 380–95.

theology affirms that, in any sense, 'God was in Christ' then it seems an inescapable conclusion that God suffered 'in Christ' at the cross. If God was involved with the person and career of Jesus, then he was implicated in the experience of the crucified Christ. To say thus much does not in itself demand a particular model of Christology, beyond belief in a deep participation of God in the human life of Jesus. While Christian theology has, until quite recently, been hesitant to speak of the presence of God in the suffering of all mankind, it has always wanted to affirm the presence of God in the suffering and death of Jesus. Here at least then we might expect to find theological talk about the suffering of God. As a matter of fact, however, traditional theology has wanted to escape this conclusion, usually by the route of asserting the 'two-natures' doctrine of Christology; that is, it has affirmed that the divine Son suffered in the flesh, but only in the strict sense that the human nature of Jesus suffered, the divine nature remaining impassible.

This kind of approach was popularized in European theology by Calvin,[26] though it goes back through the canons of Chalcedon to the formulations of the Church Fathers, where both the Alexandrian and Antiochene schools were agreed at least upon the presupposition that the divine Logos himself could not change or suffer.[27] Indeed, this was also common ground with their common enemy, Arius. It was because Arius took the sufferings of the whole person of the historical Jesus seriously that he was driven to the logical conclusion that the pre-existent One who became man could not have been the authentic divine Logos, but only a kind of honorary Logos.[28] The modern refusal to take this route of merely humanizing the sufferings of Christ is marked by three levels of argument, which display an increasing profundity.

In the first place, reflection upon the wholeness of a 'person' should make clear that we cannot isolate experiences and attributes within

---

[26] Calvin, *Institutio Christianae Religionis* (1559), II. xiv.

[27] e.g. Athanasius, *Orationes Contra Arianos* 3. 32, 3. 34–5, 3. 54–7, cf. *De Incarnatione*, 17, 'When the Virgin gave birth, he did not suffer himself'; Nestorius, *The Bazaar of Heracleides* 132–6 (trans. and ed. G. R. Driver and L. Hodgson, Clarendon Press, Oxford, 1925, pp. 91–5), cf. Theodore of Mopsuestia, *On the Incarnation* Fragments 5, 9 in R. A. Norris, *The Christological Controversy* (Fortress Press, Philadelphia, 1980), pp. 119, 121. For an earlier statement, see Tertullian, *Adversus Praxean* 29. For a strong modern example of this approach, see Friedrich Von Hügel, *Essays and Addresses on the Philosophy of Religion*, Second Series, p. 223: 'fellow-suffering . . . is supplied by the Humanity of our Lord'.

[28] See Robert C. Gregg and Dennis E. Groh, *Early Arianism: A View of Salvation* (SCM Press, London, 1981), pp. 68–70.

sealed compartments labelled 'divine' and 'human', and still present Christ as 'one person'. Patristic theology had itself recognized this problem and proposed a *communicatio idiomatum* (an exchange of attributes) between the divine and human elements in Christ; birth, suffering, and death could be predicated of the Logos in so far as he was one person with the passible humanity he had taken. However, in the West this affirmation did not get beyond a paradoxical assertion, in which the Logos remained absolutely impassible and untouched in himself. Typical of the paradoxical method was Tertullian's triumphant flourish that 'The Son of God was crucified . . . It is certain because it is impossible.'[29] One school of thought in the East, the Alexandrian 'one-nature' Christology, certainly stressed the reality of the *communicatio* under the catchword that the Virgin Mary was '*Theotokos*' (God-bearing), but the Alexandrians were struggling to understand how an impassible Logos could be the subject of human growth and suffering. Where they could not convincingly isolate these phenomena within the flesh of Christ they were forced to weaken the character of Christ's psychological experiences of suffering. Athanasius, for example, suggested that Christ feigned anguish and ignorance for our sake.[30] Perhaps Cyril of Alexandria was the most innovative in expounding the *communicatio idiomatum*, proposing that the human nature was actually constituted as a human reality by the Logos.[31] However, his presuppositions led even him to declare that the Logos 'suffered impassibly',[32] and to deal with the cry of forsakenness by concluding

---

[29] Tertullian, *De Carne Christi* 5 (trans. E. Evans, SPCK, London, 1956, p. 19). The Antiochene two-nature Christology was suspicious of the *communicatio*; though Theodore gives qualified approval to *Theotokos* (Fragment 11, ed. Norris (n. 27 above) pp. 121–2), Norris judges that he failed to formulate a doctrine of *communicatio idiomatum*: see R. A. Norris, *Manhood and Christ*, (Clarendon Press, Oxford, 1963), pp. 260–1.

[30] Athanasius, *Contra Arianos* 3. 37–8. See R. A. Grillmeier, *Christ in Christian Tradition*, Vol. 1, Revised Edition, trans. J. Bowden (Mowbrays, London, 1975), pp. 314–15.

[31] Cyril of Alexandria, *Ep.* 46. 3 (Second Letter to Succensus, ed. and trans. L. R. Wickham, *Oxford Early Christian Texts*, Clarendon Press, Oxford, 1983, p. 89), cf. ibid. 5 (ed. Wickham, p. 93), *Ep.* 17 (Third Letter to Nestorius) Anathema 11 (ed. Wickham, p. 33).

[32] Cyril, *Ep.* 4. 5 (Second Letter to Nestorius): 'within the suffering body was the Impassible' (ed. Wickham, p. 7); *Ep.* 17. 6: 'he was in the crucified body claiming the sufferings of the flesh as his own impassibly (*apathos pathē*) (ed. Wickham, p. 21). It has been suggested that the designation *apathos* should be taken in the strict Aristotelian sense of 'not passively', and hence actively or voluntarily. Then Cyril would be

that Christ was not actually speaking for himself here but only on behalf of other men.[33]

The problems found by the Fathers confirm the modern understanding of personality, deepened by the social and psychological sciences. It is now impossible to think of 'person' as any kind of union between two totally different 'natures' with their own characteristics, as Chalcedon had finally proposed ('to be acknowledged in two natures . . . concurring into one person'[34]). John A. T. Robinson aptly suggests this would mean a person who 'functioned on [two] different circuits'.[35] Expressing the same point more organically, it is now clear that persons become what they are through their experiences and their relationships, and so personality cannot be placed at a different level of reality from something which has fixed potentialities for only certain kinds of experiences and actions, and which is called a 'nature'.[36] As a matter of fact, we ought to notice that the Fathers themselves had problems with the suggested distinction between 'nature' and 'person'; the formula of Chalcedon makes no attempt to define these terms or to provide a metaphysical account of their relationship, but uses them in a rather doxological fashion as sign posts to truth.

Today we must affirm that if Christ is one with God and one with humanity, he must be so as a whole person. God cannot be safeguarded from suffering by preserving an area of experience in Christ from contamination by change, suffering, ignorance, and death. This must be the case whether we think of the 'oneness' of Jesus with God as a matter of function (God's acting through Jesus) or as a matter of ontology (God's being one with Jesus), and recent writing on Christology from either perspective has made this clear.[37] Nor is it adequate to replace a

affirming that the Logos suffered in himself by his own will, foreshadowing the theopaschite formula of the sixth century that 'one of the Trinity has suffered'. This does not seem to accord with Cyril's insistence, in reply to the criticisms of Nestorius, that the human flesh is the place of Christ's sufferings (see above). Anyway, any notion of *merely* 'willed' suffering falls short of true vulnerability. See below, pp. 60–3.

[33] Cyril, *Quod Unus Sit Christus*, in J.-P. Migne. *Patrologiae Graecae*, 75: 1325c., 1328a. For a discussion, see Werner Elert, *Der Ausgang der Altkirchlichen Christologie* (Lutherisches Verlaghaus, Berlin, 1957), pp. 91–3.

[34] Text in Stevenson, op. cit. (Ch. 1 n. 1), p. 337.

[35] John A. T. Robinson, *The Human Face of God* (SCM Press, London, 1973), p. 111.

[36] Especially see Wolfhart Pannenberg, *Jesus–God and Man*, pp. 342 ff.

[37] From the functional perspective, see Anthony T. Hanson, *The Image of the Invisible God* (SCM Press, London, 1982), pp. 18–19, 142–3. From the ontological perspective, see Brian Hebblethwaite, 'The Moral and Religious Value of the Incarnation' in Goulder, op. cit. (ch. 1 n. 7), p. 91.

two-nature view of the suffering of God with a two-stage one. Luther, for example, had protested against a merely verbal *communicatio idiomatum*, speaking of 'the death of God', but with the explanation that while God suffered in the incarnation he could not suffer in his eternal nature.[38] This recalls the early expression of Ignatius about 'the passion of my God' upon earth.[39] The second level of modern thought about the suffering of God at the cross therefore opens up, by contrast, an eternal perspective.

For we must move on to affirm that the cross is an actualization in our history of what is eternally true of God's nature. If indeed God suffers in the cross of Jesus in reconciling the world to himself, then there must always be a cross in the experience of God as he deals with a world which exists over against him. In the often-quoted words of Horace Bushnell from the nineteenth century:

It is as if there were a cross unseen, standing on its undiscovered hill, far back in the ages, out of which there were sounding always just the same deep voice of suffering love and patience that was heard by mortal ears from the sacred hill of calvary.[40]

This has been a characteristic theme of Anglo-Saxon theology since the end of the last century; in Wheeler Robinson's comments on Jeremiah quoted above we note, for instance, his speaking of a 'glimpse of the eternal cross in the heart of God'.[41] The sacrifice of God must at the very least be woven deeply into the whole painful story of human evolution. Current German theology has discovered this theme of 'the eternal cross' rather late (via a renaissance of interest in Hegel), but early

---

[38] See Luther, *Confession Concerning Christ's Supper* (1528), American Edition (n. 18 above), Vol. 37 (1961), p. 210, where he calls 'Lady Reason' the 'grandmother' of figurative language; cf. *This Is My Body* (1527), op. cit., p. 62: 'he who kills Christ has killed God's son, indeed, God and the Lord of glory himself.' Luther's concern to go beyond a verbal *communicatio* in the person of Christ has been stressed by recent *Kreuzestheologie*; e.g. Moltmann, *The Crucified God*, pp. 233–4; Jüngel, 'Vom Tod des lebendigen Gottes' (ch. 1 n. 36 above), pp. 113–4.

[39] Ignatius, *Ad Romanos*, 6.   [40] Bushnell, op. cit. (n. 1 above), p. 31.

[41] See also H. Wheeler Robinson, *Suffering Human and Divine*, p. 189: 'this actual victory in time (is) the downward extension of that victory wrought in eternity by the suffering God over the sin of the whole world'. The suffering of God in the whole of man's evolutionary process was portrayed by Lionel Thornton in *The Incarnate Lord* (Longmans & Green, London, 1928), pp. 279 ff. and later by Canon Charles E. Raven in *Natural Religion and Christian Theology*, Vol. 2 (Cambridge University Press, 1953) pp. 157–8. Cf. also P. T. Forsyth, *The Justification of God* (Independent Press, London, 1917), pp. 164–5.

or late, theologians have not shown as much serious interest as they ought in considering whether, or how, the historic cross occupies a decisive place within the cosmic process. As we have already seen, this is the case even where a theologian *wants* to affirm its uniqueness. Recent German theological work has, however, been impressive in establishing a third level of insight about the suffering of God in the cross of Jesus—a strand of theological thinking which has been dignified by the title '*Kreuzestheologie*', or 'Theology from the Cross'.[42]

Those who offer a theology 'from the cross' affirm that the cross is not just an indication of an eternal truth about God, but that it actually expresses what is most *divine* about God. God will be Godlike above all in the cross, and so all doctrine of the nature of God must begin from the cross as the revelation of God. This insight is based upon Luther's distinction between a 'theology of glory' and a 'theology of the cross', that is between the attempt to find God by the exercise of the human reason, deducing aspects of the invisible God from the visible things of the world, and by contrast a reflection upon the way that God himself has chosen to be found—in the suffering and humiliation of the cross of Jesus.[43] From this Lutheran background Barth formulated the dialectical statement that the divinity of God is displayed most clearly in the lowliness of the cross, while the glory of man is displayed in the resurrection.[44] This smartly reverses the classical view that it is the human nature of Jesus which suffers in the cross, and the divine nature which breaks through in triumph in the resurrection from the dead. Rather, affirms Barth, God is most divine in his humility. More recently other theologians have taken up the same theme. Eberhard Jüngel speaks of God as 'defining himself in a dead man' since he identifies himself with the crucified Christ.[45] J. Moltmann speaks of God as revealing himself in what is most unlike himself, in 'Godlessness and abandonment by God', for if God revealed himself in what was exactly like him then only God could know God.[46] This insight leads Moltmann to a contemporary Christian ethic, urging the Christian

---

[42] Literally, 'Theology *of* the cross'; see above, pp. 12–13.

[43] Luther, *Heidelberg Disputation* (1518), Thesis 21, cf. Theses 19 and 20; see *Luther: Early Theological Works*, Library of Christian Classics, Vol. 16, ed. and trans. J. Atkinson (SCM Press, London, 1962), pp. 290–2: 'God is not to be found except in sufferings and in the cross'.

[44] Barth, *CD* IV/1, pp. 204, 555–8.

[45] Jüngel, *God as the Mystery of the World*, pp. 362–4.

[46] Moltmann, *The Crucified God*, pp. 26–8.

church not simply to look for the like-minded in making its fellowship, but to offer an open friendship to those who are quite unlike it in order to share fellowship with the crucified Christ.[47]

These various theologies of the cross have usually appealed to an exegesis of Mark 15:39, understanding the evangelist to mean that the centurion is brought to his confession of the divine sonship of Christ *by* Christ's cry of desolation and the act of his dying, rather than despite it.[48] In this way Mark intends us to understand that the divine sonship of Christ and the derived sonship of Christians is fittingly expressed in suffering. This gospel pericope crowns the triple riposte of current theology to the notion that only the humanity of Christ suffers in the cross: God suffers in the cross in *oneness* with the person of Christ; God suffers *eternally* in the cross; God is most *Godlike* in the suffering of the cross.

3. THE PROBLEM OF HUMAN SUFFERING

Reflection upon the problem of human suffering also seems to demand a belief in the suffering of God, or so it has appeared to much contemporary thought. Though it is not our primary task in this study to formulate a theodicy, the question of theodicy *is* deeply bound up with the notion of the possibility of God. Suffering will always have a dimension of mystery, as the Book of Job assures us, but a great deal of light is nevertheless cast by the affirmation that God suffers with humanity.

1. At the most basic level it is a consolation to those who suffer to know that God suffers too, and understands their situation from within. The psychological effect upon a sufferer of being aware of a suffering God who understands his predicament may be below the level of theological argument, but it may in the end soar on wings far higher than any formal theodicy can. No theological argument can justify the mountain of misery represented by an Auschwitz, a Babi Yar, or a Hiroshima, yet the fact remains that 'the *Shema* of Israel and the Lord's prayer were prayed in Auschwitz'.[49] Though the Book of Job does not

---

[47] Jürgen Moltmann, *The Open Church: Invitation to a Messianic Lifestyle*, trans. M. D. Meeks (SCM Press, London, 1978), pp. 60–3; *The Church in the Power of the Spirit*, pp. 114–20.

[48] So e.g. Eduard Schweizer, *The Good News According to Mark*, trans. D. H. Madvig (SPCK, London, 1970), pp. 358–9.

[49] Moltmann, *The Crucified God*, p. 278: 'There would be no "theology after Auschwitz" . . . had there been no "theology in Auschwitz"; cf. Simon, op. cit. (ch. 1 n. 11), p. 83: 'Even Auschwitz held and holds the secret of redemption'.

as yet hint at the concept of a suffering God, it does embed a powerful statement about the mystery of suffering within a theophany, thereby pronouncing in no uncertain terms that God is with the sufferer, and leaving the way open for further reflection about the mode of this presence.[50]

If we do appeal to the psychological validity of belief in a sympathetic God, we ought however to notice two necessary corollaries. On the one hand, we must be able to speak of a God who at the same time is victorious in his sufferings, since in our experience of human comforters we find that the fellow-sufferer who can help us is the one who has not been overwhelmed and disintegrated by his suffering. On the other hand, we must speak of a God who suffers universally, since a God who suffered only in the particular historical context of Jesus of Nazareth would seem to have a restricted range of empathy, at least in the view of the contemporary sufferer.

2. At a second stage of prologomena to a theodicy proper, the conviction that God suffers will forbid the structuring of any theological argument where God directly causes suffering. By 'directly' here I mean any sequence of cause and effect where the effect follows necessarily from the cause, even in the scholastic refinement of a final cause within secondary causes. If God suffers then he too is a victim and not a torturer, not even a disciplinarian using suffering for reasons 'which he knows best but which are hidden from us', as popular piety often suggests. Much recent theology has been concerned to say that the concept of a suffering God cuts away the ground from beneath an atheism of protest against a cruel God,[51] as it does from beneath any theology where the omnipotence of God is envisaged as moving events and people around like pieces on a chess board; indeed this sort of view of divine power is what protest atheism usually assumes theology to be. But the omnipotence of God cannot be the human power of an absolute monarch multiplied to infinity if the cross testifies to a God whose love is made perfect in weakness. Belief that God suffers forbids the thought altogether that God sends suffering, though he may allow it.

---

[50] See H. H. Rowley, *Job*, The New Century Bible (Nelson, London, 1970), p. 20: 'It is of the essence of its message that Job found God *in* his suffering'.

[51] See H.-G. Geyer, 'Atheismus und Christentum' (ch. 1 n. 36), pp. 269 ff; Paul Ricoeur, 'On Consolation', in A. MacIntyre and P. Ricoeur, *The Religious Significance of Atheism* (Columbia University Press, New York, 1969), pp. 87 ff., speaks of the 'tragic faith' of 'the crucified, the dying God'; Jüngel, *God as the Mystery of the World*, pp. 63 ff.; Moltmann, *The Crucified God*, pp. 226–7.

However, we must not appeal too glibly to the crucial distinction between what God allows and what he brings about, without recognizing its consequences for a doctrine of God. Any real distinction between divine permission and divine causation requires some view of limitation in God, for if God permits suffering when he could do something to remove it, this is equivalent to causation. On the other hand, if the limitation upon God is imposed from outside himself, there is no meaning to his permission. Thus we arrive at the notion of God who freely accepts self-limitation for the sake of the freedom of his creation, and this brings us to theodicy proper.

3. If we judge that the most adequate (or the least inadequate) explanation for human suffering lies in human free will, the affirmation that God suffers is still needed to give credibility to such a defence of the world as God's creation. For the free-will defence cannot stand alone. We may claim that in order for human beings to be truly free persons they must have the possibility of refusing God's purpose for their lives, so making choices which are damaging and self-destructive. But if we say this, other things must be said about *God's* choice in creation. On the one hand, as John Hick has argued, for man to be able to turn from God he must have been created in conditions which made this possible, so that a Fall is 'virtually inevitable' in such a world. Hick himself proposes (in a manner reminiscent of Origen) that man was created at an 'epistemic distance' between himself and God, to allow room for response.[52] Thus, although God does not create evil and suffering, and though man's own immediate responsibility is not denied, God must bear an ultimate responsibility in choosing to make man as a free creature at all. If we follow Origen and Augustine in speaking of evil as strictly 'nothing', or a parasitic negation of Being without any ontological reality of its own, then there is no question of its being directly created by God. But this does not absolve the creator from an ultimate responsibility; it is the 'risk' he takes in moving out beyond himself to create beings other than himself.[53]

The question of divine responsibility can also be raised from another angle. There is the problem of 'natural evil'—disturbances in the order of nature causing disaster and suffering among humankind—which cannot be traced to free human choices. It might be argued that since

---

[52] John Hick, *Evil and the God of Love*, p. 317, Cf. Origen, *De Principiis* 2. 9. 2: Origen argues that created minds are granted free movement towards and away from an ineffable God, so that 'the good that was in them might become their own'.

[53] See at greater length ch. 8 below.

man is a person in the making, then the making of persons requires as an environment the kind of self-evolving structures in the world from which suffering cannot be excluded. For example, for sailors to develop a sense of moral responsibility there must be storms at sea. We shall have occasion later on to insist that the superfluity of natural evil cannot *all* be traced to moral instrumentality, but even if we allow only a minimum of the instrumental view of natural evil, then again God bears an ultimate responsibility for this 'Vale of soul-making' in choosing to make persons rather than machines.

Now, Hick argues that for this kind of ultimate responsibility to be consistent with a God of love, two things must be the case. First, the good attained by suffering—that is, the creation of our personhood—could not be reached by any other means than the risk of suffering. We may add here that this need not entail a denial that God could have created other 'possible worlds', or other possible persons enjoying moral good, by other means;[54] all that is being claimed is that this particular world and the particular kind of persons *we* are with our freedom and associated values could not be attained without the very high risk of suffering. The question is whether this particular game is worth the candle, not whether there could be other games. In fact, the theological judgement that there could be other possible worlds underlines the ultimate responsibility of God for this one. The responsibility remains even if we argue, with some process theologians, that any other creation would have involved the 'evil' of triviality.[55] The second criterion Hick rightly argues for is that God should do everything that is in accord with his nature to overcome evil and suffering; it need hardly be said that the whole of this present study is concerned with asking what *is* 'in accord with his nature'.

To these two criteria for a theodicy I believe we must add a third. As a God of love, the Creator must not only limit himself by taking the risk that human persons may suffer through their freedom; he should also limit himself by sharing that suffering. Only the fact that God himself suffers can make credible the tracing of suffering to the free will of the

---

[54] Alvin C. Plantinga attempts to argue the stronger form of the Free Will Defence, that there could not be another possible world containing moral good without moral evil: see *God, Freedom, and Evil* (W. B. Eerdmans, Grand Rapids, Michigan, 1977), pp. 34–53. But all that need be argued is that there could not be beings *exactly like us* without the freedom to do evil; so Cobb and Griffin, *Process Theology*, pp. 74–5 (from a process perspective).

[55] See David R. Griffin, *God, Power, and Evil*, pp. 284–7.

creation. This alone makes credible the creation of the world as an act of love. We may affirm God's own freedom by putting the situation like this: it is not that God must suffer, the world being what it is, but God has made the world as it is *because* he chooses to suffer with it. It is in this sense we can say that 'God must suffer'. This is what Karl Barth has in mind when he remarks 'in passing' that

> . . . the fact that from all eternity God resolved to take to Himself and bear man's rejection is a prior justification of God in respect of the risk to which He resolved to expose man by creation—and in respect of the far greater risk to which He committed him by His permitting of the fall . . . We must insist upon man's responsibility. . . . But much more we must insist upon the responsibility which God Himself shouldered . . .[56]

Any theodicy which includes God's ultimate responsibility for the predicament of the world must affirm the suffering of God, and Barth here alerts us to the fact that an assigning of responsibility to God is a genuine religious feeling which ought not to be suppressed. It breaks out in popular forms such as the comment of a social worker serving the wards of a hospice for the dying, reported in a national newspaper, that she is glad she believes in God because 'that means I've got somebody to be flaming mad with'.[57] There is an Old Testament idiom which is relevant here, when the early writers speak of God's sending evil as well as good upon the world.[58] Their view that there could be no rivalry to the activity of Yahweh lay behind their speaking in this way of a direct causation of evil, and later Israelite faith found ways of speaking about a more indirect link between God's creative sovereignty and the presence of evil in the world, such as the figure of 'the Satan' or accuser;[59] but the early idiom is surely to be interpreted theologically as an instinctive feeling about the ultimate responsibility of God for the world as it is. Barth in the quotation above rightly adds the Christian insight that God takes responsibility by suffering himself; he shoulders man's responsi-

---

[56] Barth, *CD* II/2, p. 165.

[57] *The Guardian*, 17 August 1979.

[58] See Walther Eichrodt, *Theology of the Old Testament*, trans. J. A. Baker, Vol. 2 (SCM Press, London, 1967), pp. 176–8. Relevant texts include Amos 3:6, Isa. 45:7, Exod. 4:21, Deut. 2:30, 2 Sam. 17:14, 2 Sam. 24:1, 1 Kgs. 12:15.

[59] See G. B. Caird, *Principalities and Powers* (Clarendon Press, Oxford, 1956), pp. 32–3. A notable text in this development is 1 Chr. 21:1.

bility in order to reconcile him, as the cross witnesses. Something of this emerges in an ironic manner in the popular song by Sydney Carter:

> It's God they ought to crucify instead of you and me,
> I said to the carpenter a-hanging on the tree.[60]

This sentiment becomes an unhealthy one only when it is used to excuse man from his responsibility for his own free choices, or when it portrays God as responsible in the more direct sense of causing suffering, such as in a scheme where all suffering and evil are the logically necessary consequences of creation rather than a 'risk'. The epitome of this kind of thinking is found in Jung's account of the cross of Jesus as God's clearing of his own guilty conscience: 'The sacrifical death was a fate chosen by Yahweh as a reparation for the wrong done to Job on the one hand, and on the other as a fillip to the spiritual and moral development of man.'[61] Later I shall be arguing that God cannot be said to experience suffering recognizably like ours, if he enters into a creation where suffering is a strictly necessary element of his own works.[62] But the urge to trace responsibility for suffering to God in some manner is an essential part of a theodicy, and can only be met by the conviction that God also suffers.

It is true that some contemporary political theology which affirms the suffering of God refuses to raise the question of ultimate responsibility for evil. It is enough, it is said, to know that God suffers with us and struggles for us; it is not important to know who is responsible for suffering in theory, but all-important to know whether God is going to take responsibility here and now in practice by taking the side of the oppressed.[63] We ought to take notice of their objection that to find explanations for suffering can lead to doing no more about it; theory can oust praxis. But this need not happen. Nor need the seeking of

[60] Song, 'Friday Morning', in *Sydney Carter in the Present Tense*, Book 2 (Galliard, London, 1960).

[61] C. G. Jung, *Answer to Job*, trans. R. F. C. Hull (Routledge & Kegan Paul, London, 1954), p. 78. Cf. ibid. pp. 91–2: 'The atonement [is] not the payment of a human debt to God, but [a] reparation for a wrong done by God to man'. In Jung's view, the Job story shows a conflict in God between his light and dark (unconscious) nature, which he unsuccessfully projects onto Job. Similarly, Jim Garrison in *The Darkness of God* (SCM Press, London, 1982), describes the experience of the cross as 'Divinity, wrestling with its own dark side' (p. 177). I have already commented that the notion of a conflict between love and wrath in God is a false trail of thought.

[62] See below, ch. 8–9 *passim*.

[63] e.g. Cone. op. cit. (n. 9 above), pp. 178–83.

reasonable explanations for suffering, fragmentary as they must be, entail a destruction of faith as some theologians object. The notion of the risk of creation implied by the free-will defence is by no means a substitute for faith. It still remains to decide whether God's creative choice *is* worth the cost; it remains open, with Ivan in Dostoevsky's novel *The Brothers Karamazov*, to return the entrance ticket to God with the polite observation that the price is too steep.[64] Is God's purpose worth the tears of one tortured child, even if God himself suffers? Only faith can answer that question, after all reasonable talk is silent.

4. THE WORLD-PICTURE OF TODAY

A final major influence behind the present theological conviction that God must be a suffering God is the overall picture of the world with which we work today. The way we think the world is will inevitably shape the way we think of the creator of the world. In the period of the Fathers and the medieval Schoolmen the world was pictured as a *hierarchy*: all entities from the pebble on the shore to the highest archangel occupied a rung on the ladder of reality according to the degree in which they participated in the transcendent world of Being. It seemed to the theologians of this period, following Platonic philosophy, that the only possible cause and ground for the world in which we live—a world of change, flux, and decay—must be a world which is unmoving, unchanging, static perfection. The necessary basis for a world of Becoming must be a world of pure Being. Such Being was therefore defined as the opposite of Becoming: Being Itself could have no part in Becoming, although things that were trapped in Becoming could gradually rise to share in Being. God as Absolute Being, either at the top of the pyramid or beyond it altogether (depending upon the particular school of Platonism in vogue), must therefore be absolutely unmoving, unchanging, and unaffected by the world of Becoming. His nature could be deduced from the appearance of the world by the *via negativa*—reversing whatever was characteristic of this world, such as change and development.

There is no need here to labour the point that has been made so often in recent theological discussion: that the early Fathers of the Church

---

[64] Dostoevsky, *The Brothers Karamazov*, trans. C. Garnett (Heinemann, London, 1912) p. 252. See Stewart R. Sutherland, *Atheism and the Rejection of God: Contemporary Philosophy and* The Brothers Karamazov (Blackwell, Oxford, 1977), pp. 30 ff.

recast the God of scripture in the mould of Greek philosophy.[65] God's unchanging faithfulness became an unchanging immobility; his moral otherness from the world (his holiness) became a philosophical otherness which effectively excluded him from direct involvement in the turmoil of history. We ought, however, to notice that the Christian version of the absolute transcendence of Being was in fact more extreme than its Greek sources.[66] The Neo-Platonist view of a graded divinity, or plural principles at different levels of divinity, allowed for the lower reaches of divine Being to be involved in change and suffering. But once the Christian theologians had insisted that *their* Logos-mediator between God and the world (Christ) was of equal divinity with the transcendent Father, then both the fount of Godhead and his Logos were equally immune from suffering and change. The whole essence of God as Being Itself abode in absolute calm, untouched in his inner self by the world in which people suffer, grow, and die. Today there is a widespread reaction against such a notion of an immutable God; we suspect that the apex of the pyramid of Being is what we call today 'an ivory tower'.

The Rational Theology of the eighteenth century replaced this model of a pyramid or hierarchy by the model of the world as machine. God was conceived as the great Designer of the machinery of the cosmos which ran by the laws of cause and effect which he had built into it at its manufacture. Once again, deducing the nature of God from the appearance of the world—this time as an artefact or piece of technology—led to the concept of a God remote from the world and not involved in its day-to-day running (even if, in theistic versions of the model, he could interrupt its running from time to time with a miracle). Like the God of the hierarchy of Being, this God must also be impassible as the unchanging lawgiver. The protest of German theology in this century against any kind of natural theology stems from the assumption that any attempt to think about God from the appearance of the world must lead to this immobile God—the God of the Philosophers and not the God of the Cross.

But in fact the picture of the world that we work with today ought

[65] For elaboration of this point see Wolfhart Pannenberg, 'The Appropriation of the Philosophical Concept of God as a Dogmatic Problem of Early Christian Theology', in *Basic Questions in Theology*, Vol. 2, trans. G. H. Kehm, (SCM Press, London, 1971), pp. 119–83, esp. 157–73; Hans Küng, *Menschwerdung Gottes*, Exkurs 2, 'Kann Gott Leiden?', pp. 622–31; R.A. Norris, *God and World in Early Christian Theology* (A. & C. Black, London, 1966), pp. 45–56, 134 ff.

[66] This is argued by Mackey, *The Christian Experience of God as Trinity*, pp. 170–1, cf. pp. 125 ff.

not to lead to such conclusions about its creator. After the rise of the biological sciences and evolutionary theory, we now think of the world as a living organism, a community of relationships in the process of growth and development, a macro-process that requires as much sacrifice and pain as the building of any human community. One of Hume's objections to natural theology was that the world looked less like a designed machine than 'a plant or animal',[67] and any attempt at a theology of nature today must greet his observation with acclaim. The old form of the teleological argument must take on new shape: while the designer of a machine stands back from his work (the celestial watchmaker), the designer of a community has to work *inside* it, suffering its growing pains and leading it to the aim he has for it. The cosmological argument too must be converted to the contemporary model of the world; instead of mechanical causation, factors like influence and persuasion become paramount ones in the building of a community. Thus the concepts of design and cause are replaced by purpose and persuasion, both of which will involve vulnerability and suffering. It is unfortunate that a great deal of discussion about the validity of natural theology among philosophers of religion is spent either defending or attacking forms of the argument which no longer correspond to the world-view of today.

There can be, of course, no question of *proving* the fact of God from the phenomena of the world. God cannot be the conclusion of a logical argument, since he is not available to us like an object in the world. But faith can clarify its understanding of God by reflecting upon the world that God creates. A strong objection to natural theology used to be not only that it attempted too much in offering a rational proof of God, but that even as 'suggestive' language about God it projected an image of God that was out of tune with the personal, active God of Israel and Jesus. Now, for perhaps the first time in the history of Christian thought, a reflection upon the 'visible things' of the world is not likely to lead to affirmations about God that are discordant with the suffering God of the cross. It ought to be no longer possible to suppose with Luther (in Thesis 20) that a knowledge of God gleaned from his works will project merely a God of power and so bolster the power-hungriness of men, while only knowledge of God from the cross will witness to a God of lowliness. Through his work both in the cross and creation God can manifest himself as 'the one who is hidden in suffering',[68] and thus

[67] David Hume, *Dialogues concerning Natural Religion* (1779), Part 7.
[68] Luther, *Heidelberg Disputation*, Thesis 20 (ed. Atkinson (n. 43 above), pp. 290–1).

theology of nature and 'theology from the Cross' ought to join hands, though so far they hardly seem to have touched fingertips. There can also be an integration between natural theology and existential theology which begins from reflection upon human experience since both are concerned with forms of organic community.

Thus the model of the world as organism with which we work today will lead us to conceive of a suffering God as its creator and sustainer. In this a strong contribution has been made by process theology, in urging us to think of the world as a living society, growing towards the aims God sets for it through a network of mutual influences, with God himself sharing in the conditions of its becoming.[69] Throughout this study we shall be in dialogue with process thought, in both appreciation and dissent, so it would be well to keep in mind from the outset the fundamental model of dipolar existence with which process thought works, and which includes the suffering of God as a necessary element.

The basis of process theology is the co-creativity of God and his world. Indeed, it is the power of creativity possessed by all creatures that involves God in suffering. The basic building blocks of reality at a subatomic level are understood as being momentary events of extremely brief duration, which reach a peak of satisfaction and then perish, to be succeeded in the stream of life by other events. These droplets of becoming or 'actual entities' can also be called 'actual occasions' or occasions of experience, and they enjoy some kind of feeling appropriate to their level of existence. They have some freedom to create themselves, growing towards a feeling of satisfaction through a process of 'concrescence', during which they 'prehend' (i.e. grasp) data of experience from a number of sources.[70] According to Whitehead's system of thought, they can receive influence in this way from previous entities, and pre-eminently from God who offers to every entity an 'initial aim' or a set of ideals which he knows will result in its maximum satisfaction. By providing this initial aim, God invites every entity to set forth on its path of growth towards satisfaction.[71] But in its process of concrescence, the entity is free to aim for intensity of feeling in ways that may accept, modify or reject the influence of God. Though God supplies an initial aim, luring the entity towards the goal of his purpose

---

[69] See ch. 1 n. 40 above for introductory works on process theology.

[70] A. N. Whitehead, *Science and the Modern World*, pp. 129–30; *Process and Reality*, pp. 27–39, 163–6, 323–6; Charles Hartshorne, *The Logic of Perfection*, pp. 196–7, 229–30.

[71] Whitehead, *Process and Reality*, pp. 373–5.

for it and the whole world, the entity has freedom in the way that it forms its own 'subjective aim' or sense of purpose.[72]

Each entity is dipolar, having a mental and a physical aspect to its being. Through its physical pole it prehends past entities in its environment as well as God, and thereby grows to satisfaction. Through its mental pole it can grasp ideals and values—called 'eternal objects'— quite apart from the physical occasions through which they may originally have come; this vision of possibilities for existence is called 'conceptual prehension'.[73] When the entity has reached satisfaction and perished, it ceases to be a subject and becomes an object to be prehended by others in their turn in a process of 'transition'.[74] Entities build up into societies, which are the large-scale objects in the world which we normally perceive—sticks, stones, people. The sorts of objects produced depend upon the nature of the transition from one entity to another. For instance, if there is a build-up of mentality in the stream of entities, then entities of a high degree of mentality are formed which finally result in consciousness; such a transition is also a build-up of novelty from one entity to another since it is the mental pole that is able to do and think new things. If there is a build-up merely of physical stability, then inanimate objects are formed. Moreover, animate 'societies' have dominant or controlling occasions such as the highly mental entities making up the human soul; in other 'societies', like a tree, all members contribute equally—which Whitehead calls a 'democracy'.[75]

This then is an organic view of the world, moving in a process of becoming towards a purposeful goal in which values are gained. We notice three features of this process which will be important for our later discussion of divine suffering. First, causation is a matter of influence and persuasion. Entities influence others by presenting themselves to be objectified within an other's experience; entities are influenced *by* others when they freely grasp hold of them. This is true whether we are thinking of causation by God or elements within the world. Past entities in the world provide efficient causation ('causal efficacy') through the process of transition, while God provides final causation through initiating the process of concrescence. But neither kind of cause is coercive. Second, everything in the universe enjoys some kind of experience or feeling, whatever kind of transition it is involved in. Some

---

[72] Ibid., pp. 130–4.
[73] Ibid., pp. 49–50, 69–73.   [74] Ibid., pp. 29–30, 129–30, 320–2.
[75] Whitehead, *Adventures of Ideas*, p. 264; *Process and Reality*, pp. 151–67. Cf. Hartshorne, *The Logic of Perfection*, pp. 202–3.

amount of feeling is passed on when an entity prehends the physical pole of another entity, but a much larger amount of feeling is passed on when an entity prehends the mental pole of a perished entity, that is when a present entity directly grasps the concepts and ideals which the previous entity had been envisaging in its own mind. Because an entity is grasping mental concepts though the instrument of its physical aspect, Whitehead calls this a 'hybrid prehension', and entities employ this kind of prehension above all when they grasp God's initial aim for them.[76] They prehend God's own concepts, his vision of possibilities for the world. Third, there is a place for sacrifice within this world system, since an entity might willingly forgo its own maximum satisfaction for the good of future entities, inspired by its vision of God's purpose for the whole world, which Whitehead calls a sense of 'peace'.[77] Thus influence, feeling, and sacrifice are three universal features of this view of the world.

We should now more explicitly examine the impact of this scheme of things upon God. According to Whitehead, God 'keeps the rules' of the process and is himself an actual entity, though unlike all other entities he does not perish.[78] God's mental pole is his 'primordial nature' in which he envisages all the possibilities there are for the world ('a vision of eternal objects'), which are the source of both stability and novelty within the cosmos. He sorts these into values, graded by their relevance to all particular situations whatever, and from them he presents each entity with its initial aim as it prehends his primordial being.[79] While his primordial nature is independent of the world, he also has a 'consequent nature' corresponding to his physical aspect, by which he himself prehends the world.[80] That is, he absorbs influence from the world, receiving the effects of worldly action and decision into himself. In feeling the world like this he suffers, for while all entities contribute value to God they also actualize both good and evil through the choices they make, and God receives the effect of these; he also feels their experience of suffering.

Thus God is the supreme cause of all things, luring on the world to an

---

[76] Whitehead, *Process and Reality*, pp. 343–4, 469.

[77] Whitehead, *Adventures of Ideas*, pp. 367 ff., 380 ff., cf. pp. 86, 109. Also see *Science and the Modern World*, p. 238.

[78] Whitehead, *Process and Reality*, pp. 135, 521–2. Therefore God is the only actual entity which is not also an actual occasion, conditioned by temporality; cf. *Religion in the Making*, pp. 90–9.

[79] Whitehead, *Process and Reality*, pp. 69–73.   [80] Ibid., pp. 46–7, 523.

intensity of beauty and satisfaction by presenting it at every level with an aim derived from his vision of possibilities. At the same time he is supremely effected, influenced, and moved by the world. Indeed, entities have their eternal life in God, an 'objective immortality' in being preserved within the divine being.[81] This means that Whitehead can speak of God's suffering love as 'a tender care that nothing be lost', and as 'the patience of God, tenderly saving the turmoil of the world'.[82] This amounts to God's pain as 'the great companion, the fellow-sufferer who understands'.[83] Whitehead acclaimed Plato's insight that 'the divine persuasion is the foundation of the order of the world',[84] but in opposition to Plato he affirmed that the ideals by which God influences the world involve his own actual suffering presence in the world.[85]

In a later development of process thought, Charles Hartshorne presses even further the notion of God's suffering immersion in the process, by shifting the focus of attention to the aspect of God's being which Whitehead called 'consequent' and which Hartshorne calls 'concrete'. Hartshorne disagrees with Whitehead that the possibilities contained within the primordial nature of God are to be thought of as 'eternal objects' which God contemplates. This seems to him to restrict the freedom of actual entities within the world. Surely, he argues, ideals must be able to emerge from the creative advance rather than being entirely imposed upon it from God's vision.[86] So the primordial nature of God, which he calls the 'abstract essence' of God, is the ground of possibility for God's concrete nature, and since this concrete nature includes all reality, the abstract essence of God is 'the eternal possibility for creative actualization'.[87] The necessary, independent aspect of God (his abstract essence) is indeed rich in possibility, but not in the form of particular possibilities which God surveys; it is the undefined possibility itself for all actualities, God's infinite capability for actuality. This fits in with Hartshorne's understanding of God as a society of entities rather than as a single actual entity. God is like a person, with his abstract essence like the enduring character of a person over against the many

---

[81] Ibid., pp. 46–7, 89, 364.   [82] Ibid., pp. 525–6.   [83] Ibid., p. 532.

[84] Whitehead, *Adventures of Ideas*, p. 205, cf. pp. 213–14.

[85] Ibid., p. 215.

[86] Charles Hartshorne, *Creative Synthesis and Philosophic Method*, pp. 58 ff. Cf. David R. Griffin, 'Hartshorne's Differences from Whitehead', in L. S. Ford (ed.), *Two Process Philosophers*, pp. 37–40.

[87] Hartshorne, op. cit. (n. 86 above), p. 68; cf. *The Divine Relativity*, pp. 70 ff.

concrete states of his life. God's abstract essence is his 'essential core of identity', his 'bare, individual existence'.[88]

Later we shall have occasion to judge the effectiveness of these two models for Christian theology, but what is important to notice here is that Hartshorne's account stresses the enmeshing of God in the world and its tragedies. While the abstract essence of God 'does not include the actual world and is not relative to it', his concrete state is supremely related to the world.[89] God is unsurpassably interactive.[90] Only he is related to all actualities at once; he is to be thought of as 'the all-inclusive reality' like a person who has the whole world for his body.[91] As including all events within his concrete nature, the qualities of responsiveness, participation, and sympathy come to the fore. God does indeed persuade the world, as in Whitehead's thought, by the beauty of his ideal for us, but in practical terms this means setting limits to our free decisions rather than presenting us with specific aims. His setting of limits means 'mitigating the risk and maximizing the promise of freedom'.[92] So his desire for all-inclusive beauty moves the world to greater and greater harmonies, by his constant setting and readjusting of boundaries within which worldly creative choices take place. God redeems all that is possible to redeem, but 'he will do this for the cosmos and his own life, and for us only as items in the inclusive reality, members of the inclusive society'.[93] It is because Hartshorne has already secured God's identity by the notion of his abstract essence that he is able to speak in this way of God as the ultimate receptacle for all experience and achievement, making a creative synthesis by including and evaluating all actualities within the harmony of his being.

At a number of points in our study we shall need to return to these basic ideas of process thought, to draw out more of their implications, to gain from them, and to question them. Here I only wish to register two

---

[88] Hartshorne, *Creative Synthesis and Philosophic Method*, p. 233, *A Natural Theology for Our Time*, p. 27.

[89] Hartshorne, *A Natural Theology for Our Time*, p. 27; cf. *The Divine Relativity*, pp. 80–1.

[90] Hartshorne, *A Natural Theology for Our Time*, p. 40.

[91] So also Schubert Ogden in agreement with Hartshorne; see S. M. Ogden, *The Reality of God* (SCM Press, London, 1967), p. 178.

[92] Hartshorne, *The Logic of Perfection*, p. 204; cf. *The Divine Relativity*, p. 135.

[93] Hartshorne, *A Natural Theology for Our Time*, p. 110. Since, according to Hartshorne, actual entities are past, God himself only knows past occasions rather than present ones (which are 'becoming' actual; see *Creative Synthesis and Philosophic Method*, p. 109).

fundamental disagreements with the process vision of the world, despite its enormously attractive view of God's action as suffering persuasion. The primary tenet of process thought is that creativity is the supreme value, which requires the various contributions of God and the world for it to happen. God is co-creative with the world because he can do no other; it is the nature of the process that he should have a restricted freedom and be involved in suffering; all is subservient to the creative advance towards fuller value. In this study I shall be rooting God's limitations and sufferings firmly in his own will as a Creator who offers real freedom to his creation. I believe that this more traditional view of divine self-limitation can in fact be vastly illuminated by views of divine action and reaction in process thought, without the incoherence that is sometimes claimed to result.

I also believe that we need to take issue with the view that a dipolarity in God would preserve his being in the face of suffering. Process theology is rightly concerned to affirm both God's universal immersion in suffering and his remaining other from the world as God; but I am not convinced that we can think of this by distinguishing sharply between two aspects in God corresponding to body and mind, or contingency and necessity, or actuality and possibility. Nor do we have to take the whole package of the process view of the world as having dipolarity and thus 'mentality' at every level of existence, in order to learn from its vision of a responsive creation bound together in mutual influence. It is this kind of world view, stressing factors of feeling, persuasion, and sacrifice, which makes the idea of a suffering God not only cogent but supremely desirable.

In this chapter we have surveyed four factors which promote the theological conviction that God suffers—the meaning of love, the implications of the cross of Jesus, the problem of suffering, and the structure of the world. But if these themes are given their full weight, we cannot escape from the conclusion that a suffering God is a God who is *changed* by his world, who is even under constraint from it. It is this implication we must now go on to examine.

3

The God Who Suffers Change

IF we are to answer such questions as 'Does God suffer?' or 'How does God suffer?', it seems sensible to begin by asking what we mean by suffering in our own experience. What is human suffering like? How well can this language be stretched for symbolic talk about God? One way of approach would be to survey different kinds of suffering, and to enquire in a scientific manner about their differing causes. After all, one might protest, to deal with the concept of suffering as an overall category would be to lose the real human situation in abstractions. Can any one category cover the pain caused in a Western family life by someone's having to work 'unsocial hours', and the pain of a family in India suffering from basic malnutrition? Can any one concept cover the suffering caused by war, genetic defects, toothache, and unemployment? Surely, one might assert, the only way of proceeding would be to analyse the various causes of suffering in their concrete social contexts, and then ask what light these actual events throw upon the notion of a suffering God. But this would be a very lengthy procedure if we were to take the social analysis seriously, and for most of the time the tools of enquiry we would be using would not include a theological interest in the meaning of suffering which went beyond charting its conditions.

If we do begin the other way round, however, with certain generalizations about the universal features of suffering, we must take care that we do not produce a theological scheme that implicitly condones suffering. It would be all to easy to speak of a suffering God and so to accept the state of a suffering humanity—to conclude that if God suffers, then we should hardly complain. Even, then, if we do not begin by analysing the various social-political causes for human suffering, our theological thought should create a motivation for dealing with such causes of suffering as can be cured. A theology of a suffering God must be tested by the yardstick of whether it builds up an intolerance towards those conditions of human suffering which can be abolished. With this qualification, we may risk a rather generalized analysis of what suffering entails.

I.   SUFFERING AS FEELING AND INJURY

We may discern two aspects of the experience of suffering; it is both an inner *feeling* and an *impact* from outside ourselves; that is, suffering is both felt and received. (*a*) On the one hand it is a movement within a person's psyche, a feeling, an emotion, an impulse. As an inner troubling or disturbance of equanimity it may be called 'pathos'. (*b*) On the other hand it is a conditioning from circumstances and causes other than ourselves. This impact or constraint need not only be physical, such as a blow from a fist; it can be social, such as the blow of losing one's home to the building of a motorway, or psychological, such as the blow of finding oneself misunderstood. Suffering, then, is both felt and received; it is both an emotion and an impression, a feeling-tone and a constraint.

Much of classical theology has denied both these dimensions of suffering to God. The first aspect seemed to destroy his blessedness, his eternal and untroubled bliss. The second seemed to destroy his aseity. This was because the idea that God had the origin of his existence only from himself (*a se*) was extended into his total self-sufficiency, needing nothing other than himself to be himself; so absolute Being was defined as being totally uncaused and unconditioned—in short, as having 'necessary' rather than 'contingent' existence. Moreover, both dimensions of suffering—feeling and constraint—were rejected as being suitable predicates for God because alike they meant movement in the sense of *change*. As far as feeling was concerned, an emotion was a motion from one state of being to another, and so meant *changing oneself*. The situation of receiving the impact of something causing pain seemed even more unsuitable for God; it meant being moved by something other than onself, and so *to be changed*. Since God was envisaged as absolute Being which excluded any becoming, there was no place for any change in God, from causes either outside or within himself. Again and again the argument was produced (deriving from Neo-Platonism) that God as the most perfect Being cannot change; if he changes for the better then he was deficient in his being before and so not God, while if he changes for the worse then he has become degraded in being and is certainly not God any longer.[1] This argument in fact assumes that 'perfection' is a fixed maximal quantity of value, so that

[1] See e.g. Augustine, *Sermones* vii. 7; Anselm, *Monologion* 24; Aquinas, *S. Th.* 1a. 9. 1. For a refutation from a non-process perspective, see Richard Swinburne, *The Coherence of Theism* (Clarendon Press, Oxford, 1977), pp. 212–15.

change will either get nearer to it or further from it. Much of my later discussion will challenge this assumption.

This picture of an unchanging and a-pathetic (literally, 'non-suffering') God was characteristic of traditional theology. Though the massive criticism of this portrait in recent years has perhaps tended to parody it, nevertheless there is some truth in the view that an apathetic God makes apathetic believers. As Dorothee Sölle suggests, 'When a being who is free from suffering is worshipped as God, then it is possible to train oneself in patience, endurance, imperturbability, and aloofness from suffering.'[2] The ideal believer becomes one whose coolness and placidity mirrors the divine peace, and this can lead to the dangers of political quietism and the characteristic modern desire to insulate oneself from the facts of suffering in the world. Evidence of this latter trend can be seen both in the evasion of suffering, as in the removal of the aged and dying from the home to institutions when it is not strictly necessary, and in the blunting of sensitivity to suffering through its trivialization in the media, as in the sensational reporting of war and starvation.

Traditional theology bound together the immutability of God with his impassibility; it insisted that to suffer meant to change, and therefore God could not suffer. At the foundation of this was a wedding together of the two dimensions of suffering; inner feeling was understood to be inseparable from external constraint or injury. Recently however there has been a tendency to separate these two dimensions—to speak of the suffering of God as a feeling, but to admit no constraint upon God. Some theologians thus admit a feeling-tone of suffering in God, but insist that he is not changed by suffering in any way.

An easy way to slip into this kind of thinking is to begin by differentiating quite properly between physical pain and suffering. Many medical authorities distinguish between the 'pain sensation' and 'pain experience',[3] the first being a matter of the bodily senses and the second a matter of a state of mind. It might well seem an appropriate theological move to use this distinction as a defence of talk about God as suffering; we might claim that although God has no pain sensation, since he does not have a body and a mass of nerve endings, he can still suffer in a way analogous to the human 'pain experience'. We might point to the

---

[2] Sölle, *Suffering*, p. 43.

[3] This precise terminology is used by J. D. Hardy, 'The Pain Threshold and the Nature of Pain Sensation', in C. A. Keele and R. Smith (eds.), *The Assessment of Pain in Man and Animals* (E. & S. Livingstone, London, 1962), p. 172. See further Hick, *Evil and the God of Love*, pp. 328 ff.

fact that in human experience the link between physical pain and inward suffering is a variable one anyway. People in a certain psychological state of mind can make light of the sensation of physical pain; soldiers in the excitement of battle, accident victims in shock, even victims of torture in a state of a religious exaltation can suffer pain without great inner feeling of distress. Conversely, people can experience considerable distress of mind while in physical safety. However, we make a careless step of thought if we go on to suppose that an injury inflicted upon us from outside is always a matter of biological pain, and that when human misery cannot be traced to strictly physical pain it is purely an *inner* state of mind; we forget that such causes of suffering as bad housing conditions, the threat of poverty, and psychological warfare are also impacts upon us from outside. Much suffering is caused today by conditions which promote isolation and loss of meaning. Sensation and stimulation is more complex than the pain caused by the damaging of nerve endings. If we forget this, we may draw hasty conclusion that 'the real experience of suffering is an activity in our inwardness',[4] and so pass quickly to the theological notion of a God who feels suffering as his own inner act without actually being changed by anything external to him. But no coherence can be given to this notion of suffering from our human experience; suffering is always a matter of feeling *and* constraint, even if the constraint is more subtle than a strictly physical injury. As long as we are drawing any analogy at all from human suffering, we must think of something in God which corresponds to both aspects of suffering, or abandon the analogy altogether.

Before we go on to criticize some extensive attempts in recent thinking to make exactly such a distinction between God's feeling of suffering and his being changed by the world, we should look more closely at the classical insistence that the two dimensions of suffering belong together.

2.   THE UNITY OF SUFFERING AND CHANGE

The classical theists demonstrated impressively that suffering meant being changed; on those ground they *denied* suffering in God. If we are to *affirm* it, it must be on the same grounds. Thomas Aquinas clearly intertwines suffering as feeling with suffering as constraint when he restates the philosophy of unchanging Being in terms of God as pure actuality. He rightly perceives that to suffer is to be acted upon by

4 Lee, *God Suffers for Us*, p. 19, cf. pp. 40–1.

something other than oneself. But according to Aquinas this cannot happen to God, because God would have to possess the potentiality to receive such an impression, and he has no potentialities that he does not eternally actualize.[5] This consideration is supported by the definition of God as simple and perfect; as perfect he cannot acquire anything such as an injury, and as simple he cannot be changed either, for only composite things change.[6] So much for suffering as receiving an impact from outside. Thomas likewise claims that suffering as a feeling is also impossible for God; all emotions are excluded from God because, as passions, they arise from receiving something from an external force through the senses.[7] In other words, suffering as an emotion is prompted precisely by the stimulus of suffering as an impact from outside. Moreover, God cannot even change *himself* by choosing to feel suffering within; as pure act there are no unrealized potentials in God, no goals which God sets before himself to achieve in the future such that there could be a feeling of effort or striving within God.[8] As simple Being, one part of God cannot act upon another to produce suffering and change. As perfect Being, God cannot add to himself in any way, such as by gaining an experience of suffering or being released from it.

With this image of God as *actus purus*, simple and perfect, the classical theist binds together the assertions that God is not changed and does not suffer. When he speaks of God as love it is within that framework. Conversely, we may compare this statement from a modern process theologian, who also links together suffering and change but with the opposite conclusion:

There can be no love without suffering. Suffering in the widest sense means the capacity to be acted upon, to be changed, moved, transformed by the action of, or in relation to, another. The active side of love requires that we allow the field of our action and its meaning to be defined by what the other requires.[9]

In the last chapter I suggested that love must mean suffering. Now I suggest, in agreement here with Daniel Day Williams, that suffering must mean change and being changed. To love is to be in a relationship where what the loved one does alters one's own experience. The person who loves must take the other into account as he is, not imposing his own view upon him but receiving what the other has to contribute; at

5 Aquinas, *S.Th.* 1a. 2. 3; 3. 1; 9. 2; cf. 19. 7; 22. 1.
6 Aquinas, *S.Th.* 1a. 9. 1.   7 Aquinas, *S.Th.* 1a. 20. 1.
8 Aquinas, *S.Th.* 1a. 9. 2.
9 Williams, *The Spirit and the Forms of Love*, p. 117, cf. pp. 127–8.

the same time the lover's existence is shaped by the other's needs. The lover does not impose a structure of 'doing good' on the other, but has his existence threatened and then transformed by the reality of what the other is. When we apply this thesis about the nature of love to God who is love, I believe we must affirm some of the insights in a theology of process: to some extent God must be influenced by the world as well as the world by God; to some extent God must 'become' what he is in reaction to the environment of the world as the world becomes in the context of God. God's inclusion of the world within his experience must have some effect upon him. As Charles Hartshorne remarks:

To love is to rejoice with the joys and sorrow with the sorrows of others. Thus it is to be influenced by those who are loved.[10]

But if we are to grasp the true force of the claim that to suffer in love is to be changed, we must pin down more exactly the differences between such theological statements as those of Aquinas and Williams. Aquinas perhaps more than most past theologians has suffered recently from parodies of his view that God cannot move and change. 'Classical Theism' has been made too easy a target for those who want to speak casually of a suffering God. David Burrell, in his book *Aquinas: God and Action*, exclaims with some exasperation about the men of straw that have been set up in place of the Angelic Doctor. In the critics' version of Thomist theology, he complains, 'the God which emerges is unresponsive and aloof, a useful tool for ecclesiastical tyranny and a convenient symbol for the super-ego, but hardly fit for Christian worship'.[11] This God who is detached and unconcerned is not, he insists, the God Aquinas is talking about, and he singles out Hartshorne as one process theologian who seems to him to be guilty of this misunderstanding. However, I believe that Hartshorne, with other process theologians, does have a valid critique of Aquinas' concept of God, whatever excesses some critics might run to. If we isolate some features of Aquinas' thought, we should be able to see the real point of opposing his denial of suffering and change in God, as well as the need to keep these concepts together as he rightly does.

1. In the first place, we ought to notice that when Aquinas states that God does not move himself, he does not mean that God is inert and static but that he always acts effortlessly. As Burrell points out, Aquinas is insisting that God is beyond the human category of motion with its

---

[10] Hartshorne, *A Natural Theology for our Time*, p. 75.
[11] David B. Burrell, *Aquinas: God and Action*, p. 36, cf. ch. 6 *passim*.

alternating movement and rest.[12] The statement that God is unchangeable is a parallel one; it forbids thought of activity connected with
striving and achieving. Thus Aquinas allows a certain movement in God
when he thinks it does not involve change—that is, he recognizes the
activity of the will; in line with this he argues that love, like knowing, is
a matter of intention and thus a desire and movement of the will rather
than an emotion. Burrell concludes that Aquinas is not really following
a very different programme from Hartshorne in aiming to preserve the
transcendence of God, since Hartshorne also reserves immutable aspects
to God, in an 'abstract' nature.[13]

However, we notice that there is still a substantial difference between
Aquinas and the process theologians here; Aquinas forbids the
movement of suffering in God because it is a movement from
potentiality to actuality, and it is precisely this movement that is central
to Hartshorne's thought. In his abstract or transcendent nature God is
pure potentiality, and these potentials are actualized in his 'concrete'
nature which includes the world within itself. God grasps all
potentialities *and* all actualities, but he does not grasp potentials *as*
actuals. This idea is basic to process theology, but it is also an insight
which I believe is basic to any assertion of the suffering of God. Aquinas
denies it and consistently denies also the suffering of God; if we are to
affirm the one we must accept the other. A suffering God is one who has
potentialities within him which he has not yet actualized; only in this
way can we speak of a God who suffers change in suffering.

2. But, in the second place, we must notice that Aquinas is in fact
extremely cautious about saying such things as that God is unchanging.
Burrell's study of Aquinas' language makes clear that his method is not
to describe God in himself as unchanging, and then to unpack the
implications of this assertion. Rather, Aquinas takes the negative way of
proscribing certain talk about God as unsuitable, so pointing more
clearly towards an unknown God who is ultimately indescribable.[14]
Thus he is asserting that we cannot think of God as changing *in a certain
way*, with the kind of change which we know in our experience, namely
moving from potentiality to actuality, or setting and achieving goals.
He is hesitant to make the absolute verdict that God does not change,
and thus leaves a good deal of room open for further exploration, even
after the bulk of the *Summa Theologiae*. In contrast to this method, if we

[12] Ibid., p. 82, cf. pp. 37–8; see Aquinas, *S. Th.* 1a. 9. 1–2.
[13] Burrell, *Aquinas: God and Action*, pp. 81–3.
[14] Ibid., pp. 13 ff., 59 ff., 87 ff.

are now to say positively that God does suffer and change, then we are undeniably being ambitious about describing the being of God. Some may object that it assumes a strict analogy between the experience of loving and personhood as we know it and as it might be true in God. Though any attempt to talk about God in himself requires the use of some kind of analogy, this kind of talk seems to presume that the human experience of suffering has a *high* degree of reference to God.

One defence of this positive method might be to begin by constructing an ontological system, a theological vision of how things are, such as the process scheme where reality is characterized by 'feeling' at all levels, and where 'God is not to be treated as an exception to all metaphysical principles, invoked to save their collapse', but is instead 'their chief exemplification' (A. N. Whitehead).[15] However, I am proceeding on a more pragmatic basis than this. In the previous chapter we found that certain religious concerns prompted us to speak of God as a suffering God; some of these were inherited from the Christian tradition, arising from reflection upon fundamental religious experiences that we can only call 'revelation', and some arise from our experience of faith today. Our starting point is the *concern* to speak of a suffering God, in order to make sense of our experience as Christian believers. We are now going on to face the implications of that concern, and to see whether we can make this kind of talk about God consistent with our human experience of how things are, and coherent in relation to other parts of Christian believing (such as a recognition of the transcendence and ultimate mystery of God). Our method is to take an existential concern and test it for reasonableness. In doing this we should be able to discover some of the scope and limits of analogical talk about God as personal. Anyway, we might judge of Aquinas' method that, however limited it might claim to be, it still raises all kinds of problems about the relation of God to the world.

3. This brings us to a third observation about Aquinas, concerning his denial of a 'real relationship' between God and mankind. He asserts that 'being related to creatures is not a reality in God'.[16] Burrell, in his study of Aquinas, admits that this sounds rather shocking, but asks us to consider carefully what Aquinas means. Aquinas gives the illustration of our viewing an object such as a pillar: 'Just as we can say that the pillar has changed from being on my left to being on my right, not through

[15] Whitehead, *Process and Reality*, p. 521. Also Ogden, op. cit. (ch. 2 n. 91), p. 175.
[16] Aquinas, *S. Th.* 1a. 13. 7; translation from Blackfriars Edition, Vol. 3 (1964), p. 75.

any alteration in the pillar but simply because I have turned around', so
it is that we can apply to God 'words implying temporal sequence and
change, not because of any change in him but because of a change in the
creatures'.[17] It would be preposterous to think that Aquinas is drawing
the conclusion that God is as inert towards us as a stone pillar. The point
is that the relationship between God and his creatures is not a
symmetrical one. In Burrell's exegesis, when Aquinas maintains that the
creatures have a 'real relationship' (*relatio realis*) to God, he means that
they have natures that need him. Conversely, God's relationship with us
is a 'conceptual relationship' (*relatio rationis*), or something we merely
attribute to him with our minds, in the sense that he does not have a
nature that inherently needs the relationship; he wills it freely.[18] Thus,
by defining a 'real relationship' as one which happens by a necessary and
natural process, Burrell is able to claim that God relates himself freely,
and thus more intimately, to the world without it.

But we notice that this supposedly intimate relationship still means
that God is not changed by the world that he knows and loves. Here the
analogy of the pillar holds good. According to Aquinas, when a creature
knows or loves another, he turns to the image (the phantasm) of the
known in his mind by means of his active intellect, and is thereby
affected by it.[19] A key feature of the 'real relationship' is that the
knower is changed by the object known; in the terminology used by
Hartshorne, who acclaims Aquinas' theory of perception thus far, the
knower is 'internally related' to the object he takes into his mind.
However, as Hartshorne points out, Aquinas exempts God from this
logic of knowing. Although God is the Supreme Knower, he is not
changed by the image of his creatures;[20] he seems then, like the pillar, to
be only an object and not a subject of knowing. Hartshorne, with
justice, protests that this can hardly be called knowing or loving at all,
and that if God truly knows the world he must be affected by it.
Thomists will, of course, riposte that God knows in a special mode, by
perfectly willing or intending the knowledge of the beloved.[21] But can

---

[17] Ibid.

[18] Burrell, *Aquinas: God and Action*, p. 85. See Aquinas, *S. Th.* 1a. 28. 1 cf. 1a. 14. 8,
1a. 19. 4.

[19] Aquinas, *S. Th.* 1a. 13. 7, 1a. 34. 3, 1a. 19. 3, 1a. 85. 2. Also *Summa Contra Gentiles*
4. 11. 13, 4. 19. 3.

[20] Charles Hartshorne (with William L. Reese), *Philosophers Speak of God*, pp. 120
ff., cf. *Man's Vision of God*, pp. 235–6.

[21] See e.g. F. X. Meehan, 'Efficient Causality: A reply and a Comment', *Journal of
Religion*, 26 (1946), pp. 50 ff. Burrell, *Aquinas: God and Action*, pp. 141, 151, 155–6,

God actually know the world as it is if its own peculiar reality has no effect upon him, or is God simply loving his own image of it? Again, we must ask whether God can be said to do anything remotely analogous to the 'repenting' of which Old Testament writers speak;[22] can he be intimately related to us if he does not form new purposes in the face of human reaction to him, but only appears to do so by changing *our* circumstances so that we see him, like the pillar, from new perpectives?

We can only answer these questions by taking into account what seems to be most consistent with the nature of human love, within a coherent concept of God. We can agree that Aquinas' denial of 'real relations' to God does not portray God as inert, and that it points correctly towards God's free will at the heart of his relationship with the world. But we must attempt to combine this freedom with the process insight that God is internally related to the world, for in so far as a denial of real relations denies this, it is not continuous enough with any experience of knowing and loving that we have. A preliminary step would be to guard against immediately assuming that if God needs the world within a reciprocal relationship, then such a necessity must be an intrinsic part of God's nature, like the creature's need of God; we notice that both Aquinas and process thought do in fact make this assumption from opposite sides of the argument.

If however, in opposition to Aquinas, we ascribe suffering love to God we must face squarely what it implies about change. There must be some gap between what God already knows and what the world does at any point in time. It must be possible for the world to bring something new to God each morning, for this is what is involved in a 'real relationship'. One way of conceiving this would be to distinguish between what God knows perfectly in potentiality, and what he knows perfectly in actuality as it happens. For God, the 'other over against him'—mankind—would have existed already in his mind as a potentiality, but the actuality of a community of persons can never be quite the same as the possibility of it in the creator's mind. To love within the growth of a community is to allow it to develop in its own way and to make its own impact and contribution; otherwise it is not a community of free persons but a puppet show. We might also appeal to

argues that God's inner act of understanding the world does not, like ours, produce an inner articulation and so does not increase self-knowledge.

[22] Relevant texts include Gen. 6: 6, 1 Sam. 15: 11, Jer. 18: 8, cf. Jonah 3: 4–10, Isa. 38: 15, Hosea 11: 8. Calvin takes a similar view to Aquinas: see *Institutio Christianae Religionis* (1559), I. xvii. 12–13.

the analogy of an artist painting a picture; he will have the potential form of it in his mind as he begins, but in his interaction with the materials of his creation he will discover new aspects to his purpose, and the actuality will have novel features to it. There is some co-creativity between artist and medium, some playful development of artistic purpose. In these kinds of ways we might conceive of God as suffering the impact of his world, moving from the potential to the actual.

If we could think in this way, it would fit in with another aspect of suffering love as we know it in human experience. Daniel D. Williams draws attention to what he calls 'the pilgrimage of love':

We cannot know fully the meaning of love until it has done all its work . . . what love may do and will do, what creative and redemptive work lies ahead, can only be known partially in the history of love until the 'end'.[23]

The essence of love is not to insist on knowing the end of the story, not to weigh up and calculate the gains of loving. Relationships begin with a journey of love into the unknown. Even within the family the mystery of another's personality means that there is a journey of discovery into strange territory. In a marriage where there is nothing new to discover about the other, because one partner insists on prying open all the other's thoughts, there will be a voyage to disaster. To treat each other as persons is to respect the mystery of the other. So in the re-making of relationships after a breach there is also an element of risk, an uncertainty about how things will turn out. Without a pilgrimage of trust and risk there will be no reconciliation: 'There is nothing love cannot face; there is no end to its faith, hope and endurance.'[24] To take this step into the unknown, not knowing fully how things will turn out is for us to grow in being a person. If we were in any sense to apply this analogy of Personhood to God, then we should think of his creating a covenant partner and taking a risk of faith on him. He creates one who is other than himself, a stranger to his being, and goes on pilgrimage with him. The very act of creation is a kenotic event for God. As J. Macquarrie expresses it:

God risks himself, so to speak, with the Nothing; he opens himself and pours

---

23 Williams, *The Spirit and the Forms of Love*, p. 212.
24 1 Cor. 13:3, *NEB* version. On the journey of love, see below, pp. 158–63. Cf. F. W. Dillistone, *The Christian Understanding of Atonement* (Library of Constructive Theology, James Nisbet, London, 1968), p. 266: 'Yahweh went forth . . . seeking the man, the succession of men, to whom he could relate Himself as friend to friend . . . This god is in the begining the Stranger'.

himself out into nothing . . . and in giving himself in this way he places himself in jeopardy . . . but a God who securely hoarded his Being would be no God and perhaps nothing at all.[25]

So, at the deepest level, when mankind has broken the relationship with God, God heals it by knowing the suffering of a love that does not calculate what it may achieve, but exposes itself to the unknown of death. A suffering God like this would be affected and changed by the world, not to become less God but to become more richly himself, fulfilling his being through the world.

This kind of theological sketch raises, of course, problems about limited omniscience, temporality, and incompleteness in God. In order for it to be acceptable we shall have to cope with these issues in the next chapter. More immediately I want to deal with one result of this way of thinking—the implication that the world is in some way necessary for the being of God. If God fulfils his being through the suffering of creation and redemption, if he becomes more fully himself by pouring himself out in kenotic love for the world, then it seems that the world is necessary for God to be God. It was, naturally, this conclusion that Aquinas was trying to avoid with his definition of a *relatio rationis* between God and mankind. But perhaps, it may be objected, there is no need to press on either to this conclusion or to Aquinas' solution. Despite the masterly achievement of Aquinas in weaving together the two dimensions of suffering as feeling and constraint, upon which our thought has relied so far, there are some theologians today who prefer a compromise path: they will admit that God feels suffering, while denying that he is changed by his world which is the occasion of that suffering.

3. ONE-DIMENSIONAL SUFFERING?

In the Patristic period there were some attempts already being made to loosen the bond between the two aspects of suffering, particularly among Western theologians. Tertullian tentatively suggested that, while God's substance was not liable to change, yet he must have feelings (such as anger and mercy) of some kind; 'he is moved by all these affections in his own way'.[26] Lactantius more firmly opposed the

---

[25] John Macquarrie, *Principles of Christian Theology*, p. 256.
[26] Tertullian, *Adversus Marcionem* 2. 16 (cf. *Adversus Praxean* 29 on the immutability of God).

current view that 'God is not moved by any feelings', maintaining that to rule out any emotional reaction of God to the world would be to undercut his vitality and providence; at the same time, he insists that God must remain free from external constraint, the principle of his movement residing entirely in himself.[27] But it is today that there is a sustained attempt to speak of God's feeling of suffering without being changed by the world, though there are harder and softer lines taken about this one-dimensional suffering.

1. The strongest line taken suggests that God feels suffering, but is not changed in any way at all, either from outside or by changing himself from within. For example, H. P. Owen approves the view that 'God is incapable of suffering change from either an external or an internal cause', but he also thinks that God must suffer for his world, feeling 'sorrow, sadness, and pain' since he is a God who is loving and incarnate.[28] He attempts to reconcile the suffering and the immutability of God by proposing that God's experience of suffering is wholly vicarious, in the form of an 'imaginative response'.[29] This can only mean that God imagines what it might be like to experience the suffering that his world knows. Basic to this approach is the distinction that Owen makes between 'response' and 'change'; he maintains that God can respond to the needs of his world without actually being changed by making his response, though Owen goes a little beyond this Thomist point with the notion of suffering in imagination.

Similarly, E. Mascall affirms that God by his very essence is changeless and necessary, while at the same time he asserts that 'the intensity with which our actions as personal beings affect God is infinitely greater than that with which they affect our fellow beings.'[30] He is more cautious than Owen in not venturing upon an explanation of 'imaginative suffering', though it would seem that some such idea is required if one is to attempt to integrate a feeling of suffering with strict immutability. R. E. Creel, for instance, agrees that God can respond to the world without its making any change in his very being, but then he also denies that this response could involve any possibility in feeling. He suggests that, since an immutable God actually 'responds' by making eternal resolves about how to deal with all possible choices that human beings might make, a better word than 'response' might be 'pres-

---

[27] Lactantius, *De Ira*, 2, 4, 8, 15–17.
[28] H. P. Owen, *Concepts of Deity*, p. 23.
[29] Ibid., p. 24.
[30] E. L. Mascall, *He Who Is*, p. 111, cf. pp. 95–6.

ponse'.[31] While this is a consistent argument, it depends upon being able to conceive of such a non-sympathetic interaction as being love. Owen rightly wants to speak of a more sympathetic involvement, even though in the diluted form of an imaginative response.

There are, however, a number of fatal defects in this idea of imaginative suffering. First, it is hard to see the difference between suffering in imagination and experiencing the actual mental pain which Owen denies to God. Even if God takes on the experience of his creatures vicariously, he must be conditioned by it. This objection stands out even more sharply in the face of an ingenious extension of Owen's kind of idea along the lines of role play. D. Attfield[32] suggests that God, in the person of the Logos, plays the role of a suffering and dying man in union with a real man, Jesus. The divine Logos does not, however, know that he is only playing a role and so achieves considerable imaginative identity; he does not know that he is impassible and so enters imaginatively into dying, imagining himself to be 'snuffed out' irretrievably. Along these lines, believes Attfield, he can make sense of the notion of a crucified God, and such an argument is perhaps the end-point of Owen's approach. But if this experience can actually happen to the divine consciousness, it is hard to see how it has no causative effect upon it. Similarly, it is questionable whether one can talk of an imaginative response anyway unless the responder knows what it is *like* to suffer. Some recent philosophy of religion has doubted whether one can speak of a God who knows the world with perfect sympathy and yet is not changed by it, since to know the world truly as it is means to know it as it knows itself, i.e. in a state of change.[33] Indeed, the idea of a merely imaginative response of God to the suffering of his world hardly does justice to the religious experience of the Old Testament prophets, who believed that *they* were being called into sympathy with *God's* unique pain.

2. A second, softer form of claiming that God suffers without being changed is to suggest that God feels suffering and thus *changes himself* in a

---

[31] Creel, *Divine Impassibility*, pp. 17, 23, 30. For a criticism of such divine 'planning in advance', see Richard Swinburne, *The Existence of God* (Clarendon Press, Oxford, 1979), pp. 238–9.

[32] D. G. Attfield, 'Can God be Crucified?: A Discussion of J. Moltmann', *Scottish Journal of Theology*, 30 (1977), pp. 45–57.

[33] See Anthony Kenny, *The God of the Philosophers* (Clarendon Press, Oxford, 1979), pp. 39 ff. Cf. A. N. Prior, 'The Formalities of Omniscience', *Philosophy*, 37 (1962), pp. 114–29, and N. Kretzmann, 'Omniscience and Immutability', *Journal of Philosophy*, 63 (1966), pp. 409–21.

limited way. Hans Küng, for example, professes himself dissatisfied
with Aquinas' idea of a mere *relatio rationis* between God and the world,
especially as it bears on the incarnation.[34] It is not enough, he asserts, to
say that the Logos only seems to suffer and change in so far as the
humanity of Christ changes its *relatio realis* to the Logos. That would not
be to speak of the Word become flesh, but of the flesh become Word.
However, he inherits the mantle of Aquinas in that he also accepts that
there can be no unrealized potentials in God; he believes that if God
were to move from potentiality to actuality, achieving some possibility
that was not so far achieved, then God would not be God. On the other
hand, Küng invites us to consider what 'actuality' signifies; it means
livingness, vivacity, energy, and the ability to do new things that suprise
us with the unexpected. He suggests that 'mutability' in the sense of
God's changing himself to meet the needs and conditions of the world is
the highest form of life. God changes himself and his will (he 'repents')
in the face of what people do with his love, though he is not actually
changed by any external force. He changes himself in response to the
world; the world does not change him. God as active energy is in a state
analogous to what we call becoming, suggests Küng, 'not however out
of a potentiality, but out of the highest actuality'.[35]

There are problems, however, in the notion of a suffering God who
changes only by altering himself in response to the world (an approach
which is also adopted by Emil Brunner[36]). To begin with, this kind of
change still appears to be an actualizing of a potential. J. Y. Lee, who
takes a similar line, offers a modified formula here, speaking of God's
'active potentiality' in contrast to a 'passive potentiality'. He appears to
mean that God has a potentiality for acting in empathy with the world,
but not a potential for being acted upon by it, since 'men's action never
causes or affects but always *occasions* divine "reaction"'.[37] Even if we
were to accept that this formula makes more sense of self-change as a
supreme form of actuality, we still have to ask whether self-alteration
can truly be called suffering. To say that God chooses to suffer without
enduring external constraint is a very weakened notion of suffering,

[34] Küng, *Menschwerdung Gottes*, pp. 639–44.   [35] Ibid., p. 640.

[36] E. Brunner, *The Christian Doctrine of God: Dogmatics* Vol. 1., trans. O. Wyon
(Lutterworth Press, London, 1949), p. 268: 'God "reacts" to the acts of men, and in that
He "reacts", He changes.' cf. Barth, *CD* II/1, pp. 370–1: 'He is moved and touched by
himself'.

[37] Lee, *God Suffers for Us*, p. 41. The terminology of active and passive potential was
used by Aquinas (*S. Th.* 1a. 9. 2.), but as applied only to creatures and not to God.

since part of the meaning of our suffering is the feeling of helplessness, a falling victim to what we cannot regulate. Origen perceived this when considering the human sufferings of Christ: 'pain is an experience outside the control of the will'.[38] If God, in choosing to suffer, knows no vulnerability to suffering with its unexpected attacks, then he is hardly sharing our experience. Men have no choice in much of the suffering they have to undergo. In addition, to propose that God's suffering consists only in his changing himself is to depict a masochistic God, and so to come perilously near to condoning human suffering as an offering God requires.

It surely only makes sense to say that God *chooses* to suffer in love, if what he chooses to do is to put himself into a situation where he can be injured. He must, like Jesus facing the cross, be exposed to the risk of suffering which remains a risk rather than an absolute certainty, even if it is a virtual certainty. It is not masochism for Christian people also to choose suffering, if the suffering is inflicted upon them by others who do not have to inflict it. This was the conclusion Origen came to about the sufferings of Jesus, in reply to the criticisms of Celsus that his divine intention to suffer must have meant that he did not suffer in the fullest sense; Origen suggests that what Jesus willed was to fall into the hands of evil men, so that pain was not under his control but 'in the power of the men who were disposed to inflict the pains and griefs upon him'.[39] If we now apply this to the nature of God himself (which Origen did not do) then we must speak of God's choosing that suffering might befall him, being open to suffering with its final unpredictability. It is not adequate to speak of God's only changing himself.

An illuminating analogy for this kind of chosen suffering is the human experience of 'active suffering', to which Kierkegaard drew attention, speaking of suffering as 'the highest action in inwardness'. This is a taking hold of the suffering that befalls us, accepting it for ourselves and doing something with it, 'grasping misfortune' or 'reconstructing existence in action'.[40] To choose suffering in this way is to suffer victoriously, for 'what I take belongs to me in a differing sense from something I only bear' (D. Sölle).[41] Though suffering has befallen

[38] Origen, *Contra Celsum* 2. 23; trans. and ed. Henry Chadwick (The University Press, Cambridge, ²1965), p. 88. Origen is not, of course, thinking about the suffering of the Logos in his divine nature.

[39] Ibid., cf. 2. 10 (ed. Chadwick, p. 75).

[40] S. Kirkegaard, *Concluding Unscientific Postscript*, pp. 386–8.

[41] Sölle, *Suffering*, p. 103.

us, we choose it as our own; or for the sake of love we choose a path where it is likely that suffering will be imposed upon us, and we make that our own. If we apply this analogy to God then we can say that when God chooses to make our suffering his own he is subject to suffering, but not subjected by it; he is under constraint from suffering, but it has no power to overwhelm him because he has freely chosen it as part of his own being. He triumphs over suffering because he chooses it for a purpose. Such a suffering is redemptive, as Berdyaev maintains:

Divine suffering exists and this divine suffering is evoked by a lack of congruity between God and the condition of the world and man. There is a dark suffering which leads to ruin, and there is a bright suffering which leads to salvation. Christianity changes the path of suffering into the path of salvation. It is a divine-human suffering, and that answers the tormenting questions of theodicy.[42]

Central, therefore, to the human experience of active suffering is a dialectic between fate and action, between suffering which befalls and suffering which is chosen. If we are to apply this analogy to God in any meaningful way, we must retain the dialectic. This is what theologians fail to do when they speak of God's only changing himself. Seizing upon the idea of active suffering, they suggest that divine suffering is to be understood only in terms of inward action. J. Y. Lee, for example, finds this to be a way of coping with the problem of the effect of evil upon God. He notes the customary objection to the suffering of God that, if suffering is an evil, this would seem to allow evil a place within the divine being. In reply he maintains that God's suffering is not directly caused by human sin but only occasioned by it as God *undertakes* suffering to overcome evil: 'evil is the providential occasioning of divine passibility'.[43] In this way of thinking, God's suffering is redemptive because it is a purely inner action. It would in fact be better to solve this question along the lines of suffering not being intrinsically evil; just as in human experience suffering can have ultimate good or evil effects depending upon the reaction of the sufferer, so God's victory over evil consists in the way that he deals with the suffering that befalls him, whatever evil causes lie behind it.[44] If we sever the dialectic of suffering

---

[42] Nicolas Berdyaev, *The Divine and the Human*, trans. R. M. French (Geoffrey Bles, London, 1949), p. 73.

[43] Lee, *God Suffers for Us*, p. 50. (Cf. Heschel, *The Prophets*, pp. 225–6.) The objection being answered, that suffering is intrinsically an evil, is voiced by e.g. Friedrich Von Hügel, *Essays and Addresses, Second Series*, pp. 199–202.

[44] So Wheeler Robinson, *Suffering Human and Divine*, p. 178.

which befalls and suffering which is chosen, whether we do so in the interests of divine goodness or divine aseity, we are no longer meaningfully talking about suffering at all. It is tempting to slip into this way of thinking, since to speak of something befalling God ('fate') is immediately to raise problems about the omniscience and eternity of the divine nature. Even Moltmann speaks of God's suffering as 'the supreme work of God on God himself',[45] but if it is not also the work of man on God it is not suffering.

4. THE FREEDOM OF GOD TO BE IN NEED

The suffering of God must, then, include the two dimensions of feeling and change in their full sense. To feel suffering is to be under constraint from external forces, and so for God to suffer means that he is changed by the world. However, we now seem to be facing a major problem of thought. If God is changed by the world, it can only be to become more truly himself or to fulfil his being, for if his being were degraded he would no longer be God, and anyway his suffering of change is an exercise of love which must be life-enhancing. But then the world seems to be necessary for God to be what he is. This chain of thought can in fact be started further back, with creation itself. In creation, God engages in relationship with free beings; these cause him suffering, which inflicts change upon him through which he makes himself more truly himself. Thus creation contributes something to the being of God (or to the becoming of God) and is necessary in some sense to him. A further implication of this appears to be that God and the world must coexist, for God must always have had a world to fulfil himself through. It ought to be clear now why the classical theists such as Aquinas were so alarmed by the notion of a suffering God, and why we cannot hold a merely sentimental belief in it. If we are to hold to it we must follow through the consequences, though I believe they will lead to a concept of God which will be more adequate to our experience of suffering than a God who merely hoards his being up in himself. Traditional theology has usually offered at least three reasons why the world cannot be necessary to God: he would not be infinite, the world would have no explanation, and God would not be self-existent. The third of these presents the most challenge to any theology of a suffering God, and will occupy us longest.

1. First there is the question of the *infinity* of a suffering God. Much

---

[45] Moltmann, *The Trinity and the Kingdom of God*, p. 99 (see below, ch. 5. 3).

traditional theology has protested that for an infinite God to include even a trace of finitude would be a contradiction in terms, and this would rule out any effect upon God by the world. We might make the quick riposte, with Karl Barth, that it is not for us to lay down demands as to what God can or cannot include within his divine life; if we object that an infinite God cannot encompass the finite then we are simply showing our 'pagan' and idolatrous outlook in denying God's freedom to be what he wills to be.[46] It is not for us as creatures to accuse God of contradicting himself. Less polemically, we might point out that the idea that the infinite cannot include the finite stems from a notion of the simplicity of the divine being. The argument here, as adopted by Aquinas from Aristotle, is that what is completely unlimited cannot contain any limits, and hence cannot include any finite boundaries. The underlying assumption is that God must be logically 'simple', so that what is true of any part of God is true of the whole. But, as Keith Ward suggests, 'It is quite coherent, however, to suppose that God, while indivisible, is internally complex.'[47] Then we could conceive of God as exhibiting his infinity not in excluding the finite, but including it as part of his being.

If we think of God as internally complex, then we are not compelled on the other hand to insist that an infinite God who contains the finite must be infinitely finite, i.e. including *everything* finite. The point is that, according to his good pleasure, an infinite God can include what finitude he will; he is not obliged, for instance, to retain evil actions within himself eternally. We may observe here in passing that the doctrine of God as Trinity is precisely one way of attempting to express the nature of God as complex being. In fact, it is very hard to conceive of a God who did not participate in the finite as having any kind of contact with the finite world at all. The logical conclusion would be a God who was totally self-absorbed, for whom the fitting symbol would not be a cross but a narcissus.

2. A second, and stronger, traditional objection to a suffering God runs like this: if the world is the means through which God becomes what he is (through suffering in it), then there is no *explanation* for the existence of the world. It is asserted that only a God who is wholly independent, necessary, and infinite can explain the existence of a world which is dependent, contingent, and finite. So E. Mascall objects that a God who fulfills his being through the world may be an explanation of

[46] Barth, *CD* IV/1, p. 186; II/1, p. 314.
[47] Keith Ward, *Rational Theology and the Creativity of God*, p. 216, cf. p. 71.

the purpose of the world, but not of the sheer fact of the world. Such a God would explain *why*, but not *that* the world is: 'Nothing less than a strictly infinite God can provide the explanation of the world's existence, and . . . in the fullest sense the world must be altogether unnecessary to God'.[48] This rules out the kind of change which suffering makes to the being of God. The claim is that God must have 'necessary' being, in the particular sense of being totally unconditioned and uncaused by anything other than himself; the world cannot be necessary to God in any way, or theology can no longer provide any ultimate explanation for the world (and explaining the world is supposed to be one of the glories of doing theology!).

This claim, however, is not as strong as it looks. In the first place, its advocates admit that a totally self-sufficient God explains *that* the world is at the expense of *why*. If the world is totally unnecessary to God, then creation rests upon a decision of God's will for which no reason can be found. As soon as we begin to offer reasons why God should have made the world—for example, to have fellowship with man—then we infringe the sort of absolute freedom of God's will that this view presupposes. (There can be another meaning to the freedom of the will of God, as we shall see in a moment.) It is much to the credit of theologians like Mascall that they boldly admit this: 'It is possible to assign motives for the acts which our human wills perform, precisely because their freedom is limited; in the case of God there is no reason whatever.'[49] But this looks like a very peculiar explanation for the fact of the world; it is an explanation without reason. One is tempted to suppose that God created the world in a fit of absent-mindedness.

Moreover, it is not quite right to say that the notion of a suffering and changing God sacrifices the reason *that* creation is for the sake of the *why*. Even if there is a partnership between God's creating the world and the world's creating itself, and even if the partnership includes the world's conditioning of God as well as God's conditioning of the world, God is still the reason *that* things are as long as he plays the decisive role in this co-creativity. It is not required that God should be the sole cause as long as he is the primal cause. In terms of process theology, for example, since God supplies the initial aim for every entity to grow towards satisfaction, he can be the ultimate reason that things are. Indeed, it is the *why* and the *how* which he shares with creatures; when

---

[48] Mascall, *He Who Is*, p. 112.

[49] Ibid., pp. 103–4, cf. Etienne Gilson, *The Spirit of Mediaeval Philosophy*, trans. A. H. C. Downes (Sheed & Ward, London, 1936), pp. 96–7.

one asks why things are as they are, the answer lies partly in their own decision to be. But they could not even get started on that decision without the initial input from God.[50]

There is a further weakness in the view of a totally self-sufficient or necessary God. A strong case can be made that only a contingent God can be the cause of a contingent world. Only a God who can choose one thing rather than another can create a world which might be one thing rather than another, a world in which—we might say—there was more than one way for Leonardo to paint the smile on the face of the *Mona Lisa*. The thought of a God who chooses among possibles runs counter to the idea of a wholly necessary God, who ought not to do anything other than he does. If God creates by a necessary act, then the world appears to issue from him by a changeless decree, and must itself be necessary. Keith Ward judges that, despite all the ingenious attempts to get round this problem, 'if the world is to be contingent, and man really free, contingency and mutability must exist within God himself'.[51]

But if we accept that God is still the explanation for the world even though his being is in some sense conditioned by it, these considerations lead us on to the third and most substantial objection to the idea of a God who suffers change and so needs the world to be what he is: can he be self-existent?

3. Traditional theology has insisted that for God to be God, the explanation for his existence must lie only in himself. God must be the reason for God; he is 'the one who is himself' (*ipsum esse*). This basic affirmation seems at first sight to be disturbed by the claim that the world can change and condition the being of God. This is the crucial point for any theology of a suffering God, whenever it dares to face the logical conclusion that the world is in some way necessary for God. How can the world be necessary for a self-existent God? We cannot begin to answer this until we make an important distinction: self-existence is not simply the same thing as self-sufficiency. Traditional theology assumed that if God were the ground of his own being, then he

---

[50] See John B. Cobb, *A Christian Natural Theology*, p. 214. Cobb makes the further point that eternal objects are only effective agents because God envisages them (p. 158).

[51] Ward, *Rational Theology and the Creativity of God*, pp. 80–1. Creel, *Divine Impassibility*, p. 168, agrees that there must be some contingent aspect in God's will; but he denies that this entails passibility on the grounds that what God is dependent upon is only a realm of abstract possibilities, which Creel terms 'the Plenum' (ibid., pp. 62, 85). This has a remarkable resemblance to Whitehead's realm of 'eternal objects', and is subject to the same criticisms: see below, pp. 158–63.

must be unconditioned by anything else in every conceivable way. But this does not have to follow. To affirm that God is 'self-sufficient' for the fact of his existence (or self-existent) does not necessarily mean that he is self-sufficient for the whole mode of his divine life.[52] We can think of a God who determines himself, and yet also allows his creation to participate in the causes of his own becoming. The essential point is that God should play the decisive or sovereign role in this process, as he does in a co-creation of the world. The associated notion that God has 'necessary being' might then have a limited usefulness in denoting that God is self-existent and self-explanatory, but in fact it has generally been used with the meaning that God is completely unconditioned and self-sufficient as well; for this reason I have avoided using the term wherever possible in this discussion.

One way in which self-existence might be ascribed to God without self-sufficiency is in the form of the *will* of God. The freedom of God is not a matter of freedom from conditioning, but the freedom of his will. God is free to be what he chooses to be. This principle has received its most majestic enunciation in the work of Karl Barth, who asserts that the highest designation for God is not 'the One who is necessarily', but 'the One who loves in freedom'.[53] He is self-existent (*a se*) in the sense that he has absolute freedom to choose himself and his relationship to others. He is unconditioned only in the sense that he is free to choose whether to be conditioned or not:

According to the biblical testimony, God has the prerogative to be free without being limited by His freedom from external conditioning, free also with regard to His freedom . . . God must not only be unconditioned but, in the absoluteness in which He sets up this fellowship [i.e. with mankind], He can and will also be conditioned.[54]

Unlike Aquinas, this is not the concept of a God who has 'necessary being' and *therefore* has freedom of will, but rather a God whose freedom of will constitutes his being. Barth thinks it to be a regression that the early idea of God's aseity was interpreted by later notions of the 'unconditioned' or 'necessary being'. The heart of the divine lordship is

---

[52] The same distinction is made by Ward in the course of his argument; *Rational Theology and the Creativity of God*, pp. 10, 81 ff., 85–6, 121. He usefully distinguishes between 'existential self-sufficiency', i.e. self-existence (p. 10), and self-sufficiency in general (p. 86): 'it is a mistake to try to preserve an idea of Divine self-sufficiency, by denying that he depends upon any finite thing in any way'.

[53] Barth, *CD* II/1, pp. 301, 307.　　　　　　　[54] Barth, *CD* II/1, p. 303.

the freedom 'to be determined and moved by oneself'.[55] Thus, building a little on this thesis of Barth, we may say that God can actually *fulfil his being* through the world in suffering because he chooses to do so; he chooses that the world should be necessary to him. Barth himself affirms that as God chooses his own being he also chooses the world and his suffering in Christ; he 'says yes' to us, to suffering, and to death when he says yes to himself.[56] Since suffering must include change it is surely a logical step to add that he chooses to be completed through the world, to be fulfilled through giving himself away in suffering. Barth comes close to this when he says that God 'ordains that He should not be entirely self-sufficient as He might be'.[57] Keith Ward, who takes a remarkably similar line to Barth, declares more firmly that as creator,

[God] is no longer the completely self-sufficient eternal one; he is one who both expresses and creatively determines his own nature in relation to creatures . . . Thus when God returns to himself from his encounter with the other, he returns enriched.[58]

I believe, then, that it *is* coherent to say that God is changed by the world in suffering and that this contributes to his being, *if* he freely chooses that this should be so. However, to place such a premium on God's act of choice immediately raises two further questions: (*a*) can God then choose to do anything? (*b*) could God have chosen otherwise?

The first of these two questions recalls the ancient discussion as to whether God creates by his will or out of his nature. If we say that God can create, and therefore suffer, simply because he chooses to do so, we appear to open the door to the possibility that he might be capricious or arbitrary in his choice. Like Big Brother in George Orwell's *1984*, he might decree that henceforth $2+2=5$ in order to test his subjects' obedience to him. Christian theologians who have stressed the will of God in creation have therefore usually looked for a harmony between the will and the nature of God, suggesting that his free choice is at the

---

[55] Barth, *CD* II/1, p. 301, cf. pp. 303, 306–8. According to my argument, therefore, Barth falls short of the true meaning of suffering when he thinks of God's suffering as being a matter of self-movement or self-change (see above, pp. 60–1), though he makes the essential point that God is free to suffer. Employing this latter insight of Barth, we should say that God is free to be changed.

[56] *CD* II/2, pp. 161 ff., 177; cf. 116 ff., 352 ff. See Herbert Hartwell, *The Theology of Karl Barth: An Introduction* (Duckworth & Co., London, 1964), pp. 106–7.

[57] Barth, *CD* II/2, p. 10.

[58] Ward, *Rational Theology and the Creativity of God*, pp. 138, 140.

same time an overflowing of his abundant goodness and love.[59] In the matter of the suffering of God, therefore, his choosing to suffer is in some way appropriate to his nature. But we cannot be allowed to get away with this solution quite so easily, though I believe it does point the way forward. What is this harmony between will and nature? How can a choice be at the same time an overflow? One answer is that given by Keith Ward; he tidies up the ambiguity by proposing that God has a necessary nature which 'governs' his contingent choice. Ward believes that rational theology has been right to require that God should have necessary being if there is to be any explanation for the fact of the world. On the other hand, he believes that a doctrine of creation requires there to be contingency in God, since this world cannot be the only possible world. Ward's solution is to suggest (rather like process theology) that God can be necessary in some respects and contingent in others; he has some qualities in which there are real alternatives, and others in which there are none. Accordingly, his necessary being provides the conditions, or lays down the limits, for his contingent choices;[60] God chooses to be self-giving love, but the basis for that choice is his essential goodness. Thus God needs the world 'in a qualified sense'; he does not need it to be himself, but he needs it to be what he chooses to be. He does not need it to be good; but he needs it to be good in the particular way he has chosen to be good, that is in expressing love to others.[61]

A quite different way of harmonizing the will and the nature of God is put forward by Barth, who keeps the will of God central. The choosing of the world by God is indeed a 'free overflowing' of his goodness, 'an expression and application of the love in which He is God',[62] but God does not 'need His being' in order to be who he is or to make the choices he does.[63] His own being, like his activity in the world, is a matter of his free will and determination. God in himself is an act or event in which he posits his own reality: in short, 'God is His own decision'.[64] So there is no question of a divine nature laying down

---

[59] The classical expression is in Origen, *De Principiis* 1. 2. 10; 2. 9. 1. See Henry Chadwick, *Early Christian Thought and the Classical Tradition* (Clarendon Press, Oxford, 1966), p. 84: 'Origen is well aware that he is confronting an insoluble problem in trying to reconcile the affirmation that creation is an outflow of the divine nature with the affirmation that it is dependent upon the divine will.'

[60] Ward, *Rational Theology and the Creativity of God*, p. 232, cf. p. 73.

[61] Ibid., p. 144, cf. Keith Ward, *Holding Fast to God*, p. 33.

[62] Barth, *CD* IV/2, p. 346.

[63] Barth, *CD* II/1, p. 306. [64] Barth, *CD* II/1, p. 272, cf. 271; I/1, p. 433.

conditions for choice; God's choice of us is a free overflowing of his choice of himself. This overflow 'matches' or corresponds to his essence of love, but this essence is itself personality which is 'absolutely its own, conscious, willed, and executed decision'.[65] Thus God's will for us, including his will to suffer for us, is altogether consistent with his will for himself.

It seems to me that Barth's is the more satisfactory answer to the question about whether God can choose to do anything, and it should become clearer why this is so if we move on to the related question: could God have done otherwise than loved us and suffered for us? It might at first glance seem obvious that if God has freely chosen to suffer, then he could have done otherwise. Barth and Ward in their different ways state this. For Ward, God is necessarily good in his being, but freely chooses to love. Without his love for mankind, 'he would not have been completely what he is . . . though he need not have been just what he is in every respect'.[66] For Barth, God necessarily decides to be the one who loves himself in the fellowship of the Trinity, but he need not have chosen to love *us*. 'God's loving is necessary, for it is the being, the essence, and the nature of God. But for this very reason it is also free from every necessity in respect of its object'.[67] It is important to understand here that according to Barth, God is necessarily loving, not because he has an essence which includes love as a necessary attribute, but simply because he has determined himself as loving. There is no otherwise in God's will to be himself; he affirms himself as 'a matter of empirical fact'.[68] God loves because he loves, because this act is his essence.[69]

Barth thus distinguishes between two kinds of freedom of will in God. In one there is an otherwise, but in the other there can be no otherwise. With regard to the world, God has freedom to will it or not to will it; but with regard to himself, his freedom consists *in* his determining of himself, not in his deciding *whether* to do so. Commenting upon Aquinas' dictum *Deus vult esse Deum* ('God wills to be God'), Barth says:

God cannot not be God . . . His freedom or aseity in respect of Himself

[65] Barth, *CD* II/1, pp. 271, 273.
[66] Ward, *Rational Theology and the Creativity of God*, p. 144.
[67] Barth, *CD* II/1, p. 280.
[68] Barth, *CD* II/1, p. 307.
[69] Barth, *CD* II/1, p. 279.

consists in His freedom, not determined by anything but Himself, to be God, and that means to be the Father of the Son.[70]

We may add from elsewhere in Barth's thought that this also means to be the one who loves. We shall have to return to this dual notion of freedom, but for the moment we observe that both Barth and Ward think that God need not have loved *us*, though Barth (unlike Ward) includes love as well as goodness in the necessary being of God.

But there seems to be something profoundly unsatisfactory about this notion of God's choosing to love the world in such a way that we can say 'he need not have done so' or 'he could have done otherwise'. It does not seem to touch the core of the meaning of love, which must be more than willing the good of another as one alternative among other possibilities. The belief that God's love for the world is an overflow or revelation of his true nature seems to be prejudiced if in fact God need not have loved us in his essential being. J. Moltmann surely reaches the heart of the matter when he objects, 'Does God really not need those whom in the suffering of his love he loves unendingly?'[71] It cannot be truly love if one can choose otherwise. It is not hard to think of an 'otherwise' in our loving, but this is because ours is limited by circumstances and lack of knowledge. We are not fully free to love. Since it is a matter of fact that God does direct his love towards us, it seems odd to say that 'he need not have done so'. Faced with this difficulty, we might be tempted to look for an alternative to the notion of the free *will* of God as the basis for divine change and suffering, and some who have done so have found an answer close at hand in the idea of the *desire* of God.

5. THE DESIRE OF GOD

Christian reflection upon the 'desire' of God is at least as early as the Lady Julian of Norwich who believed that there was a 'desire, longing and thirst' in God 'from without beginning'.[72] Berdyaev suggests, as does Moltmann more recently, that the key to divine suffering lies in God's desire for fellowship beyond himself. Love is a longing for self-

---

[70] Barth, *CD* I/1, p. 434. Barth also calls this 'the inner necessity of His freedom': *CD* IV/1, p. 175.

[71] Moltmann, *The Trinity and the Kingdom of God*, p. 52.

[72] Julian of Norwich, *Revelations of Divine Love* ch. 31, ed. G. Warrack (Methuen, London, [8]1923), p. 64. See K. J. Woollcombe, 'The Pain of God', *Scottish Journal of Theology*, 20 (1967), pp. 129 ff. See further below, ch. 4 n. 26.

communication, a thirst to communicate what is good.[73] Such a desire, it is claimed, transcends the distinction between will and nature.[74]

A desire for relationship and fellowship is certainly essential to love, and it is right to highlight this. But when we are asking how it can be that God should need the world, it is doubtful whether it helps to elevate the idea of the 'desire' of God above the free decision of God's will, as a supposedly more adequate concept.[75] After all, we still need to justify the claim that a desire for fellowship reaches out beyond the harmony of God's own being, especially if this is understood in a Trinitarian way as a society of relationships. If simply 'desire' is the key, why does God desire an other? Here Moltmann tries a piece of quick theology by etymology, claiming that 'freedom' really means 'friendship', and so God's freedom must be understood as his vulnerable love, the kindness with which he meets human beings who are other than himself.[76] But this is less an argument than an illustration. Again, both Berdyaev and Moltmann affirm that God's going out beyond himself in a desire for relationship springs not from deficiency of being but from the abundance of his creative fullness. While this is an important claim, it still has to be justified. In fact, both Berdyaev and Moltmann do have an explanation as to why the desire of God is desire for an other; they both reach behind the notion of 'desire', and do not in the end make the desire itself final, but some other factor.

For Berdyaev, the thirst of God is grounded in freedom itself, which is 'an ultimate frontier'.[77] While this freedom is akin to the *Ungrund* of Boehme's system, Berdyaev explains that he differs from the earlier mystic in not locating it within God; rather he conceives it to be 'outside' God, preferring not to speak about this 'unspeakable and

---

[73] Moltmann, *The Trinity and the Kingdom of God*, p. 57; Nicolas Berdyaev, *Freedom and the Spirit*, pp. 136–7, 209–12, and *The Meaning of History*, trans. G. Reavey (Geoffrey Bles, London, 1935), pp. 46 ff., 75–6.

[74] So Moltmann, *The Trinity and the Kingdom of God*, pp. 99, 105–8; cf. *God in Creation*, pp. 79–86.

[75] In his most recent book, *God in Creation*, p. 85, Moltmann more clearly allows the idea of the divine will for creation to contribute towards the deeper concept of the love of God, *if* will is redefined as an 'essential resolve', in order to exclude decision or choice. But, as I show in my exposition of Barth, divine will must include choice, and it is in this sense that I am using it.

[76] Moltmann, *The Trinity and the Kingdom of God*, p. 56.

[77] Nicolas Berdyaev, *Spirit and Reality*, p. 106.

ineffable apophatic mystery of God's life'.[78] That is, freedom is the
Absolute, transcending the being of the personal God who creates us,
longs for us, and relates to us. God desires fellowship beyond himself
because he values this freedom, and therefore wants communion with
another who is also free like himself. God's desire for man is a desire for
the other to be free. He longs for one who can in freedom reciprocate his
love, and he knows tragedy because man throughout his history has
distorted freedom: 'It is not man but God who cannot get on without
human freedom'.[79] But this means that a dark, primordial freedom is
the final factor to which God himself—or at least the known God—is
subordinate. This, we observe, is quite different from Barth's view that
what is final is God's own free decision.

Curiously, Moltmann too has an ultimate value underlying desire.
This is a particular notion of love. Moltmann begins by defining God's
love for himself as love of like for like, while his love for us is love of the
unlike; the first is a 'necessary love', while the second is a 'free love'. He
then argues that 'like is not enough for like', since for God to love freely
as well as essentially he must move from love of himself to love of one
who is different from himself. In this way, 'Creation is a part of the
eternal love affair between the Father and the Son'.[80] In a later chapter
we are going to have occasion to question whether it is really
illuminating to make this sharp distinction between two kinds of divine
love—love of like and unlike. What we should notice here is that
Moltmann seems to be placing some value anterior to God himself, to
which God must conform. To love freely, God must apparently move
from love of like to love of unlike. Either, like Berdyaev to whom he is
much indebted, this is making freedom itself absolute, or he is making a
certain expression of love absolute. In the latter case, the world also is
not truly contingent, since it seems to be a necessary emanation from
God's love which takes this particular form of love for the different.

If then we propose the 'desire' of God as an *alternative* to the free-will
choice of God, or even claim it to be a more profound concept than
'will', we still find ourselves looking for a rationale of this desire, with

[78] Nicolas Berdyaev, *Dream and Reality*, trans. K. Lampert (Geoffrey Bles, London,
1950), p. 99, cf. p. 179. This concept of 'freedom' is reminiscent of the 'Gottheit' of
Meister Eckhart's mysticism. For a good discussion, see Carnegie S. Calian, *The
Significance of Eschatology in the Thoughts of Nicolas Berdyaev* (E. J. Brill, Leiden, 1965),
pp. 15–17, 69–70, 73–4.
[79] Berdyaev, *Freedom and the Spirit*, p. 128.
[80] Moltmann, *The Trinity and the Kingdom of God*, pp. 58–9.

resulting problems. I believe that the solution lies in not attempting to distinguish God's free will from desire; the longing or desire of God for his creation is simply his will regarded from a certain perspective. God desires us because he chooses to be like that; his desire *is* his will. We have come back to Barth's conviction about the freedom of God's will, but with an important modification. Understanding God's will as desire indicates that there can be no 'otherwise' in the love of God for mankind. Because he thirsts and longs for fellowhip with his creatures it makes no sense to say that he need not do so. But if we ask why he so thirsts, we cannot get back behind the choice of God. Each aspect, will and desire, defines the other. Barth has made the crucial point that in the choosing of his own being, God's freedom consists in his being free to be God, not in being free to be otherwise than he is. Unlike Barth, we may include within this kind of freedom his choice of mankind. God is what he chooses to be, and as a matter of fact he chooses to be not just for himself but for us. It has then as little meaning to say that 'he need not have loved us' as it has to say 'he need not have been himself'. This is admittedly an extension of Barth's concept of God's freedom, but perhaps not such a very great one after all. Such critics as Moltmann are not quite fair to Barth in their depicting him as a nominalist, as if the sovereign liberty of God were in the end 'his power of disposal over his property—creation'.[81] Barth actually insists that 'in the free decision of his love God is God in the very fact . . . that he does stand in this relation, in a definite relationship with the other', so that 'we cannot go back on this decision if we would know God and speak accurately of God'.[82] Again, he underlines that 'we cannot go back behind this event'[83] of God's gracious choice of man as covenant partner. The primordial choice of God is the final fact, and we must surely add that there can therefore be no otherwise, though in Barth's own view this can only be said of God's choice of his own being as Father, Son, and Spirit.

   I suggest then that talk of God's 'desire' is a way of saying that God's choice of his creation is the furthest frontier of our knowledge of God. God does not 'need' the world in the sense that there is some intrinsic necessity in his nature, binding his free choice (thus far Aquinas is right); but he does need the world in the sense that he has freely chosen to be in need. His desire and his will are one, and because what he freely chooses is his manner of being, there can be no meaning in the phrase 'he need

81   Ibid., p. 56. Similarly, Mackey, *The Christian Experience of God as Trinity,* p. 201.
82   Barth, *CD* II/2, p. 6.   83   Barth, *CD* II/1, p. 281.

not have done so'. In our ensuing discussion I shall be further justifying the claim that God's suffering springs from his will-as-desire, in preference to the other approaches we have surveyed. I believe this to be more cogent than thinking of divine suffering either as an act of will which could have been otherwise, or as an act belonging to a contingent pole of God's nature as distinct from a necessary one. But let us for the moment remind ourselves of the point to which we have come. If God suffers then he is changed by the world, and he can only be changed to become more truly himself; but he opens himself to this suffering because he chooses mankind for fellowship, and so chooses to be fulfilled through his creation. While this suffering love is a matter of free choice for God, it is at the same time a desire in which there can be no question of God's not longing for our love.

This equation of will and desire in God also provides a strong theological foundation for the idea that the material universe coexists eternally with God, though of course this does not apply to any particular form it takes (such as in our own world). For process thought, the coexistence of God and the universe derives from the ultimate value of creativity—rather like Freedom in Berdyaev. The absolute factor of the creative process requires both God and other actualities as necessary component parts. It is for this reason that there can be no literal creation *ex nihilo*. But if we follow through the clue of the desire of God, then there is a different basis for an eternal coexistence of God and the universe; it derives from the good pleasure of God, in which there can be no otherwise. Creation is *ex nihilo*, but only in the sense that it is ultimately 'from nothing except' God's will and love, not in the sense that there ever 'was nothing except' God. This means that there was no 'point', often defined as marking the beginning of time, when reality external to God began. The universe then is dependent upon God as existing and being held above nothingness by his will, but God also is dependent upon the universe by his own desire. That primordial will or desire means a longing for a cooperative enterprise at all stages of creation, including a fellow-working with humankind in due time, so that in another sense creation is 'from' God *and* creatures. To this conjunction we may apply the words of the wedding rite, suitably adapted: 'What God joins together let no man put asunder'.

The mystery whose curtain we can never finally lift is not the mere self-existence of God, but his 'yes' to himself which includes his 'yes' to us and the suffering we cause him as his creatures. We find ourselves in a situation of faith where we want to affirm that God suffers; by following through this affirmation consistently we arrive at the belief that as God chooses himself as Father, Son, and Spirit he also chooses us in an act of will in which there can be no otherwise. The mystery of God is not an act of will for which there is no reason, which would be the case with the utter aseity of God, but an act of will which is desire for fellowship with another. If it be objected that this lifts mankind beyond the status of creature, we might ask what would have the greater religious value of humbling us. Is it the belief that we are totally unnecessary to God, that we can neither contribute to his life nor wound him? Or is it the amazing thought that God is so humble that he wants us as much as he wants himself?

4

A Future for the Suffering God

HAS God a future? At first sight this seems to be a theological version of
the ancient trick question, 'Have you stopped beating your wife (or, for
that matter, husband) yet?' Neither 'yes' nor 'no' seems entirely
satisfactory. To answer yes, God has a future, implies that there is some
unknown area lying ahead of God which he has yet to experience and
discover, and for some Christian theologians this would be unthinkable.
They would find quite absurd the final chorus of the recent musical
Godspell, where the cast invited the audience to stand and join with
them in singing 'Long live God!' (though it was reported that the then
Archbishop of Canterbury did so with enthusiasm at the performance
he attended). Yet to answer no, there is no future for God, is to envisage
a God who is not God at all. Is the question then a theological nonsense,
smuggling in notions of time where they have no business to be? I think
not. It is a proper thing to ask because it belongs with the question,
'Does God suffer?' In our experience, to suffer means to have a real
future, and talk about the suffering of God must have sufficient
continuity with our experience to be meaningful, even while we
recognize the discontinuity that permits such talk to refer to God at all.

In human experience, suffering is linked with having a future because
it involves having unrealized possibilities. John Hick aptly diagnoses
suffering as the desire that our situation should be other than it is,
'involving the elements of memory of the past, anticipation of the
future, and the capacity to imagine alternatives'.[1] The gospel scene of
the agony of Christ in Gethsemane is a paradigm of suffering, where the
heart of the matter is anticipation of what is going to happen; it is the
expectation of the cross that prompts the anguish and the bloody sweat.
We find the same elements in a modern Gethsemane, as recorded by a
young Danish cabin-boy who underwent torture during the Second

---

[1] Hick, *Evil and the God of Love*, p. 354.

World War. After an experience of suffering that left him unconscious he wrote in his diary:[2]

Immediately afterwards it dawned on me that I have now a new understanding of the figure of Jesus. The time of waiting, that is the ordeal . . . the waiting in the garden—that hour drips red with blood.

Suffering which involves expectation, a 'waiting', means a participation in time, and that means being in a state of change from possibility to actuality. The sufferer has a future in another sense too; he awaits liberation from his suffering, and may hope for victory over suffering.

If then we are to speak of a suffering God, we must try to speak as carefully as possible about the future of God. If we affirm that God suffers for us and with us, then for this to have meaning we must answer yes to the enquiry, 'Has God a future?' even though we must add immediately that it is not exactly like our future. We must try to speak of something 'new' lying ahead for God, yet not exactly as it would for us, of a path that God treads towards a goal, yet not exactly as we would. In this way we are taking up the agenda which we set ourselves in the last chapter, when we saw the need to speak of God's desire to fulfil himself through creation.

I.   THE COMING OF GOD TO HIS GLORY

In our task of speaking coherently about the future of a suffering God, there is a biblical symbol at hand to help us, that of the 'glory' of God. This one image is used to express both the nature of the divine being and hope for the future. Thus, according to the biblical witness, to proclaim the future of God is not at all to diminish the glory of God, for there is a sense in which God 'comes' to his glory.

The Hebrew term *kāḇôḏ* has the meaning of 'weight', or worthiness and honour, and as applied to the being of God it serves most obviously to describe the outshining of the divine majesty, or the making manifest of invisible godhead. The *kāḇôḏ* of Yahweh is given content as a light-phenomenon, drawing upon the imagery of thunderstorm (Ps. 29: 3,

---

[2]   Related in H. Gollwitzer, K. Kuhn, R. Schneider (eds.), *Dying We Live: The Final Messages and Records of Some Germans Who Defied Hitler*, trans. R. C. Kuhn (The Harvill Press, London, 1956), p. 71; the boy was Kim Malthe-Bruun. (My attention was drawn to this story by D. Sölle, in *Suffering*.) For similar experiences, cf. Alexander Solzhenitsyn, *The Gulag Archipelago*, trans. T. P. Whitney (Collins/Fontana, London, 1974), pp. 451–5.

Exod. 19: 16). Yet this radiance also points more deeply to the very
nature of God's being; especially in the Priestly theology and the
thought of Ezekiel, where the *kābôd* itself is distinguished from its
protective envelope of cloud, there is 'the strongest possible emphasis on
the nature of God as light',[3] Here the 'glory of the Lord' evokes what is
impressive and splendid in the actual being of God. In the New
Testament use of the equivalent term *doxa* we can detect both these
inner and outer dimensions of the glory of the being of God,
particularly in the ascription of the title 'the Lord of Glory' to Jesus.[4]
Now, in the later parts of the Old Testament and throughout the New
Testament, 'glory' is also used as a focus of eschatological hope.
Building upon the expectation that Yahweh would 'get himself glory'
in the history of Israel, there is a priestly and prophetic announcement
that Yahweh's claim to rule the world will finally be actualized as the
earth will be filled with his *kābôd* (Num. 14: 21, Isa. 40: 5,
Hab. 2: 14). Similarly, the New Testament writers associate the
resurrection of Christ from the dead with the divine 'glory', Paul for
example speaking of his being raised 'by the glory of the Father'
(Rom. 6: 4), by which they seem to mean that Jesus is a representative of
the future realization of the glory of God.[5] Christ appears in the final
glory which should have been manifested at the last day; what was
expected to happen at the end of history in the new creation had
happened surprisingly ahead of time.

The biblical appeal to 'glory' as a way of expressing both the being of
God and the hoped-for future announces that, in moving towards the
goal of his cosmic work of creation and redemption, God is entering
upon his own glory. Now, if we lay stress upon the fact that 'glory' can
mean the inner nature of the divine being as well as its outer
manifestation to mankind, we shall find at least a hint in the biblical
witness that in getting himself glory, God comes to the actual fulfilment

---

[3] Article 'dokeo, doxa' (G. Von Rad and G. Kittel), in G. Kittel (ed.), *Theological
Dictionary of the New Testament*, Vol. 2, trans. and ed. G. W. Bromiley (W. B. Eerdmans,
Grand Rapids, Michigan, 1964), p. 239. See Exod. 24:15 ff., Exod. 40: 34–5, Ezek. 1:28.
Cf. G. Von Rad, *Old Testament Theology*, Vol. 1, trans. D. M. G. Stalker (Oliver and
Boyd, Edinburgh, 1962), p. 240: *kabod* according to the Priestly Writing was 'something
belonging immediately to Yahweh, part of his supernatural being'.

[4] e.g. 1 Cor. 2: 8, Acts 7: 2, Rev. 4: 9, 5: 12.

[5] Cf. C. K. Barrett, *A Commentary on the Epistle to the Romans* (A. & C. Black,
London, ²1962), p. 123: 'For Paul, "glory" is a word with a predominantly
eschatological meaning . . . glory is that which will be revealed on the last day'. Also
see 1 Tim. 3: 16, John 12: 28, Acts 7: 55–6, Luke 9: 29.

of his own being. H. Gollwitzer does so, when he suggests that God 'finally defines himself, makes himself known, and brings himself to full divinity, that is to his *doxa*'.[6] However, this notion that God's future glory might be something to do with his own increase in beatitude and not merely with the universal *acknowledgement* of his deity, requires a justification beyond an argument about biblical texts. J. Moltmann is one theologian who simply assumes that biblical writers have the actual godhead of the Father in mind when they speak of the future glory of God,[7] and we must return to this question shortly. But for the moment we should notice the sensitive way in which Moltmann discerns the element of suffering woven into the pattern of God's future. In effect, he suggests that we might say of the Father, as well as the Son, that 'he must first suffer and then enter upon his glory'.

Here Moltmann points to a further cluster of New Testament texts about 'glory'. He recalls that the New Testament writers speak about God's glorifying of mankind,[8] and also portray the perfected creation as glorifying God in its joy and its hymns of thanksgiving.[9] His important insight is that these two actions of glorifying, by God and by his creatures, are intimately related. God's purpose for human beings to be glorified can mean nothing less than their sharing in fellowship with the God of glory, being united in community with God's glorious life. There is a foretaste of this whenever sins are forgiven, the bound are liberated, the sick are healed, and outcasts are accepted. Such a liberation of man also glorifies God; wherever it happens, even if only partially at present, God's joy increases, and in the ultimate deliverance of creation from frustration into the liberty of the glory of God, God himself will be finally glorified.[10] But now we remember that the liberation of man is achieved through the suffering of God, since we experience freedom as we take our place deliberately in the fellowship of God's sufferings. So we can truly say, concludes Moltmann, that God moves towards his glory by way of the path of his suffering. In this sense there is a future of liberation, and even salvation, for the suffering God; he dwells in the

[6] H. Gollwitzer, *Die kapitalische Revolution* (Munich, 1974), p. 105.

[7] Moltmann, *The Church in the Power of the Spirit*, p. 58; cf. id., *Theology and Joy*, pp. 58–64.

[8] Moltmann, *The Church in the Power of the Spirit*, p. 59. See Col. 1: 27, Phil. 3: 21, Rom. 8: 21, 2 Cor. 5: 5.

[9] Moltmann, *The Church in the Power of the Spirit*, pp. 60, 61, 63, citing mainly the book of Revelation 1: 6, 7: 10, 19: 1, cf. Rom. 11: 36.

[10] Ibid., p. 60. Cf. Moltmann, *The Future of Creation*, pp. 94–5.

world in suffering because his aim is to dwell in the world in glory.[11]

Moltmann is giving, as he admits, a version of the mystical Jewish image of the redemption of the Shekinah. According to this tradition, God in the form of his Shekinah-glory not only dwells with his people but in that dwelling suffers slavery himself; in the summary offered by Franz Rosenzweig,

God himself separates himself from himself, he gives himself away to his people, he shares in their sufferings, sets forth with them into the agony of exile, joins their wanderings. . . . Nothing would be more natural for the 'God of the Fathers' than that he should 'sell' himself for Israel and share its suffering fate. But by doing so, God puts himself in need of redemption.[12]

Akin to this is H. Wheeler Robinson's notion of the 'Kenosis of the Spirit' in his dwelling in humiliation with 'such men as we are . . . [which] cannot mean anything but continual suffering for God'.[13] These ideas imply that the redemption of man in the new creation also means release from servitude for God.

But at this point we must squarely face the assumption being made in drawing like this upon the biblical image of glory. Why should the final glorifying of God affect his being, implying the beatification and even the liberation of God? Why should it not mean simply the eschatological unveiling of God's glory and its recognition by the whole of creation? In their release from suffering, men could glorify God in the sense that the holy being of God would be finally displayed in the full glory it always had. In reply, we can urge some biblical support for the idea that God comes to a new fullness of being since, as we have seen, *kābôd* and *doxa* indicate the very nature of God as well as its radiant unfolding to man, especially where 'glory' is linked with an interest in the 'beauty' of Yahweh.[14] But more than this biblical image is needed,

[11] Moltmann, *The Church in the Power of the Spirit*, p. 64, *The Trinity and the Kingdom of God*, pp. 124–8, *The Future of Creation*, pp. 88–92.

[12] Franz Rosenzweig, *The Star of Redemption*, trans. W. W. Hallo (Routledge & Kegan Paul, London, 1971), pp. 409–10. This passage is cited in most of Moltmann's major works, e.g. *The Church in the Power of the Spirit*, p. 61. T. E. Fretheim, *The Suffering of God*, pp. 144–8, finds a basis for these ideas of the 'capture' and humiliation of God in such Old Testament passages as Psalm 78: 61, Psalm 18: 35, Isa. 63: 9, and especially Isa. 42: 14.

[13] H. Wheeler Robinson, *The Christian Experience of the Holy Spirit* (The Library of Constructive Theology, Nisbet, London, 1928), p. 151.

[14] e.g. Exod. 33: 18–19. See Hans Urs Von Balthasar, *The Glory of the Lord: A Theological Aesthetics*. Vol 1: *Seeing the Form*, trans. E. Leiva-Merikakis, ed. J. Fessio and J. Riches (T. & T. Clark, Edinburgh, 1982), pp. 53 ff.; also G. Von Rad, op. cit. (n. 3 above), p. 364.

impressive illustration though it is, upon which to base a claim about the real future of God. After all, a theologian in the Thomist tradition such as E. Mascall can echo the biblical dimension of glory as the unveiling of God, in order to make a distinction between the 'accidental' and the 'essential' glory of God.[15] When we give glory to God, he argues, we do not contribute to his essential being but only to the manifesting of his glory for our sakes. If, then, we are to say more than this we shall have to move beyond the compiling of biblical fragments into a mosaic; we must appeal to a wider perspective of the Trinitarian nature of God.

God can only be essentially glorified by man if he has identified himself with man's cause in an essential way; he must have committed his being to the being of the world. Hegel expressed this in terms of the world as a relative form of God's own Spirit, so that God comes to consciousness of himself through creaturely minds.[16] A number of contemporary theologians have rewritten Hegel in suggesting that God comes, not to self-consciousness, but to fellowship with himself, and that the doctrine of the Trinity is the appropriate way of expressing this. God comes to fellowship, coming not only *from* himself as source of all that is, but *to* himself as goal. God attains 'union' with himself (Moltmann),[17] or as E. Jüngel puts it, 'God comes to God' in a movement which is portrayed in the doctrine of the eternal generation of the Son. God is not only his own origin; 'God encounters himself out of this origin in such a way that he becomes his own partner. God is also his own goal.'[18] God moreover does not only come to God; he has come to man, taking the journey into the far country in the person of Jesus Christ. If however we are now to take a further leap of thought, as I believe we should, and say with Jüngel that in the death of Jesus, 'God comes in one and the same event as God to God, and as God (definitively) to man',[19] we must not neglect the indispensable notion of the desire of God. If God aims at the goal of himself *in so far as* he aims at man, this can only be through his own desire to be this kind of God. Thus the theological foundation for the belief that God has a future is an

[15] Mascall, *He Who Is*, p. 97; cf. his sequel, *Existence and Analogy*, pp. 140–1. F. Von Hügel makes the same distinction between 'essential' and 'accidental' glory, *Essays and Addresses, Second Series*, p. 154.

[16] See below, ch. 9, 1 for a closer exposition of Hegel.

[17] Moltmann, *The Church in the Power of the Spirit*, p. 61, cf. *The Trinity and the Kingdom of God*, pp. 149–50.

[18] Jüngel, *God as the Mystery of the World*, pp. 382–3; cf. E. Jüngel, 'Das Verhältnis von "ökonomischer" und "immanenter" Trinität', *Zeitschrift für Theologie und Kirche*, 72 (1975), pp. 363–4.

[19] Jüngel, *God as the Mystery of the World*, p. 383.

interweaving of the concepts of the Trinity and the desire of God. That is, our glorifying of God can only contribute to the being of God if he has his own history of coming to fellowship with himself to which our fellowship can add something, and if God has a desire for this fellowship with man which needs to be satisfied.

It is in accord with this that Moltmann sets the glorifying of God through suffering in the cosmic perspective of the life of the Trinity. He declares that the doctrine of the Trinity is not an abstract formula, but the concept which matches God's dealing with the world throughout history. Indeed, it describes the inclusion of our history within God himself. The Trinity is a happening, not a static 'group in heaven'; God happens as an event of personal relationships, which is open to embrace human relationships.[20] The Trinity depicts the history of God's own life, a history of suffering between the Father and the Son, and this is open from all eternity to take in the history of human suffering. When we suffer we can take our stand within God's own life, in the fellowship of the cross.[21] But this also provides, says Moltmann, the basis for man's glorification. Here Moltmann appeals to yet another cluster of scriptural texts about 'glory', namely New Testament references to the mutual glorifying of the Father and the Son in the Spirit. The father glorifies the Son through his exaltation in cross and resurrection, raising him into his own future glory; the Son for his part glorifies the Father through his obedience in the cross. The Spirit glorifies the Father and the Son by transfiguring the world, freeing men for fellowship with them. 'He glorifies Christ in believers and unites them with him.'[22] So there is a Trinitarian history of glorification as well as suffering, and mankind plays a part in the former too; as the Spirit unites creation with God he glorifies the Father through glorifying the Son in the world, and in this way unites God with himself. The history of glorifying is at the same time a history of unifying:

The unity of the triune God is the goal of the uniting of man and creation with the Father and the Son in the Spirit. The history of the Kingdom of God on earth is the history of the glorification of God.[23]

---

[20] Moltmann, *The Church in the Power of the Spirit*, pp. 54–6. *The Crucified God*, pp. 246–7, *The Trinity and the Kingdom of God*, pp. 94–6.

[21] Moltmann, *The Church in the Power of the Spirit*, pp. 62–4. *The Crucified God*, pp. 254–6.

[22] Moltmann, *The Church in the Power of the Spirit*, p. 59, cf. *The Trinity and the Kingdom of God*, pp. 124–8, *The Future of Creation*, pp. 90–1. Some of the relevant New Testament texts are Rom. 6: 4, 1 Tim. 3: 16, Phil. 2: 11, 2 Cor. 3: 7, John 17: 21–2.

[23] Moltmann, *The Church in the Power of the Spirit*, p. 62.

Moltmann does not notice the distinction between 'accidental' and 'essential' glorifying of God, but in effect he is intending to speak of the latter. Man glorifies God essentially in that he completes the fellowship of God. God comes to his own 'union' through including man in the fellowship between the Father and the Son. In suffering, God opens himself to include within his life all who suffer; then he comes to his glory by glorifying them.

This account of the suffering and glorifying of God has some important strengths, as well as at least one weakness. By means of heaping together some glittering fragments of scripture on the theme of 'glory', Moltmann is setting out a pattern of God's action in the world. The pattern itself, which stands beyond the particular mode of exegesis, is of a God who comes to fullness of being through involvement in the history of human suffering and glory. It is a bold and unashamed attempt to talk about God, where much contemporary theology has contented itself with talk about the experience of human existence, even if illuminated by divine revelation. Theology has often modestly limited itself to talk about human experience because it has rightly recognized severe problems of language in trying to talk about God who is by definition unique and unclassifiable. Moltmann's approach seeks to talk about God while taking account of the problems. By speaking about God in terms of the suffering and glorifying of God through mankind, he does not separate God from human experience; by speaking of God as an open event of relationships rather than as *a* being, he attempts to avoid making God an object like other objects in the world. He is speaking about God as personal without reducing him to *a* person.[24] In this latter enterprise, of course, Moltmann is hardly a pioneer. He is one in a whole movement of recent German theology which has taken its inspiration from Barth's talk of God as a self-related 'event' or 'happening'.[25] I think myself that we can attempt talk about God in this way, and that it is only possible in the context of notions of a suffering God; in further chapters this method will be worked out more extensively.

But Moltmann's mosaic of scriptural texts has either resulted in, or been prompted by, a curiously limited notion of that 'desire' of God

[24] Moltmann, *The Crucified God*, p. 247. But we need to take issue with this view that the 'persons' in God are analogous to individuals. See below pp. 139–42.

[25] See Barth, *CD* I/1, pp. 350–1, 358–9; II/1, pp. 181, 263–8: 'With regard to the being of God, the word "event" or "act" is final' (op. cit., p. 263). See Eberhard Jüngel, *The Doctrine of the Trinity*, pp. 61–8.

which we have seen to be fundamental to a belief in the future of God. If God is to be glorified 'essentially' (to use Mascall's category), then God must have a desire for fellowship with human beings which needs to be satisfied by *them*. Behind the coming of God to fellowship there must be a drive or thirst for fellowship with persons who enrich the being of God through their freely contributing to the project of creation. Otherwise we are simply speaking of the unveiling of the glory of God, not its fulfilling. If we are indeed to trace the path of God from suffering to glory along the *via dolorosa* of creation, then we must try to understand suffering as unfulfilled desire, and essential glory as satisfied desire. Moltmann has this in mind, particularly in his later work: 'God does not desire to be glorified without his liberated creation.'[26] But in Moltmann's scheme of reciprocal glorifying, the world completes or glorifies God in so far as it is transformed by the Spirit of God. This does not in itself take seriously a real contribution by the world to God's satisfaction, since God is apparently pleased by his own work of transfiguration. God's desire is met by his own achievement, as humankind glorifies God by being the place where God's own glory manifests itself.[27] This comes remarkably close to the notion of an 'accidental' glorifying of God; in fact, Moltmann fails to distinguish between notions of glory as essential and manifest, using the range of the biblical image indiscriminately. If the making of the world were indeed (as Moltmann proposes) a 'one-sided relationship' in which God 'stands over against himself', then it is hard to see how there could be the mutual relationships between God and creatures which Moltmann wants to affirm, relationships such as 'indwelling, sympathizing, participating, accompanying, enduring, delighting, and glorifying'.[28] We have already had occasion to remark that Moltmann steers close to the idea of the suffering of God as being 'all his own work'; the same might be said with even more reason of his glorification.

To augment the glory of God essentially must mean that the creation enriches the glory of God by works of love that are co-creative with

---

[26] Moltmann, *The Church in the Power of the Spirit*, p. 60. The slight hint here is expanded in *The Trinity and the Kingdom of God* (pp. 45–7, 58–60, 230 n. 84), perhaps assisted by new acquaintance with ideas of the Lady Julian of Norwich about the 'thirst' and 'desire' of God; cf. *The Future of Creation*, p. 187 n. 23.

[27] Moltmann, *The Trinity and the Kingdom of God*, pp. 103–5, 116–18.

[28] Moltmann, *God in Creation*, pp. 15–16; cf. p. 206, where creation is described as 'an interplay between God's transcendence in relation to the world, and his immanence in that world'.

him. Moltmann speaks of God's desiring response from his world, but the response of the creation to the urging of the Spirit must be more than a passive allowing of God to display his glory within it. Correspondingly, the suffering of God must be more than his patience in waiting to dwell in the world in glory. The issue is vividly set out when Moltmann employs the biblical picture of the Sabbath rest as the location for the impact of creation upon the Creator; it is in the blessing of the Sabbath that God is portrayed as beginning to 'feel' the world, 'to experience the beings he has created . . . to be touched by each of his creatures'.[29] But the Sabbath moment in the continual interplay between God and the world is completely disconnected from the moments ('days') of work. It is apparently not in the works of his creatures that God 'comes to himself', but in their resting in him. Yet if God has a desire for fellowship, his own being will be enhanced by the active response of his world, in all its worship *and* work. This is what God suffers to enable, and this must be at the heart of his satisfaction and joy.

Those who openly argue, in the Thomist tradition, that the glory we give to God augments only his 'accidental' glory, miss seeing this even more badly. E. Mascall, for instance, appeals to a human analogy about satisfaction to illustrate his argument, without perceiving that it works against him. He wants to establish that our glorifying of God cannot add anything to him, or make his being in any way richer:

Now most fathers receive presents from their small children on their birthdays, and receive them gladly, in spite of the fact that the presents are usually quite useless and in any case have to be paid for by the parent in the last resort. They are none the less readily accepted because of that, and the normal human parent has a joy in receiving such a gift which far exceeds the satisfaction obtained from a much more expensive and useful present given by a business client or even by a grown-up friend.[30]

Mascall's conclusion is that the world is equally 'useless' to God, and that therefore 'God created the world by an act of love for which no reason can be assigned except the free operation of his creative will'. But what does 'useful' mean in the context of this example? If God as a Father receives satisfaction from the giving of his children, a satisfaction that he

---

[29] Ibid., p. 279. While Moltmann occasionally affirms that creatures contribute to their own evolution, he denies that this can be conceived as contributing to God's own creative work (ibid., pp. 196, 212, 224).

[30] Mascall, *He Who Is*, p. 110.

could not otherwise have, is not this 'useful'? Mascall seems to have succumbed to a highly materialistic understanding of 'usefulness', if a child's present can give higher satisfaction than anything else, but is still apparently useless and adds nothing to the Father. In fact, it adds considerably to his real wealth of being, if nothing to his purse. With this outlook however, Mascall can assert that 'although created beings can be of no utility to God, it is of their very essence to be for his glory', by manifesting his grace.[31] According to the Hebrew concept of *kābōd*, the glory of God is his 'weight' or worth, and yet it is being suggested here (as also by Maritain, Gilson, and Von Hügel, among others[32]) that what is worth while to God cannot enhance his essential glory. We certainly cannot add to his glory in the sense of increasing his wealth of ethical goodness, but this does not automatically imply, as Hartshorne points out, that we cannot add *any* 'goods' to God; we can increase God's happiness by our actions, which is a good, and which answers to 'our noblest need' of offering the value of our being to God.[33] We must learn to think in more personal and relational terms about what adds worth and richness to personality.

Similar in some ways to the distinction between 'accidental' and 'essential' glorifying is R. E. Creel's suggestion that creatures can enrich the being of God 'extensively' but not 'intensively'. He maintains that our response to God can alter the 'texture' or 'flavour' of his life, but not its depth of bliss or satisfaction. This distinction stems, according to Creel, from the fundamental will of God in creation; what God desires is not that creatures should choose to enter his kingdom, but that they should simply choose one way or the other. Since, in Creel's view, a true lover is mature enough not to grieve if he is rejected by the free choice of another, God is emotionally impassible and 'can be perfectly happy no matter what happens to us in this life and no matter whether we choose for or against his kingdom'.[34] If my previous argument for the sympathetic quality of love has any validity, however, it is impossible to

---

[31] Ibid., p. 109, cf. his *Existence and Analogy*, pp. 145–6. Curiously, Wheeler Robinson, despite his insistence upon the suffering of God, also judges that the participation of God in human history 'can add nothing to God himself, save the manifestation of his grace' (*Suffering Human and Divine*, p. 173).

[32] J. Maritain, *The Degrees of Knowledge* (Charles Scribner's Sons, New York, 1938) pp. 458–60; E. Gilson, op. cit. (ch. 3 n. 49), pp. 96 ff.; Von Hügel, *Essays and Addresses, Second Series*, pp. 153–4.

[33] Hartshorne, *Man's Vision of God*, pp. 118–19, cf. p. 235.

[34] Creel, *Divine Impassibility*, p. 146, cf. p. 141.

accept this view of God as the supreme exponent of liberal individualism. In sharp contrast to all these rather meagre notions of worth and satisfaction we might set the meditations of Thomas Traherne; in his 'First Century' he firmly links God's 'treasure' and 'joy' with 'wanting' mankind as images and companions:

He is from Eternity full of Want: or els He would not be full of Treasure. Infinit Want is the very ground and Caus of infinit Treasure. It is Incridible, yet very Plain: Want is the fountain of all His Fulness. . . . Infinit Wants Satisfied Produce infinit Joys.[35]

We must consider once again the meaning of the will of God: what is it that God wills? Mascall argues that he simply wills there should be a creation, with no discernible motivation behind the will. Creel argues that God simply wills that his creatures should have choice, but feels no distress about what they do with it, either to him or each other. In both cases God's self-sufficient nature is untouched by the result of his will to create, and his self-sufficient glory is untouched by the result that human beings glorify him.[36] The world is strictly unnecessary to him, and it is as an act of sheer condescension or magnanimity that he allows it to give him glory, in the sense of making his glory manifest in it. We are reminded of the rationalization, sometimes heard in sermons, that 'magnifying' God simply means seeing God more clearly, as with a magnifying glass. But we can think otherwise of the will of God: what our minds can never reach behind is not his bare will, but his will to be for us, his will to be completed and fulfilled by fellowship with the world. This is his primary decree or desire, to be for us as he is for himself, choosing us in the same act of being by which he chooses himself.

2.   THE PROTEST OF GOD AGAINST THE PRESENT

God therefore treads a path from suffering to glory along the track of desire in search of fulfilment. If we think through this concept of divine desire, then there are a number of implications which are important for the idea of the suffering of God. The first is that a God who has a future protests against the reality of the present world; above all, he protests against suffering and death. This has something to say to the argument

---

[35] Thomas Traherne, 'First Century', 43, in *Poems, Centuries and Three Thanksgivings*, ed. A. Ridler (Oxford University Press, London, 1966), p. 183.

[36] Mascall, *He Who Is*, pp. 110–11; Creel, *Divine Impassibility*, pp. 145–6, 163–4.

of Don Cupitt against the doctrine of incarnation, in his contribution to the symposium, *The Myth of God Incarnate*. There he judges that the result of such a doctrine has been to create Christendom as a hierarchy of power and authority; the belief that God has been manifested in a unique way in Christ has, he concludes, simply sanctioned the divinizing of the Emperor one step below Christ in the hierarchy.

> Christ's Lordship was originally eschatological, and manifest in this age only indirectly and by ironic contrast with temporal lordship. But the dogma of the incarnation brought it forward into this present age. As the manifest Absolute in history, Christ became the basis of the Christian Empire and of political and ecclesiastical power in the present age.[37]

Christ's lordship was really, he argues, a pointing forward to the future coming of the kingdom ('My kingdom is not of this world'), a dimension which is lost when Christ is understood as the open manifestation of glory here and now. But the undisputed fact of history that the Christ of Christendom did become a 'manifest Absolute' and thus a political guarantor, does not exhaust the possibilities for understanding the glory of God as supremely displayed in Christ. Indeed, it may be argued that a belief in the unique presence of God in the crucified Christ means that God has chosen to identify himself as God in a dead man; he has chosen to define his deity in weakness. This strikes a blow against all human self-aggrandizement and self-deification, where power is defined as the ability to inflict suffering upon others or to avoid suffering for oneself, and where the weak and suffering are despised as of no real account and as failures of the system. Whatever we think in our better moments, we often act on the basis that refugees have no votes and starving children have no armies. But the belief that God is uniquely at one with the crucified Jesus turns all human values upside down; God is revealed not as the one who causes suffering, or has escaped great suffering, but who suffers. This discovery contradicts the power structures of the present world, and leads the followers of Christ into dissatisfaction with the *status quo*, moving them forward into the future of which Cupitt speaks.

The 'Theologians of Hope' therefore insist that God both protests against the world of the present from the standpoint of his future glory, and that he also reveals this protest through identifying himself with the suffering Jesus in a way that shakes us out of the present and its

---

[37] Don Cupitt, 'The Christ of Christendom' in J. Hick (ed.), *The Myth of God Incarnate*, (SCM Press, London, 1977), p. 141.

assumptions. Moltmann, for instance, makes the former point in his first book, *Theology of Hope*,[38] and the latter in the sequel, *The Crucified God*.[39] It is ironic that very different theologies can be employed to sanction a common political concern, Cupitt arguing against incarnation and Moltmann arguing for it, in the same interest of overthrowing authoritarian political structures. Indeed, it is a virtue of Moltmann's Trinitarian theology that it opposes not only theological but political monarchianism, arguing that a God who exists in Trinitarian fellowship is open to suffering where a sovereign Monad hoards his being protectively to himself.[40]

But if we are to prefer a theology of Trinity and incarnation as a base for political action, it is important not to lose sight of the theme of the divine desire. The protest of God must be understood as a desire and longing *for* the future rooted in the present, and not simply as a kind of royal manifesto delivered *from* the future. An excessive dwelling upon the future as a contradiction of the present, a total denial that there is any correlation between the reality of God and the reality of the world as it is now, can lead to what Rubem Alves has called a failure to care for the present:

And the future to be liberated by revolutionary action . . . becomes the absolute positive. As metaphysics and religion denied the earth for the sake of heaven, the present is here denied for the sake of the future. Man is absolved from inhumanity and brutality in the present, as the time of transition, the time which does not count.[41]

Tragically, a protest against the suffering of the present can lead to a promotion of greater suffering in the name of the future. 'Flowers sprout from the barrel of a gun', says a well-known slogan in Latin America. A theology of hope centred upon God's coming to us from the future in the form of a list of promises makes a programme central, and is in danger of making a manifesto absolute. However, to find our desires for the future taking on the dimension of promise in fellowship with a God who also has longing, is to be flexible and 'situational' about

[38] Moltmann, *Theology of Hope*, pp. 21–2, 190–7, 334–8, cf. J. Moltmann, 'Ernst Bloch and Hope without Faith', in id., *The Experiment Hope*, ed. and trans. M. D. Meeks (SCM Press, London, 1975), pp. 40–1.

[39] Moltmann, *The Crucified God*, pp. 68 ff., 327 ff., cf. *The Future of Creation*, pp. 14–17.

[40] See Moltmann, *The Trinity and the Kingdom of God*, pp. 192–200.

[41] Rubem Alves, *A Theology of Human Hope* (Corpus Books, 1969, repr. Abbey Press, St. Meinrad, Indiana, 1975), p. 155.

the strategies we might adopt. A stress upon the desire of God looks for experience of God through the sacrament of the present world—'epiphany'—as well as for the promise which contradicts the present situation. Otherwise, as John Macquarrie has put it pithily,[42] we are in the position of the White Queen in *Alice Through the Looking-Glass*, for whom 'the rule is, jam tomorrow and jam yesterday—but never jam today'.

3. THE PERFECT INCOMPLETENESS OF GOD

But the idea of a God who has desires, and who comes to his glory by the way of suffering, involves a further major implication: we cannot think of God as absolutely complete. It would be merely naïve, of course, to observe that a human sufferer has to await the resolution of his suffering, and so God must do exactly the same. But the more we think through what it means for God to suffer in sympathy with mankind, the more we are compelled to speak of the incompleteness of God, and the more the concept of a 'desire' for complete fellowship makes this incompleteness coherent with his perfection. In the previous chapter we noted that H. P. Owen wanted to maintain that God felt suffering for us, and yet was not in any way changed by it. In Owen's view, God responds to the world with a sympathetic suffering, but does not in any sense grow in response to it. God suffers in imaginative response while remaining immutable.[43] However, elsewhere in his account, Owen entirely undermines his own assertion and provides—perhaps unwittingly—a clue about the way we can think of the movement of God towards the completion of his essential glory. In dealing with the theme of the omniscience of God, Owen argues that unless God experienced the world in the sequential time which the world itself knows, he would not really be experiencing the world at all, and so could not be omniscient. Temporal events cannot be known timelessly if they are to be known as they really are.[44] We might illustrate this point for a moment with reference to suffering. A refugee is hungry and cold and desperately needing medical help on Monday; on Wednesday he is given relief by an Oxfam agency. If God is to know the suffering of the man on Monday as it really is, he cannot at the same time and in the same manner be aware of his experience of relief on Wednesday. If we were, he would not know the refugee's condition as the refugee himself

---

[42] John Macquarrie, *Thinking about God* (SCM Press, London, 1975), p. 229.
[43] Owen, *Concepts of Deity*, p. 24.   [44] Ibid., p. 31.

knows it, and so God would not have a complete knowledge of human mentality and would not know everything.

In the face of this sort of problem, Owen offers a possible redefinition of the omniscience of God, in terms of God's perfect knowledge of 'such things as are knowable'.[45] That is, 'God, in knowing himself, knows timelessly all the possibilities that the world actualizes, but he does not thus know them as actual.' While God knows immediately and completely 'every possibility of choice and every consequence of it', he only knows actualities as they actually happen in the world at each point of time. Thus God knows the future perfectly, but only as possibility, not prediction. Owen himself believes he can retain the immutability of God together with this view of omniscience; he believes that he can say that God knows the world successively yet is not temporally conditioned. However, if God does not know possibilities as actualities until they happen, the conclusion appears inescapable that he moves in some sense from the one to the other, and so must suffer change. This seems to involve God's being, especially when we consider that the possibilities there are for the world include God's own actions. Another philosopher, A. Kenny, recognizes the implication of this kind of argument, and judges that 'if there is a God who knows all that we know, he must be subject in some degree to change'.[46]

The issues are brought out particularly sharply by R. E. Creel, who agrees with Owen that God's being is not involved in temporality, and yet also affirms (with Kenny) that a knowing relation must result in 'change' in the knower. Creel's solution is to propose that God is indeed involved in the passage from potentiality to actuality, but only in his changing *awareness* of those who make this transition. Creel affirms, with Owen, that there is no sequential movement in God's own being, on the grounds that God knows all possibilities eternally. But he goes on to conclude that although God possesses his own life all at once he cannot possess the lives of others all at once; there must be 'internal change' in God in the sense of his *awareness* of actualities, though still no 'internal relation' to the world which would involve a change in God's *being*.[47] This latter distinction, however, depends upon a view of God's knowledge and love as being totally non-sympathetic, so that God is emotionally impassible and passible only in his *knowledge* of actualities. If we agree with Owen that God does feel our sufferings (and my whole

---

[45] Ibid., pp. 31, 33.
[46] Kenny, op. cit. (ch. 3. n. 33), p. 51, summing up the argument from p. 40.
[47] Creel, *Divine Impassibility*, pp. 105–11.

argument so far supports this), while agreeing with Creel that God must be said to 'change' internally in his awareness, then we are naturally brought to consider the view of omniscience held by the process theologian Charles Hartshorne, whom Owen is intending to oppose.

Hartshorne too describes God as possessing all the reality of the world that can be possessed at any one time, and so possessing possibilities only as possibilities. But on this basis he makes the distinction, crucial for our enquiry, between *perfection* and *completion*.[48] Hartshorne speaks of God's 'relative perfection' in the concrete (or world-experiencing) state of his being. It is 'relative' in being a perfection relative to any particular moment in the process of history, but it is also 'relative' in the sense of relatedness: God is perfectly related to all the reality there is at any one moment.[49] Thus God is perfect, i.e. whole and all-inclusive, but his completion lies ahead. He can be perfect and yet still have a future because his perfection is dynamic. J. Macquarrie speaks similarly of perfection not being a 'static end-state' for God: 'This does not rule out the idea of ever higher grades of perfection and goodness as the context is widened', that is, as God creates more time and history. Macquarrie pleads for acceptance of this idea by offering the illustration that 'what can properly be called 'perfection' in a child gets replaced by new ideals of . . . perfection in the wider context of adult life.'[50]

At each stage of human history God is perfect in relation to it. He is unsurpassable by others but, as Hartshorne maintains, he still surpasses himself in some respects. Completion lies ahead of God as a goal, or as his coming to glory. Plato's argument has been wearily repeated—that God cannot change because, if he becomes more perfect he was not God before, and if he becomes less perfect he is not God any longer. But this envisages 'perfection' as a fixed totality of states of being, whereas God must be the origin of ever new possibilities for his world and hence for himself. The notion of an absolute maximum of reality and value is no more consistent than 'the pseudo-ideas of "greatest-possible number"'.[51] God has ever new and surprising ways in which he expresses himself in his creation, and this means also that God experiences it in new ways, for even if he knows all the possibilities of

[48] Hartshorne, *A Natural Theology for our Time*, pp. 16, 18–19, cf. *The Divine Relativity*, pp. 20–2, 41–2, 76–7.

[49] Hartshorne, *Man's Vision of God*, pp. 7 ff., *A Natural Theology for Our Time*, pp. 70–2, *The Divine Relativity*, pp. 79–82.

[50] Macquarrie, *Principles of Christian Theology*, p. 209.

[51] Hartshorne, *A Natural Theology for our Time*, p. 129, cf. pp. 19–20.

what he and the world can be together (and we shall need to qualify this in a moment), he cannot experience them as actualities until they happen. If God is free to do new things, he is free to have new experiences:

He is the Whole in every categorial sense, all actuality in one individual actuality, and all possibility in one individual potentiality. This relatively simple idea was apparently too complex for most of our ancestors to hit upon.[52]

The ancestor particularly in his gunsights is Aquinas, who maintained that as pure and simple being, God actualized all his potentialities simultaneously. But 'possibility is in principle inexhaustible: it could not be fully actualized'.[53] For instance, Hartshorne points out that some states of reality that are possible taken singly exclude each other by definition in actuality.[54] To embroider our previous illustration, we might say that God cannot experience the refugee both as stateless and as granted British citizenship at the same time, though both are possibilities.

With the help of these insights from process thought, we can draw up some principles about the future of God. Because God knows all possibilities something cannot be new for him in the same way as it is for us when it is actualized; but when it becomes actual it does contribute something fresh to his experience. He knew it before, but not like this. Thus there is something new for God in the future, though not as for us. This is especially the case when possibilities are people, free personalities. There is a gap between God's knowing persons as potential and as actual which is also the gap between his perfection and his completion, and I suggest that it is bridged by his *desire*. Whereas he knows us perfectly in all our possibilities, he desires to be united with us in actuality, in the actual state of our liberation from suffering. Thus his desire springs from his perfection of knowledge and relationship; it is *because* he is perfect that he desires, rather than despite it. We recall again the analogy of God as a creative artist, who sets out with the desire to paint a picture; he has the possibility of the finished work in his mind, but the actuality has new elements in it which arise from his grappling with the materials—the canvas, brushes, paint. When God has free personalities for his materials,

---

[52] Ibid., pp. 20–1.
[53] Ibid., p. 21, cf. Hartshorne, *Man's Vision of God*, pp. 121–3.
[54] Hartshorne, *Man's Vision of God*, p. 21: 'all values are not "compossible", cannot all co-exist'.

he is bound (by his own desire to create in this medium) to 'grow and develop in his own creative action'. It is this sort of illustration that W. H. Vanstone movingly depicts at the heart of his book about the cost of divine love; from watching two boys build a model of a waterfall from sticks and stones as a work of love, Vanstone concluded that 'the activity of creating included the passivity of waiting—of waiting upon one's workmanship to see what emerged from it'.[55]

But if we are going to make this view of the 'perfect incompleteness' of God coherent, we need to probe rather more carefully the assertion that God knows all possibilities, even if he does not know them as actualities. What are these possibilities, and does he know them eternally? H. P. Owen seems to grant God a knowledge of *all* possibilities, in the sense of whatever might possibly come to existence in the world, and to conceive of his having this awareness timelessly.[56] Curiously, he comes close here to the process theologian Whitehead, with his notion of 'eternal objects'.[57] Whitehead proposed that God in his primordial nature envisages all possible values for the world in a way untouched by time. This portrays the divine mind as something like a vast computer memory, containing all possible permutations of human action and consequences, valued according to the degree of satisfaction (or intensity of feeling) which they would yield in every conceivable situation. But if this is so, the gap between possibility and actuality is minimal, if not entirely missing. It lies simply in *whether* one possibility or other will be actualized, not *how* they will be so. God does not know the future only in the sense that he does not know which possibilities, among those which he eternally visualizes, will be actualized by a free being. This still seems a form of determinism, with the world as a duplicate of at least a selection of the ideas in God's mind. If we take seriously the analogy of the creative artist, as we have reflected upon it above, then there must be 'new possibilities' for God in two senses: *first*, there will be those that arise from the interaction between Creator and creatures as the Creator's work has an effect upon him, and *second* there

---

[55] William H. Vanstone, *Love's Endeavour, Love's Expense* (Darton, Longman & Todd, London, 1977), p. 33.

[56] Owen, *Concepts of Deity*, pp. 32–3. So also Creel, *Divine Impassibility*, pp. 28–9.

[57] Whitehead, *Process and Reality*, pp. 62–4, 69–73, cf. pp. 46, 523–4; *Science and the Modern World*, pp. 195–214. For an attack on this idea as determinism, see William A. Christian, *An Interpretation of Whitehead's Metaphysics* (Yale University Press, New Haven, 1959), pp. 271 ff. For a defence, see Lewis S. Ford, 'Whitehead's Differences from Hartshorne', in L. S. Ford (ed.), *Two Process Philosophers*, pp. 58 ff.

will be those that God himself conceives spontaneously from his own creative imagination as the work proceeds. In this context one must say, with Keith Ward, that

> there is no sum total of eternal ideas, but a constantly changing stock of imaginatively created ideas, limited only by God's character as wise, good, and loving . . . . The Creator will not only be ignorant of what will be actual in future . . . he will not know everything that is possible.[58]

Hartshorne lays stress upon the first kind of new possibility mentioned above. In dialogue with Whitehead's concept of 'eternal objects', he protests that there are 'emergent as well as eternal universals'.[59] Pursuing the analogy of the artist, he refuses to believe that the colours that an artist uses have to be a matter of God's eternal conceptual envisagement: ' . . . the blue, the red, why may these not emerge for the first time in some individual's experience, and originally in the whole of reality?'[60] A determinate colour is not 'something haunting reality from all eternity, begging for instantiation'.[61] Hartshorne proposes that in the necessary aspect of his being, God possesses simply the power of possibility itself, including abstracts such as 'quality' and 'specificity' which are the basis for colour. Distinct possibilities, such as a colour itself, can only arise in interaction with the world and its past, in the concrete nature of God; but even these possibilities can only be general, as parameters or limits for detailed happenings. The name of a colour still refers to something relatively vague. A *particular* tinge of pigment on a *particular* place on the canvas is not a possibility at all, but a detail of actuality which simply happens: 'There is no such thing as a possible particular.'[62] Ahead of time 'the painter knows roughly what he can do. But that he can do just *this* which he subsequently does, not even deity can know until it is done . . . Creativity does not map the details of its future actions, even as possible.'[63]

Hartshorne's account is a valuable reminder of the sheer novelty of some elements within any true creative process, but I do not think that it leaves God as creator with sufficient initiative to do new things himself. It severely limits God's activity in the world, and especially his ability to

---

[58] Ward, *Rational Theology and the Creativity of God*, p. 154.
[59] Hartshorne, *Creativity Synthesis and Philosophic Method*, p. 58.
[60] Ibid., p. 63, cf. Hartshorne, *Man's Vision of God*, pp. 247–8.
[61] Hartshorne, *Creative Synthesis and Philosophic Method*, p. 59.
[62] Ibid,. p. 122.   [63] Ibid., p. 65.

react to the response of his creation to him. He can, it seems, influence us only by the beauty of a being which is rich in experience, and cannot create new qualities and ideals to inspire us, for example in the face of suffering. This underplays the second kind of 'new possibility' I drew attention to above—the originality of the artist himself in imagining details, and especially that of the Supreme Artist. Here Whitehead's concept of God's own supreme vision of values has a kind of truth which should not be neglected. We might obtain a more convincing picture of God as creator if we think of God as setting the boundaries of possibilities out of the resources of his primordial will, much as Hartshorne thinks of God as conceiving such things as colour in general. (Hartshorne, however, restricts this to the concrete state of God's being.) Because God is self-existent and self-explanatory in the sense that he is, in his free will, the prior condition for all beings,[64] he must eternally know the general outlines of all possible events. These, as Ward suggests 'set the limits of all possible worlds, though they are not exhaustively specified to cover every actual eventuality'.[65] Then in his interaction with the world new, specific possibilities arise which he does not know either eternally or ahead of their time; but these are a blend of the effect of his workmanship upon him *and* his own spontaneous imagination of new possibilities. He can envisage detailed possibilities, down to the last fraction of a pigment; yet man is still free not to brush on the pigment, or to make his own original contribution to mixing a new one.

If we think of creation like this, then we can indeed say that God knows all possibilities that can be known, although it follows that the only possibilities that are knowable are those that have been conceived, whether by creature or Creator. At any one point in time, God knows all the possibilities there are to be known, but he does not know possibilities which have not yet been creatively thought of, and which do not therefore exist. (Ward usefully names these 'negative poss- ibles'.[66]) As long as we accept that God can suffer change, this kind of approach does, I think, satisfy the criteria both for God's omniscience and for his future. God's future, created by his own desire for his creation, is a matter of the gap between his knowledge of all possibilities

---

[64] The term 'necessary being' could be used to denote a self-existent and self-explanatory God, as long as this were not misunderstood in the sense of unconditioned or totally self-sufficient. See above, ch. 3, pp. 66–8.

[65] Ward, *Rational Theology and the Creativity of God*, p. 165.

[66] Ibid., pp. 154–5.

(in the sense I have just defined them) and his experience of their actualities. He is nevertheless perfect in that he has total knowledge of, and relation to, everything that actually exists and all possibilities there are for existence at any one moment. Such a notion is required for the belief that God suffers, for suffering has a future in two senses: the sufferer anticipates his suffering and he awaits release.

What has been said so far about the 'perfect incompleteness' of God naturally requires the basis that God has temporality. It judges that God takes our history so seriously that he experiences it as history: he takes our future so seriously that he experiences it as future. It is not only that God would fail to experience the world as we do if he did not know it successively; he would also fail in love, for time is important to us and must mean something to a loving God. Mascall, seeking to underpin the Thomist statement of God's timelessness, nevertheless urges that a God who experiences history in an instantaneous flash has more compassion for us than one who experiences it in our time; he argues that God can be of more help to us if he can be in all times simultaneously.[67] Thus, in a *tour de force* of argument, he suggests that history is more important to God if he is not involved in it. We are bound to doubt whether the history for which God is so concerned is in fact recognizable as ours.

Mascall also argues for the timelessness of God along the lines that time is not a single 'receptacle' (as in the Newtonian view) into which things and events are put. Physical entities have their own time-scales arising from their relation to other events, as modern relativity theory has shown, and there are likely to be many time-frames in the universe as there are many space-frames. Mascall concludes that the only way that God could be related to many time systems would be to be timeless.[68] But, while Mascall rightly draws attention to a 'relational' rather than a 'receptacle' view of time, his argument by no means follows. It is just as coherent to say that God can relate to all time-scales because he can participate in them all concurrently, along their individual time-paths, where we are limited to our own. He is 'eternal' in that he surpasses time by being able to indwell all systems of time, not by being above them. Indeed, for God to create new possibilities in the

---

[67] Eric Mascall, *The Openness of Being: Natural Theology Today* (Darton, Longman & Todd, London, 1971), p. 176.

[68] Ibid., pp. 164–5. Mascall therefore criticizes Pike's arguments against the notion of timeless Person, on the grounds that he has failed to take the scientific view of relational time into account: see Nelson Pike, *God and Timelessness* (Routledge & Kegan Paul, London, 1970), pp. 121–9.

way we have been contemplating, there must be something like successive states in his experience. There must be something corresponding to 'before' and 'after' in his own experience of his actions, as indeed there must for God to suffer from the actions of others. Time is a necessary property of God's creative will, which promotes change and humbly suffers change. Indeed, we might even take one step further in thought and dare to suggest that God can indwell all systems of time because he has his own kind of 'time' or 'history' which is capable of intermeshing with them. Though we cannot say exactly what this might mean, once again the doctrine of the Trinity supplies an image, since talk of God's begetting, being begotten, and proceeding speak of a God in movement. Within this inner 'history' of his triune being in which there is no before and after, he can make room for all our histories in which there is. As Barth suggests, God's repetition of himself makes space eternally within himself for time, so that 'God has time, because and as He has eternity'.[69]

The belief that God suffers involves the belief that there are times at which God exists. In a moment we shall be considering another way in which God's temporality transcends ours, in his *victory* over suffering. Here we must add that God is also 'eternal' with regard to his character: that is, during all the changing states through which God projects himself, he remains consistent with himself. This is the aspect of God's character that was developed into the classical concept of 'necessary being', with all its unfortunate implications of self-sufficiency.[70] A dimension of that changeless character is, we have seen, his knowledge of the limits for all possible worlds; this persists through all the change which God instigates. This reflects the biblical concept that God is unchanging in his faithfulness. Indeed, the view of the future of God outlined here has a good deal of support in the biblical records of the faith of ancient Israel, where God's relation to the future of human persons is seen not as exact prediction but as promise. One only need see what unlikely events the prophets claimed to be fulfilments of previous prophecy to understand that in Israelite faith 'God fulfils his promises in unexpected ways' (Zimmerli).[71] We might find here a witness that the

---

[69] Barth, *CD* II/1, p. 611: Barth, of course, denies that God's being has a successiveness like ours, but refuses to define eternity as 'an abstract opposite to the concept of time'. Cf. *CD* II/1, p. 593.

[70] See above, n. 64.

[71] Walther Zimmerli, 'Promise and Fulfilment', in C. Westermann (ed.), *Essays on Old Testament Interpretation*, trans. J. L. Mays (SCM Press, London, 1963), p. 107. This

future is real for God, though not in quite the same way as for us: in making promise rather than prediction, God leaves himself room for the new and the yet unknown, both in human response and in his own creative imagination.

The classic text here is the revelation of the Lordship of God to Moses in Exodus 3:14, with the word-play on the name Yahweh: exploiting its similarity to a tense of the verb 'to be' (*'ehyeh*, from the verb *hayah*), the narrator gives us the name of God as 'I am what I am', or 'I will be what I will be', or even 'I am what you will discover me to be'.[72] This is no declaration of God as unmoving being, for God here defines his being as interested and involved in his people; the verb here has the implication 'I will be for you', for his being will be manifest in his future acts, as an efficacious being present for his people. There is thus no divorce between God and the world, but at the same time there is otherness and mystery; God eludes being pinned down to any position where he would simply be the tool of his people; in refusing to give them his name as they wanted he declares his freedom to do the new and the unexpected. This is not a philosophical aseity but a declaration of his freedom of will, which is at the same time a promise of the future and not a prediction. Finally, in this rich text, he discloses his being as faithfulness, for the formula 'testifies that the reality of God will not be different from that made known in his revelation'.[73]

4. THE VICTORY OF GOD OVER SUFFERING

So God experiences our history and our future in a way that is both like and unlike the way we do. In his journey from suffering to glory along the path of his desire there is, however, another way in which his experience transcends ours: he has victory over suffering. If it is essential that a God who helps us should sympathize with our suffering, it is also essential that he should not be overcome or defeated by suffering. Even

phrase has become a leitmotif among the 'theologians of hope'—e.g. Moltmann, *Theology of Hope*, pp. 102–12. See further Paul S. Fiddes, 'God and History', *The Baptist Quarterly*, 30 (1983), pp. 85–8.

[72] This is the translation offered by G. Henton Davies, in *Exodus: Introduction and Commentary* (Torch Bible Commentaries, SCM Press, London, 1967), p. 72. Similarly, see Brevard S. Childs, *Exodus: A Commentary* (Old Testament Library, SCM Press, London, 1974), pp. 60–4. In contrast, Mascall argues for Aquinas' understanding of the phrase as denoting the self-sufficiency of God (*Existence and Analogy*, pp. 11–15).

[73] Childs, op. cit. (n. 72 above), p. 76.

in the human analogy, the sufferer is not helped by a counsellor who is disorientated and disintegrated by sympathy. But how then should we think of God's victory over suffering? Classical theists who believe that God's eternal blessedness must not be disturbed, that his peace of mind and happiness must be uninterrupted, and yet who want to allow for some kind of suffering in God, envisage that God's sorrow and pain is always instantaneously dissolved away in his joy.

Any suffering that God endures through his love for his creatures is immediately transfigured by the joy that is necessarily his within his uncreated Godhead. (H. P. Owen)[74]

He sympathizes with our sorrows . . . but even this is infinitely surpassed by the beatitude which God enjoys in the interior fullness of his own divine life. (E. Mascall)[75]

Yet we must doubt whether this kind of continuous transfiguration of suffering can in fact be called suffering. Can there be suffering which does not disturb equanimity? Owen draws the analogy of a doctor whose joy in healing obliterates his loathing for the disease: but if the doctor is so taken up with the victory of his art and the triumphs of medicine that he fails to feel with the patient in his condition, he is unlikely to be a good doctor. After all the final object of the doctor's attention is not the disease but the patient; it is the suffering of the patient and not the loathing of the disease that most disturbs him.

Another way of expressing this suffusion of suffering would be to say that God's delight in the values he possesses outweighs his sympathetic suffering with the world. Thus Ward proposes that:

God is supremely happy in the contemplation of all those values which he possesses in his own being. He is happy in the contemplation of those values which are being realized in the world. These sorts of happiness are overwhelmingly greater than even the whole sum of the sorrows of the world.[76]

But this notion of the bliss of God requires us to separate a value from the creatures which embody it, so that God can enjoy the value even though a creature is suffering from a lack of it. In fact, the final logic of this sort of argument is that in his essential being God is not self-giving love at all, but a cherisher of values. Ward does not hesitate to take this

---

[74] Owen, *Concepts of Deity*, p. 24.   [75] Mascall, *He Who Is*, p. 111.
[76] Ward, *Holding Fast to God*, p. 37, cf. *Rational Theology and the Creativity of God*, p. 199.

step: 'God on his own cannot be self-giving love; for there is nothing to give himself to'.[77] Ward thus distinguishes sharply between necessary and contingent properties of God. In his necessary being God has the personal attributes of power, knowledge, goodness, wisdom, and happiness. But once he has made creatures, as an expression of his goodness and from a delight in the values which he knows eternally within himself, he relates to them in a contingent way; he loves them in a costly manner that means suffering, and allows them to enrich his own being. Although he has not made creatures out of any desire, but as a free display of his goodness, he develops a real sensitivity to them and even desire for them. He is 'the Aristotelian aristocrat'[78] who has got involved. We might comment, unkindly, that he seems to be slumming in the world. In the next chapter we must question similar attempts to bifurcate the being of God into 'necessary' and 'contingent' areas, but for the moment we must ask whether it is possible to appreciate values without also desiring the creatures who might possibly exemplify them. It is clear why Ward wants to say God can; he wants to exempt God from any unfulfilled desires:

His desires cannot be frustrated, and require no difficult endeavour; he cannot be dissatisfied with what he necessarily is.[79]

But can God appreciate values without yearning for those who might actualize them? Hartshorne judges, I believe rightly, that 'cosmic beauty as a value must be actualized in concrete experience, and this . . . can only be a cosmic love.'[80] Moreover, even if God could like values without loving creatures, it is doubtful whether a suffering based on this ability would be anything like suffering as we know it. If there is no element of frustrated desire in the divine suffering, then it seems to be simply an omniscient awareness of *our* suffering. We have seen that a belief in God's omniscience should lead us to speak of a temporal and a suffering God; but suffering cannot be simply defined as omniscient sensitivity to our pain. We cannot then think of God's triumph over suffering as his blissful vision of values which soothes away his suffering. A suffering God must be a disturbed God.

Rather, we can think of God's victory over suffering in two ways—as his certainty of final victory, and as his choosing of it for himself. First, we can say that God knows that at the last he will be all in all, though he suffers limitations willingly on the way to that ultimate victory. Such

---

[77] Ibid., p. 137, cf. p. 139.   [78] Ibid., p. 146.   [79] Ibid., p. 144.
[80] Hartshorne, *A Natural Theology for Our Time*, p. 15.

joyous certainty need not be at odds with the desire and thirst of God which aims towards a real future, and with the deepest meaning of love itself. True, love is a pilgrimage into the unknown; it takes the risk of abandoning calculations; it cannot reckon on a return for its outlay and it does not seek to know the whole of the story before the end; it is patient (1 Cor. 13: 4). There can be no suffering love unless there is an element of the unknown which calls for trust. Suffering love abandons securities and goes out like Abraham into a desert journey. But all this is not incompatible with God's certainty of final victory over suffering, though it might appear at first glance to be so. Desire and certainty belong together in God, we may say, because while there is an unknown in the future for God, it is not unknown in the way that it is for us. I have already suggested that God, unlike us, knows all possibilities that can be known; at the same time he knows the power of his love to persuade and influence his creation. So he has the certainty of perfect hope, where ours can only be partial, and hope 'is the evidence of things not seen'. The divine certainty is not prediction, but confident hope. How could we experience the 'Spirit of hope' who comes from the 'God of hope' unless we were participating in God's own hopefulness? The strength of this hope, amounting to beatitude in God, is confirmed by a closer inspection of the contrast between time and eternity.

The classical notion of eternity, expressed by Boethius,[81] is a timelessness where God experiences past, present, and future simultaneously ('the complete and perfect possession at once of an endless life'); we have already seen that this is not coherent with the belief that God suffers. A suffering God is implicated in time. We might then conceive of a different kind of transcending of time, a different sort of victory over the successiveness of the passing moment which we endure. Heidegger has pointed to the nature of our human predicament as being fragmented in time; it is not the flow of past, present, and future that is the problem, but our inability to unify our experience of them.[82] We are unable to bring our past, present, and future into a whole. We cannot integrate our present with our past because we either regret the loss of the past in nostalgia, or we try to obliterate our memory of it in guilt. We cannot integrate our future with our present, because we either try to escape into it in wish-fulfilment dreams, or feel threatened by it. Most acutely, suffering defeats us because we cannot unify our time; suffering overwhelms us because we cannot live with our past or

---

[81] Boethius, *De Consolatione* 5. 6: 'interminabilis vitae tota simul et perfecta possessio'.   [82] Martin Heidegger, *Being and Time*, pp. 236–7, 279–80.

face our future. If we were whole in time we would not be broken in our personalities by suffering. This perception of our predicament gives us a clue to the nature of eternity, and God's mastery of time: we might think of his eternity not as an abolition of time but as a healing of it. At every moment of his divine life he would be integrating the flow of past, present and future into a new wholeness, redeeming the past and anticipating the future in a new harmony. Thus, although there would be an element of the unknown in the future for God, and he would know a real desire for the realizing of possibilities, he would experience the future in a different way from us. His hope would be perfect in ways that we cannot conceive.

If in fact we think carefully about the experiences we have which we call 'timeless moments' or epiphanies of eternity, we find that they do not dissolve time but heal it. We sometimes speak of being absorbed in a piece of music as a 'timeless moment', not noticing that an hour has slipped by. But this experience is not strictly timeless; the whole effect of the music depends upon a sequence of time in rhythm, repetition, and variation. Rather, we have experienced a new relationship to time; in terms of modern relativity theory, the time itself was defined by the relation, and was not something absolute. Time is not a single 'container', whose contents might be viewed from above by a divine observer in such a manner that for him there would be no difference between past, present, and future. However, the 'relative' view of time also means that, while a difference remains, there can be no rigid *separation* between the past and the future, and no absolute present. We might then conceive of a God for whom the past is still present and open to his transforming vision. J. Macquarrie speaks of God's bringing the past into 'an ever widening reconciling context' as 'the horizons of time and history continually expand'.[83] It is therefore perhaps a little misleading for Macquarrie also to refer to this integration of time as 'the *simultaneity* of [God's] universal experience',[84] as he is thinking of the healing of the past in the context of a real future with 'expanding

---

[83] Macquarrie, *Principles of Christian Theology*, p. 361, cf. id., *Christian Hope*, pp. 120 ff. See also Jüngel, *God as the Mystery of the World*, pp. 212–14: 'what is past is not without possibility'; id., *Death*, pp. 117–20.

[84] Macquarrie, *Christian Hope*, p. 118. Similarly, Pannenberg attempts to speak of eternity as the 'concurrence of all events in a single present', while insisting that this does not cancel the particularities of history: Wolfhart Pannenberg, *What is Man? Contemporary Anthropology in Theological Perspective*, trans. D. A. Priebe (Fortress Press, Philadelphia, 1970), pp. 74–6.

horizons'. It is the harmonizing of time, not its obliteration in a simultaneous moment, which belongs to God.

If, in accordance with this, we think of God's victory over suffering as his having a 'sure and certain hope' of bringing about the reconciling of all things and a new creation without end, then we cannot think of God's venture in creation as a total risk. The belief that God 'takes a risk' in creation is often stated in an emotive way, without considering its implications. Vanstone, for example, states that God is prepared for either the triumph or the tragedy of love, and describes the tragic issue of love as meaning that '*all* has been given in vain'.[85] We must rather think of God as embarking upon an enterprise with what we might (rather clumsily) call a 'limited risk'. If the end is in one sense 'certain', the route has an openness about it that stems from human freedom and the choices open to human personalities. The goal of God is nothing other than the making of persons, and the kind of persons we become is based upon the choices that we make, the kinds of values we hold to, the ways in which we respond to challenges and disappointments. The personality is not a ready-made entity, but is formed through experience. The Apostle Paul speaks of our reactions to everyday afflictions as building the body of glory:

Though our outer nature is wasting away, our inner nature is being renewed every day. For this slight momentary affliction is preparing for us an eternal weight of glory beyond all comparison. (2 Cor. 4:16–17)

Decisions and experiences in this life matter: they are building what we are. Since God's aim is the making of persons, he has the certain hope that we will be 'glorified', but the *content* of that end depends upon human responses, for the content of the end is persons. There is no standard model of a human personality which God is constructing in a cosmic factory, and so not only the route to the end but the content of the end is something which God has put into the hands of his creatures. When we are dealing with persons, we cannot separate the road from the destination. Thus the risk upon which God is embarked is real and serious, though not a total one. He has a certain hope of the fact of the end, but there is a genuine openness about the route and therefore the content of the end. There is room then for tragedy as well as triumph in God's victory over suffering; while creatures will know bliss in the comtemplation of their creator, God may know that they are not all that they could have been. There will be no deficiency in their beatific

85 Vanstone, op. cit. (n. 55 above), p. 77.

vision, for they will be perfectly related to God, and God will have healed their past, as I suggested above. Whitehead speaks of the judgement of God as 'a tenderness which loses nothing that can be saved' and as 'a wisdom which uses what in the temporal world is mere wreckage'[86] as he includes it within his own being; all values that have been actualized in the world will contribute to the richness of God's life. Each creature is felt for the worth of its life, however little that may have been.

Process thought at this point is often criticized for apparently making evil eternal within God, for the effects of all past actions are present to him and make an impact upon him. But this misses the point that God transmutes[87] or sums up[88] the effect of human lives rather than gathering them indifferently into himself. The possible tragedy lies not in the presence of evil within God, but the absence of some good that the world might have produced. As God cherishes all human experiences, he opens himself to 'the tragedy of unfulfilled desire'.[89] We must not forget, however, that the 'end' of which are speaking in traditional Christian imagery can only be a decisive shifting of creation onto a new level of existence, not an absolute end, if God's being is indeed in the process of becoming. So his hope too is without end, each goal a new beginning, each disappointment with his creatures the basis for a new enterprise in what J. Macquarrie felicitously calls a 'continuing consummation'.[90] In this way, I believe that we can conceive of a blend of triumph and tragedy in God in his experience of suffering, as we can also think of a future which is certain and yet also unknown.

There is also a second reason why God suffers victoriously and is not

[86] Whitehead, *Process and Reality*, p. 525.
[87] Whitehead, *Religion in the Making*, pp. 148–9, *Process and Reality*, p. 531. Whitehead also calls God the 'valuation of the world' (*Religion in the Making*, p. 159). On the importance of 'transmutation' in a process theodicy, see Griffin, *God, Power and Evil*, pp. 302–4.
[88] Hartshorne, *The Logic of Pefection*, pp. 174–5.
[89] Hartshorne, *Man's Vision of God*, p. 294; also see C. Hartshorne, 'Whitehead and Berdyaev: Is there Tragedy in God?', *Journal of Religion*, 37 (1957), p. 77. Whitehead speaks about tragedy in God, despite transmutation: see 'Immortality', in M. Schilpp (ed.), *The Philosophy of Alfred North Whitehead* (Northwestern University, Evanstone and Chicago, 1941), p. 698, and *Adventures of Ideas*, p. 381.
[90] Macquarrie, *Principles of Christian Theology*, p. 356. This has a similarity to Process Thought where God's satisfaction is related to successive phases in his becoming; see Whitehead, *Process and Reality*, p. 135, and Cobb, *A Christian Natural Theology*, p. 189.

degraded by suffering: he chooses his suffering. Gregory Thaumaturgus seems to have been the first to suggest this, saying that God triumphs over suffering because he wills to suffer for a definite purpose:

But of him who, while his nature remains impassible, is of his own will immersed in sufferings that he may overcome them, we do not say that he becomes subject to suffering, even though, of his own will, he has shared in sufferings.[91]

This is a penetrating insight, though Gregory blunts it by limiting the extent to which God shares in suffering, since he is attempting to maintain the impassibility of God at the same time. Gregory believes that God cannot experience 'the sorrows that come from human sufferings'; because God has not been constrained to suffer but has freely chosen it, Gregory concludes that the actual suffering which God undergoes can have no element of constraint or hurt in it. God triumphs over suffering in the sense of nullifying it, like a flame being cut by a sword and taking no hurt into its essence.[92] In the previous chapter we have already seen that for God to suffer in any meaningful sense of the word, he must choose to be affected by external forces; while he is not constrained *to* suffer, *in* suffering he undergoes constraint. But we can agree that one who chooses his suffering is not thereby ruled by it; he is subject to suffering but does not become subjected to it in the sense of being dominated by it. Even in human experience, when someone suffers actively by accepting suffering as something belonging to them, it ceases to have the power of an alien force over them. I have already quoted D. Sölle's comment that 'what I take belongs to me in a different sense from what I only bear'. This is akin to the urging to 'love' suffering that we find in the medieval mystical writings.

If we follow through the human analogy of active suffering for a moment, we shall be led to several important reflections upon the idea of a suffering God. When someone accepts as his own the suffering that is inflicted upon him, the person who inflicts it loses all power over him; the torturer or oppressor loses the ability to dominate him in any ultimate sense. When the sufferer has lost his fear of suffering as something strange to his being, he has the strength to resist and rebel against the tyrant, even if only mentally. D. Sölle has again pointed out that we cannot therefore conceive of God as someone who directly sends suffering as a means of keeping us in order, punishing, or even

[91] Translation in Mozley, *The Impassibility of God*, pp. 66–7.
[92] Ibid., p. 68.

educating us, since we would only need to make suffering our own in order to 'dethrone' God.[93] Only a God who suffers with us can be our God, once we have learned to suffer actively. Likewise, his own triumph over suffering must be of this kind for us to recognize it as victory, and accept it as a religious value.

Further, in the human analogy, to make suffering our own is not mere resignation or Stoic toleration. Once we have ceased to be resentful about suffering and have accepted ownership of it, we are free over it to see whether it can be ended, and what causes of suffering can in fact be dealt with in the present. The notion of God as an unbending monarch who sends suffering for reasons he best knows can lead to a religious fatalism, a resigned submission to a God who lays down stern decrees. This is not true 'acceptance' of suffering, but apathetic resignation, and it can be invoked to block social change. We can detect a flavour of this in the verse not now usually printed in the Victorian hymn 'All things bright and beautiful' (by Mrs C. F. Alexander), which gives a social meaning to the phrase 'all creatures great and small':

> The rich man in his castle,
> The poor man at his gate,
> God made them high and lowly,
> And ordered their estate.

The image of an unfeeling ('a-pathetic') God will naturally lead to an apathy in matters of social justice, as the Liberation theologians have emphasized. But the idea of a God who triumphs over suffering by choosing it for his own includes the notion of his protest against the suffering of the world, and motivates believers in a suffering God to change the conditions which cause suffering. To 'love' suffering, in the phrase of the mystics, should not mean believing that God sends it, or regarding it in itself as something of final value.

Once again we see the centrality of the idea of the 'desire' of God. God chooses to suffer, but his desire and thirst is not for suffering itself but for fellowship with his creation. This is why we must say that he chooses that suffering should *befall* him, rather than making himself suffer, as we saw earlier. To desire suffering would be a kind of divine masochism, and would detract from the conviction of God's victory over suffering; he would be the eternal auto-victim of the universe. Rather, out of his desire for his creatures he chooses to suffer, and

---

[93] Sölle, *Suffering*, pp. 109–11.

because he chooses to suffer he is not ruled by suffering; it has no power to overwhelm him because he has made the alien thing his own. He fulfils his own being *through* suffering, since he can only become more truly himself through suffering with the world, but the suffering itself is not the fulfilment of his purpose. What actually fulfils God is the satisfaction of his desire. The God who has a future suffers to bring many sons and daughters to glory, and in this he is glorified.

5

The God Who Suffers and Remains God

THERE is a story told of Archbishop William Temple that he was once listening to a lecture when the person sitting next to him whispered, 'Do you understand what he's talking about?' Temple is said to have replied, 'Well, I understand perfectly what he's saying, but I don't understand what he's saying it *about*.' We must always take care that our theological talk is actually about God, in the sense that it remains meaningful to use the word 'God' of the subject of our discussion. It is fairly easy to talk about the *suffering* of God, but it is less easy to speak of the suffering of God. If God's suffering is to be of healing effect for a suffering world, then it must be recognizably God's, and not merely our human suffering projected onto God. We cannot simply analyse what suffering means in human experience and transfer the results to God without recollecting the uniqueness of his Being. In this chapter we must therefore pay further attention to the need to hold our beliefs in the suffering of God and the transcendence of God together. The argument of the last two chapters has been that if we attribute suffering to God in a manner that can meaningfully be called suffering, then this implies that God changes in response to his world, and that his change takes the form of a pilgrimage to his future glory. Throughout I have been concerned to make these affirmations coherent with the idea of a creator God who is self-existent, the explanation for the universe, and incomparable with all beings. In doing this, I have found the concept of God as Trinity indispensable.

From time to time I have alluded to one solution to the question of how a transcendent God can suffer, which has proved attractive to much recent theological thought and which we must now criticize more directly. Some have wanted to accept the conclusions about change and futurity in God, and yet at the same time retain the image of God as unchanging, timeless, and self-sufficient. Some want to claim that God *is* thoroughly involved in the winding path of the world's history, and yet also is *not*. That is, God's transcendence over his world and his immanence in it, his otherness and his interest, may be simply driven apart into two compartments of the divine Being. This might be pictured in a paradoxical fashion as an inner Holy of Holies in God's life where there is timeless peace and untroubled bliss, while in the outer courtyard there is all the hurly-burly of time and history; in the words of a nineteenth-century theologian, Martensen, 'in the outer chambers is sadness, but in the inner ones unmix'd joy'.[1] More subtle distinctions would be between God in his essence and his activity, or between necessary and contingent natures of God, or God 'in himself' and God 'for us'. Some hinterland is reserved in God which is untouched by the world, and this is named his transcendence. Suffering and transcendence are conceived as opposites, though enormous efforts might be made to harmonize them.

This supposed solution is surprisingly pervasive, and appears in different areas of theological interest. A. Heschel, for instance, whose concern is with the nature of prophetic experience and whom we have already credited with insisting upon the prophet's feeling of sympathy with the pathos of God, nevertheless excludes pathos from the very Being of God. Pathos, he believes, belongs to God's outward relationship with mankind, to the 'situation' in which God involves himself in sharing the history of his people, not to the attributes of God's being; it is 'modal', not 'essential'.[2] In his own theological concern to develop a Christology, A. T. Hanson refers to Heschel's distinction with approval; it not only, in his view, solves a need to combine the philosophical idea of 'an unchanging divine principle' with the personal, living God of Hebrew tradition, but is also supports a functional understanding of the presence of God in Christ. Accepting the view that God suffers with all men only in his relationships with them and not in his being, Hanson concludes that we can think of the incarnation in Christ as not touching God's being either:

It is surely also significant for our study that Heschel rejects any suggestion that the pathos of God is of his essence. To this corresponds our claim that the incarnation should not be understood in substantialist terms, but in terms of a relation of indwelling and grace between the Word and Jesus.[3]

Actually, it is hard to see how the two sets of concepts—modal pathos and functional Christology—are necessarily linked, and they certainly

[1] H. H. Martensen, *Christian Dogmatics* (T. & T. Clark, Edinburgh, 1866), sect. 51, p. 101.   [2] Heschel, *The Prophets*, pp. 225–6, 229.

[3] Hanson, op. cit. (ch. 2 n. 37), p. 139.

do not verify each other. A functional view of the divinity of Christ, in which God is seen as acting uniquely through him, could entail the suffering of the inner essence of God as much as an ontological view could. In fact, I shall be arguing later that a belief in the essential suffering of God helps to explain *how* God could be uniquely at work in the particular person of Christ.[4]

Neither Heschel nor A. T. Hanson make much attempt to reconcile the two dimensions of impassible essence and suffering action which they identify in God. Two sustained attempts to conceive a duality like this and also to harmonize it are those made by Karl Barth and process theology. Barth conceives of the dual dimension in terms of the traditional doctrine of the immanent and the economic Trinity, and process thought proposes a dipolarity of absolute and contingent aspects in God. We have already briefly surveyed these approaches, and now we must give them extended attention. Then we shall examine the recent attempt by Jürgen Moltmann to unify the two dimensions of God's transcendence and worldly action, bringing them together into a single experience of suffering. However, as we shall see, in distinguishing between the inner and outer dimensions of God in terms of his love for the like and his love for the unlike, Moltmann continues some of the old problems.

I.   SUFFERING IN THE 'ECONOMIC' TRINITY: KARL BARTH

The classical expression of a twofoldness in the being of God has been the distinction made between the immanent and the economic Trinity. (We should recall, of course, that these traditional labels are unfortunately liable to confusion, for the term 'immanent' in this context refers to God's dwelling in himself and not in the world; perhaps 'transcendent Trinity' or 'essential Trinity' would be clearer.) The early Church Fathers noted that God manifested himself as Father, Son, and Spirit for the purpose of dealing with the world in creation, redemption and renewal; he acted thus in his *oikonomia* or his ordering of history. As such he was implicated in the material cosmos and in the life of his people on earth. But they also believed that God must be more transcendent, more mysterious, more separate from the world in his very Being.

In the early period in the West, this distinction between the being and the activity of God tended to be a contrast between the eternal unity of God (his *monarchia*) and his diversity for the sake of creation and

---

[4] See below in ch. 6, pp. 166–9.

salvation. Tertullian, for example, held this kind of merely 'economic Trinitarianism'; while God was eternally one in substance, he only extended himself into three 'persons' (distinct identities[5]) for the period of the *oikonomia*; the Father certainly knew the Logos eternally as his 'thought', but not as 'son' or 'persona' until he put him forth for the sake of creation.[6] The later work of the Cappadocian Fathers in the East made clear that the immanent being of God was eternally Trinity, three persons (*hypostases*) who are the same in essence (*ousia*), and thus indivisible in their actions towards the world.[7] But to give real content to the distinctions between the persons, they also rather paradoxically continued the older model of an ordering in the divine being, with a highest level of divinity which was mysterious and ineffable. Gregory of Nyssa occasionally hints at the one *ousia* itself as the incomprehensible factor, and they certainly all represent the Father as the utterly transcendent source (*arche*) of the other *hypostases*, and perhaps even of the divinity in the Godhead.[8] In this way theologians were able to think

[5] It is essential not to confuse the Latin 'persona' with the modern sense of person as a centre of consciousness or an individual mind; the force of 'persona' is that one encounters a distinct form which is 'other' (*alius*) from oneself, for instance in the functions of speaking and acting (Tertullian, *Adversus Praxean* 11). See J. N. D. Kelly, *Early Christian Doctrines* (A. & C. Black, London, [4]1968), pp. 114–15. The Greek term 'hypostasis' also expresses an objectivity or concreteness of presentation; see G. L. Prestige, *God in Patristic Thought* (SPCK, London, [2]1952), pp. 176 ff. This historical insight is valuable for the modern debate; see below pp. 139–42.

[6] Tertullian, *Adversus Praxean* 2; 6–7; *Adversus Hermogenem* 3. On this point see J. Danielou, *The Origins of Latin Christianity*, trans. D. Smith and J. A. Baker (Westminster Press–Darton, Longman, & Todd, London–Philadelphia, 1977), pp. 363–6.

[7] A major analogy used for the relation of *ousia* to *hypostasis* is of a universal and its particulars: see Basil the Great, *Ep.* 38. 5 cf. *Ep.* 214. 4, 236. 6; Gregory of Nazianzus, *Orationes* 25. 16, 26. 19, 29. 2. For identity of operation, see e.g. Basil, *Ep.* 189. 6 (actually by Gregory of Nyssa); Basil, *Adversus Eunomium* 3. 4. See Kelly, op. cit. (n. 5 above), pp. 264 ff.

[8] e.g. Gregory of Nyssa, *Adversus Eunomium* 2. 3; Gregory of Nazianzus, *Orationes* 20. 7, 31. 14; Basil, *On the Holy Spirit* 47. See Maurice Wiles, *The Making of Christian Doctrine: A Study in the Principles of Early Doctrinal Development* (Cambridge University Press, 1967), pp. 136–7; Mackey, *The Christian Experience of God as Trinity*, pp. 144 ff., 151–2. O'Donnell, op. cit. (ch. 1 n. 42), p. 65, concludes that this coupling of ideas tended 'to sever the connection between the economic Trinity and the immanent Trinity'. Lossky, however, denies that there is any 'mysticism of the divine essence' in the Cappadocians or in later Orthodoxy: see Vladimir Lossky, *The Mystical Theology of the Eastern Church*, trans. Fellowship of St Alban and St Sergius (James Clarke, Cambridge–London, 1957), p. 65. Similarly, John D. Zizioulas, *Being as Communion: Studies in Personhood and the Church* (Darton, Longman, & Todd, London, 1985), pp. 40–1, 87–92, insists that the person of the Father 'causes' the divine essence.

in a compromised Platonic fashion of God as Absolute being, while at
the same time allowing for him to be operative and known in the world;
he was both known and unknown.

Though these theological ventures distinguished in various ways
between economic and immanent aspects of God, they hardly presented
two forms of Trinity, immanent and economic. It is in Augustine that
we find something approaching an immanent Trinity detached from
the activity of the triune God in the world. A sharp contrast is drawn
between the inner being of God characterized by mutual relationships,
and the outer action of God towards the world where the persons act
together in an indistinguishable manner.[9] The key thought here is of a
society of relationships within a divine mind, sufficient unto itself.[10]
Because God is related to himself eternally as Father Son and Spirit, he
thinks of himself, enjoys himself, and loves himself without any need of
an outside world. In his *oikonomia* he graciously enables creation to share
in this changeless state of self-enjoyment. Through his work of creation,
he impresses his own triune image upon the human mind, so that all
human loving participates in the divine Being which is love, and in the
loving humility of his act of redemption he draws us anew to the good
as the source of our being; but the eternal festival of love would still go
on without us as guests.

The Fathers only made tentative probes towards using the distinction
between God in himself (immanent) and in the world (economic) in
order to speak of the suffering of God, and then only in the form of a
qualified 'suffering' of the Son.[11] But Karl Barth in recent times has

---

[9] The Cappadocian formula of identity of operation is thus made more absolute
('opera ad extra sunt indivisa'), with a shift from inseparability to indistinguishability. The
divine substance is immutable, and thus the Son can be said to be 'sent' by the Father
only in the sense that the three persons work together (and indistinguishably) in using
changeable substance to make one of the persons visible (Augustine, *De Trinitate* 5. 9, 11,
13, cf. 2. 32—'a changeable creature subject to an unchangeable God'). For modern
criticism of this approach in general, see Karl Rahner, *The Trinity*, pp. 11 ff., 23 ff.

[10] The 'social' aspects of the relations, present in the imagery of begetting and loving
(*De Trinitate* 5.7–10, 6. 7, 15. 4–5, 9–10, 27–31), are integrated into the dominant
psychological analogies, of which Augustine finds the most adequate to be the Trinity of
memory, understanding, and will (op. cit., 10. 17–18); thus the will is defined as love of
self, which is perfect in God. Further on self-sufficiency, see *De Trinitate* 6. 9, 9. 17–18;
Sermones 34. 8; 117. 5, and generally, John Burnaby, *Amor Dei: A Study of the Religion of
St. Augustine* (Hodder & Stoughton, London, 1938), pp. 160 ff.

[11] For the orthodox meaning of the phrase that the Son of God 'suffered in the flesh',
see above ch. 2, pp. 26–8. Earlier patripassianism was, of course, modalist rather than
Trinitarian; when Praxeas confessed that 'while the Son suffers, the Father co-suffers'

taken up a bold distinction between the whole Trinity in God himself
and the whole Trinity in action in the world, in order to speak of the
worldly suffering of both Father and Son. The two Trinitarian spheres
of the being of God are re-employed by him to speak of the triune God
as impassible and passible at the same time. On the one hand he endorses
Augustine's image of a self-sufficient God, giving the picture his own
characteristic colouring in terms of God's being satisfied by speaking his
word to himself. God does not need us as a conversation partner, and it is
out of his free grace that he opens up the circle of the word between the
Father and the Son, and addresses us.[12] But then Barth says that since
God has opened himself to us, in his actions towards the world there are
no limits such as the human mind might think appropriate to God. God
can immerse himself in the finite, God can suffer, God can die. The God
who is impassible in himself can also be passible in the world. He does
not merely, as the Fathers hesitantly suggest, 'suffer' in the indirect sense
that the divine Son is united with a suffering *human* nature. God suffers
in his divine being when he takes on the 'form of a servant' in the world.
At the same time he wears the 'form of glory' and remains immutable
and unlimited over against the world:

He is absolute, infinite, exalted, active, impassible, transcendent, but in all this
He is the One who loves in freedom, the One who is free in His love, and
therefore not His own prisoner. He is all this as the Lord, and in such a way that
He embraces the opposites of these concepts even while He is superior to
them.[13]

God can do these things, and if we say that he cannot then we are simply
imposing our human ideas about what God is like upon what God
actually is. God does not contradict himself or come into conflict with
himself by being both exalted and lowly, but rather shows his freedom;
within these polar elements of the divine and worldly in God, Barth
includes impassibility and suffering or 'the active and the passive'.

Barth's argument here is built upon an even more fundamental re-
employment of the traditional distinction between immanent and
economic Trinity, which Barth likes to name the 'essence' and 'work' of

---

(see Tertullian, *Adversus Praxean* 29), he understood 'the Son' to be the man Jesus Christ.
The nearest the Early Church came to conceiving that the Logos suffered in his divine
nature while the transcendent Father did not, was the Theopaschite formula of the sixth
century, that 'one of the Trinity has suffered'; while approved by the Second Council of
Constantinople in 553, it was finally rejected by the Western Church.

[12] Barth, *CD* I/1, p. 40. [13] Barth, *CD* IV/1, p. 187, cf. II/1, p. 313.

God, and which lies at the base of his whole theology. All talk of God begins from God's revelation of himself which is his 'work', but because God speaks the truth about himself we can follow the track of revelation back into the eternal being of God, as long as we do not imagine that his work is exactly the same as his essence.

> To the unity of Father, Son and Spirit among themselves corresponds their unity *ad extra*. God's essence and work are not twofold but one. God's work is His essence in its relation to the reality which is distinct from Him and which is to be created or is created by Him. . . . Though the work of God is the essence of God, it is necessary and important to distinguish His essence as such from His work, remembering that this work is grace, a free divine decision . . .[14]

God in himself is holy mystery, but we can be confident that the being of God *corresponds* to his self-revelation. In the one God himself there is 'something like fatherhood and sonship . . . and then a third thing common to both', though the three modes of his being which exist in mutual relationship cannot be as 'relatively distinct' among themselves in his essence as they appear to be in his work.[15] There is thus an 'analogy of relations'[16] between the Triune God in essence and the Triune God as revealed, or between God 'in himself' and 'God for us'. There is, however, bound to be a gap between the immanent and the economic Trinity since this leaves room for God's freedom to reveal himself as a work of sheer grace.[17] Given this background of Barth's theological method, which is always to move from the revealed God (as thrice one Lordship) to the essential Godhead, we must ask whether the gap is too large if it means that God is both impassible and passible. Is God consistent in his being if he embraces such opposites in his inner being and outer actions? While Barth successfully shows that God can contain a polarity of exaltation and humility, the question is whether the polarity can also be specified in such terms as absolute and relative, infinite and finite, impassible and passible.

Barth, of course, works hard at bringing the inner and outer being of God together. Above all, he insists that 'as Father, Son and Holy Spirit

---

[14] Barth, *CD* I/1, p. 371.

[15] Barth, *CD* I/1, p. 363, cf. p. 362.

[16] Barth, *CD* I/1, p. 372, cf. III/2, p. 220, IV/1, p. 203.

[17] Barth, *CD* I/1, pp. 172, 332–3. Similarly, E. Jüngel, 'Das Verhältnis von "ökonomischer" und "immanenter" Trinität' (ch. 4 n. 18 above), p. 364 (cf. pp. 354–5.) calls for the retaining of a distinction in thought ('distinctio rationis') between the economic and immanent Trinity in order to be able to hold their identity as a mystery of God's grace.

God is, so to speak, ours in advance'.[18] This does not only mean that since God relates to himself he has the potential to relate to creatures; Barth believes that 'God in himself' cannot in fact be separated from 'God for us' since God has chosen to be for us. There is 'no man-less God'.[19] God need not have spoken his word to us, but *de facto* he has eternally spoken his word with man in mind, so that 'hearing man, as the object of the purpose of the speaking God, is included in the concept of the Word of God as a factual necessity'.[20] Again, as a matter of fact our human history is already included in the eternal story of God's movement (or 'becoming'[21]) within himself; the begetting of the Son 'before all time' does not exclude time, but includes 'our time, the time and history of the sinful creature'.[22] All this means that God's determination of his own manner of being cannot be separated from his free choice of man as his covenant partner. Since he eternally elects the man Jesus of Nazareth to be one person with the divine Son, God's free choice of mankind takes place in the same act of his being in which he determines, in eternal repetition of himself, to be God in the mode of Son as well as Father.[23] Thus, in 'positing himself' as the Son, as another reality over against himself, God takes the first step in his journey into the far country of the human world, to create and redeem us. In choosing to be ours in advance, God chose to expose himself to

[18] Barth, *CD* I/1, p. 383.

[19] Barth, *CD* IV/3. 1, p. 119. The English translation misses the force of the key phrase 'es gibt zwar eine Gottlosigkeit des Menschen . . . es gibt aber . . . keine Menschenlosigkeit Gottes' (*Kirchliche Dogmatik* IV/3. 1, p. 133). Cf. K. Barth. *The Humanity of God*, trans. J. N. Thomas (Collins, London, 1961), pp. 44–7. There are good exegeses of this idea in E. Jüngel, '. . . keine Menschenlosigkeit Gottes . . .', *Evangelische Theologie*, 31 (1971), pp. 376–90, and John Thompson, *Christ in Perspective: Christological Perspectives in the Theology of Karl Barth* (Saint Andrew Press, Edinburgh, 1978), pp. 102–9.

[20] Barth *CD* I/1, p. 140.

[21] Barth, *CD* I/1, p. 427, cf. p. 430.

[22] *CD* I/1, p. 426. R. H. Roberts doubts whether the 'history' in which God is involved is actually our history; see 'Barth's Doctrine of Time: Its Nature and Implications', in S. W. Sykes (ed.), *Karl Barth: Studies of his Theological Methods*, (Clarendon Press, Oxford, 1979), pp. 126 ff. Barth will only be convincing on this point if we accept his basic view of the freedom of God to relate to mankind.

[23] Barth, *CD* II/2, pp. 5–6, 101 ff., 115 ff.; III/1, pp. 50–1. Jüngel, *The Doctrine of the Trinity*, p. 72, finds Barth to mean that, in so far as God determines the Son to be the mode of his being which elects to be one person with the man Jesus Christ, 'we shall have to understand God's primal decision as an *event* in God's being which *differentiates* the modes of God's being'. (cf. ibid., pp. 96–8.) My own exegesis is greatly indebted to that of Jüngel.

negation, suffering and death: 'God wills to lose in order that man may gain'.[24]

In giving Himself to this act He ordained the surrender of something, i.e., of His own impassibility in face of the whole world which . . . can only be the world of evil. In Himself God cannot be affected either by the possibility or by the reality of that will which opposes Him . . . But when from all eternity He elected to be one with man in Jesus Christ, He did it with a being which was not merely affected by evil but actually mastered by it . . . What a risk God ran.[25]

All this ought to mean that in his primal decision to be himself, God also suffered pain in himself in the deepest recesses of his being. In choosing the journey into the far country he was choosing the road to Gethsemane and Calvary. This external work of God must have affected his immanent Trinitarian life with no reservation. But here Barth draws back; when he considers the immanent Trinitarian relationships within God, he maintains that there is an eternal *obedience* of the Son to the Father which is the basis for the temporal suffering of the Son in the world. Humble obedience must take the form in human history of suffering and death; it is appropriate for God in the Son to be obedient unto death on the cross, to exhibit his deity in this way, for eternally there is *obedience* in God himself.[26] E. Jüngel, in his scintillating commentary on the *Dogmatics*, suggests that this obedience can be regarded as a 'passivity' which corresponds to the 'passion' of the Son of God.[27] But word-play cannot disguise the fact that suffering itself is being isolated within the work of God in human history, and not carried back into the essence of God. Jüngel shifts quickly between the notion of 'passive being' in God to 'God's-being-in-the-act-of-suffering'. He rightly underlines that for Barth the final word about the being of God is that it is act or event; this is true of the essence as much as the work of God.[28] God 'happens' in relationship to himself. Jüngel further makes the point that 'passivity' and suffering are also the highest activity in so far as they are 'affirmed' by God, and so are proper to the being of God as act. But he slides over the fact that for Barth, God's 'being-in-the-act-of-suffering' refers to his work or 'economic' being only. The same is

[24] Barth, *CD* II/2, p. 162.
[25] Barth, *CD* II/2, p. 163, cf. pp. 166, 169; IV/1, p. 79; IV/2, pp. 225, 357.
[26] Barth, *CD* IV/1, p. 201. Obedience takes the form of suffering in the world, because in becoming a human obedient son Jesus identifies himself with the human sons of God (notably Israel), who are disobedient and thus under judgement: see *CD* IV/1, p. 171.   [27] Jüngel, *The Doctrine of the Trinity*, p. 84.
[28] Barth, *CD* II/1, pp. 263–4.

true of Jüngel's conclusion that God's being is 'a being-in-a-becoming threatened by perishing'. Despite Barth's appeal to the doctrine of *opus dei ad extra internum*, which Jüngel identifies as a key to Barth's thought,[29] the internal 'work' of God is not really the same as his external work. Of course, Barth has laid the foundations for speaking of a passion of God in the immanent Trinity, with his ideas of God's eternal choice of man and God's being as event. He could have spoken of God's immanent being as being defined by exposure to suffering and 'nothingness'; but he has not done so.

The reason for Barth's reluctance is clear: he wants to hold on to the statement that God need not have chosen man and the way of the cross, though as a matter of 'factual necessity' he has: 'He could have remained satisfied with Himself and with the impassible glory and blessedness of His own inner life. But He did not so do'.[30] I have been suggesting in previous chapters that we should indeed accept Barth's idea that God's suffering is based in his choice, but with the qualification that there is no more 'otherwise' in it than there is in God's choice of himself. We can now see the problems which Barth runs into by wanting to maintain the alternative, 'He could have . . .'. What possible meaning can there be to say, 'He need not have done so'? In anybody else's theology it might mean that there was a 'before' and an 'after' in God's choosing to suffer, so that we could say that God *was* impassible but now is no longer impassible. The impassibility and passibility of God would then be a matter of sequence. Indeed, Moltmann in his critique of Barth seems to suppose that this is what Barth is saying.[31] However, we must recall that for Barth, God is what he chooses to be and *de facto* he has chosen to be for us. Barth himself sometimes becomes impatient about stressing the 'otherwise':

We can only say that He has actually done so, and that this decision and act invalidate all questions whether He might not have acted otherwise.[32]

As a matter of fact, God's making covenant with mankind in Christ is 'a relation in which God is self-determined, so that the determination belongs no less to Him than all that He is in and for Himself'.[33]

---

[29] Jüngel, op. cit., p. 69.
[30] Barth, *CD* II/2, p. 166. Cf. IV/2, pp. 345–6, IV/1, p. 79.
[31] Moltmann, *The Trinity and the Kingdom of God*, p. 54.
[32] Barth, *CD* IV/1, p. 80.
[33] Barth, *CD* II/2, p. 7: 'Without the Son sitting at the right hand of the Father, God would not be God'.

Normally, the statement that a person 'need not have done it' makes sense because we can conceive of what he would have been like if he had not so acted. But this cannot apply to God if, as Barth maintains, his being is (unlike ours) totally and freely determined by his own primal choice. We can only think of God in the way he has actually chosen to be. As soon as, with Barth, we make the category of God's free will the heart of his godhead in place of the category of necessary being, it becomes artificial to distinguish between the 'inner necessity of his freedom' in which God chooses to be himself, and the 'practical necessity' of choosing to be for us. In the light of this, we could only give any meaning to the notion that 'he need not have made us' if we could conceive of God as not having chosen us and yet still as being in all essentials what we *actually* know him to be. Now we can to a certain extent think of God as speaking to himself, loving himself, moving himself, and being obedient to himself, so that we can fail to notice the incongruity of these statements with Barth's own insistence that as a matter of fact God does *not* exist by himself. But we cannot begin to think of God as suffering without us, for there could be nothing in God by himself which could give rise to suffering. The suffering of God is the test case which shows up the oddness of saying that God 'need not have done so' if he is what he chooses to be. Perhaps this is why Barth, in his view of the being of God, preserves an area which is *always* impassible. This seems to be an attempt to give content to the notion that he need not have suffered, though it conflicts with his whole method of thought, based upon God's correspondence to himself in his acts and his being. We notice the strain in passages like the following:

In this primal decision God does not choose only Himself. In this choice of self He also chooses another, that other which is man. Man is the outward cause and object of this overflowing of the divine glory. . . . In ordaining the overflowing of His glory, God also and necessarily ordains that this glory, which in Himself, in His inner life as Father, Son, and Spirit, *cannot* be subjected to attack or disturbance, which in himself *cannot* be opposed, *should* enter the sphere of contradiction [my italics].[34]

It might at first glance seem odd to say, as I propose, that while God has freely chosen to be God for us he could not have done otherwise, but this is precisely what Barth wants to say about God's freedom to choose himself. Freedom in the true sense is not a mere choice between

---

[34] Barth, *CD* II/2, p. 169, cf. IV/2, pp. 345–6: 'This God is self-sufficient. This God knows perfect beatitude in Himself . . .'.

alternatives but a creativity, a way of being which has the power to shape itself.[35] Barth rightly objects to the view of classical theism that God cannot choose in the freedom of his love to be subjected to the conditioning of the world and its sufferings, but he fails to carry through his own insight when he retains the qualification that he could have done otherwise. It appears that the only way he can give meaning to this qualification, within his framework of the freedom of God, is to retain an untouched hinterland in the immanent being of God, while affirming of God in the world that 'the Almighty exists and acts and speaks here in the form of One who is weak and impotent, the eternal as One who is temporal and perishing'.[36] Such a driving of a wedge between God in his essence and his works does not match Barth's own insight that God corresponds to himself.[37] Of course, the reason Barth does this is his implacable opposition to 'natural theology'; he fears that if he removes the 'otherwise' from God's choice of man, there would be a correlation between man and God, with the inherent ability for man to know God through the structures of his own existence. But this need not detract from the Lordship of God if the situation is there by God's choice, and if it is open to new initiatives which he can take, as I suggested in my previous chapter.

We have been exploring the way that Barth tries to bring the immanent and the economic Trinity together by the affirmation that 'God is ours in advance'. Another move he makes is to show how the opposing attributes which he identifies as belonging to these two circles of God's being are really in harmony. For example, the omnipresence of God in himself is exercised by his being able to dwell in one particular place in the world; his eternity, as his own history, enables him to enter our time; his omnipotence is displayed by his triumph within weakness.[38] Barth works hard at bringing these polar concepts together, and he does helpfully show how the God who endures 'perishing' is still God. But he does not attempt to bring together the opposites of impassibility and passibility: here there is silence, and it is a significant one. For Barth, the passion of God in the world is based upon

[35] For an exposition of freedom as creativity in God and man, see John Macquarrie, *In Search of Humanity* (SCM Press, London, 1982), pp. 13 ff.

[36] Barth, *CD* IV/1, p. 176.

[37] Barth, *CD* II/1, pp. 657–60, I/1, p. 383, cf. p. 305. Jüngel, *The Doctrine of the Trinity*, p. 24 judges that 'the Church Dogmatics is the ingenious and diligent attempt to think the proposition "God corresponds to himself" through to the end'.

[38] Barth, *CD* IV/1, pp. 187–8.

his eternal obedience. It would make no sense to say that it was a manifestation of his eternal impassibility, unless it were in the form that God's passibility is a quality which is impassible or unalterable, viz. he always suffers. But Barth, of course, does not want to say this.

Our criticism of Barth's attempt to reserve some kind of impassibility in the immanent Trinity has been that it drives too great a wedge between the being of God in himself and his acts in the world. Barth tries hard to avoid this, but in the end the rift that he denies is there cannot be ignored. At the same time, we have seen that it does not do justice to his own insight that the suffering and conditioning of God by the world is based upon the free choice of God, which I believe is fundamental to the notion of a God who suffers and yet remains God. In this, Barth also fails to carry out his own method of theology, which moves from the action and revelation of God in the world to a contemplation of his transcendent being, on the basis that God 'corresponds to himself'. If we follow this track thoroughly, we see that all talk of God as Trinity, as a divine society characterized by relationships, only arises from our experience of God in the world anyway. We only think of speaking about a second 'person' distinct from the Father, and a third who proceeds from both, because of our experience of God's work of salvation and renewal in the world. It is because of what we want to say about God manifest in time and space, focused in Jesus of Nazareth, that we are driven to speak of God in himself as complex being and not merely undifferentiated unity. Thus man and his salvation are from the very beginning included within our thought of God as Trinity; the 'Son' cannot be separated from the 'Reconciler'. So what justification can there be for speculation about some other kind of Trinity than the one we know? Karl Rahner urges in his essay on the Trinity that:

There *must* be a connection between Trinity and man. The Trinity is a mystery of salvation, otherwise it would never have been revealed. . . The basic thesis which . . . presents the Trinity *as* a mystery of salvation (in its reality and not merely as a doctrine) might be formulated as follows: the 'economic' Trinity is the 'immanent' Trinity, and the 'immanent' Trinity is the 'economic' Trinity.[39]

The projection of the immanent Trinity as a self-sufficient divine grouping from which man is, or even might be, absent is sheer speculation; this is not actually how God has manifested himself. As

[39] Rahner, *The Trinity*, pp. 21–2.

Kazoh Kitamori has pointed out, we only speak of the eternal begetting of the Son because of the giving up of the Son to death upon the cross:

In the gospel the primary words are, 'The Father causes his Son to die'; the secondary words are, 'The Father begets his Son'. The secondary words prepare for the primary. In the gospel the final word is the pain of God. To us the bitterest pain imaginable is that of a Father allowing his son to suffer and die. Therefore God spoke his ultimate word, 'God suffers pain' by using the Father–Son relationship.[40]

It has been a welcome theme of recent theology that the doctrine of the Trinity is at root a conceptualizing of the event of the cross.[41] We only speak of God as Trinity, as a complex of relationships, because we find God revealed in the cross which involves a set of relationships. When we ask, 'Who is God?' we are confronted by an event which we can only describe in relational terms: we speak of a son relating to a Father in suffering and love. There is a son crying out to a Father whom he has lost ('My God, why have you forsaken me?') and so there is implied a Father who suffers the loss of a son, with a Spirit of abandonment between them. At the same time as they are most separated they are most one, for they are united in loving purpose: in love the Father gives up the Son and in love the Son gives up himself for us, and the Spirit of love is between them. In these relationships the world and human beings are necessarily included, and any other Trinity is a spinning out of hypotheses. It is for us that the Father gives up the Son to death, and so the 'for us' is included in whatever is meant by the eternal begetting of the Son by the Father. There can be no self-sufficient, self-contained society of the Trinity, for God has not chosen to be in that way. His relationships within himself are open to the world. Such a formulation of the Trinity from the event of the cross builds upon the pioneering thought of Karl Barth, though it carries his perception of the 'lowly' God further into the immanent Trinity than he does.

2. SUFFERING IN THE WORLDLY ASPECT OF GOD: PROCESS THEOLOGY

Another attempt to retain the transcendence of a suffering God by

---

[40] Kitamori, *Theology of the Pain of God*, p. 47.

[41] In particular, in the work of Moltmann, Jüngel, Mühlen, and Kitamori, which are well represented in this study.

dividing his being into passible and impassible aspects is that offered by process theology. Its view is, unlike Barth's, basically non-Trinitarian, but it presents a curiously parallel account of 'economic' and 'immanent' divine being. Process theologians propose a dipolar God, one of whose elements is deeply involved in the world, the other being totally independent of it. God therefore suffers in his contingent nature, but remains untouched by the world in his transcendent nature. In this way, process thought tries to secure a God who 'keeps the rules' of the universe and is not exempt from suffering, while at the same time remaining other from the world as the Supreme Mind which the process of creativity demands. In his worldly aspect, which Whitehead calls his 'consequent nature' and Hartshorne calls his 'concrete states', God is influenced and created by the world; he is caused by the world in a supreme manner, and as the archetypal sufferer he grows and develops in response to the world as we do.[42] Hartshorne stresses his immersion in the world by conceiving of his consequent nature as the 'container' of all reality;[43] he is perfectly related to all the actuality there is, with its tragedies as much as its joys. But in the other aspect of his being, which Whitehead calls 'primordial nature' and Hartshorne calls 'abstract essence', far from being affected by the world, he is unconscious of it; he is 'the uncaused cause, impassible, immutable and all the rest of it'.[44]

Whereas in his world-related aspect he is dependent upon creation, in his transcendent aspect the world is totally dependent upon him as the ground of all possibility, though process theologians differ in the way they envisage God's grasp of possibilities for the world. As we have already seen, Whitehead thinks of God as having a perfect and eternal vision of all possible values which he views as 'eternal objects'. Hartshorne thinks of the abstract nature of God as pure possibility itself, as the undefined potential for the definite possibilities that only emerge in interaction between God and the actuality of the world in the concrete states of God. But both theologians consider the divine grasp of possibility to be a form of *impassibility*. In Whitehead's thought, God's primordial being is immutable because he orders the eternal objects unchangeably; he grades them perfectly according to their relevance for any specific occasion in the world, and so presents an initial aim to every

---

[42] Whitehead, *Process and Reality*, pp. 522–33; Hartshorne, *Man's Vision of God*, pp. 239–40, 321–2.

[43] Hartshorne, *The Divine relativity*, pp. 92–3, cf. *The Logic of Perfection*, pp. 267–8.

[44] Hartshorne, *A Natural Theology for Our Time*, p. 44, cf. p. 27; Whitehead, *Process and Reality*, pp. 134, 524.

entity in its drive towards satisfaction. He lures each entity persuasively towards its goal, and with a tender care that nothing be lost he preserves whatever it achieves within his consequent being. In the primordial pole of his being therefore God is 'the *unconditioned* actuality at the base of things', and he is unconscious of the world because he has purely 'conceptual feelings' without any physical element present.[45] In Hartshorne's thought, God's abstract essence is totally closed to influence by the world because it is not at all relative to it.[46] Since his abstract essence is the possibility for his perfect relatedness to the world in his concrete states, it must itself be 'neutral', having a serene 'indifference to relational alternatives';[47] in order to be capable of correlation with all, it must itself be non-relativized by them. Thus the abstract essence of God is his individuality; 'in the transcendent being the essential core of identity is infallibly secure'.[48] The abstract essence of God is like a man's character which endures throughout all the concrete states of his existence in which he expresses himself.

In these slightly different ways, the two major process thinkers present God as impassible within himself, and supremely passible for us. God is presented on the one hand as completely immersed in the process of the world, whose events are objectified in his own being; he is 'the fellow sufferer who understands', influenced and changed by the actualities of the world as they happen. On the other hand, he is totally independent of the world because of his immutable grasp of possibility for it:

God as primordial is strictly eternal in the sense of being immutable and ungenerated. God as consequent is 'fluent', reaches no final completion, contains succession and is ever in 'process' of further creation.[49]

Some critics, and notable among them is Colin Gunton in his comparative study of Hartshorne and Barth,[50] have been so suspicious

---

[45] Whitehead, *Process and Reality*, p. 522, cf. pp. 46–8.

[46] Hartshorne, *A Natural Theology for Out Time*, p. 27, cf. *Creative Synthesis and Philosophic Method*, p. 232.

[47] Hartshorne, *The Divine Relativity*, p. 81, cf. p. 72.

[48] Hartshorne, *Creative Synthesis and Philosophic Method*, p. 233.

[49] Hartshorne, *Philosophers Speak of God*, p. 283.

[50] Gunton, op. cit. (ch. 1 n. 42), pp. 41–52. Gunton also oddly supposes that Hartshorne restricts the activity of God to the abstract essence of God, resulting in a lack of any real influence on the world by God. In fact, Hartshorne makes clear that God exercises causation in both poles of his being, as I expound in my following discussion (also see ch. 6 below).

as to think that the abstract or primordial nature of God is a mere shadow of the concrete state of God. They suspect that it is a sop to traditional views of God, which dissolves away on inspection into another way of looking at God's involvement in the world, so that God has no proper self-existence. Though Hartshorne stands more accused of this than Whitehead, his very subtle argument is that God is independent of the world and so supremely an individual in his own right, just because he *is* abstract. He cannot be absorbed into the world because in his basic self-identity he cannot be pinned down into any particular situation. One is tempted to say that this makes God sound like the consummate politician, and in fact it points to a totally opposite criticism of process thought that I believe to be better founded; this dipolar way of thinking drives the two aspects of God too far apart and so—ironically—suffering does not touch God enough.

Of course, the process theologians, like Barth in his account, do attempt to bring the two natures of God together. In particular, two moves are made. First, process theologians who follow Whitehead suggest that the initial aim which God presents to actual entities cannot be formed alone by his primordial vision of all possible ideals ('eternal objects'). They ask how he could entertain a specific aim which is exactly relevant to each becoming occasion if he did not take account of the actual situation in the world. Surely, to formulate an aim that would offer the greatest possibility of satisfaction to a particular entity, he must draw upon the influences from the world which have been absorbed by his consequent nature. Thus they conclude that his aim must be formed by a synthesis of his primordial *and* consequent natures.[51] John Cobb, for example, judges that Whitehead 'has too sharply separated the two natures of God', and so has not been true to his own view that God is himself an actual entity. As far as all other actual entities in the universe are concerned, 'It is always the actual entity that acts, not one of its poles as such, although in many of its functions one pole or other may become primarily relevant'.[52] To suppose otherwise would be to omit the 'subjective unity' of the entity. The application of this to God is probably a modification of Whitehead's own thought, though much (rather too much, I suspect) can be built upon the enigmatic last page of *Process and Reality*:

[51] See Pittenger, *Process Thought and Christian Faith*, pp. 49–54; Lewis S. Ford, *The Lure of God*, pp. 83–5, 105; Cobb, *A Christian Natural Theology*, pp. 178–9, 183–4.

[52] Cobb, *A Christian Natural Theology*, p. 178. Cf. Whitehead, *Process and Reality*, p. 470.

What is done in the world is transformed into a reality in heaven, and the reality in heaven passes back into the world. By reason of this reciprocal relation, the love in the world passes back into the love in heaven and floods back again into the world.[53]

Some process theologians who lay stress upon the blending of the consequent and primordial natures of God draw attention to White-head's notion of 'propositional feelings', and deduce that God must have them too.[54] Cobb, for example, points out that according to Whitehead, God's vision of 'eternal objects' is his own aim at intensity of feeling; that is, God has an appetite for beauty. Now, for this aim to be relevant to each specific entity, Cobb concludes that it must be 'the feeling of a proposition of which the novel occasion is the logical subject and the appropriate eternal object is the predicate'.[55] In other words, God imagines what it would be like for an entity to realize the particular value which he, God, is envisaging. Further, as he imagines this, he desires its realization sympathetically: 'God's propositional feeling is clothed with the subjective form of desire that the proposition become true.'[55] Whitehead explains that all temporal entities entertain these 'propositional feelings', either about their own future enjoyment of beauty, or its enjoyment by others.[57] Cobb finds this an important clue to the way that actual entities can detect which of the infinite possibilities envisaged by God are relevant for them; they find the initial aim because they recognize God's feeling about them, and their appetite is conformed to his.[58] But looked at from God's side, if he has such 'propositional feelings' they must include some physical prehension of the world: they are always 'impure prehensions', involving the fusion of physical and conceptual feelings,[59] and so for God they must involve a working together of his consequent and primordial natures.

[53] Whitehead, *Process and Reality*, p. 532.

[54] Cobb, *A Christian Natural Theology*, pp. 180–1; Ford, 'Whitehead's Differences from Hartshorne' (ch. 4 n. 57 above), pp. 62–3, 67.

[55] Cobb, op. cit., p. 156, cf. pp. 181–2.

[56] Cobb, op. cit., p. 229. For Whitehead's view of the 'appetition' of God for realization of values, see *Process and Reality*, pp. 160–1, 134–5; cf. Whitehead, *Adventures of Ideas*, p. 357: 'We must conceive the Divine Eros as the active entertainment of all ideals, with the urge to their finite realization'.

[57] Whitehead, *Process and Reality*, pp. 391–5. Thus a new occasion can also prehend from a past entity the propositional feeling which that entity held about it; this would be a 'hybrid (physical) prehension', and it seems that such prehensions are constituent parts of the initial aim.   [58] Cobb, op. cit., p. 157.

[59] Whitehead, op. cit., p. 393, cf. Cobb, op. cit., p. 229.

One can only applaud the underlining of this element of Whitehead's thought by thinkers such as Cobb and Lewis Ford. In effect they insist that God's vision of beauty for the world is much more (we might say) than viewing scenes on a cinema screen, or storing data in a computer memory. It points to an aspect of God's inner being which might be called vicarious love, emphasizing his character as a suffering God, and we shall return to this perception later. However, we are bound to ask *where* such a synthesis, or any other integration of the two poles of God's being, takes place. It is not sufficient simply to say that it takes place in God 'as a whole actual entity', for in other entities this means in practice that integrations of physical and conceptual feelings occur in one pole as it draws upon the feelings of the other. Whitehead makes clear that all the higher phases of experience involve a mixture of physical and conceptual feelings,[60] but in worldly entities there is a leading edge of either the physical or mental pole in this synergism; there is no altogether distinct 'third thing',[61] but a kind of overlap or interplay from one pole to the other. In the case of 'propositional feelings' in worldly entities, Cobb observes that 'this complexity belongs to the mental pole of the experience'.[62] If we find such feelings in God we must ask where the locus of the synthesis is in the divine experience.

Some Whiteheadians[63] appear to suggest that it takes place in the consequent nature of God, so that entities receive their initial aim through prehending his consequent nature which has had woven into it the conceptual feelings of the primordial one. Indeed, Whitehead himself seems to attribute such a synthesis to the consequent nature of God.[64] But in that case the primordial nature of God is still left detached as an area which is itself untouched by the world, as an unconscious reservoir of indeterminate feelings. On the other hand, if we were to suppose instead that the primordial vision of God has been shaped by his

[60] Whitehead, op. cit., pp. 49, 470. In worldly entities, an instance of an impure *physical* feeling is a 'hybrid' prehension: ibid., pp. 343, 469. Conversely, a 'propositional feeling' is an impure *mental* feeling.

[61] Ford, *The Lure of God*, p. 110 n. 8, rightly dispenses with the notion that the 'superjective' aspect of God provides a kind of third nature.

[62] Cobb, op. cit., p. 34.

[63] e.g. Pittenger, *Process Thought and Christian Faith*, pp. 49–54; Ford seems to suggest this in 'Whitehead's Differences from Hartshorne' (ch. 4 n. 57 above), p. 62.

[64] Whitehead, op. cit., p. 524. This reversal of the situation which obtains in worldly entities might be due to the fact that God originates in his conceptual pole whereas they originate in the physical pole (ibid., p. 54). God would then be a sort of reversed actual entity, but not an actual occasion.

consequent experience of the world,[65] so that God is not working blind in his eternal choices, this would deny the fundamental Whiteheadian idea of the transcendence of God. The otherness of God from the world consists in his feeling only 'pure' concepts in his supreme mentality,[66] and so being unconscious of the world in his mental nature. Once we chip away at that, then there seems to be no other way in Whiteheadian terms of affirming the separate identity of God over against the world.

Faced with the difficulties involved in integrating the two poles of God as an actual entity we might adopt a second approach to the question. Instead of following Whitehead's description of God as an individual actual entity, we could consider him as a Person, that is a temporal *society* of occasions. In fact, Cobb's insistence that God acts as a whole actual entity is supplemented by his description of God as a person. He points out that the process within the consequent being of God, which Whitehead himself describes, is much more like the transition between individual entities which make up the larger society of a person, than the concrescence of a single entity itself.[67] The factors he points to include God's experience of satisfaction, and the availability of God to be prehended by other entities during his becoming, both of which are only true of a single entity when it is completed and perishes. God, of course, does not perish. Moreover, God in his consequent nature experiences time, though it is admittedly not our experience of fragmented and lost time, and therefore Whitehead does not call it time but everlastingness.[68] Cobb himself attempts to combine Whitehead's notion of 'eternal objects' with a view of God as a living person, but Hartshorne carries through a more radical revision along personal lines.[69] For him, there is no question of locating God's transcendence in some conceptual pole of his being. The dipolarity of God should be considered by analogy from human persons, where the independence of a person is a matter of his enduring character, in contrast to the successive states of his existence.

Hartshorne therefore envisages God as the eminent instance of the dipolarity which he observes in personal creatures. A man has a 'weak'

---

[65] Curiously, Ford seems to hint at this in claiming that we cannot prehend directly the consequent nature of God; see *The Lure of God*, pp. 83, 85, 110 n. 8, cf. Ford, 'Whitehead's Differences from Hartshorne' (ch. 4 n. 57 above), pp. 66–7.

[66] Whitehead, op. cit., p. 50.   [67] Cobb, op. cit., pp. 188–92.

[68] Whitehead, op. cit., p. 524.

[69] See Hartshorne, 'Whitehead's Idea of God' in Schillp (ed.), *The Philosophy of Alfred North Whitehead* (ch. 4 n. 89 above) pp. 530 ff.

form of both his elements of independence and relatedness with regard to other people. On the one hand he is a 'person' with a partial set of relationships to other persons; on the other hand he is an 'individual' with abstract qualities which are partially independent of changes around him in his environment.[70] He has an abstract essence which is included in all his concrete states and actions, but which is at least partly untouched by them. Hartshorne admits that in the case of human beings, 'extreme changes in weather or scenery might temporarily or permanently rob even Abraham Lincoln of his moral humaneness'.[71] In the case of God, however, he has a perfect degree of both abstract and concrete modes. On the one hand he is 'supreme' in being related to the whole of reality; he is all-inclusive and dependent upon the world. In this way he is 'internally related' to all creatures; that is, he is the subject who knows all and so is affected by all, since the knower is always changed by the objects he knows.[72] On the other hand, he is the 'Absolute' in his abstract qualities and so is independent of the world. In this way, he is 'externally related' to all; that is, he is the universal object which is known by all, for 'only God can be so universally important that no subject can ever wholly fail . . . to be aware of him'.[73] As 'object-for-all-subjects' he changes them without their affecting him in the slightest. As Supreme, then, he is related to all; as Absolute he is related to nothing in particular, though since everything relates *to* him he might be said to be 'related to the possible as such', while being indifferent to particular relational alternatives.[74] Thus God is both all-inclusive and immutable at the same time.[75] Indeed, in this way of thinking, the one concept actually requires the other. 'The absolute can exist in the supremely relative, in serene independence, serene exemption, from relativity.'[76]

The question, I suggest, is whether one can construct an analogy for God like this, in which the dual dimensions in the human personality are made eminent, each in their own right, without losing the idea of personality altogether. Hartshorne has in mind the religious value of the idea of a suffering God; he is anxious to portray God as suffering without being 'dragged down into helpless misery',[77] but I doubt whether making a person's limited independence unlimited is the way to achieve this. Hartshorne argues effectively that, as far as the concrete

---

[70] Hartshorne, *The Divine Relativity*, pp. 74–5.   [71] Ibid., p. 75.
[72] Ibid., pp. 6–7, 18–19.   [73] Ibid., p. 70.   [74] Ibid., p. 72.
[75] Ibid., p. 94.   [76] Ibid., p. 86.   [77] Ibid., p. 45.

states of God are concerned, the notion of One who includes all others within himself accords well with the nature of personalness;[78] in human experience persons do include others within themselves, as personalness is essentially inter-personalness, the loss of oneself in another and the gain from another in oneself. But this surely cannot be combined with an absolute independence of character or enduring identity. In human terms, it is fundamental to personality that someone's abstract identity should *be* only partially independent; the dipolarity is not complete, but there is an overlap from one side to the other, because persons always exist in relationships. With his comment that even Lincoln's humane approach to life might be affected by the weather, Hartshorne makes the partial ('weak') independence of the character appear always regrettable. So he goes on to say that while God's concrete acts of goodness will be different in the case of a righteous or sinful person, the abstract quality of his goodness remains unchanged.[79] But change, as Hartshorne himself argues in the case of the concrete nature, is not necessarily for the worse; so there is no reason, according to the logic of an eminent personality, why God's concrete actions should not shape the nature of his goodness; in the human analogy they certainly would. Though Hartshorne sometimes calls the abstract essence of a person his 'personality', in contrast to his 'person', he is really talking about his individuality, and it is basic to personality that this should not be totally immutable, though it should of course be resistant to degradation and to being swayed by casual sensations. There should be no *instability* about basic traits of character. It is this kind of mutability that the 'way of eminence' should be excluding from God, not all mutability whatsoever.

I believe that a Trinitarian development of the personal analogy for God can be more successful than a 'dipolar' one in preserving both the transcendence of God and a suffering which inhabits every corner of his Being. Transcendence cannot be equated with immutability and impassibility without diminishing the reality of suffering. By contrasting process thought with Trinitarian theology in this way, I am not ignoring the fact that efforts have been made by process theologians to interpret the elements of dipolar theism in terms of the Trinitarian

---

[78] In *A Natural Theology for Our Time*, pp. 9–12, Hartshorne gives the example of a teacher whose pupil's achievements become part of himself.

[79] Hartshorne, *The Divine Relativity*, p. 81.

symbols of Father, Son, and Spirit.[80] In referring to a Trinitarian theology, I mean the attempt to understand the complexity of the divine being in terms of an interweaving of personal relationships. Process thought cannot make divine personality, in the sense of immanent mutual relationships, the criterion for understanding unity and diversity within God, though it can, of course, speak of God's self-identity, his relationship to the world, and the interplay between them.[81] Indeed, we must recognize that process thought rightly affirms a correlation between God and the world that has often been lost in traditional Trinitarian schemes. Process thought is making a crucial contribution to the doctrine of God when it insists that there can be no 'otherwise' in God's suffering relationships with creation. Nevertheless, the advantages of a Trinitarian model of a personal God over a dipolar model can be seen if we consider the role which creativity and actuality play in process thought with regard to the divine suffering.

In the first place, we notice that Hartshorne presents the reality of God over against the world as a logical independence, in a new version of the classical argument of necessary being. He develops this from the dipolarity of eminent relativity and absoluteness. Because God in his concrete existence is all-inclusive, in his abstract essence he must be Absolute in the sense of not relating to any reality in particular.

---

[80] For a concept of Trinity in the Whiteheadian mode, see Ford, *The Lure of God*, pp. 103–4. He suggests that the Father is God as a unified actual entity, the Son is the primordial nature, and the Spirit is the provision of aims to our everyday experience. Thus the Spirit makes us aware intuitively of the consequent nature of God, which cannot (according to Ford) be prehended directly; for criticism of this idea, see below, pp. 156–7. For a Trinity in the Hartshornian mode, see S. Ogden, 'On the Trinity', *Theology*, 83 (1980), pp. 97–102. He suggests that the Father is the whole abstract essence of God (his individuality), the Son is the objective aspect in God which is externally related to the world (being loved by all), and the Spirit is the subjective aspect which is internally related to the world (loving all). O'Donnell, op. cit. (ch. 1 n. 42), pp. 84 ff., finds Ogden's approach supportive of Barth's view of the Son as object of divine love; but we notice that it does not accommodate Barth's perception that the Son is also *subject* of the divine act of loving in a mutual indwelling.

[81] Joseph Bracken, however, argues from a process perspective for the Trinitarian God as a society of primordial, consequent, and 'superjective' natures, which are 'personalised centers' for a single all-embracing activity of interrelating. See his two articles, 'Process Philosophy and Trinitarian Theology' 1, 2, in *Process Studies*, 8 (1978), pp. 217–30, and 11 (1981), pp. 83–96. But there is an unresolved tension in this account between the process concept of an act of being which is 'instantiated' in several distinct activities, and the distinctly non-process language of the natures 'deciding' for each other and 'responding' to each other (op. cit. (1981), pp. 86–9).

Correspondingly, therefore, this sort of Absolute requires some kind of relativity to make sense of itself; it needs a world in which it can be object for all knowing subjects. The conclusion is therefore drawn that God need not have created *this* world, but that he must have created *some* world: 'he is *bound* to create, provided that he is not thus bound with respect to any given creature or set of them'.[82] But this way of defining God's otherness from the world seems to say at once too much and too little about God's involvement in the world for the notion of a truly suffering God. On the one hand it binds God to a metaphysical principle to which he has to conform—the correlation of the relative and the absolute, which in the end exemplifies the advance of creativity. Certainly, the principle of creativity, together with other metaphysical categories, belongs to God's own eternal, necessary essence; but it is still a category to which his actions are bound, beyond even his own decisions. Thus God is bound to suffer; his only choice is which world he is to suffer in. Such an obligation detracts from the freedom of God which we have seen to be basic not only to personality but to a suffering which is victorious, as 'active suffering', freely chosen. On the other hand, this kind of necessary creativity says too little about God's commitment to this world. While there is no 'otherwise' about creating *a* world, there is an otherwise about *the* actual world we have. Thus, ironically, in its proper concern for a pan*en*theism ('everything in God') where God is more than the 'all', process thought separates God too much from the suffering world. As in Barth's thought, God could have done otherwise—at least with respect to the world we have. In contrast, I have been arguing that the concept of a God who chooses to create and suffer has room for there being no otherwise in that desire, when it is inseparable from his decision to be himself in the relationships of Father, Son, and Spirit. The great virtue of process thought is to remind us that Trinitarian thinking has often separated the one decision from the other.

The more Whiteheadian strand of process thinking does in fact attempt to make God's primordial decision basic to creation. Lewis Ford claims for Whitehead almost exactly the point I have been making about there being real divine decisions, and yet in practice no 'otherwise' about the values chosen. He suggests that God decides upon the metaphysical principles by his ordering of the 'eternal objects' in his

---

[82] Hartshorne, *The Divine Relativity*, p. 74; also Hartshorne, *Man's Vision of God*, p. 164: '*some* other lives he must have'; cf. Hartshorne, *A Natural Theology for Our Time*, p. 102.

primordial vision, yet 'the primordial act is not a decision amid antecedent possibility, for it is the very creation of possibility itself'.[83] God does not choose between 'sets of logically consistent metaphysical alternatives', because his primordial choice set up the whole situation as it actually is. However, those Whiteheadians who argue in this way are faced with the problem that the entire system of actual entities still requires creativity as an ultimate notion which God does not himself decide upon. As Whitehead puts it, God is 'in the grip of creativity' and even 'a creature of creativity'.[84] They try to reconcile this with God's primordial decision about metaphysical principles either by suggesting that 'creativity' is too general to be strictly a principle,[85] or that it is not an agency or cause;[86] the reason *why* new processes of creativity keep occurring is said to be in the decision of entities, and above all the decision of God. But this exceedingly fine distinction between creativity as an ultimate notion and an ultimate cause cannot blur the fact that God is still subject to it, and is not free in the sense that personal suffering requires.

We reach the same conclusion by examining what process thought says about the actuality of God in his consequent nature, or concrete states. Once more we see that God is too absorbed into the world in this pole of his being, which leads to over-compensation in the other in terms of immutability. The problem is not that God is eminently conditioned by the world; after all, the more perfect the suffering love of God, the more he will be affected by his creation. Nor is the problem that God desires the world for the completion of his being, as 'the Eros of the Universe'; we have seen that any divine suffering means that God will be completed by his creation. The point is that in process thought, God needs the world in the sense that it adds a dimension to his being which would otherwise be entirely absent, namely actuality. God needs the world to actualize himself, either realizing his conceptual feelings (Whitehead) or expressing his vague potentiality in definite forms (Hartshorne). Certainly, Whitehead speaks of God as having a sort of non-temporal, non-conscious actuality in his primordial nature (a 'deficient actuality'), but this is quite different from the actuality he achieves in the world. In this sense God has a 'yearning after some

---

[83] Ford, 'Whitehead's Differences from Hartshorne' (ch. 4 n. 57 above), p. 69.
[84] Whitehead, *Process and Reality*, pp. 529, 129.
[85] Ford, art. cit. (n. 83 above), p. 70.
[86] Cobb, *A Christian Natural Theology*, pp. 211–14.

actuality'.[87] In contrast, the desire we have been speaking of in the Trinitarian being of God is the completion of what is already there in God; the yearning for fellowship is the continuation of his fellowship with himself. While there is no question of his being complete without us, because he has not chosen to be that kind of God, yet we add a glory to what is already present, new levels of satisfaction without end. In a Trinitarian concept of a personal God, he is an event of relationships—a happening—in himself, though he desires to be open to the events of the world and chooses that these should enhance his being. So the suffering of God is rooted in his will and goes to the very heart of his being which is act.

Process thought makes valuable affirmations about the suffering of God, notably its insistence that there can be no 'otherwise' about God's involvement in a suffering universe. However, in attempting to retain the transcendence of God in an impassible pole of his being, it both undercuts the commitment of God to suffering in *this* world and subordinates God to a principle of creativity which is beyond his decision. Hartshorne makes valiant efforts to overcome this with his view of an eminent Person; but although the kind of 'personality' which emerges includes all human suffering, it is hard to describe it as suffering in a way analogous to the way we suffer.

3.   THE SUFFERING OF GOD IN HIS TRANSCENDENCE: JÜRGEN MOLTMANN

At first glance, the Trinitarian theology of Jürgen Moltmann seems to satisfy our demand for a suffering which penetrates to the inner being of a God who still remains transcendent. Moltmann is highly critical of any attempt to divide the immanent Trinity from the economic Trinity, in terms of there being any self-sufficient inner life of God.[88] It is the great contribution of Moltmann to the present debate about the suffering of God to insist that the cross is the event in history which discloses the inner nature of God without reservation. There can be no untouched hinterland in the being of the God who is revealed in the cross. Nor ought it to be held against Moltmann that he retains *some* distinction between the economic and the immanent Trinity despite this.[89]

[87] Whitehead, *Process and Reality*, p. 50.
[88] Moltmann, *The Crucified God*, pp. 239–40, and *The Trinity and the Kingdom of God*, pp. 147–8, 158–61.
[89] Mackey, *The Christian Experience of God as Trinity*, p. 208 does criticize Moltmann on this score.

Though Moltmann does not always seem to notice that he is doing so, at least implicitly he justifies talking about the immanent Trinity in order to affirm panentheism and avoid pantheism. In order not to collapse God into the process of the world, it is necessary to talk about the God *who* is acting in history, or in Moltmann's words, about 'the interaction between the substance and the revelation, the "inwardness" and the "outwardness" of the triune God'. So Moltmann speaks of the completion of history 'when the economic Trinity completes and perfects itself to immanent Trinity'.[90] The principle which Moltmann announces is that 'statements about the immanent Trinity must not contradict statements about the economic Trinity. Statements about the economic Trinity must correspond to doxological statements about the immanent Trinity.'[91] In *this* sense, the economic Trinity is the immanent Trinity.

We must enquire then, how well he succeeds in keeping to his principle in the distinctions he draws between God's inner and outer actions. He does speak felicitously of an intertwining of God's action and passion;[92] it is not just a question of God's inner actions leading to outer passion in the world, or God's deciding in favour of the world, which Moltmann criticizes as the way of 'eternal efficacy'. God's inner *passion* also leads to outer acts, for Moltmann adopts Jewish mystical theology in thinking of a withdrawal of the divine being into himself as a foundation for creation outwards; the idea here is that in order to make room for creation *ex nihilo*, God must make a space of nothingness inside himself, for if creation is *ex nihilo* there can be no area already outside himself where creation might take place.[93] Thus an inner 'passion' (withdrawal) leads to outer action. Conversely, his outer passion leads to inner acts, as his suffering in the world is the path towards his inner glorification. Moltmann helpfully then urges a total reciprocity between action and passion in God, inner and outer in both modes. But something nevertheless seems out of kilter, as Moltmann concludes from all these permutations that 'the suffering of God is God's supreme work on God himself'.[94] We discover, if we examine the moments of divine passion as Moltmann describes them, that the interaction is really in terms of the effect of God's own acts upon his inner passion. He is the source of his own suffering.

[90] Moltmann, *The Trinity and the Kindom of God*, pp. 160, 161.
[91] Ibid., p. 154.   [92] Ibid., pp. 98–100, cf. pp. 118–19.
[93] Ibid., pp. 108–11; Moltmann, *God in Creation*, pp. 86–9.
[94] Moltmann, *The Trinity and the Kingdom of God*, p. 99.

Thus, Moltmann speaks of God in creation as humiliating himself by withdrawing and making room for others, but there is no thought of his humbling himself further by allowing *them* to contribute to the creative processes. Creation is simply mobilized by 'an alteration' in the loving relationship between Father and Son, as the eternal Godhead 'breathes in' in order for the Father to utter himself creatively in the Son.[95] The problem here is a literal and temporal creation *ex nihilo*, which prevents Moltmann's thinking of a more cooperative enterprise between Creator and creatures. Then again, in his suffering among his people Israel in the mode of the Shekinah, God is said to open up a rift in himself and confront himself as 'another', by imprisoning himself in this alien form.[96] In the incarnation this self-confrontation of God by God comes to a climax, as the human son 'confronts the Father in the world', and as God suffers utter dislocation of his own being in the cross, where the Son is forsaken by the Father.[97] Moreover, the continual suffering of God with humankind since then is his patience in allowing them time to respond to him by taking their place with the crucified Christ in the fellowship of the suffering God. God gives us time to fall in with his plans to dwell in the world.[98] Now, if moments of divine passion are all basically God's acts upon himself like this, we are bound to ask whether the impress of the world upon God is being taken seriously. I have already suggested that Moltmann's concept of the glorifying of God is too much God's own operation; now we have to amplify the similar hint I made earlier about his suffering. God seems less the supreme victim than the supreme self-executioner.

Moltmann is certainly pointing a way forward. He is underlining the human experience of God's suffering as something which is peculiarly his own, deeper and more awful even than any human suffering can be. Earlier on we recognized this testimony in the Old Testament prophets. We might speak (with Kitamori)[99] of a 'transcendent' suffering of God, rather than a transcendence of God in immunity from suffering. He remains God in that he suffers more deeply than anyone else. Further,

---

[95] Ibid., p. 111; cf. Moltmann, *God in Creation*, p. 114: 'a self-alteration of eternity'.

[96] Moltmann, *The Trinity and the Kingdom of God*, pp. 118–19, cf. p. 29.

[97] Ibid., p. 118, cf. pp. 80–1. For the general idea of God's confronting himself in the world, see also Moltmann, *God in Creation*, pp. 15–16, 206.

[98] Moltmann, The *The Trinity and the Kingdom of God*, pp. 209–10.; cf. *God in Creation*, pp. 210–11.

[99] Kitamori, *Theology of the Pain of God*, pp. 101–4, cf. p. 45: 'pain is the essence of God'.

Moltmann underlines the desire of God to include creation within his own being. But in all this, there is not enough of God's experience of suffering as something *befalling* him from without, that we have seen to be essential to the true notion of suffering. Despite Moltmann's criticism of 'eternal efficaciousness' which he finds in Barth, he himself has God as eternal sole cause—but of his own inner suffering. I make this criticism hesitantly, becaue I am appreciative of Moltmann's intention to affirm the suffering of God as 'with us, from us, for us'. If we ask why, oddly, the intent does not seem to have been carried out, we notice two significant features of Moltmann's thought about the immanent Trinity.

First, Moltmann maintains that in God's inner being there is a love of 'like for like', so that the loving response of the Son to the Father is a 'necessary' one. It is because divine love cannot be satisfied with love of the alike, that God moves out in creation to love of the unlike; thus, in his economic activity God receives the 'free' response of creatures who are not Sons, but 'images' of their Creator. In order to evoke this free response, God sends forth the Son to become the archetypal 'Image' himself, or the Logos.[100] Such a distinction between love of the alike and love of the unlike does seem to drive the immanent Trinity apart from the economic Trinity, despite Moltmann's principle of correspondence. It leads Moltmann to think of the cross as the unique, most terrible instance of divine suffering because here the *inner* divine life is disrupted; here the relationship of like with like is torn apart. The cross is understood only in terms of suffering in the immanent Trinity, and so what is missing in this interpretation is the human response of Jesus. Surely, at the heart of the pain of God in the cross must be the disruption of a relationship between God and an obedient son, whose response is free and not necessary. It is such an alienation that would be the greatest tragedy for God. At this crucial point, Moltmann therefore appears to neglect the contribution of the world to the suffering of God. Anyway, ought we so sharply to distinguish love for like and unlike in God's being and his activity respectively? Moltmann himself speaks of man as the 'image' of God, and conversely he refers with approval to the traditional view that 'person' in God ought not to be understood as a common, generic concept obliterating the differences between Father, Son, and Spirit: 'The "three Persons" are different, not merely in their relations to each other, but also in respect of their character as

100 Moltmann, *The Trinity and the Kingdom of God*, pp. 68–9, 117, 121.

Persons . . .'.[101] In the light of this, the simple contrast between love for like and unlike seems too divisive a way of conceiving the difference between the immanent being and the economic activity of God.

I believe that Moltmann is right to point to a unique suffering of God in the cross of Jesus, and to indicate that this might even be called a transcendent suffering in comparison with his suffering elsewhere. We can speak of God's taking our suffering into himself universally, out of a more profound and terrible suffering which remains his own. Later we shall explore ways in which the cross of Jesus might be understood as transcendent suffering, but such suffering cannot be a matter of God's act alone, in dislocating his own life. The world and human response must be involved intimately in the deepest dimensions of divine suffering.

A second feature we notice in Moltmann's account of the Trinity is his conception of the three persons as each analogous to a human person. Moltmann is arguing for a social analogy of the Trinity in the strict sense of the 'persons' being 'individual, unique, non-interchangeable sub-jects . . . with consciousness and will'.[102] Though he adds a relational and historical dimension to Boethius' classical definition of person, he agrees with it as far as it goes: *persona est naturae rationabilis individua substantia* ('the individual subsistence of a rational nature').[103] He defends this against the charge of tritheism by pointing to our experience of human persons as having open boundaries, existing in a unity of relationships with others as much more than separate individuals; this inter-personalness is eminent in God, so that in the perichoresis of the persons there is truly One God.[104] He is, of course, aware that there is another way in which our human experience of inter-personalness could be conceived as eminent in the being of God; we might think of God as one complex personality, in which the 'persons' are really existing relationships, or movements of being characterized by relationship. Augustine and Aquinas both spoke of the persons as relationships,[105] but Moltmann rejects this as too modalist. He is rightly

---

[101] Ibid., p. 189.

[102] Ibid., p. 171. The context makes clear that Moltmann approves of the definition, though it needs supplementing.

[103] Boethius, *Contra Eutychen et Nestorium*, ch. 3. This is cited and discussed with approval in C. C. J. Webb, *God and Personality* (George Allen & Unwin Ltd., London, 1919), pp. 47 ff.

[104] Moltmann, *The Trinity and the Kingdom of God*, pp. 174–8.

[105] Aquinas, *S. Th.* 1a. 40. 2 cf. 1a. 30. 2. Augustine first formulated the theory of subsistent relations as a way of escaping the alternative presented to him by the Arians,

concerned that we should not project an image of God as a dictatorial monarch, and he (again I believe rightly) believes that the notion of a God who is in himself social prevents this kind of absolute monotheism. A God who exists in relationship can be open to the relationships of the world. But he assumes that conceiving the 'persons' *as* relations will leave us without sufficient sociality in God, and will represent God as the absolute subject or supreme individual: 'there are no persons without relations; but there are no relations without persons either'.[106]

In this I believe that Moltmann is mistaken, and that there is much more to be said for Barth's definition of the persons in God as modes of being characterized by their mutual relationships. In this way of thinking, God is the one personal God, though not *a* person in the sense of *a* being, for the affirmation of God as 'thrice of the one divine I' radically prevents such reduction to an object in the world.[107] The clue which we should glean from the mystery of human personality, open in relationship to others, is that the divine personality can only be thought of as an event of relationships, or as supremely self-differentiated Being. Human personality is mysterious because it happens in 'the realm of the between' as Buber puts it,[108] in the midst of a reciprocity of 'I' and 'Thou'. We might stretch this language of human personality to refer to God as a single personality *in* whom there is a 'between'; so in opposition to the classical view that God is simple Being, we must insist that God is complex Being, so complex that we can only think of him as a Son relating to a Father and a Father to a Son, in the Spirit of fellowship.

If we attempt to think of God as three subjects with their own consciousness, we may end as Moltmann does with a divine society which is admittedly not independent of mankind in the sense of being

---

that distinctions within God must be either substance or accident; e.g. *De Trinitate*, 5. 5–7, *De Civitate Dei*, 11. 10, *Ep.* 238–41. However, his perception has enduring value beyond its cultural context.

106 Moltmann, *The Trinity and the Kingdom of God*, p. 172. Mackey, *The Christian Experience of God as Trinity*, pp. 203–4, agrees here with Moltmann's criticism of God as Absolute Subject. In *God in Creation*, p. 266, Moltmann nevertheless comes near to conceiving the person of the Spirit *as* a relationship.

107 Barth, *CD* I/1, pp. 351, 364–5.

108 See e.g. 'What is Man?', in M. Buber, *Between God and Man*, trans. R. Gregor Smith (repr. Fontana Library, Collins, London, 1961), pp. 244 ff. R. Gregor Smith, *The Doctrine of God*, pp. 131–2, points to the importance of the category of 'the Between' as the realm of relations, and suggests that Buber himself obscures this by his concentration upon the individual 'I'.

impassible and self-sufficient, but whose suffering can still apparently be conceived as caused by the divine persons alone. In contrast, to think of God as a network of relationships is inevitably to involve man and his response, because it is impossible to think of God as a complex of relationships without *our* participation in God. This is because this manner of speaking of God cannot be objectified like other objects in the world. It is not possible to visualize or portray three interweaving relationships, or three 'movements' of being which are defined by their relations to each other. This sort of talk about God only makes sense in terms of our participation in God. In fact, Moltmann himself came close to affirming this sort of thing in his earlier book *The Crucified God*, when he spoke of God as 'the event of Golgotha' and to the question 'can one pray to an event?' answered that one can 'pray *in* this event'.[109]

Let us spell out what this might mean in religious experience. To say that the event of the cross reveals God means that we can only conceive of God as a complex of relationships, like a father relating to a son in a spirit of suffering and hope. But we conceive of this by a particular kind of thinking which is 'marked by participation' rather than spectatorship, so that we find in our suffering we are taken into a movement of suffering that is already there, like the movement of a forsaken son towards a father, and a desolate father to a lost son. Moltmann speaks similarly of sharing in the event of a suffering God, but without apparently making the relationships themselves the key to the experience. In affirming that we pray 'in' God, Moltmann draws attention to the New Testament description of prayer, which is through the Son, to the Father, in the Spirit. We might go on to interpret this as meaning that when we pray to God as Father, we find that our address is fitting into a movement like that of speech between a son and a father, or that when we have moments of joy, we can find that our exhilaration is supported by a movement of joy that is more profound than our own. H. Mühlen has taken up this pattern of thought in suggesting that the Trinitarian Being of God must be understood as reciprocal movements of self-giving, so that we have 'access to the Father' through Jesus when we experience the 'process of giving-away produced in us through the Spirit of God in service to our fellow men'. To be one and the same being (*homoousios*) with the man Jesus of Nazareth means that God 'is for us

---

[109] Moltmann, *The Crucified God*, p. 247; cf. Moltmann, *The Future of Creation*, p. 82: 'God is not an object to be defined by a concept . . . knowledge comes about because the knowing person is included in this (divine) history'.

exactly as for Jesus . . . the non–objective Whence of the giving-away which is produced by the Spirit'.[110]

This kind of thinking builds upon Barth's insistence that God is an event or happening, and that the modes of happening can only be described in terms of personal relationship. But it adds that we can never think of this event without humanity; if one could, then the modes might well collapse into a simple monarchian being in the way that some commentators fear. Here we must agree with process thought, that there can be no 'otherwise' in the relationship of God and world. For it only makes sense to speak of a divine field of force of relationships from the viewpoint of a participant within it. Augustine was able to think of the three 'persons' in God as relationships because of his Neo-Platonist idea that relationships were existent realities; it still makes sense in terms of a more dynamic kind of thinking, where the category of substance is replaced by event, 'person' by a movement of being, and contemplation by participation.

Now, this makes a fundamental contribution to our understanding of the transcendence of the suffering God. This cannot be an otherness beyond suffering, but must be an otherness in suffering. While the interlacing of relationships which is the personal God is open to us and embraces us, it is at the same time other than us and the relationships we make. There is of course no circle of relationships which is already enclosed without us, and which is then opened up subsequently for late-comers; God is open to us in his very form, for it is for the sake of the world that the relationships within God are movements of suffering and self-giving. He determines that when he determines his own being. Our circles of relationship always interlock with those of the divine being or event, for God is at the centre of them all. But the circle of relationships which is the Father, Son, and Spirit is always deeper and more inexhaustible in personalness than our relationships are. The interweaving movements of his being are richer in suffering, giving, and joy, so that the mystery of God is not what we do not know of him, but what we do know. We only know that he is mystery because he has revealed himself for, as Barth insists, it is the revealed God who is the hidden God.[111] The mystery of the Trinity is not a hidden Trinity beyond the manifest Trinity, like the other side of the moon turned away from the earth; it is the mystery of the personalness of God. Even in relationship

---

[110] Mühlen, *Die Veränderlichkeit Gottes*, p. 37.
[111] Barth, *CD* II/1, pp. 181–4, cf. pp. 283–4.

with human persons, we cannot plumb the mystery of another's personality, and it is even more so with God who is hidden because he is known.

The transcendence of a suffering God can only be understood as a transcendent suffering, not a transcendence beyond suffering. Only the thought of God as Trinity can make sense of transcendent suffering, for only a God who happens as an event of relationships can be both other than and yet inclusive of the world. He can include all suffering in himself as he includes all human relationships, yet he is other than the world in his unique suffering, taking our suffering into himself out of the depths of the more profound and terrible suffering which remains his own.

6

The Power of the Suffering God

'THE power of God is the worship he inspires.'[1] With this dictum, A. N. Whitehead suggests that human ideas of power as force and aggressive strength fall wide of the mark of true power, which is a matter of winning people's minds and changing their attitudes. If a suffering God can inspire this kind of allegiance, then his weakness is indeed stronger than men. But it is precisely here that some traditional theists argue that the idea of a suffering God fails. Surely, they maintain, the idea of a suffering God only depresses the worshipper, especially when suffering is taken to mean that God is changed by his world and so includes the finite within his infinite being. It is often said that what the worshipper needs is a vision of God in a majesty which is untouched by trouble and unclouded by disturbance: this is alone the kind of God who will give us confidence. Would not a God who is threatened by the finite inspire *either* despair, since we will be afraid that he might go out of existence, *or* at the most an esteem that differs from our admiration of human persons only in degree, falling short of inspiring the genuinely religious feeling of absolute dependence?

I.   THE POWER OF PERSUASION

In response to the first worry mentioned above, the notion of a suffering God can still provide assurance that he will never cease to be. I have been arguing that it is coherent to think of God as having both an open future and a certainty of final triumph, since God may have the sort of certainty which is a perfect hope. While he has a sure hope that in the end he will unify all things with himself, the content of that event depends upon the response of his creatures. Tragedy and triumph are not mutually exclusive in the divine history with the world, for the world that God reconciles to himself may not have become all that he

---

[1] Whitehead, *Science and the Modern World*, p. 276.

intends it could be. In this sense God can be threatened by the finite, without the possibility of his ceasing to be altogether. Later we shall need to consider how we might even think of God as experiencing death without being dead.

In reply to the second worry of our supposed objector, we may wonder whether he is in fact thinking of a religious feeling of being absolutely *dependent*, or whether he is not rather thinking of being absolutely *dominated*. A suffering God cannot, of course, inspire the kind of awe that would be involved in adoring One who had the absolute power to order people about without their consent. But then we should ask whether such a fearful feeling is a genuinely religious one anyway. Obeisance to a tyrannical father-figure can lead to an immaturity and infantile repression which is unhealthy, and which Freud in fact judged to be characteristic of all religion. Religious worship then becomes a ritual which we perform to suppress our anxieties, and particularly our guilt at having rebelled against this authoritarian God. One symptom, for example, of its having been made into an obsessive ritual like this is the refusal to allow any changes in a familiar liturgy.

Belief in a dictatorial Father leads to correlative views of the suffering of Jesus. When understood as a *human* act of suffering, the cross may then be conceived as something offered to appease an angry monarch who demands retribution. When understood on the other hand as an act of *divine* suffering, the cross may be presented as the ultimate human crime of slaying God in revolt against his authority, which comes uncomfortably close to the Freudian concept of the guilty killing of the primal Father who represents the super-ego.[2] Such unhealthy trends in religious feeling arise from the concept of a dominating God. But a God who suffers with us in compassion is one upon whom we can be absolutely dependent, in the sense of being dependent upon an absolute love, which in its turn is willing to have a relative dependence upon our partial love. So the weakness of God provides a basis for a healthy feeling of dependence, but not for the desire to be dominated. David Jenkins has made this crucial distinction between the two terms, pointing out that 'so much of the dependence that we know now is in fact part of a series of dominance/dependence relationships which we are more and more discerning to be humanly crippling, at the psychological, social, and political levels'.[3]

---

[2] See R. S. Lee, *Freud and Christianity* (Penguin Books, Harmondsworth, 1967), pp. 116–25.

[3] David Jenkins, 'The Liberation of God', in Moltmann, *Theology and Joy*, p. 6.

There seems to be no strong case against Whitehead's contention that a suffering God can inspire worship, as long as there is a place here for the typical religious feelings of assurance that God will not cease to be and of ultimate dependence upon God. It is not contradictory to claim that the vulnerable God whom we adore in worship still has the power to change human wills and to shatter proud and self-enclosed egos. The suffering of God has the compelling power not of coercion but of persuasive influence. This is not the sentimentality of the plea 'O dearly, dearly has he loved, and we must love him too',[4] for the 'must' has no force unless God himself moves us to respond to him; Abelard saw this point when he insisted that the divine love has power to 'incite' or create human love.[5] It is the suffering of God, we may say, that has the power to alter human attitudes to God and to other people, and there can be no stronger power than that. Such influence enables us not only to cope with our own suffering, but also to destroy the causes of needless suffering in the world. Yet if there is nothing to contradict the belief that a suffering God exercises this kind of influential power, in what ways might we positively conceive of this happening? Recent thinking has explored three levels of answer to that question, which we might identify successively as the power of God's story, God's situation, and God's feelings.

2.   THE STORY AND SITUATION OF A SUFFERING GOD

At the first level of understanding, appeal is made to the effect of a meaningful story.[6] Much of human suffering is apparently meaningless in itself, and because we experience suffering as senseless we are driven into silence and numbness of spirit; we are paralysed by it in our will and emotions. We cannot use suffering actively to promote what is life-giving, making something out of it. There is thus no hope of learning from suffering, or of using it to overcome what has caused it, letting a protest against oppression be born from the experience of suffering. But

---

[4] Hymn, 'There is a green hill far away', by Mrs C. F. Alexander (1818–95).

[5] Abelard, *Expositio in Epistolam ad Romanos*, 2. 3–4. Abelard's view of God's love as a transforming power is well expounded by Richard E. Weingart, *The Logic of Divine Love: A Critical Analysis of the Soteriology of Peter Abailard* (The Clarendon Press, Oxford, 1970), pp. 124–8.

[6] The approach of Dorothee Sölle and Hans Küng is considered below; also see Lee, *God Suffers for Us*, pp. 84–7, and Ulrich Simon, *Story and Faith in the Biblical Narrative* (SPCK, London, 1975), pp. 55–8.

there *is* hope if we can place alongside our story of meaningless suffering a story of suffering which has meaning. Many of the great tragic dramas do exactly this for their audience, assuring people who suffer and die hidden from the spotlight of history that some human beings are able to interpret their ending, 'dying well' in the sense of using the occasion of death to make public affirmations about the human condition. Othello affirms love and Hamlet affirms loyalty even in face of the mess they have made of their lives.[7] Beyond these human stories, we may say that God's suffering has a plot, or an aim in view, and so is triumphant; as we have been arguing, it is his way of setting out on a pilgrimage of love towards his future glory.

So, as we set our suffering in the context of the suffering of God, we can 'make our pain serve the pain of God', as Kitamori expresses it. As we place the meaningful story of the suffering of God alongside our own, we begin to find words to cope with our suffering; we emerge from dumbness, first towards rightful protest and then to healthy acceptance. We find ways to make our suffering serve the cause of life. Dorothee Sölle points out that those who suffer without apparent reason or purpose depend especially upon the story of those who suffer for the sake of a cause or just end:[8]

Those who suffer in vain and without respect depend on those who suffer in accord with justice. If there were no one who said, 'I die, but I shall live,' no one who said, 'I and the Father are one,' then there would be no hope for those who suffer mute and devoid of hoping . . . There is a history of resurrections, which has vicarious significance. A person's resurrection is no personal privilege for himself alone—even if he is called Jesus of Nazareth.

Above all, then, we depend upon the story of the suffering of God which comes to a focus in the story of Jesus. Here comes to visibility a suffering which has a purposeful content, in compassion for mankind and hope of life through death. So we can choose our suffering as a suffering with Christ, 'filling up that which is lacking in the sufferings of Christ' as one New Testament text puts it (Col. 1: 24).

If, however, we follow this line of thought we must be careful to notice two factors. Firstly, there is no question of finding a meaning that

---

[7] See Helen Gardner, writing on Othello and Shakespeare's tragedies in general, in 'The Noble Moor', *Proceedings of the British Academy*, 41 (Oxford University Press, London, 1955), p. 203: 'But the end does not merely by its darkness throw up into relief the brightness that was. On the contrary, beginning and end chime against each other. In both the value of life and love is affirmed.'　　[8] Sölle, *Suffering*, p. 150.

already and inherently lies behind an instance of human suffering, as if we could trace a reason why God has 'sent' suffering to someone. To think like this would be to go back to the idea of a God who inflicts suffering rather than one who endures it himself; it would be to revert to an authority-figure to whose omnipotent choice, in this case a choice of meaning, we must simply submit. Rather, the power of the story of divine suffering is that we can find a meaning *for* our suffering rather than one *behind* it; that is our suffering can acquire a meaning. We can put the word of the cross alongside our apparently senseless suffering, or the suffering of others, and then we can see what meaning emerges. This is a prime example of what Hartshorne has called 'emergent values'. We can never say to another person that this or that is without doubt the meaning of their suffering, for that implies that God can be proved or demonstrated from the fact of suffering as the first cause. All we can do is tell the story of the cross and other cross-like events, and wait to see what meaning the sufferer discovers. As Hans Küng says: 'In the light of Jesus' definitive Passion, his suffering and death, the passion of each and every man . . . could acquire a meaning.'[9]

But this brings us to another factor we must take account of: we must take seriously the actual shape of the story, the kerygma of the early church about the suffering of Christ. At the heart of it is a cry of forsakenness, summing up the apparent contradiction of all that Jesus had proclaimed in his ministry. He had announced the nearness of God ('the kingdom of heaven is at hand') and therefore the possibility of a new kind of fellowship with God, which he exemplified himself in his intense awareness of God as Father; but now he was suffering a loss of the sense of God's presence ('My God, why have you forsaken me?'). So taken as a story in its own right, regardless of the historicity of the actual cry of desolation, the passion of Christ apparently presents not a paradigm of meaning, but a tale of senseless suffering as perplexing as our own. If we are to say that our suffering can acquire a meaning as we identify it with the suffering of Christ, and that the cross has meaning as the supreme story of the compassionate suffering of God, we have to reconcile this with the desolation at the heart of the story.

One way of coping with this has been suggested by Dorothee Sölle,[10] in understanding the cry of desolation itself as a triumph. Here,

[9] Hans Küng, *On Being a Christian*, trans. E. Quinn (Collins, London, 1977), p. 432, cf. pp. 433–6.
[10] Sölle, *Suffering*, p. 147: 'His "Eli, Eli" is a scream of growing up, the pain of this cry is a birth pang'; cf. p. 140.

she suggests, Jesus learns to do without an external Father figure, perceiving that the only God is the one whom he himself represents as a man; this is the point of the claim that 'I and the Father are one'. Sölle draws the conclusion that the suffering of God means the absence of God himself from the world; having made himself weak, he allows himself to be represented by others who suffer meaningfully. Jesus, then, is the first of those who see that if they face up to the fact of forsakenness, then they can do the work of God in so far as their suffering can change and heal the suffering of others; because they can say, 'I die but I shall live', and 'I and the father are one', then there is hope for those who suffer without meaning. This interpretation of the story asserts that the cry of forsakenness is not senseless because it is a cry of victory, giving hope to others. Yet we must ask whether in fact this does justice to the story of the cross as one of deepest desolation and abandonment. If we allow the story to make its effect upon the hearer, we surely cannot make a lament for being forsaken by a Father into a triumphant manifesto of growing up and doing without a Father.

There is another way of understanding, indicated by Hans Küng when he says:

This senseless death acquires a meaning only with the resurrection of Jesus to new life with God, as known by faith . . . this senseless human suffering and death thus acquires a meaning which man as he suffers and dies simply cannot produce himself, which can only be given to him by Someone who is wholly Other, by God himself.[11]

That is, just as our own suffering has to acquire a meaning, without there being a total meaning inherent within it, so likewise does the cross of Jesus. Nor is the Father absent from the story, because he is present to give the passion meaning. For anything else to be the case would be either to over-glorify or to belittle suffering; we give suffering too much significance if we think it has a total pre-existent meaning, and we give it too little if we think it must remain senseless. The meaning of the cross is the compassionate presence of God in the deepest human desolation. Even the cry of suffering acquires a meaning. But if this is so, I suggest that Küng limits the power of the story by restricting the moment of the giving of meaning to the episode of the resurrection. That would be merely a reversal of the cross, an opposing of one stage of the story to another. There is also a possibility here of speaking about a 'transcendent' suffering of God in the cross of Jesus, a unique suffering

---

[11] Küng, op. cit. (n. 9 above), p. 433.

that is unsurpassed by any other involvement of God in the predicament of mankind. We can say that the cross acquires meaning through the very depth of the divine participation in its lack of meaning. God was present in a unique way in the cross, since he so fully identified himself with this dying man that the loss of meaning experienced by Jesus entered into the very being of God himself. Here God was exposed to the threat of the meaningless, of nothingness, and to say that he gives meaning to the cross is to affirm that he is not destroyed by this threat even as he suffers it. Faced by an ultimate loss of purpose, God gives it purpose by his very sharing in it. Thus, 'God defines himself when he identifies himself with the dead Jesus' (E. Jüngel).[12] But for God to identify himself in this way with a human son makes most sense in the context of Trinitarian thinking about God; it requires the precondition that there is already a differentiation in the being of God, something about God which can only be described as son-like as well as Father-like; then we can say that God loves the Son as the murdered man Jesus, who has thoroughly made himself at one with estranged human beings, so much so that he shares their own sense of alienation and loss of meaning. God identifies himself with the man who has identified himself with sinners.

We gain confidence that we can affirm this kind of uniqueness about the cross of Jesus, by the actual phenomenon of the effect of the story; this story which has a profound loss of meaning at its heart has nevertheless proved to be a key narrative which has the power to give significance to other events, and has gone on being open to new levels of meaning itself.[13] It is a universal story, rich in application to new contexts, inexhaustible in its relevance to human suffering. That it can acquire such a meaning calls out for explanation, and it is at least reasonable for Christian faith to account for it in terms of the unique presence of the suffering God in this event. Of course, the statement that the merely human story of the cross of Jesus lacks meaning needs some qualification. The Christian understanding finds some meaning in it as the account of a man who willingly immerses himself in the human predicament of estrangement despite his own sense of the nearness of God. There is a meaning in his self-identification with the forsaken and

---

12 Jüngel, *God as the Mystery of the World*, pp. 363–4.

13 The 'paradigmatic' and 'iconic' nature of the cross is stressed, though without the conclusions I draw from it, by Van Austin Harvey, *The Historian and the Believer* (SCM Press, London, 1967), pp. 270–5.

the outcasts of society; the one who opposed the religious law with the way of simple acceptance found himself almost inevitably the victim of the legal process. But until God gives the event of his death further meaning, it is an open question whether he or the Pharisees were right in their conflicting views of how God deals with human beings.[14] From the momentum of the story itself we can say that Jesus becomes 'accursed' on the cross, in that he enters the same realm of meaningless death as we inhabit. But the story still needs to acquire meaning, in terms of saying that God made this death his own; then we can say that 'Christ was accursed *for us*' (Gal. 3: 13), as a means of *overcoming* our own alienation.

The second level of contemporary thinking about the powerful influence of the suffering God moves beyond the story to the situation of God. While on the first level of understanding the story of the cross illuminates our story, here the history of the cross includes our history. We have already met this approach in the thought of Jürgen Moltmann, who envisages God as an event of suffering in which human beings can take their place. He insists that what is visible at the cross is true of the being of God throughout history; there is an ever-present situation in which a divine Father suffers the loss of a Son, a Son suffers the loss of a Father, and a Spirit of self-giving love and hope flows between them. In his own Trinitarian history of suffering, God opens himself to include the uproar of all human history; oppressed and forsaken people can find themselves within the situation of a suffering God, and so can also share in his history of glorification.[15]

Several contemporary theologians speak in this way of God's 'opening up room' in himself for us through suffering. Adrienne Von Speyr, in an influential saying, proposed that the cross is 'the moment when the distance separating Father and Son has been widened to embrace the whole world'.[16] Similar expressions can be found in the writings of E. Jüngel and H. Mühlen,[17] and I have already urged in this

[14] For a recent reconstruction of the conflict of interpretation between Jesus and the Pharisees, see Peter Stuhlmacher, 'Jesus als Versöhner', in G. Strecker (ed.), *Jesus Christus in Historie und Theologie: Festschrift für H. Conzelmann*, (J. C. B. Mohr, Tübingen, 1975), pp. 97–9.

[15] Moltmann, *The Crucified God*, pp. 252–5, *The Trinity and the Kingdom of God*, pp. 74–5, 94–6.

[16] Adrienne Von Speyr, *The Word: A Meditation on the Prologue to St John's Gospel*, trans. A. Dru (Collins, London, 1953), p. 26, cf. pp. 60–4.

[17] Jüngel, 'Vom Tod des lebendigen Gottes' (ch. 1 n. 36 above), p. 120: 'God endures negation within himself, which creates room in his Being for other beings'; Mühlen, *Die Veränderlichkeit Gottes*, p. 34; cf. *Die abendländische Seinsfrage*, pp. 58–61.

study that the suffering of God makes most sense in terms of our participating in the 'happening' which is the Trinitarian God. But then, in what sense are we influenced or transformed by this inclusion within the life of God? We seem to be speaking in a rather abstract manner when we refer to God's 'making room' in himself, and our occupying this room, Here, I believe, we need the help of some of the insights of process theology, taking the idea of the influential suffering of God onto a third level, which affirms the power of the feelings of God.

3. THE INFLUENCE OF THE FEELINGS OF GOD

We return to Whitehead's dictum that 'the power of God is the worship he inspires'. Process theologians find a transforming effect in our feeling that our experiences have entered into the experience of God. They suggest that we are powerfully persuaded by God when we experience him as the one who has felt the depth and universal scope of our human condition. We 'prehend' or grasp God's prehension of the world. God objectifies his being for us to grasp, as divine being in which the world has for its part already been objectified. This kind of influence can of course be parodied into the kind of thing that the Methodist preacher W. Sangster once recalled as the worst opening to a sermon he had ever heard, namely 'I feel I have a feeling that I feel you feel as well'.[18] But it is another dimension altogether when we feel another's actual sympathy with our feelings. The term 'feeling' here does not simply mean emotion; rather like Schleiermacher's use of the term *Das Gefühl* it refers to an apprehension which transcends rational argument and involves intuition. The process thinkers are trying to express the conviction that we do not merely conceive intellectually of our experiences being taken into the being of God; we know this as a 'felt knowledge'. God's including the effects of all past states of the world within himself has a transforming effect upon the present world; he has power over the creation precisely because he is receptive of the lives of his creatures, which enrich the divine life:

Power over others consists in this, that one's own reality is rich in value which fits the needs of others and is therefore attractive to them as data for their awareness. To furnish suitable and valuable content to an awareness is to exert the only kind of influence upon it to which it is subject.[19]

18 W. E. Sangster, *The Craft of the Sermon* (Epworth Press, London, 1954), p. 127.
19 Hartshorne, *The Logic of Perfection*, p. 275.

Above all, the datum which influences us is the divine experience of human tragedy. Let us be careful here: the impact upon us is not a feeling of pity for a suffering God; this would indeed destroy worship in the way that is claimed by objectors to the suffering of God. As a matter of fact, some Christian hymns do invite us to pity the sufferings of Christ, and so by implication the sufferings of the God who is at work in Christ, but the danger here is that our sorrow for God can merely be disguised self-pity. As H. H. Farmer once suggested, we tend to pity ourselves as never having been properly appreciated, and we are delighted to welcome Christ to 'the great class of the unappreciated' too, so enabling us to go on feeling sorry for ourselves.[20] But far from increasing complacency, the process theologians are suggesting that when we apprehend God as receptive of our experience we find ourselves being assessed; God places a value on our feelings as they enter his being. In Whitehead's system, God values all ideals eternally within his primordial nature, and then evaluates their realization in time and space as he accepts the experience of actual entities into his consequent nature. Hartshorne, though without such a total notion of eternal valuation, speaks of an 'ever-new summation' of the lives of all creatures as they enter the consciousness of God's concrete nature, 'integrating' values and preserving 'what can be salvaged from our failures'.[21]

Exactly how the acceptance of our feelings by God, and so his suffering with us, works a powerful change upon us might be clarified by analogy with human relationships. The process thinker Daniel D. Williams draws attention to the two factors of judgement and transformation at which we have already hinted. In the first place, when we apprehend someone as being affected by the way we feel, it enables us to face up to the truth of our situation. We are brought up against judgement, as 'we are made aware of the significance of our acts by the way in which they are received in the feelings of others'.[22]

[20] H. H. Farmer, *The Healing Cross*, (Nisbet & Co., London, 1938), p. 191. Simon, op. cit. (n. 6 above), p. 55, comments that in the gospel passion narratives, 'both hero worship and pity are equally excluded by the story'.

[21] Whitehead, *Religion in the Making*, pp. 153–6, 159, *Process and Reality*, pp. 46, 63–4; Hartshorne, *The Logic of Perfection*, pp. 274–5; *The Divine Relativity*, p. 141. Cf. Wheeler Robinson, *Suffering Human and Divine*, p. 204: 'God has always been transforming the fact of sin by his own attitude towards the suffering which it occasioned in him.'

[22] Daniel Day Williams, 'How does God Act?: An Essay in Whitehead's Metaphysics', in W. L. Reese and E. Freeman (eds.), *Process and Divinity: The Hartshorne Festschrift*, (Open Court, La Salle, Illinois, 1964), p. 177.

Furthermore, to have our feelings taken in by another person and reflected back like this is to experience their being transformed. When we are aware of our feelings being accepted in love, this results in the 'strengthening or weakening, purgation or enhancement of feeling'.[23] It is not hard to think of situations which illustrate the truth of these insights. For example, when someone absorbs our bitter feelings into himself without rejecting us, we are able to grow up and develop beyond them. In the relationship between a young child and a parent the child may not grasp what he has done wrong, and may be confused by his conflicting feelings of guilt and defiance, until he feels the effect of his feelings upon his mother. Then he comes under judgement, and is moved to awareness and sorrow.[24] Again, when a child feels sad or unhappy, the parent may say, 'You feel sad, don't you?' and the child is helped to recognize his feeling and build upon it. The parent here acts as a kind of amplifier, enhancing feelings by accepting them in what is often a painful experience of empathy. So we find two dimensions interwoven, judgement and transformation, in the acceptance of our feelings by others.

Process thought also points towards another sort of duality in the experience of having our feelings received into another, which has particular force when applied by analogy to God's reception of the world. That is, feelings may be accepted preveniently or consequently. D. D. Williams himself only refers to the consequent nature of God, that is to the pole of God's being which is shaped and created by the world, when considering our apprehension of God's feeling of the world. But in the case of fellow creatures, we do not only feel the experience of others *after* they have realized their aims; in a mode of feeling which Whitehead calls 'propositional feeling',[25] we can anticipate what they would feel *if* they were to enjoy—or fail to enjoy—certain values. In the light of this we can aim at our own intensity of feeling, influencing others through what we become. Thus we can choose to sacrifice our own immediate enjoyment for the sake of the future; that is, we persuade others by the kind of object we become, our experience being prehended by them in their turn. We have already remarked that some process thinkers believe that this mode of

---

[23] Ibid.
[24] This family analogy was developed by R. C. Moberly, in *Atonement and Personality* (John Murray, London, 1901, repr. 1924), pp. 121–4.
[25] Whitehead, *Process and Reality*, pp. 393–5.

'propositional feeling' must also be ascribed to God,[26] so that he does not merely 'preview' those values which will produce the most intense enjoyment by each actual entity, but passionately desires their realization. He longs for what will make for beauty. It is a short step from here to conclude that God's appetite for these eternal objects is his experiencing in advance what it would be like for a worldly entity to pursue various possibilities; hence, in grasping the initial aim which God presents, the creature prehends not only the values held out to it, but what it would be like to achieve them. In this way the creature is persuaded by two modes of the feelings of God; as he prehends the being of God, he is moved by God's anticipated experience of his experience, and he is moved by the way God receives his actual experience into himself. In process terms, we may call the first final causation and the second efficient causation.

There seems to be a place in both modes of divine persuasion for the suffering of God, as he feels potential suffering in vision, and actual suffering in recollection. In forming an initial aim for a creature he feels what it would be like to fall short of it, and in his consequent nature he feels the actual effects of what the creature makes of it. It seems to be of great religious value that both should be true, for the first affirms that God *has* aims for human life, underlining the element of judgement in our experience of God's feelings, while the second stresses that we are accepted by God despite our failures to incarnate his purposes. There is judgement and justification. Within the varieties of process thought, the Whiteheadian notion of God's vision of eternal objects in his primordial nature seems to be required to give any real force to this dual affirmation. However, even this form of process thought cannot, I suggest, do justice to the very insights that it identifies. Dipolar theism cannot properly express the personal elements of judgement and transformation in their double mode of God's prevenient and consequent acceptance of the world.

Of course, process thought does attempt to describe the relationship of personal beings to God. Persons, according to process ideas, are large-scale organisms, or societies of the minute organic events which are the basic building-blocks of reality. Not only the basic 'actual entities' but a whole person (as an 'enduring object' or 'actual whole-synthesis') can be persuaded by God and enter into his being.[27] God offers aims to a

---

[26] e.g. J. B. Cobb and L. S. Ford; see above, ch. 5 pp. 127–9.

[27] Hartshorne, *The Logic of Perfection*, pp. 192–3, 200–3; Whitehead, *Process and Reality*, p. 439, *Science and the Modern World*, pp. 98–9.

person, or sets boundaries to his choices, as much as he does to each element of the person's being; indeed, a person as a conscious organism attains the degree of moral responsiveness in which he can be consciously aware of God's directing activity, though his awareness of this tends to be sporadic. So we have been speaking, in a way quite consistent with process thought, of personal 'creatures' as having a history of being persuaded by God. The problem, however, lies in speaking of God as relating to these persons in both the prevenient and consequent way which would give meaning to the notion of God's sacrificial suffering. If we conceive of God, in a Whiteheadian manner, as an actual entity among others, then we have to allow that in relating to creatures he breaks the rules of actual entities in ways that seem quite arbitrary within the dipolar system. We have already seen the problem of locating 'propositional feelings' within God, and other difficulties arise too. Actual entities are not supposed to be prehended twice,[28] and yet creatures are said to be influenced by prehending both God's initial aim for them, and the consequent effects of their actions upon him. Moreover, the consequent nature of God is not complete since it is continually being augmented by the world, yet it can apparently be prehended by us; entities are only supposed to be available to be grasped by others (as 'superjects') because they have reached satisfaction and perished as subjects.

To cope with these problems, Lewis Ford suggests that we do not directly prehend God's consequent nature at all, but only know it indirectly through the aims which God offers to us out of the resources of his ever-complete primordial nature. From these we can glean an intuition into God's responsive experience of the world.[29] This explanation, however, vastly diminishes the impact upon us of God's feeling of the world, so that it becomes hard to say with Hartshorne that we 'enjoy God's enjoyment of ourselves',[30] and are correspondingly moved by his suffering with us. If, however, we follow Hartshorne in conceiving of God as a person rather than an actual entity, within the context of dipolar theism this means a person with an absolutely abstract nature, and so one who does not entertain specific aims for human persons. As we have already seen, such a concept of a supreme person is of one who cannot act with 'the particular providence for particular

---

[28] See Whitehead, *Process and Reality*, pp. 34, 38–9. I am indebted to Dr Randall Morris for drawing my attention to this point.

[29] Ford, *The Lure of God*, pp. 103–5, 110 n. 8, 121.

[30] Hartshorne, *The Divine Relativity*, p. 141.

occasions' which Whitehead ascribed to God in his own system of initial aims.[31] According to Hartshorne's concept of a suffering God, we can certainly speak of his absorbing and transfiguring our failures in the concrete reality of his being, but we cannot speak of his suffering our failure to realize any *particular* aims he might have for us, nor of any prevenient suffering caused by envisaging the possible future tragedies of the world.

4. THE CREATIVE JOURNEY OF FORGIVENESS

Process thought, then, points in a valuable way to the powerful effect which an exchange of feelings between us and a suffering God can have upon us, but I believe this insight can be carried through better with the more thoroughgoing personal analogy for God which is offered by Trinitarianism. A great deal of light is shed by one personal experience in particular, that of forgiveness, which is at the heart of the Christian tradition about the suffering of God in the cross of Jesus. As we have seen, the story of the cross illuminates problems of human suffering which are not directly to do with sin as personal rebellion against God, but the Christian church has also from its beginning related the experience of reconciliation in the present to the past event of the cross as the central act and offer of God's forgiveness to sinful humanity. Recent writings on the suffering of God have had much more to say about theodicy than about the doctrine of Atonement,[32] but this lack only underlines the need to bring together our thinking about the sufferings connected with sin and the wider problems of human suffering. As a matter of fact we find that forgiveness, whether human or divine, operates through exactly the same kind of process of exchange of feelings as we have been discussing in general. An act of forgiveness involves embarking upon an experience which is costly in terms of suffering, and which for this very reason has a powerful effect upon the experience of others. We often miss seeing this because we

[31] Whitehead, *Process and Reality*, p. 532.

[32] For example, critics of Moltmann's book *The Crucified God* have complained that it neglects the doctrine of Atonement in favour of theodicy and political action for the oppressed; perhaps Moltmann has not sufficiently clarified the way in which these *are* part of Atonement. See Ulrich Asendorf, 'Eschatologia crucis?', *Theologische Beiträge*, 4 (1973), pp. 150–64, especially pp. 161–2; Bertold Klappert, 'Die Gottverlassenheit Jesu und der gekreuzigte Gott', *Verkündigung und Forschung*, 20 (1975), pp. 35–53, especially pp. 50–1.

have turned forgiveness, and pre-eminently the proclamation of God's forgiveness of sins, into a mere transaction to be understood through legal or commercial images. 'Of course God will forgive me; it's his business', said the poet Heine as he lay dying. However right he was in his view of the mercy of God, he was as wrong in his choice of metaphor as the severest Calvinist. Forgiveness is no mere business, no kind of contract or bargain. It is indeed an exchange, but one of feelings rather than merits or punishments. H. R. Mackintosh gets to the heart of the matter when he speaks of forgiveness as a 'shattering experience' for the one who forgives as well as for the one who is forgiven,[33] and in the course of his argument he offers a metaphor for this experience which deserves unpacking and expanding:

How true it is that in heart and mind the forgiver must set out on 'voyages of anguish'! It is an experience of sacrificial pain, of vicarious suffering.[34]

If we analyse what happens in any human act of forgiveness we find a costly and painful 'voyage' of experience, a journey of imagination and sympathy into the situation of the offender. It is this journey which, as Mackintosh points out, is a creative act enabling the offender to accept the forgiveness offered to him and so to come back into fellowship with the one he has wronged.[35] Forgiveness is a costly matter because it aims at reconciliation, or the restoring of relationships, and this requires an acceptance of the experience of another into oneself that is nothing less than a journey of painful discovery. When someone perceives that a forgiver feels with him like that, then he is won to sorrow and response. The acceptance of feeling has a powerful effect, promoting both the elements of judgement and transformation which process thought has already brought to our attention. Indeed, forgiveness creates transformation of attitude and personality precisely *through* the fires of judgement. As Paul Tillich aptly summarizes it, the New Testament witness to 'justification by faith' is about 'the acceptance of the unacceptable sinner into judging and transforming communion with God'.[36]

To understand better how this happens, we should notice that any 'journey' of forgiveness in human experience has an active and a passive

---

[33] H. R. Mackintosh, *The Christian Experience of Forgiveness* (Library of Constructive Theology, Nisbet & Co., London, ²1934), p. 191.

[34] Ibid., p. 188, cf. pp. 198–9, 209–13. The following analysis is indebted to the study by Mackintosh.   [35] Ibid., pp. 211–12, cf. pp. 28 ff.

[36] Paul Tillich, *The Courage To Be*, p. 161.

dimension. They are not successive stages on the journey but are deeply intertwined with each other, and recall our earlier discussion about active and passive suffering. First there is an active movement of discovery, an awakening of awareness. If the forgiver is truly to heal the broken relationship he cannot just forget about the offence that has been done to him. It would, no doubt, be more comfortable for him just to put it out of mind, but there is a brokenness in relationship that has to be faced up to if it is to be mended; truly to forgive is more than ignoring the other and leaving him in the mists of forgetfulness. The forgiver has to bring the wrong done to him back to mind, painful though it is to relive it, and then he must try to think himself into the mind of the offender. As Mackintosh finely says, 'Sympathy brings him close to the guilty life, actually by intense feeling putting him where the other is.'[37] He stands in the shoes of the other, feeling his shame, trying to understand why he said or did what he did. Like Father Brown, the priest in the stories by G. K. Chesterton who solves mysteries of crime through imagining himself to be the criminal, he can say 'I thought and thought about how a man might come to be like that, until I realized that I really *was* like that, in everything except actual final consent to the action.'[38]

This painful voyage of identification is a key part of reconciliation, because the forgiver is trying to win the offender to accept his offer of forgiveness. To accept forgiveness from another is a humbling and disturbing matter, and it will only happen if the forgiver is experienced as a certain kind of person, someone of fellow-feeling who has truly drawn alongside the one who is in the wrong. If the offender feels that the other is a harsh critic, standing over against him in judgement, then he will not be enticed back into relationship. The one who has offended is after all on the defensive; he will not be helped if he is faced by a critic offering pardon from a height of superiority. We all know people who offer us forgiveness in a way that makes clear they will use it as a weapon against us, if not now then later. 'She might decide to be forgiving / And gain an advantage', remarks the Unidentified Guest in T. S. Eliot's play *The Cocktail Party*.[39]

[37] Mackintosh, op. cit. (n. 33 above), p. 188.

[38] G. K. Chesterton, *The Secret of Father Brown* (repr. Penguin Books, Harmondsworth, 1974), p. 12. Significantly, Chesterton has his character claim that this identification has the power to create remorse in the criminal: 'It solves the whole problem of time and sin. It gives a man his remorse beforehand' (ibid., p. 174).

[39] *The Complete Poems and Plays of T. S. Eliot* (Faber and Faber, London, 1969), p. 360.

But there is another reason for this journey of identification, this participation in the state of the other's being. It calls for a journey of discovery also to be made by the offender; he too must be awoken to the wrong he has done and the hurt he has caused. There can be no healing of relationship unless he faces up to it, unless he feels remorse. Forgiveness depends upon response, not because the offender has to make himself worthy of forgiveness, but because a relationship cannot be mended without the participation of both partners. Forgiveness can be offered freely from one side only, but for it to achieve its aim, it must be received. When the forgiver enters with sympathy into the turmoil or dark tunnel of the other's mind, and says (by word or by gesture), 'I forgive you', then he is bringing the offence out into the open. The wrong is brought to clear daylight. Even though the forgiver is not 'rubbing the nose' of the offender in his own dirt and destruction, he is shaking him awake to the fact of what he has done. He is calling him and enabling him to sorrow, so that this movement of identification is an act of judgement in its very mood of acceptance. It is a painful voyage, but a deliberate action, corresponding to what we have earlier called 'active suffering'.

There is also, however, an aspect of passive suffering, a moment of sheer endurance in this voyage of forgiveness. In opening himself to the dark experience of the other, the forgiver has left himself vulnerable to effects upon himself which are unknown and incalculable. What it will be like to bear the experience of the other, to relive the past hurt to oneself, cannot be under planned control. Moreover, the offender may well be hostile towards the one he has wronged, and this hostility will have to be endured. A sense of guilt may, it is true, manifest itself in an anxiety which numbs and paralyses a person, so that the act of forgiveness will create an assurance that the wrongdoer is accepted; as Paul Tillich stresses, forgiveness enables the guilty person to take the courage to accept that he is accepted.[40] But a sense of guilt can also break out in the form of hostility, and often anxiety and hostility are present in a subtle mix. So the forgiver must absorb the hostility of the other, and foster healing through receiving it into himself. By forgiving he takes the first step across the gap which separates them, and so exposes himself to attack. The offender is resentful at having the offence called to mind, fears blame, and wants to justify himself by blaming the other; he is likely to feel, if not to say, 'It's your fault. How dare you

---

[40] Tillich, *The Courage to Be*, pp. 160–1, 181–3.

presume to forgive me!' If there is to be reconciliation the forgiver must not react to justify himself and accuse the other; he cannot argue his neighbour back into relationship, but must bear his anger, drawing out the venom of hostility. He has brought the matter out into the open in the first place; he has acted to awaken awareness and now he must neutralize the hostility against him by bearing it in love. Once again, as with the more active movement within forgiveness, he is seeking to win the other back into friendship. He is making an agonizing voyage into the mind and heart of the other in order to persuade him to respond.

Such a human experience cannot provide an exact analogy to the divine forgiveness of sins, for in any human relationship it is not a mere matter of one partner's being in the right and the other in the wrong. There is no simple 'guilty party'.[41] The forgiver has no doubt himself contributed something to the breach in relationships. But the fundamental insight in this analysis is that the one who makes the forgiving move is setting out to remove some blockage in the other person's attitude or approach to the relationship, enabling him to face up to his wrong and to accept that he is accepted. The forgiver does this through entering into the situation of estrangement in which the other is existing, and through the other's feeling this identification with him. This is what Tillich rightly sees as lying at the very heart of the divine act of atonement:

The suffering of God, universally and in the Christ, is the power which overcomes creaturely self-destruction by participation and transformation. Not substitution, but free participation, is the character of the divine suffering. And, conversely, not having a theoretical knowledge of divine participation, but participation in the divine participation, accepting it and being transformed by it—that is the threefold character of the state of salvation.[42]

Daring to retell the story of the prodigal son, we might say that the son fails to come to his right mind in the pigsty and return home, since he is disabled by anxiety and hostility. So the Father himself takes a journey into the far country to fetch his son.[43] This is the journey of forgiveness, when the Father offers pardon in the most costly way possible in order to move us to repent, and we can see this offer clearly portrayed in the cross of Jesus. The cross, at the apex of the ministry of

[41] The situation is not quite so simple with regard to the divine–human relationship either. See above for the notion of the responsibility of God; ch. 2, pp. 35–6.

[42] Tillich, *Systematic Theology*, Vol. 2, p. 203.

[43] Barth does dare to use this metaphor; *CD* IV/1, p. 185.

Jesus, exhibits the twofold character of the journey as active and passive suffering, and shows how personal transformation can happen through judgement. First there is a voyage of discovery, as the one who proclaims the Father's acceptance of sinners into the Kingdom of God identifies himself with those who are estranged and alienated in life. Throughout his ministry Jesus deliberately seeks out the company of the outcasts of society whom the respectable religious establishment had discarded as unfit for the Kingdom, so carrying out the programme inaugurated in his baptism when he identified himself with the penitent sinners of Israel. He requires only an attitude of repentance, and trust in himself as the agent of the Father whose Kingdom is even now breaking in with his ministry. Finally in his death he enters an experience of utter forsakenness, crucified as a religious blasphemer and political rebel, bearing the curse of exclusion from his community which was the deepest point of shame according to the traditions of Israel's faith. Though himself living in tune with the mind of the Father, he consents to participate in the experience of estrangement which is the lot of a humanity which has lost communion with God.

To undergo such an alienating death is in fact to experience the judgement of God upon distorted human existence, for (as we have seen in an earlier chapter), the wrath of God can be best understood as his underlining of the self-destructive consequences of human actions. Jesus enters the realm of death in its most bitter form, as the place where all relationships are broken. It is this complete identification with the human predicament of estrangement that the gospel narratives mark by his cry of forsakenness, and the Apostle Paul explains as 'being made sin for us'.[44] There is no question of God's *inflicting* any penalty upon Christ; rather, Christ participates in the alienation which man brings as judgement upon himself. Moreover, because God has committed himself to Christ as his agent of forgiving love, making himself one with him, we may conclude (with astonishment at the mercy of God) that the Father himself embarks upon this agonizing voyage of discovery. Far from simply forgetting about the sins of the world, he journeys deeply into the heart of man's condition. We have seen that a forgiver must always stand where the offender is, and here God himself enters into the human experience of death in its most estranging form. He participates in our brokenness, to win us to the offer of healing. Therefore this is at the same time a journey of discovery for mankind.

[44] 2 Cor. 5: 21, cf. Rom. 6: 21, 8: 3. The Pauline theology of the self-identification of Christ with sinners is ably expounded by J. A. T. Robinson, *The Body*, pp. 34–48.

Jesus in dying as he does brings us to judgement; he awakens us to what the sin of man against man can do, as the authorities and the crowds execute the one who has disturbed and challenged their lives. This is what man does with goodness when it confronts him; he crucifies love. We also see the consequences of the deeper, more universal estrangement of man from the source of his being in God; this is what death looks like when the most fundamental relationship of life is distorted.

Interwoven with this active suffering of Christ is 'passive suffering'. There is a sheer vulnerability about the moment of forsakenness, a loss of meaning which befalls him whatever his deliberate, sacrificial intentions might have been to share the state of outcasts to the uttermost. There is no such thing as programmed suffering in such an act of acceptance, and the implications of this for God's own journey into death and 'non-being' will be explored further in the following chapters. One part of the passive suffering, as in human acts of forgiveness, is the enduring of hostility. The cross of Jesus demonstrates that when God offers his forgiveness in Christ, he does so in face of human anger and hostility against himself, and that he knows the cost of absorbing it into his being. Jesus is the target of extreme hostility, provoked by what seems to be his blasphemous offer of God's acceptance to the outcasts and law-breakers of society. The cross sums up the whole ministry of Jesus which has been the offer of the forgiveness of sins on his Father's behalf, accepting those who were ritually 'unclean' into his personal company. This mission evokes resentment from the religous authorities; throughout his ministry Jesus is absorbing their hostility, and in the end the passion narratives depict his drawing out of the venom from soldiers, priests, and the crowds. The author of the Letter to the Hebrews provides an apt title to the picture: 'Consider him who endured from sinners such hostility against himself' (Hebrews 12: 3).

5. THE POWER OF A UNIQUE SUFFERING

The cross of Jesus thus focuses the journey of suffering that God makes into human experience. In the present state of creaturely rebellion against God, a central form this journey will take is the voyage of forgiveness, though we must add that a God whose nature is suffering love would have been present within his world to share its growing pains, regardless of whether there was human sin or not.[45] Nor must we

---

[45] For a justification of this viewpoint see below, ch. 8 *passim*.

suppose that to speak of a journey is to imply any divine intervention 'from outside'; its starting-point is from within God's continuous experience of the world. It is a matter of going deeper in, rather than breaking in. The exchange of feelings between God and his creatures which this forgiveness brings is able to transform human personality, and is an event of such power that it is appropriate to use metaphors of victory over hostile forces to describe it; forgiveness as a performative word brings liberation from sin and death, because it turns a person away from allegiance to those powers in human existence which hold him in slavery, and towards the living God. There is nothing sentimental about the forgiveness which is proclaimed and enacted in Christ, since it creates a new situation for those to whom it is offered.

If we ask how the suffering of God in one human person, Jesus Christ, can create a new situation for us here and now, then part of the answer lies in the power of a story, which we have already reflected upon. Though God is always entering into our human predicament to reconcile us to himself, the story of the cross focuses this saving action so clearly that it comes to us with the force of revelation. The story of the cross discloses the love and the wrath of God in a new way; the death of Jesus, in the context of his life and resurrection, enhances our human capacity to respond to God, and such response is the very stuff of which true existence is made. In fact, this response is so basic to life that we can only describe it as an act of co-operation with the hidden and persuasive work of the Holy Spirit. As Norman Pittenger neatly says, it is 'Response with an upper case R, since we are talking about a truly divine operation'.[46]

But the power of the cross to create a new situation, and thereby a new response, exceeds the effect of a story alone. Process thought reminds us that an event contributes to the life of future events in such an organic way that it is really present in them. This applies in the first place to the effective causation which one creaturely entity has upon others in the future, since they have to take account of it in some way; if they persist in rejecting the experience which it offers to them, then its influence dies out, but if they incorporate its experience in formulating their subjective aims, then its life goes on being really present in its successors. The Church of Christ may then be understood as the community whose members have chosen to go on being constituted by

46 Norman Pittenger, *The Lure of Divine Love*, p. 137; cf. id., *The Word Incarnate*, pp. 182–3, 228–30.

the effect of the life and death of Jesus Christ. Cobb and Griffin use the image of a 'field of force' to describe the influence of Jesus in his truly human obedience to God, and his supreme representation of God's aims for man.[47] The church, in being willingly conformed to the living and dying of Jesus has gone on preserving and amplifying this field of force, so that the experience of Jesus is really present and available for disciples of all ages. Further along the same lines, Lewis Ford finds that the resurrection of Jesus witnesses to the emergence in creation of a new kind of organism, in which a whole community can share a common directing mind; the Spirit of Jesus, a subjectivity which is supremely open to the purpose of God for humanity, goes on living in the community like a mind in a single body.[48] Thus process philosophy, building upon the organic relationships in the world and extending the New Testament picture of the Body of Christ, suggests that the particular suffering of Jesus (which is inseparable from its impact upon God) goes on being present to us in a more actual mode than mere historic remembrance. It is a present experience which we can share, and so enables our response.

Moreover, process thought conceives of a second manner in which an event has influence upon the future. As well as its direct causation upon other creatures, it will affect them indirectly through being taken into the consequent nature of God. In his mutual interaction with the world, God takes account of what is done there, and that is the God of whom *we* have to take account. We prehend the being of a God who has shaped himself in reaction to the achievements and failures of the world. So, as Hartshorne says of God, 'To alter us, he only has to alter himself.'[49] Applied to the particular event of Jesus Christ, we may say that it creates a new situation for us because it creates a new situation for God. Pittenger provides a good summary of this insight of process thought applied to faith in Christ:

. . . the total event of Jesus Christ, reaching its climax on the cross, is a matter not of the *dead* past but of the *living* past in the divine life. And in God's continuing relationship with humanity, that living past plays its central role in God's dealing with men and women.[50]

[47] Cobb and Griffin, *Process Theology*, pp. 104–5, 108–9; cf. J. Macquarrie, *Principles of Christian Theology*, p. 326. Also see J. Cobb, 'The Presence of the Past and the Eucharist', *Process Studies*, 13 (1983), pp. 218–31, esp. pp. 223–8.

[48] Ford, *The Lure of God*, pp. 77–9.

[49] Hartshorne, *The Divine Relativity*, p. 139; cf. Hartshorne, *Creative Synthesis and Philosophic Method*, p. 277.   [50] Pittenger, *The Lure of Divine Love*, p. 124.

The role of which Pittenger speaks is on the one hand the influence of the past upon God's formulation of new aims for the world now. But on the other hand, as stressed by Hartshorne, it is the sheer effect of encountering the divine life in which previous events of the world are treasured and transformed; God can change our minds because he is the supreme object of our awareness. This latter insight is of special value in explaining the ongoing power of the particular sufferings of Jesus, but it is just this that is better expressed in the more personal models of God as Trinity and God as forgiving. We must enquire what scope there is for God to change himself in order to change us in this manner. Hartshorne claims, with some cogency, that for God to bring his abstract essence to a summing up of the whole of reality will make a difference to the sum.[51] While God brings no specific values (as in Whitehead's thought) to the rich harmony of the social whole which he contains, he does bring himself with his absolute potential for values, and this will result in the setting of new boundaries for creaturely choices. Whiteheadian thinkers produce a number of different accounts of how the primordial nature of God, with its vision of eternal objects, can affect the consequent nature of God embracing the world. But there are, as we have seen, strains in these often arcane explanations,[52] while there are limits upon divine action in what Hartshorne has to say instead.

In contrast, there are considerable gains of clarity in a more thoroughgoing personal model. We have already seen that in the human experience of forgiveness the forgiver has to learn how best to win the offender to himself. The result of the agonizing journey of discovery is the ability to draw a hostile and alien mind into forgiving love. The most perfect forgiver that could be conceived still has to change—not from reluctance to forgive to a willingness to do so, not from anger to mercy, but rather into new areas of experience. He has to move in his experience from having the *desire* to forgive to such an immersion into the experience of the other that he *can* win the other to himself. The other finds him to be the sort of person from whom he can

---

[51] See Hartshorne, *The Logic of Perfection*, pp. 274–5, *Creative Synthesis and Philosophic Method*, p. 240, *Philosophers Speak of God*, p. 284.

[52] See above, ch. 5, pp. 126–9. A further problem is whether God's prehension of the world in his consequent nature can involve elimination or abstraction, ('negative prehensions') as with other actual entities. See Hartshorne's criticism of Whitehead in 'Whitehead and Berdyaev: Is There Tragedy in God?' (ch. 4 n. 89 above), pp. 77–8, and the discussion by Griffin in 'Hartshorne's Differences from Whitehead' (ch. 2 n. 86 above), p. 52.

accept reconciliation. Talk of God's 'learning' through his suffering must of course be a highly metaphorical language, but it points to the reality of God's suffering in order to present himself to us in a way that is shaped to our needs. He enters into a new situation so that we should find him marked in that particular way by the experience of human failure and suffering, and so be moved to respond to him. We apprehend God as one who is shaped by the experience of the cross. A suffering God who was and is always willing to forgive gains through the cross a new experience of the human condition that gives him access into our resistant hearts. He suffers changes in order to change us. This is the permanent validity of those so-called 'objective' models of the atonement which present a change in God as well as in the sinner. They certainly mistake the sort of change involved by presenting it as a change of attitude on God's part, as if God needed to have his law satisfied before he could forgive. There can be no question of a change of attitude in a merciful God, but there can be what we might call a 'change of approach', gained through new experience.[53]

Process thought therefore points to the enabling power of the being of a God who has entered new situations of suffering, though it takes a more personal model to clarify this. Process thought (or at least the Whiteheadian version of it) also supplies a clue as to how the event of Jesus could be such a 'new' experience of suffering for God that it is uniquely formative for others. All human beings incarnate to some extent the aims of God for humanity, but there is room in this system of thought for one person to embody them to a unique degree. A Whiteheadian theory of initial aims can conceive of God's offering to one particular person the possibility of being the perfect expression of his purpose for human life. Such a person need not merely emerge haphazardly from the flux of history, or just happen to give the greatest scope to God's aims.[54] He could be chosen intentionally by God and offered a special aim,[55] although within the context of a community

[53] Cf. Moltmann, *The Church in the Power of the Spirit*, pp. 62–3.

[54] Process theologians who maintain that the specialness of Jesus came solely from his responsive prehension of God and not from special divine initiative include Schubert Ogden, *The Point of Christology* (SCM Press, London, 1982), pp. 79–85, and Peter Hamilton, op. cit. (ch. 1 n. 40 above), pp. 205 ff.

[55] Process Theologians who propose a special divine aim include David R. Griffin, *A Process Christology* (Westminster Press, Philadelphia, 1973), pp. 218–20 ('the content of God's ideal aim for men varies'), and Ford, *The Lure of God*, pp. 51–4, 75–6. Pittenger, *The Word Incarnate*, pp. 182–4, is more ambiguous. See also my article, 'God and History' (ch. 4 n. 71 above), pp. 83–7, for an expansion of the proposal made briefly here.

where there had been an increasing 'intensification of divine aim',[56] that is in the covenant people of Israel. He would of course, like them, have the freedom to reject this offer. The New Testament way of putting this is to speak of Jesus both as an 'elect Son' and an 'obedient Son'.

If we think of Jesus as one who was made a unique offer and made the free response of realizing it, then we begin to see a way of conceiving the unique or 'transcendent' suffering of God in Christ. Though God is always offering forgiveness to men, at the cost of entering into their situation and suffering human hostility against him, in the event of the cross of Jesus there is a unique experience of the human condition, because of the unique response of the one involved. Following the analysis of a human act of forgiveness, we may say that in the cross there was the 'awakening' of one man to a clear understanding of the predicament of human sin, and there was the response not of antagonism and self-justification but of consent to God's judgement upon human life. As Christ identified himself with alienated human beings at the cross, the response to his Father was as it had been throughout his life; he says 'Amen to the judgement of God'.[57] He confesses the rightness of the Father's viewpoint upon spoiled human existence. That very consent could mean nothing other than a sense of total forsakenness; consent meant in this case a breaking of communion with the Father, in being at one with those who were broken. Thus we can say that the cross of Jesus was a unique experience of human life, in its thoughts and emotions, for a forgiving God. Here God was drawn uniquely into human flesh because of the quality of the human response involved. At the same time the particular historical circumstances provided a theatre of typical human hostility to God, expressed by the other actors in the scene. The description of forgiveness as a journey of experience makes clear that God has always been entering into the human experience of death and alienation; the particularity of his suffering in the cross cannot be an experience of death for the first time.[58] But a God who journeys like this can enter a new depth of the human predicament when the one so intimately bound up with him, as a Son, himself suffers desolation and makes response from that abyss.

If the more personal model of forgiveness takes us further in the

---

[56] Ford, *The Lure of God*, p. 75.

[57] This is the memorable phrase of J. McLeod Campbell, a pioneer in exploring the power of feelings in Atonement, in *The Nature of the Atonement* (Macmillan, London, [4]1873), p. 118.

[58] This was the problem I drew attention to in ch. 1 above, pp. 3, 7–12.

direction to which process thought points us, so also does a more Trinitarian model of the being of God. In fact, we need such a model in order to justify our thorough use of a personal analogy for God. One Christian theologian employing process thought, Norman Pittenger, values the Triune concept of God as a 'unity of three interpenetrating modes of activity'; he regrets, however, that the mode of God's eternal self-expression (the Logos) should be described as 'son', because in his view this confuses the divine operation with the human son through whom it happens.[59] It has been my argument that this identity of sonship is precisely what is needed for Jesus fully to embody the divine aims of justice and self-giving love. It is because there is something 'son-like' about the active being of God that he can choose to identify himself with an obedient, human son. He wills to identify himself in act, and while I believe that this has inevitable implications also for his being (as W. Pannenberg has exhaustively shown[60]), our task here is not to develop a detailed Christology but to explore the meaning of this for the suffering of God. We have been thinking of the powerful effect upon us of encountering a God whose being is marked by the particular suffering of Jesus; while process thought can speak of Christ being 'alive in God' in the mode of the divine memory,[61] a more Trinitarian concept can speak of encountering God in a mode of sonship which is now inseparable from the human sonship of Jesus. The dedication to the Father of this unique human son, his openness in relationship to the Father, and to the future which the Father promised him, means that we cannot participate in the complex of relationships in which God happens without meeting the human personality of Jesus Christ.

6. THE FULFILMENT OF LOVE

God changes himself through suffering, out of his self-giving love for us which takes form in forgiveness. But if this be granted, a perplexing

[59] Pittenger, *The Lure of Divine Love*, pp. 132–3.

[60] Pannenberg, *Jesus—God and Man*, pp. 334–7; also 'Person und Subjekt', *Neue Zeitschrift für systematische Theologie und Religionsphilosophie*, 18 (1976), pp. 146 ff.

[61] e.g. Pittenger, *The Lure of Divine Love*, p. 124. The claim that entities (and persons) that have perished are 'alive in God' would be stronger if they were present to God in their subjective immediacy. Hartshorne believes this is possible and is what Whitehead meant by objective immortality (see e.g. *Creative Synthesis and Philosophic Method*, p. 110) but both these points are denied by Christian in *An Interpretation of Whitehead's Metaphysics* (ch. 4 n. 57 above), pp. 65–7.

conundrum about love emerges. God can only change to become more fully himself, to fulfil his being, as I have argued in our earlier discussion; can this really be called pure love, since it evidently benefits God? The conundrum then is this: is it more selfish of God to suffer or not to suffer? On the one hand, a God who does not suffer, remaining at rest in himself, undisturbed in his bliss and enjoying the fullness of self, presents a picture of 'a certain complacency in the divine love. . . . The word egocentricity may be too strong, but it points to the issue' (D. D. Williams).[62] But on the other hand, if God suffers in the full sense of being changed by his suffering, then he fulfils his own being in love since he cannot change to become any less himself. While God suffers to bring many sons to glory, he completes his own glory as well. Critics of the notion of a suffering God, such as E. L. Mascall, therefore object that if in creating and loving the world God is fulfilling himself, 'then creation, while it might be an act of love, would certainly not be an act of purely unselfish love'.[63] Surely, it is argued, the highest form of love is totally disinterested, a love in which the lover 'gains nothing for himself'. There is the conundrum: which is more selfish—a love which does not cost God suffering, or a suffering love which does something for God as well as for us?

The question may be sharpened up by considering what we mean by love. It is usual to distinguish betweeen two sorts of love in human experience, self-affirming and self-giving love. In self-affirming love, which is often called 'Eros', a person searches for an object of love to satisfy his own being; love is desire, and the object of desire fulfils the lover. The phrase 'she'll make a new man out of him' catches something of the power of Eros to bring out the true self, while the philosophers of the ancient world thought of it as a quest for beauty in the ultimate sense—beauty of art and of 'Soul'. In contrast, self-giving love, which is often called 'Agape', is understood as a person's spending himself freely and carelessly for the other person, sacrificing himself without any calculations about gain. At first sight it might seem that an impassible God who needs nothing but himself leaves no room for exercising 'Eros', and is a proper subject for showing 'Agape' as defined above. But things are not as simple as that. It should not be overlooked that in this image of God, which has never been better expressed than by Augustine, God has in fact an Eros kind of love, though admittedly

---

[62] Williams, *The Spirit and the Forms of Love*, p. 100.
[63] Mascall, *He Who Is*, pp. 108–9.

modified. God has no need to *look* for an object of desire because he eternally *desires himself*; he enjoys himself, and there is no movement towards self-realization through loving others because he *is* self-fulfilled. In the terminology of Augustine, he loves others because he already 'holds in possession'.[64] He certainly does not need man to fulfil himself, and so man is not the object of any search of love. Rather, God loves man by going to great lengths (and Augustine marvels at God's amazing humility in the incarnation) to invite man to share in God's own enjoyment of himself. This means that if the Eros kind of love is muted, though present, much more weakened is the self-giving kind of love; for God's giving of himself is simply his enabling man to share in his own love of himself within the Trinity, and this hardly seems like extravagant expense. In contrast, the image of a suffering God certainly presents Eros as a strong element in the being of God, for man is the object of God's searching love and fulfils his desire. God is 'the creative Eros' in Whitehead's telling phrase, sharing the adventure of the universe which 'reaps tragic beauty'.[65] But if Eros is strongly stressed, so is self-giving love, for in the quest for mankind God gives himself to the utmost, allowing himself to be constrained and hurt by the world. The quest of Eros is the journey of sacrificial and forgiving love.

Our conundrum is merely tightened by a simplistic distinction between Agape and Eros, but loosened by perceiving their involvement in each other. In the experience of human love, the highest self-giving love has in fact a proper element of Eros. E. Mascall, in his criticism of a suffering God, assumes that self-realization through loving others is always selfish, so that human love at its best is always mixed with a dross of self-interest; the divine love for the world must then, he supposes, be without such mixed motives. A. Nygren makes a similar judgement in his famous study of Agape and Eros, and it is a familiar motif of Protestant theology.[66] But in our human experience we find the truth of the gospel saying that 'he who loses his life . . . will gain it'; we

---

[64] Augustine, *De Trinitate*, 14. 8 cf. 15. 47, 10. 19.

[65] Whitehead, *Adventures of Ideas*, pp. 356, 380–1. According to Whitehead, God is Eros as the *object* of desire because he is also Eros as *subject*, desiring the realization of values, 'urging towards perfection' and beauty: ibid., p. 322.

[66] See e.g. Anders Nygren, *Agape and Eros*, trans. P. S. Watson (SPCK, London, 1953); K. Barth, *Evangelical Theology: An Introduction*, trans. G. Foley (Weidenfeld & Nicolson, London, 1963), pp. 196 ff.; Barth, *CD* IV/2, pp. 727 ff. A Catholic plea for the integration of Agape and Eros was made by M. C. D'Arcy, *The Mind and Heart of Love* (Faber and Faber, London, 1945), pp. 56–60, 185–93.

always become more truly ourselves when we give ourselves away, and we sacrifice ourselves only to find that we receive our selves back. We find ourselves as a mysterious by-product of losing ourselves; that is the pattern of the divine love itself, and is nothing to do with selfishness, which is a matter of setting out deliberately to realize ourselves as the main goal. E. Jüngel supplies a sensitive definition of the being of God as love, as an event of 'a still greater selflessness within a very great self-relatedness'.[67] In giving himself away to the beloved, any lover is related to himself anew. 'Lovers are always alien to themselves and yet, in coming close to each other, they come close to themselves in a new way.'[68] To recall the pattern of forgiveness, in winning the offender to himself the forgiver wins himself anew. So God himself has eternally new relationships within his (Trinitarian) being, on the basis of self-giving love to another, that is to his creation. To speak adequately of a relatedness between Father and Son which is so intimately bound up with God's relation to humanity and our response to him, it becomes necessary to talk of the Holy Spirit, or the Spirit of Love. We might then think of Agape as 'a power which integrates eros',[69] or better still of Agape as the healthy integration of self-realizing and self-giving love. If 'Agape' is going to stand for the human imitation of the divine love, we must not prejudge the issue by using the word as a label for one mode of love alone, even though it be the self-giving kind.

One particular aspect of human love makes this dialectic clear. Daniel Day Williams, in his magisterial study of the nature of love, perceives that self-love is itself nothing else than a desire to belong. The very core of selfhood is a wanting to 'feel at home in the world' and so to be in community; thus we have the paradox that selfhood (having our own being) is at base an offering of communication.[70] That the desire to belong is basic to self is seen in the nature of sin, which arises from anxiety that we do not belong, that we are not accepted. We try to overcome this anxiety by self-assertion, but in the most naked forms of this self-centredness there is still therefore a witness of our wish to participate in the lives of others. Though distorted into sin, or remaining at a submoral level, there is actually a reaching out to others in the assertion of self. Correspondingly, while this will be purified in self-giving love, the element of having our self will inevitably remain. This

---

[67] Jüngel, *God as the Mystery of the World*, p. 317 cf. pp. 298, 374–5.

[68] Ibid., p. 318.   [69] Ibid., p. 338.

[70] Williams, *The Spirit and the Forms of Love*, pp. 205–9.

observation supports the belief that love is essentially mutuality; there is a harmony between 'other-regarding love' and 'self-love'. Love calls for response. It is important to emphasize that it *calls* for it; it does not insist on response before it spends itself for another; there is no calculation on getting a return or a certain kind of return. The call to love our enemies implies that we shall not always gain a response, and the fact that love does not always win a response does not—as some maintain[71]—invalidate the view that Agape is mutuality. Self-giving love always *hopes* for a response, and the result (though not the motivation) is always a greater self-realization.

This human analogy underlines the conclusion that God is supremely selfless although—indeed, because—he fulfils his being through the pilgrimage of suffering love. It also reminds us of the element of communication in love that we have already noted. As Jüngel puts it, 'love is capable of the word',[72] and so is compelled to express itself through speech. We give ourselves away to others in words, enabling them to be themselves by words of encouragement, building them up by words which efface ourselves and thereby, in the mystery of love, finding ourselves as persons also. God, supremely, has given himself away to us in his word of self-expression. Above all, the cross of Jesus is the word in which he gives himself away most deeply. It is a self-communication in the non-verbal medium of suffering, which communicates where literal words cannot, so that we are persuaded through the very situation and the feelings of God. At the same time it *is* the point of origin of a story, which has power to give us the courage to be and to accept. As this story of suffering is retold in the preaching and worship of the church it gives new words to those whose meaningless suffering has struck them dumb. The bystander in the concentration camp at Auschwitz, suffering with no words to speak, was given words by the story of Jesus: 'God is here, hanging there on the gallows.'

---

[71] So Reinhold Niebuhr, *The Nature and Destiny of Man: Vol. 2, Human Destiny* (Nisbet & Co., London, 1943), pp. 72 ff., 86 ff. A more cautious view of Agape as mutuality, with reservations, is expressed by Gene Outka, *Agape: An Ethical Analysis* (Yale University Press, New Haven, 1972), pp. 279–85.

[72] Jüngel, *God as the Mystery of the World*, p. 298.

7

The Death of God

THE story is told of an American preacher in the 1960s who was asked
what he thought of the 'death of God' theology that was in fashion at
that time. 'God isn't dead', he is said to have replied, 'Why, I spoke to
him myself only this morning.' It was, however, no sufficient answer to
the challenge of that theological movement for one individual to profess
his own personal religious experience. For the 'death of God' theology
was not concerned with what individual instances of religious
experience might be; it was a dramatic way of speaking about a *general*
consciousness of loss of a sense of God. It observed that people on the
whole today are no longer naturally conscious of the fact of God, where
once in the past they had taken him for granted as part of their living
environment. Moreover, the 'death of God' theologians found a prime
reason for this in the fact that it no longer appears evident that God is the
necessary explanation for the world as it is. In an age of scientific and
technical progress, it is no longer an obvious assumption that God must
be the cause of events, either the immediate cause or even the final cause
behind the immediate.

I. IS GOD NECESSARY?

For a long time, of course, it has been clear to Christian theologians that
we cannot *prove* the existence of God from the state of the world, by
appealing, for example, to the intricate design of the creation (whether
snowflakes or the ozone layer) as evidence for a purposeful creator. The
Enlightenment had put paid to the kind of natural theology which
relied upon teleological and cosmological proofs. But now the 'death of
God' theologians were going one stage further. They observed that
there was something more to cope with than a recognition of lack of
proof for God; they pointed out the difficulty of even *thinking* of God as
responsible for events in the world. If God is not a necessary explanation
for the world in the sense of being a logical necessity, then what point is

there in even believing him to be either an explanation or a necessity at all? The problem was now not the proof, but the 'thinkability'[1] of God and the world as belonging together. If we do not have to resort to divine causation to explain the state of the world, then how can we think of God-and-the-world at all? The scientific challenge is also undergirded by the moral one of an increasing desire to be responsible for our own lives; in what sense can God be said to be a necessary explanation for human beings who have tasted the new wine of autonomous freedom? G. Vahanian, who was responsible for introducing the phrase 'death of God' into popular use in the 1960s,[2] detected the modern phenomenon that 'it is easier to understand oneself without God than with God'; there is a 'cultural incapacity for God'. This was the challenge laid against a merely personal and private affirmation that God was alive; the issue was a more global one than that, both in the face of a widespread consciousness of loss of God and in terms of the difficulty of thinking of God as 'necessary' for the world in its structures and history.

The force of the problem is illustrated by the difficulties that churches have in making harvest festivals relevant to the mass of people today. The problem is not just that most people are more familiar with factories than farms, and so would be attracted to offer thanksgiving to God if we replaced vegetables in the display by silicon chips. It is no more easy to think of God as the necessary explanation for a computer than for a row of carrots. Moreover, the difficulty of even thinking of God as a necessary explanation for the world is exacerbated when we consider the problems of suffering, especially in our own century.[3] Is God the reason for the miseries of Auschwitz, or the famines in North Africa? The 'death of God' theologians therefore concluded that since God is not necessary to make sense of the world as it is, there is no point

[1] The word is E. Jüngel's (Denkbarkeit), in his reflection upon the 'death of God' theology, in *God as the Mystery of the World*, pp. 12 ff., 138 ff. See also his earlier essay, 'Das Dunkle Wort vom "Tode Gottes" ', *Evangelische Kommentar*, 2 (1969), pp. 133–8 and pp. 198–202.

[2] Gabriel Vahanian, *The Death of God: The Culture of our Post-Christian Era* (George Braziller, New York, 1961), p. 147, cf. pp. 144–5.

[3] The famous cry of the poet Jean Paul, 'The Dead Christ proclaims that there is no God', stems from a sense that problems of human suffering cannot be resolved by words of religious comfort: see *Flower, Fruit and Thorn Pieces*, Book 2, trans. A. Ewing, (G. Bell, London, 1892), pp. 263–4. In his earlier work, William Hamilton found the theodicy question a stronger reason for the sense of death of God than the scientific challenge: *The New Essence of Christianity*, pp. 44–55.

in thinking of God's relationship to the world at all. We must face up to the fact that he is inactive, absent, and not available to us in any direct manner. He is 'dead' to the world in the sense of not being relevant to its ongoing life. 'Naïve theism, a direct childlike relationship to the Father above the starry sky, has become impossible.'[4] Indeed, some proposed, God himself wants us to do without him; he wants us to grow up into adults in a world come of age, not to be childishly dependent upon a father-figure. The props have been knocked away; it can even be said that God has done the knocking himself. For our own good, he has 'left us in the lurch'.[5]

Though the 'death of God' theology as a movement has itself died, the issues it raised are still with us today, often under other forms than the rather self-contradictory slogan that was chosen then. Theologians are more likely to speak of *our* 'taking leave of God' in the interests of our autonomy than of than God's 'leaving *us* in the lurch'.[6] But the question remains that if we do admit that God is not a logically necessary explanation for the world, is it nevertheless still possible to *think* of God and the world together, to think above all of God and human suffering together, to relate them in one perspective? Or must we simply retreat into the privatization of religious experience ('I spoke to him this morning'), and abandon the attempt to conceive of the Lordship of God in the world, having nothing to say about the phenomenon of a general loss of God-consciousness? Theology, I suggest, must live with the non-necessity of God for the world, and try to express the truth that 'God is more than necessary' (E. Jüngel),[7] that he is present and active in a world that we can explain quite adequately without him, but which an awareness of his presence can make more meaningful still. After all, the persuasive influence of God about which we have been speaking is a 'hidden factor' in any situation, and *an* explanation of the cause of events can be given without it. Further, I want to suggest that the mode of God's presence in a suffering world can only properly be understood as suffering and death; only the idea of a

---

[4] Sölle, *Christ the Representative*, p. 131.

[5] Ibid., p. 137. Cf. Bonhoeffer, *Letters and Papers from Prison*, p. 360: 'The God who is with us is the God who forsakes us'.

[6] The phrase 'taking leave of God' is defended by Don Cupitt in his book of that title (1980). In his more recent book, *The Sea of Faith* (BBC, London, 1984), the affinity between his thought and that of Nietzsche, to which I draw attention in this chapter, becomes more explicit: see esp. pp. 210–11, 267.

[7] Jüngel, *God as the Mystery of the World*, p. 34.

God who suffers death can answer the challenge that 'God is dead'. The theologians who spoke of 'the death of God' often appealed at some point to the idea of the suffering of God, but while they employed it as a motif for the absence of God from his world, I hope to show that we can appeal to it as a motif for his presence.

2. THE 'DEATH' OF GOD: LOSING AN IMAGE?

In fact, the rather diverse group of thelogians who hoisted the slogan that 'God is dead' meant a variety of things by it. In the first place, it could simply mean that a certain concept of God was now dead. It might merely be recognizing that a certain *kind* of human consciousness of God had been lost from European culture, the sense of God as a cosmic planning officer, an omnipotent monarch who orders all things irresistibly. That is, what is dead would be the traditional metaphysical idea of a God who heteronomously moves people and events around by his own will. This thinking is, of course, in line with our whole argument so far, and it formed a common departure point for the various 'God is dead' theologies. This leaves open the possibility that there is a God who is alive—a God who is vulnerable to the pain of his world, who is no idol sanctioning man's own urge to dominate others. The words of Dietrich Bonhoeffer were usually quoted with approval here, that God is not a *Deus ex machina* for solving needs and problems, but that 'God is weak and powerless in our world'.[8] In itself, to promote this idea under the slogan that 'God is dead' is less a piece of accurate thinking and more an advertising stunt; it is really a call for reform, asserting a stronger sense of immanence to balance transcendence.[9] What is dead is only a certain, however deeply accepted, image of God. God has always been like this; it is only now we have discovered it. But the leaders of the 'death of God' movement went on beyond this point in coming to the conclusion that *all* concepts of God are dead, or at least all concepts of God as having objective existence over against mankind, and that no human consciousness of such a God was possible at all. However, this apparently radical stance itself contained a variety of approaches, all of which are of interest for our theme.

[8] Bonhoeffer, *Letters and Papers from Prison*, pp. 360–1.
[9] Alistair Kee distinguishes between such a 'reformist' position and truly 'radical' theology: see *The Way of Transcendence*, pp. 65 ff., 110 ff.

3. THE 'DEATH' OF GOD: AFFIRMING HIS NON-EXISTENCE?

In an extreme form, the phrase 'God is dead' denoted that God did not exist as an objective reality, and had never done so. His 'death' was the cultural event of our realizing it. So Nietzsche sensed the spirit of his age which, like ours, no longer found the idea of God self-evident, and concluded, 'God is dead; God stays dead, and it is we who have killed him.'[10] But where to go from here? A. Kee usefully distinguishes between alternatives of 'reductionism' and 'escalation' built on the common foundation of the death of God in this radical sense.[11] 'Reductionist' views simply contract all talk of God into talk of humanity as we know it in our everyday experience, on the grounds that the values represented by God are only available in man himself. Nietzsche, for example, replaced belief in God with belief in the human value of the will to power. Man's own will replaces a divine will exerted over man. Kee himself does not actually classify Nietzsche as a reductionist, since Nietzsche, in the light of the death of God, calls for a 'revaluation' of all present human values; he challenges man to surpass his normal self, to go beyond the mere average and become the 'Superman'.[12] Now that God is dead, man is called to become more human than he had ever conceived possible, to voyage out onto distant seas, to venture out across the tightrope stretched over the abyss of non-existence.[13] But, as Kee also makes clear, Nietzsche bases this reaching beyond himself towards a higher life upon natural human values, and centrally upon the will to power. The label 'reductionist' does, I suggest, fit after all. More obviously still, Feuerbach offered another translation of God-talk into man-talk, with love for the ideal of the whole human species replacing the God of love.[14] The recent 'death of God'

[10] Friedrich Nietzsche, *The Joyful Wisdom*, Complete Works Vol. 10, trans. T. Common, ed. O. Levy (The Darien Press, London–Edinburgh, 1910), No. 125 (p. 169). Cf. *Thus Spoke Zarathustra: A Book for Everyone and No one*, trans. R. J. Hollingdale (Penguin Books, Harmondsworth, ²1969), pp. 296–7.

[11] Kee, *The Way of Transcendence*, pp. 184–8, 197–8, 224–5.

[12] Nietzche, *Thus Spoke Zarathustra* (ed. cit., n. 10 above), Prologue 3 (pp. 41–3): 'I teach you the Superman. Man is something that should be overcome.'; cf. *The Anti-Christ*, trans. R. J. Hollingdale, in *Twilight of the Idols and the Anti-Christ* (Penguin Books, Harmondsworth, 1968), No. 13 (p. 127), No. 61 (p. 184). See Kee, *The Way of Transcendence*, pp. 128 ff., 225 ff.

[13] These images are found respectively in *The Joyful Wisdom* (see n. 10 above), No. 343 (pp. 275–6), No. 124 (p. 167) and *Thus Spoke Zarathustra* (see n. 10 above), Prologue 4 (p. 43).

[14] Ludwig Feuerbach, *The Essence of Christianity*, trans. George Eliot (repr. Harper Torchbooks, New York, 1957), pp. 52–8, 153–4.

theologians liked to appeal to Nietzsche for his shock value (a reference to Nietzsche was virtually obligatory), but in fact they rarely went as far as his kind of atheism. The mood in which they came closest to both Nietzsche and Feuerbach was on the occasions when they interpreted love of God entirely as love of neighbour, even though they insisted that this neighbour-love was disclosed uniquely in the person of Jesus Christ.

The second type of thinking, which Kee identifies as 'escalation' and to which he himself subscribes, sets out to express an experience of transcendence without belief in an objectively existing God. This is also based upon the 'death of God' in Nietzsche's radical sense, though it rarely invokes the phrase. Instead of reducing the reality represented by God, it 'escalates' it to the 'infinite qualitative difference' from mankind, but ceases to refer this any longer to a personal God. Rather, it recognizes the presence of a mystery in human existence, the reality of a way of living which challenges all natural human values, and it finds what is revealed in Christ to be this way of 'secular transcendence'. It calls us to die to our natural judgements of value ('the way of immanence', according to Kee), and to be conformed to 'that which came to expression in Jesus Christ'.[15] Thus, Kee for example denies that all talk about God is dead; though all concepts of an existent God are certainly dead, God-talk is 'on to something' which must not be dismissed as meaningless.[16] There is an interesting contrast here with the approach of Paul Van Buren to theological language. Van Buren had confessed that he 'did not know how the word "God" was being used'. How untypical he was of the other 'death of God' theologians is shown by his comment on the basic text of the movement: 'Today, we cannot even understand the Nietzschian cry that "God is dead!". . . the problem now is that the word "God" is dead.'[17] Kee judges this opinion to be mere pragmatism, not to say doctrinaire positivism; the word 'God' can be seen, following Wittgenstein (whom Van Buren also professed to have learnt from) as having a 'grammatical' rather than a 'matter-of-fact' function, pointing to the reality of the way of transcendence which confronts mankind with the demand to die to its limited concerns and values.[18] It challenges, for instance, the elevation

---

[15] Kee, *The Way of Transcendence*, pp. 193–4, 197–8, 203–4. Also Don Cupitt, *Taking Leave of God*, pp. 85–9.

[16] Kee, *The Way of Transcendence*, pp. 190–1.

[17] Paul M. Van Buren, *The Secular Meaning of the Gospel: Based on an Analysis of Its Language* (SCM Press, London, 1967), p. 103.

[18] Kee, *The Way of Transcendence*, pp. 178–9, 196. A similar view is taken by

to ultimate value by Nietzsche of the human will-to-power, the danger of which was shown by the enployment (however unfairly) of Nietzsche's thought by Nazism. The word 'God', we might summarize, keeps the mystery open.

Now, both these types of thinking offer points of interest to our concern with the notion of a suffering God. We notice that they both fail to grapple adequately with the image of a suffering God, while at the same time actually opening the way to it with their critique of a monarchian God as the destroyer of human freedom. The 'reductionist' approach of Nietzsche, for instance, objects to the traditional notion of a God of pure infinity because this denigrates human life with its finitude and perishability.[19] On the one hand he asserts that finite beings cannot really conceive of a God who is purely infinite and imperishable; on the other hand the attempt to do so leads, he complains, to a religion of moral laws where joy in the sensual aspects of life is suppressed and mankind is always being made to feel guilty. These are shrewd insights into the failures of traditional metaphysics. But then, we might say, what of the picture of God as a suffering God? Would not this meet Nietzsche's complaint that the notion of God fails to touch the experience of perishability needed to be relevant to humankind? Nietzsche, as the son of a Lutheran pastor, is of course well aware of the Pauline preaching of a crucified God; indeed, in his own catchword he is exploiting the familiar echoes of the Lutheran phrase about the God who lies dead at the cross. Nietzsche's appraisal of the preaching of the cross is thus ambiguous. He does appreciate that it challenges the traditional metaphysical idea of the immutable God, but he cannot accept the manner in which God is joined to perishability in the message of the cross, that is in the mode of pain and suffering. For Nietzsche, the ultimate value is the will to power, and belief in the suffering and compassion of God saps the nerve of this will. Worship of a suffering God is a 'crime against life', and the cross of Jesus epitomizes the decline

---

Graham Shaw, *The Cost of Authority* (SCM Press, London, 1983): 'The only significance of the word "God" is its purely verbal function. . . . It is an integral part of human freedom, a means by which we transcend the given and transform ourselves and the world' (p. 282). God, in this view, is not an objective reality, but 'a word of the creative imagination' (ibid.).

[19] *Thus Spoke Zarathustra* (ed. cit., n. 10 above), 'On the Blissful Islands' (pp. 110–11): 'God is a thought that makes all that is straight crooked and all that stands giddy. What? Would time be gone and all that is transitory only a lie?' Cf. Prologue 4: 'What can be loved in man is that he is a going-across (*Übergang*) and a going-down (*Untergang*)' (ibid., p. 44), and 'Of the Preachers of Death' (pp. 71–3).

of life.[20] Though the image of an imperishable deity cannot actually refer to an existent God, it does have the truth of being a simile for the power which lies potentially in a perishable nature, that is in man's. For Nietzsche, with all his concern to reverence human life which is fleeting and perishing, the image of an imperishable God appears more useful than the image of a suffering God! So Zarathustra refers to the story of the death of God in the cross: 'Is it true, what they say, that pity choked him?'[21]

Nietzsche perceives very well that the cross of Jesus is 'against nature'; that is, the story of the weakness of God in the cross challenges the human value of the will to power. For this reason he rejects it. But Nietzsche's concern that we should be free from the domination of an overlording deity therefore ends in a transfer of this into patterns of human domination. Though it is not fair to regard Nietzsche as an early fascist, and we should take notice of Tillich's favourable translation of 'will to power' as 'urge towards life',[22] nevertheless his rejection of pity and sympathy as the path to the 'higher man' was attractive to later fascist movements. The political after-use of Nietzsche is an example of what might happen if we throw off the chains of an inhibiting God, without the check of the idea of a suffering God. His criticisms of pity as a form of decadence would have some validity if compassion were simply acquiescence in whatever sufferings were present in the world; we should not neglect his proper warning against a sentimental view of love and suffering. As a matter of fact, however, we have already seen that true suffering involves a rightful protest against the causes of

[20] For Nietzsche's critique of Paul's theology of the cross, see *The Anti-Christ* (ed. cit., n. 12 above), No. 47 (p. 163), No. 51 (pp. 168–9). Cf. *Beyond Good and Evil*, trans. R. J. Hollingdale (Penguin Books, Harmondsworth, 1973), No. 46 (p. 57): 'The Christian faith is from the beginning sacrifice . . . of all freedom, all pride, all self-confidence of the Spirit'. See the important discussion by Jüngel, *God as the Mystery of the World*, pp. 205–10, and also Karl Jaspers, *Nietzsche and Christianity*, trans. E. B. Ashton (Gateway, Henry Regnery Company, USA, 1961), pp. 22 ff.

[21] Nietzsche, *Thus Spoke Zarathustra* (ed. cit., n. 10 above), 'Retired from Service' (pp. 272–3): 'Is it true what they say, that pity choked him, that he saw how *man* hung on the Cross and could not endure it, that love for man became his Hell, and at last his death? . . . There he sat . . . world weary, weary of living, and one day suffocated through his excessive pity.' For a further critique of Christianity as a decadent religion of pity and sympathy, see *The Anti-Christ* (ed. cit., n. 12 above), No. 7 (p. 118).

[22] Paul Tillich, *Perspectives on Nineteenth and Twentieth Century Protestant Theology*, p. 205, cf. 197–8. Note also that, unlike Nazism, Nietzsche developed his theory of the will to defend the individual against collectivism: see e.g. *Beyond Good and Evil* (ed. cit., n. 20 above), No. 26 (p. 39).

suffering, and can have a powerful effect upon the personalities of others.[23] Nietzsche's scornful dismissal of the link between perishability and suffering in the cross receives a further critique by E. Jüngel,[24] who points out that Nietzsche appears to have a merely abstract view of the perishing of life. In our experience, it is normally linked with suffering and mourning; it is only in the ideal picture of Nietszche's Superman that perishable life is defined as the height of vitality.

Nietzsche does not, as Jüngel stresses, actually take the idea of the *death* of God seriously. It is a code for our inability to think of God, and 'it does not conceive of the idea that God *comes together* with death'.[25] We might add that it works this way for Feuerbach as well. Feuerbach finds the Christian message of a God who gives up his son to death for the sake of love to be an encoded witness that love is greater than God. According to Feuerbach's reductionism, the story that God sacrifices himself to love contains the hidden truth that love conquers God, so that 'God' is simply a word for human Love at its highest.[26] In this way he hopes to show that the Christian gospel contains the seeds of its own replacement by love of humanity. But we have seen that this by no means accords with the phenomenon of love as we experience it; sacrificial love establishes the personality of the one who loves, and so it cannot be used as a metaphor for the unreality of the divine personality. The reductionist arguments do not, then, properly consider the theme of a suffering God.

But neither do the current movements of thought which attempt an 'escalation' of religious experience without God, and which are in some ways the modern heirs of Nietzsche, though with a wider dimension of spirituality. These, we recall, replace belief in an objectively existing God with a faith in those values which call us to transcend ourselves by challenging the preoccupations of our natural life. Kee, for example, calls this 'the way of secular transcendence', and Cupitt 'the religious requirement'.[27] In fact, Kee accepts that there is a mysterious reality which invites and supports faith in this 'way' of life, and Cupitt suggests that there may be such a mystery, but both believe we cannot as yet

23 See above, pp. 88–90, 146, 157–8, 164.

24 Jüngel, *God as the Mystery of the World*, p. 207.

25 Ibid., p. 205.

26 Feuerbach, op. cit. (n. 14 above), p. 53, despite his talk of the 'suffering heart' of God (ibid., p. 62).

27 Cupitt, *Taking Leave of God*, pp. 85–6, 103–4; Kee, *The Way of Transcendence*, pp. 209–10 and Ch. 7 *passim*.

construct any satisfactory ontology for describing the mystery.[28] Here and now trust is to be placed in the 'way' itself, and the motivation is in the first place to free mankind from the immaturity and oppression of being subject to a monarchian God. Further, they understand the values of the transcendent life as a judgement upon natural human life with its egoism and tribalism, and so as a call to 'die daily' along the way of the cross.[29] Now, we are bound to ask, would not the idea of a suffering God correspond to these spiritual concerns and be the basis of the new ontology towards which they are questing? In his study, Kee does not directly address the image of a suffering God, but nearly a decade later Cupitt does, and dismisses it with vigour, not to say a Nietzschian scorn.

Cupitt's argument, like Nietzsche's, usefully points to weaknesses in popular notions of a suffering God, though it also shows the same misunderstandings about the true nature of suffering. Like Nietzsche he finds the only appropriate image of God to be of one who is impassible, immutable, and unconditioned, though of course such a 'religiously adequate God' cannot actually exist.[30] Unlike Nietzsche, however, who saw God as the personification of the natural human will to power, Cupitt finds him representing the 'religious requirement' which confronts us in life, and for which he believes a suffering God is an equally unworthy symbol. A major part of Cupitt's argument is that only the traditional image of an impassible God can symbolize the aspects of the religious requirement which judge our natural lives and summon us to victory over them. In calling upon our spirit, which is 'the capacity to exceed one's capacities', judgement is essential.[31] There are spiritual values which lay implacable demands upon us, which cannot be avoided, and which are unyielding in making us face up to the state of our lives. There is a 'categorical imperative principle' which, Cupitt believes, is aptly expressed by the image of an unchanging God and is badly expressed by the picture of a God who is all tears and sympathy. 'Is it not grotesque', he asks, 'that God himself now fails to achieve the religious ideal?'[32] However, this criticism fails to recognize the power of suffering; we have seen that even in human experience, to

---

[28] Kee, *The Way of Transcendence*, pp. 230–2 (the book ends poignantly on a footnote on this theme; see p. 234 n. 9); Cupitt, op. cit., p. 96.

[29] Cupitt, op. cit., pp. 87, 119; Kee, op. cit., pp. xv, xix, 144.

[30] Cupitt, op. cit., p. 113.

[31] Ibid., pp. 90–1, 102–3. See also now D. Cupitt, *Only Human* (SCM Press, London, 1985), pp. 189–91.

[32] Cupitt, *Taking Leave of God*, p. 112.

˙ feel another person's empathy with us is to become aware of judgement upon our situation at the deepest level. Moreover, this latter mode of judgement includes a sense of acceptance which is necessary for the transforming of personality. In contrast, we might certainly supplement the image of an immutable God with talk of love and forgiveness, but the basic image would not integrate these aspects within itself.

There is a second argument advanced by Cupitt which also raises fundamental questions about love and suffering. He finds the symbol of an impassible and immutable God proper because it expresses the true nature of the human spirit as 'sovereign' over its circumstances. The simplicity and aseity of God is a myth for the way in which the human spirit should be 'disinterested', 'freed from the constraints of natural necessity'.[33] Though Cupitt of course recognizes the need to be engaged in ethical struggle, he tips the balance towards a primary concern with self-possession as the basis for this outward action. Cupitt makes some proper criticisms of a flustered busyness which passes often for Christian ethics, but we have to decide whether the primacy he gives to calm is quite as admirable as the Buddhist tradition presents it. Our argument for a suffering love has been that it is through self-giving that we receive ourselves back in a new way. There is a truth in Cupitt's dictum that 'you cannot give it unless first you have it', but this needs interpreting by the experience that 'you will have it anew through giving'. This truth leads us to the image of a suffering God, who possesses himself through love for his creation. By his own desire, he holds himself in possession (a classic definition of being), not *before* but *through* self-communication.

The meaning which Nietzsche gives to the phrase 'God is dead', and its inheritance by some modern thinkers, thus leaves open (despite themselves) the question of whether the idea of a suffering God might fulfil the spiritual concerns expressed. We are obliged to Cupitt for the clarity with which the issue is presented: he concedes that the existence of a suffering God *is* conceivable in our modern age of autonomy,[34] but believes that the concept of such a God would not be adequate for religion. My contention has been that it is. The mainstream of the 'death of God' theologians in recent times certainly thought that it was also, and it is to their linking together of the suffering and the 'death' of God that we must now turn.

---

[33] Ibid., pp. 101, 117–19. This is reminiscent of Aldous Huxley's 'way of non-attachment', in *Ends and Means* (Chatto and Windus, London, 1937), pp. 3–6, 128–34, 297–8.   [34] Cupitt, *Taking Leave of God*, pp. 112–13.

4. THE 'DEATH' OF GOD: FACING UP TO HIS ABSENCE?

By their use of the phrase, the 'death of God' theologians were not affirming anything so straightforward as that an objective, personal God had never existed; they were registering their experience that in our time and culture he was absent. That is, they believed that no experience of God was possible at the moment, and that no concepts were at present available to talk about him (though, as we shall see, they did in fact make some exception for the language of suffering). In our day we must be content to be silent about God, and to wait for his return. Our task, they suggested, was to commit ourselves to the needs of the secular world and to the way of life embodied in Jesus, in hope that such a programme might result in due season in the return of God to our consciousness. In this stance of 'waiting', they swung between a hopeful mood that the Master of the House would return to his faithful servants, and the pessimistic mood of facing the fact that he was highly unlikely to do so. Thus in one mood Hamilton defines the radical position of the 'death of God' as being:

that there was once a God to whom adoration, praise, and trust were appropriate, possible, and even necessary, but that now there is no such God.[35]

Yet in another mood he can declare:

Our waiting for God, our godlessness, is partly a search for a language and a style by which we might be enabled to stand before him again, delighting in his presence.[36]

What is consistent here is a style of 'waiting for God', a keen sense of loss about 'not-having' God himself here and now, and not merely a relief at not-having the various idols which have supplanted God in the course of religious history—the idol, for example, of the cosmic monarch. Whether the absent God will reappear, whether we shall find the words and the frame of consciousness to meet him, receives variable answers. Now, it is of great interest for our theme that the members of this movement frequently wanted to describe the absence (the 'death') of

[35] William Hamilton, with Thomas J. J. Altizer, in the Preface to their compilation *Radical Theology and the Death of God*, p. 14.

[36] W. Hamilton, 'The Death of God Theologies Today', in Hamilton and Altizer, *Radical Theology and the Death of God*, p. 53, cf. p. 58. Expectation of the return of God is stronger in Hamilton's earlier work than his later; see the account of his theology by Thomas W. Ogletree, *The Death of God Controversy* (SCM Press, London, 1966), p. 30.

God in terms of the *suffering* of God. This was a language that they seemed, perhaps unwittingly, to find relevant for a God who appeared to have become otherwise irrelevant to an adult world.

Why should they have employed the motif of suffering to denote the absence of God? It seems first to have been an effective symbol for countering the traditional image of God as giver of orders, fulfiller of needs and solver of problems; a suffering God is not a God to be 'used' in these ways, and this opens up the hope that we might at some time find him again as one purely to be enjoyed for himself.[37] Second, the suffering of God was a symbol of commitment to the secular world which was a suffering world. Third, in the interim of 'waiting for God', Jesus Christ was 'the place to be'; his cross was not only the basis for ethics, in leading us to fellowship with all the forsaken in our world, but it also seemed to give a clue to the nature of the absent God.[38] All three of these motives are summed up in an early comment by Hamilton:

> To say that Jesus is Lord is to say that humiliation, patience and suffering are the ways God has dealt with man in the world, and thus are also the ways the Christian man is to deal with the world.[39]

The general point that the suffering Jesus offers a clue to the nature of the absent God is taken up specifically by two theologians of this movement, Dorothee Sölle and Thomas Altizer, as a basis for their whole thought. Sölle, in her theology of Christ the Representative, affirms that we can keep a sort of doubting faith in the absent God because Christ stands in for him in the world.[40] Like any act of representation, this entails both playing the role of the one who is represented, and being dependent upon him. Dependency is central, she explains, because a representative is not a total substitute for the one whose place he takes; his role can only be a provisional one. So Christ identifies with the unavailable Father, but is not identical with him. Though he faces up courageously to the fact that God is absent and we must all get along without him, he still depends upon the Father in the sense that he waits for him to attain his identity in the world and to declare himself fully.[41]

---

[37] Hamilton here commends Bonhoeffer's reference to a suffering God; see 'Dietrich Bonhoeffer', in Hamilton and Altizer, *Radical Theology and the Death of God*, pp. 122–3; cf. 'The Death of God Theologies Today', ibid., pp. 51–2.

[38] Hamilton, 'Thursday's Child', ibid., p. 100, where the suffering of Jesus is said to be 'even the meaning of divinity itself'.

[39] Hamilton, *The New Essence of Christianity*, pp. 102–3.

[40] Sölle, *Christ the Representative*, pp. 139–40. [41] Ibid., pp. 124, 128, 134–8, 144.

Christ represents the absent God by allowing him time to appear. . . . Because God does not intervene to establish his cause, Christ appears in his place. He comforts those whom, up to now, God has left in the lurch, he heals those who do not understand God, feeds those whom God allows to go hungry.[42]

Other people, following Christ, can also represent God by daring to admit his absence, and playing God for one another in circumstances of helplessness.[43] Now, suffering is at the heart of this representation, because 'dependence and the capacity to suffer are intimately related.'[44] Christ the Representative has a double agony to the end of time because he represents mankind before God and God before mankind, and is vulnerable in his dependence upon both. He suffers with people who have lost their identity, and is in pain for the God who has not yet attained his identity in the world. But this suffering of Christ is the clue to the suffering of God, who is in turn dependent upon his representatives. The absent Father is in pain because he has made himself of no identity for our sakes, removing himself from the scene and allowing himself to be represented by men, so that his existence in the world can only be partly realized. 'He put himself at risk, made himself dependent upon us, identified himself with the non-identical.'[45]

This account of the suffering of God as due to his absenting himself and being represented by others raises the question, however, as to whether in fact we can call God's act of withdrawal a kind of suffering.[46] To begin with, Sölle understands talk of God's removal of himself from the world as a mythological form of language; to say that God is 'not present' or 'has gone on a journey', or 'does not show up' is a necessary myth for expressing the fact that *we* do not experience God in our age as present and immediate.[47] If we ask what the 'death of God' theologians could possibly have meant by saying that there once was a God who could be worshipped, but now there is not, then this is one (though only one) clear answer. It is an event of human perception. But it is hard to see then how Sölle can speak so movingly of God's suffering withdrawal pains himself; these too must be a myth for our sense of loss. But even if we were to take the event of God's disappearance objectively, as a cosmic rather than a cultural happening, this still leaves

---

[42] Ibid., p. 137.   [43] Ibid., p. 142.   [44] Ibid., pp. 123–4.
[45] Ibid., p. 152; see pp. 147–9.
[46] We must also question Sölle's use of the notion of dependency. By a loop of argument, she totally equates Christ's dependence upon God with his dependence upon men whom he represents (ibid., p. 129). This seems to short-circuit and destroy the notion of representing an absent God.   [47] Ibid., pp. 132, 140.

the incongruity of saying that an absent God is the one who is suffering with the world, in being—as Sölle affirms—'mocked and tortured, burnt and gassed'.[48]

The other venture of building a theology upon the suffering Christ as the clue to the absent Father does envisage the withdrawal of God as a cosmic event. For Altizer, the death of God is not simply an event of human consciousness; rather, God has actually sacrificed his own essence, so that while he was once an objective reality distinct from the world, he no longer is so.[49] Altizer suggests that to meet the needs of man, as man grows in expertise and possibilities, God expends himself in love. In order to bring man to full maturity, in these latter times he has completely immersed himself into the world to liberate mankind from an alien deity. The incarnation of God in a human being, Christ, and then his submission to death in the cross, tells us that the nature of God is 'kenotic metamorphosis'.[50] God annihilates himself as an objective deity, yet we may hope that through our faithful 'waiting' he may emerge again in epiphanies of a new kind of spiritual life.[51]

In sketching this drama of the death of God, Altizer is drawing upon the thought of Hegel who had already employed the famous phrase that 'God is dead' before Nietzsche, though with a different intent from Nietzsche or, indeed, Altizer. For Hegel, God as Absolute Spirit comes to himself through the life of the world, which is relative spirit. God comes to true consciousness of himself through the consciousness of man. So he becomes truly himself by going out of himself, exposing himself to the nothingness of death by entering into a situation which is completely opposite to him, finite nature.[52] In this way God establishes his life as a truly vital life, not a mere static and selfish life that keeps itself to itself. The whole point of Hegel's thought is that God becomes truly himself by immersing himself into the world; he is the living God because he spends his being. But according to Altizer, though he appeals to Hegel, God simply loses himself into the world for man's sake. He has no Hegelian return ticket, though we may hope that there will be some kind of destination somewhere, in some vehicle or other. In a later

---

[48] Ibid., p. 151.
[49] Thomas J. J. Altizer, *The Gospel of Christian Atheism*, pp. 68–9, 89 ff., 102 ff.
[50] Ibid., p. 92.
[51] Ibid., pp. 120–2; also, 'America and the Future of Theology', in Hamilton and Altizer, *Radical Theology and the Death of God*, p. 33.
[52] G. W. F. Hegel, *The Phenomenology of Mind*, pp. 780–5. See further below, section 5, pp. 190–1 and ch. 9, pp. 233–6.

chapter we shall be looking further at the contributions of both Hegel and Altizer, but for the moment we must ask whether the cosmic drama portrayed by Altizer can really be called sacrifice and suffering. It seems to take the witness of Christ to a suffering God seriously, but it has little to say about the character of suffering as patience and persistence. It is an act of loving suicide, a moment of brilliant self-immolation, by which God is henceforth exempt from the continuous pain of living with the world.

5. THE DEATH OF GOD AS THE MODE OF HIS PRESENCE

The 'death of God' theologians therefore present us with an irony. They feel the problem of the relevance of God to our technological and suffering world, and their way of coping with this is to affirm the 'real absence' of God. They also find (at least from time to time) the symbol of a suffering God to be a powerful rebuttal of the monarchian God from whom we need to be liberated, but they cannot really express suffering in terms of absence, though it seems to fit naturally with the concept of 'death'. There is, however, another way forward in the face of the non-necessity of God in our world, and that is to take the death of God in the serious way that Hegel does. We can affirm that God's suffering of death is in fact at the heart of his vitality, that he is not irrelevant to our world of both science and suffering because he himself suffers death. His death is at the same time his living presence.

When Hegel in his early writings first spoke of the 'death of God', he noted the same widespread loss of awareness of God among people that the present-day theologians stress, and he called it 'the Speculative Good Friday'—a general sense of forsakenness by God.[53] But he went on to say that it corresponded to something within the life of God himself; it is not just that God has metaphorically 'died' in that people have lost awareness of him, but that God is the kind of God who actually opens himself to the assault of death, and it is precisely this that makes him the living God. That is, Hegel is using the phrase 'death of God' in the traditional sense of Lutheran theology—the exposure of God to death and his triumph over it. Good Friday is followed by Easter Sunday. In

---

[53] G. W. F. Hegel, *Faith and Knowledge*, trans. W. Cerf and H. S. Harris (State University of New York Press, Albany, 1977), p. 190. See commentary by J. Moltmann in his *Theology of Hope*, pp. 168 ff.

his later lectures, Hegel reflects thus upon the meaning of the cross of Jesus:

God has died, God is dead: this is the most frightful of all thoughts, that everything eternal and true does not exist, that negation itself is found in God. The deepest anguish, the feeling of something irretrievable, the abandoning of everything that is elevated, are bound up with this thought. However, the process does not come to a halt at this point; rather, a reversal takes place: God, that is to say, maintains himself in this process, and the latter is only the death of death.[54]

Hegel believed that the present age, when people were experiencing the hiddenness of God rather than a sense of direct contact with him, would pass as Good Friday passed into Easter morning, but this hope was based upon the nature of the being of God which was always facing and overcoming negation. He could wait not merely *for* the presence of God (like the recent 'death of God' movement) but *because* of the presence of God who embraces death and overcomes it in favour of life. He could wait for the human consciousness to become aware again of the Presence. The present-day German theologians who have a common concern to do 'theology from the cross' have unashamedly gone back to this insight of Hegel, meeting the contemporary challenge that 'God is dead' by recalling Hegel's use of the phrase, and tracing its lineage back to Luther. Despite reservations about Hegel's universal system, they revive his proclamation that the word of the cross, the word of death, touches the innermost being of God himself.[55] The story is worth remembering that on his sixtieth birthday Hegel's pupils gave him a medallion upon which was engraved an owl and a cross, showing the intimate connection between philosophy and the cross of Christ. On his death Hegel left it to Goethe, who was shocked by the suggestion that the cross entered so deeply into the structures of reality explored by the

[54] Hegel, *The Philosophy of Religion*, Part 3 (ed. Hodgson), p. 212, cf. p. 218.

[55] See, e.g., Jüngel, *God as the Mystery of the World*, pp. 63 ff. (esp. 94–5); Moltmann, *Theology of Hope*, pp. 169 ff., *The Crucified God*, pp. 34–6, 253–4; Christian Link, *Hegels Wort 'Gott selbst ist tot'*, Theologische Studien, 114 (Theologischer Verlag, Zurich, 1974), pp. 12 ff., 28 ff. Cf. Kitamori, *Theology of the Pain of God*, pp. 27 ff. Although H. Küng and H. Mühlen seek to distance themselves from Hegel, they develop their expositions of the death of God in dialogue with his; see Küng, *Menschwerdung Gottes*, pp. 207 ff., 622 ff., 665 ff., Mühlen, *Die Veränderlichkeit Gottes*, pp. 34–5. Helmut Thielicke also takes an ambiguous view of Hegel in *The Evangelical Faith*, Vol. 1, trans. G. W. Bromiley (T. & T. Clark, Edinburgh, 1974), pp. 259–64. See the review article by Allan D. Galloway, 'The New Hegelians', *Religious Studies*, 8 (1972), pp. 367–71. For a note on the 'Kreuzestheologie' movement in general, see above, pp. 12–13.

philosopher: 'To me it seems to open an abyss which I have always kept at a good distance during my progress towards eternal life', was his comment.[56]

Though later we shall have reason to criticize aspects of Hegel's dialectic, we should pay him honour for daring to plumb that abyss which Goethe shunned. With Hegel we may say that God is not dead with regard to this world precisely because he experiences death. God is not absent and not irrelevant in our age, because he knows for himself the experience of death. We began this chapter by asking how God and suffering are thinkable together; we can only think God and human suffering in one thought in the sense that God is *in* suffering, not that he is the necessary explanation for it. God is not the direct cause of suffering, and so he is not a necessary thought; but he is more than necessary in being in the situation of suffering. It is one thing for an individual to say, '*I* spoke to him this morning', and quite another to say that *they* spoke to him in the terror of Auschwitz and found courage to forgive their tormentors. God is not dead to our world because he participates in the death of our world.

Suffering is a mode of God's presence, and cannot be used as a symbol for his absence. Where the 'death of God' theologians tried to speak of an absent and a suffering God, they involved themselves in some incoherence. Sölle, for instance, approves the statement of Bonhoeffer that we are 'summoned to participate in the sufferings of God at the hands of a godless world'.[57] But she then goes on to assert that such a God is both absent from the world and helpless in it: 'The absent God whom Christ represents is the God who is helpless in this world.'[58] We must surely take issue with both these attributions to God. As far as 'helplessness' is concerned, we have already explored the peculiar power of the weakness of suffering, and that argument need not be repeated now. With regard to absence, if Sölle affirms this then she cannot also mean literally that God suffers in the world, since this requires his presence. Bonhoeffer, who was frequently appealed to by the 'death of God' theologians, does not in fact speak of an absent God; the message he reads in the story of the cross is that God forsakes us in order to be with us. We live in the world 'as if there were no God', in order to find God with us in the world; because he is not strictly needed, we enjoy his

---

[56] Cit. Karl Löwith, *From Hegel to Nietzsche*, trans. D. E. Green (Constable, London, 1965), pp. 14–15.

[57] Bonhoeffer, *Letters and Papers from Prison*, p. 361, See Sölle, *Christ the Representative*, p. 148.   [58] Sölle, op. cit., p. 150.

presence here and now. We do not have to hope for it in the misty future. 'Before God and with God we live without God.'[59]

Suffering and absence are incompatible, though not of course suffering and hiddenness. Here Kazoh Kitamori sees more deeply when he speaks of there being an immediacy of communication and fellowship in the sharing of pain. If God suffers with us, he cannot be closer to us. Yet at the same time the particular character of the pain of God means that he is hidden: 'A Father is never hidden so completely as when he sends his beloved son to suffer and finally to die. God is truly a "hidden God" in this sense.'[60] God is hidden, veiled in suffering. He is not available as the conclusion of a deductive argument from the conditions of the world, and certainly not from the suffering state of the world. But though hidden, he is immediately present and can unveil himself to us. When Sölle speaks of the suffering God as being mocked and tortured, burnt and gassed she really means only the suffering of those people who stand in God's place in the world, and God's suffering is limited to his allowing them to represent him.[61] She is, of course, right to say that God is never present in the world except through worldly mediation; he makes himself present through use of the natural, in the manner which Barth called 'sacramental objectivity' and which Rahner called 'mediated immediacy'.[62] We cannot know God in a purely immediate way, but there is *an* immediacy of God *in* the mediations of the world, including the forsaken and tortured ones. Failure to distinguish between absence and hiddenness leads to such curious phrases as 'the absent-present disturber God' (Hamilton) and 'God's absence as a mode of his being-for-us' (Sölle).[63]

The 'death of God' movement of two decades ago was not an erratic episode. It opened up essential issues, being rightly critical of a monarchian God, and rightly sensitive to the loss of awareness of God in our age. In a world which has lost the sense of the presence of God, I believe that there is an alternative to the sort of secular theology which

[59] Bonhoeffer, op. cit., p. 360.

[60] Kitamori, *Theology of the Pain of God*, p. 115; cf. p. 74 where Kitamori speaks of the 'mysticism of pain' as becoming 'immediately at one with God who denies immediacy'. He also appeals to the feeling of 'Tsurasa' in Japanese tragedy, the pain of a Father who sacrifices his beloved son: ibid., pp. 135 ff.

[61] Sölle, *Christ the Representative*, p. 151.

[62] See Karl Rahner, *Foundations of Christian Faith*, trans. W. V. Dych (Darton, Longman, & Todd, London, 1978), pp. 83–4; Barth, *CD* II/1, pp. 50–3.

[63] Hamilton, *The New Essence of Christianity*, p. 47; Sölle, *Christ the Representative*, pp. 131–2, cf. p. 141.

affirms either the non-existence or absence of a personal God. It is the sort of 'secular' (worldly) theology which takes seriously the actual death of God which he overcomes with life. This kind of thinking, while insisting upon the relative autonomy of man, also makes clear that his freedom as a creature is not absolute, for man cannot claim to be superior to God in being able alone to choose death. If God knows nothing of death, then human beings can show their final independence over against him by asserting that at least they can freely take away their own lives. Suicide, for example, is often a final fling of self-assertion against life and the Giver of life. If choosing death, in sacrifice or suicide, is only a human possibility then man is superior not only to the animals but to God. However, the belief that God can choose death in loving self-sacrifice makes clear that God is the Lord not only of the living but the dying. But, granted this, is it possible to ask *how* God can suffer death? Bonhoeffer was content to affirm the hidden presence of the suffering God in our world, and to direct his attention to the secular style of life we should adopt in the light of it, without defining more closely the manner of God's participation in death.[64] But I believe we owe it to a secular age to attempt to speak coherently about what it means to say that God suffers death, even if this runs the risk of appearing speculative.

6. HOW CAN GOD SUFFER DEATH?

Someone who has followed the argument so far, and allowed the advantages of speaking in our age of a suffering God, might object that nevertheless the concept of a God who suffers death is meaningless. Surely God cannot cease to exist and still be God, or even be subject to the threat that he could cease to exist.

1. The traditional way of giving meaning to the affirmation that God had suffered death in the cross of Jesus, where it was not simply deflected into the death of the human nature of Christ, was to diminish the significance of death. If we regard death as a mere physical barrier which man confronts, and which he just passes through like a doorway, leaving his body behind with his spirit living on, then there is less difficulty in saying that God suffers death when Jesus dies on the cross.

---

[64] These limits to what we might say were respected and indeed increased by the British theologian who learnt much from Bonhoeffer, Ronald Gregor Smith. See his *Secular Christianity* (Collins, London, 1966), pp. 167 ff., and *The Doctrine of God*, pp. 176 ff.

We might say that when the man Jesus died his biological organism perished, but his spirit simply lived on. So God, having made himself at one with Jesus stepped through the doorway of death with him; since God has no body he could not of course be touched by biological death. It is this sort of approach that Gregory Thaumaturgos has in mind, though he is uneasy about using the language of God's 'suffering' even in this attenuated sense, when he affirms that 'God enters the gates of death but does not suffer death'.[65] Yet this answer will not do, for we cannot treat death other than totally seriously. For us it is the end of the whole person, not just of an outer wrapping; we cannot any longer think, as did Greek theology, of an immortal soul as a built-in survival capsule.

For death as an ending in this complete sense, we have a great cloud of witnesses. There is the testimony of Jewish and early Christian thought to the idea of resurrection, which expressed the conviction that if man were to survive death, God had to do something new. In the face of the finality of death, God must create new life. The deaths of Jesus and Socrates have often been compared, Socrates urbanely discussing philosophy with his friends while the poison was taking effect, Jesus in a bloody sweat in the garden and crying out on the cross. The last words of Socrates were a swan-song, those of Jesus a scream. The difference was that Socrates thought of himself as stepping into immortality, released from the prison of this bodily world, while Jesus as a Jew thought of death as the utter negation of life.[66] The realism of this latter view has been confirmed by the witness of modern biology to the psychosomatic unity of the human being, an interpenetration of mind and body which fits with the Old Testament view of man as an animated body rather than the Greek view of man as an imprisoned spirit. According to Old Testament faith, a man died when the vital breath (*nepeš*) seeped out of his body, and if there was to be any future for him, God had to restore the breath of life.[67] That there is a finality about death as far as we are concerned, which throws us upon God for our hope, is underlined by pastoral experience also. Any Christian minister knows that even for people with the strongest faith there is a

---

[65] Translation in Mozley, *The Impassibility of God*, p. 68.

[66] See e.g. Oscar Cullman, *Immortality of the Soul or Resurrection of the Dead?* (Epworth Press, London, 1958), pp. 23–7.

[67] See Robert Martin-Achard, *From Death to Life: A Study of the Development of the Doctrine of the Resurrection in the Old Testament*, trans. J. Penney-Smith (Oliver and Boyd, Edinburgh–London, 1960), pp. 16–18, 31–3, 130.

sense of loss when loved ones die; funerals cannot be conducted in a triumphalist manner. If the fact of death is not faced up to and admitted in mourning, seeds of trouble are sown and suppressed grief may break out later in more dangerous ways. This experience tells us that there is no security in ourselves in the face of death; the future is not ready made and there are elements of the unknown for which we have to trust God.

Existentialist thinkers add an important witness to the finality of death; they suggest that we can gain knowledge of ourselves by facing up to the fact of death, but only if we face death as it really is, as a radical negation of life. Heidegger has emphasized that it is by having 'a sense of an ending' that we can bring some order to our lives.[68] Hegel, indeed, had already suggested that it was by dwelling with the negative, facing the fact of non-being, that we could gain further insight into being itself. Apart from the Golgotha of the spirit, mind is not mind. 'The life of the spirit is not one that shuns death, and keeps clear of destruction. . . it only wins to its truth when it finds itself utterly torn asunder.'[69] Paul Tillich similarly speaks of the 'ontological shock' of non-being; it is the threat of death that turns us to notice the possibility of meaning and support in life.[70]

Now, if 'death' has the impact of finality in such ways in our experience, to claim that God is relevant to our world because he suffers death in empathy with human beings must mean that God enters into a negative experience comparable to all this. There can be no triumphant striding through flimsy doors of death. In the next chapter we shall be exploring the claim that God himself encounters 'non-being', but in the meanwhile we must refuse the easy answer of demeaning the power of death.

2. A recent answer to the question of how God can suffer death is to distinguish between 'death' and 'dying'. J. Moltmann in his book *The Crucified God* has proposed a Trinitarian concept of death *in* God as opposed to the death *of* God.[71] His idea is that both the Father and the Son can be said to suffer, but in different ways. God the Father suffers death, that is the experience of the death of the Son or bereavement, but not dying. The Son suffers dying, but not death since no one who dies

---

[68] Heidegger, *Being and Time*, pp. 280, 285 ff.

[69] Hegel, *The Phenomenology of Mind*, p. 93; cf. pp. 780 ff., 808.

[70] Tillich, *Systematic Theology*, Vol. 1, pp. 207 ff.

[71] Moltmann, *The Crucified God*, p. 207, cf. pp. 217, 243. In his later book, *The Trinity and the Kingdom of God*, Moltmann silently drops this distinction, speaking simply of 'the death of God': see e.g. p. 80.

can know the event of his own death. So the loss of the Son by the Father can be distinguished from the loss of the Father by the Son; the Father, for instance, is the father of all the forsaken while the Son is the Lord of the forsaken since he has been forsaken too. Our forsakenness and death can then be taken up into the experience of God because the death of Jesus is *in* God, not *of* God. While the Father suffers death he does not die, for it is not his own death but that of the Son.[72] The loving grief of the Father, however, means that the suffering of the Father is no less than that of the Son; the cry 'Why have you forsaken me?' could equally well be rendered, 'Why have you forsaken yourself?'

This argument has, for all its insight, some severe flaws. In the first place there is something odd about the way Moltmann denies he is talking about the death 'of' God. Moltmann is anxious to assert that he is not being patripassian or even theopaschite;[73] God, he avers, cannot die but can only suffer death, a death that happens within the event of the Trinity in the relationships between Father, Son, and Spirit. He criticizes Barth for not being Trinitarian enough in saying that the Father suffers rejection in the Son, which amounts in the end to saying that he dies in the Son. In order to avoid the result that the Father ceases to exist, Moltmann points out that Barth has to distinguish between the immanent and the economic Trinity, God in himself who does not suffer, and God in the world who does.[74] Moltmann's solution is that while God in himself *is* the God who is in the world, he does not die but only experiences the death of the Son. But this looks like a case of the swiftness of the hand deceiving the eye: is not the Son also God in Moltmann's own thought? He continually speaks of 'God the Son' and describes the event of the cross as one 'between God and God', saying starkly that 'God abandoned God'.[75] The word 'God' for Moltmann stands for the whole event in which a Father gives up a son and the son is given up (or forsaken). Thus, on Moltmann's own terms, 'God' must be

---

[72] Moltmann, *The Crucified God*, p. 243.

[73] Ibid., pp. 203, 243. In *The Future of Creation*, p. 73, Moltmann offers the term 'patricompassionism'.

[74] Moltmann, *The Crucified God*, p. 203. See my comments on Barth's Trinitarianism, ch. 5, pp. 114–23.

[75] Moltmann, op. cit., p. 244, cf. p. 241. The incongruity of reserving the word 'God' for the experience of the father is not overcome by Moltmann's urging us to distinguish between the divine nature *in genere* and the second person of the Trinity 'in concreto' (ibid., p. 235). For further criticism of Moltmann's language here, see Richard Baukham, 'Moltmann's Eschatology of the Cross', *Scottish Journal of Theology*, 30 (1977), pp. 301–11, esp. pp. 309–10.

in the dying of the Son as much as he is in the experience of death by the Father. He cannot say that God happens as this event of giving-up and being-given-up, and then propose that only the giving-up is the experience of God. Moreover, the result of forcing apart so widely the experience of dying (the Son's) and the experience of death (the Father's) is that there is too much conflict in God. There is an over-stress upon 'God against God', so that we come near to the point which Moltmann has rightly been trying to avoid—one God who suffers with us and one who inflicts the suffering. It almost looks as if God the Father rejects the Son in order to provide us with someone who can sympathize with us in our predicament.

It is perhaps misleading to distinguish between the experiences of death and dying in this context anyway. Though of course it is true that the dead do not experience their own death, while the living experience the deaths of others, the living also in a certain sense experience their *own* death. As Max Scheler has pointed out, we discover about death from experiencing our own 'directedness towards death'—that is, the awareness of time running out.[76] We know that there are limits in life, deadlines against which we measure how much time we have left; so we experience death as that final deadline, the last limit in the face of which we feel time passing. The death of others is an offence against love, partly because we can no longer spend time on them, and they no longer have time for us. Death, whether our own or another's, is known experientially as loss of time; it is transience or perishing. Now, the dying are as yet to be counted among the living, and so the dying Jesus does, in one sense, experience his death. It is not then entirely true to state, as Moltmann does, that 'Jesus suffers dying in forsakenness but not death itself'. Given the perichoresis of the Father and the Son that Christian doctrine has always maintained against polytheism, it seems even less meaningful to distinguish so sharply between the experience of 'death' by the Father, and 'dying' by the Son, and to refuse to speak of the death 'of' God. It may be, of course, that Moltmann denies the experience of death to Jesus because he is drawing implicitly upon an anthropological assumption that we cannot gain experience of death from knowledge of our own being, but only from grief at the deaths of others;[77] but he does not actually argue this case, and anyway it seems

[76] Max Scheler, 'Tod und Fortleben', *Schriften aus dem Nachlass*, Vol. 1, (Der Neue Geist Verlag, Berlin, 1933), pp. 14–15, 25–6. See also Heidegger, *Being and Time*, pp. 279 ff.

[77] This is argued by Karl Löwith, against Heidegger; see e.g. 'Zu Heideggers

difficult to sustain in the face of our sense of perishing. Moltmann's argument, nevertheless, does make clear that those who 'suffer death', in the sense of suffering from death, are the living, among whom we must include those who are dying but not yet dead. So we arrive at a third possibility for expressing the meaning of the death of God, which does not attempt to avoid patripassianism.

3. We may speak of the 'Death of the living God', as does Eberhard Jüngel in an essay of that title.[78] That is, God suffers death in the sense that he suffers an encounter with death, but he is not dead. He enters the realm of death, but death has not won the victory in the conflict with him; God has maintained his life. Jüngel claims that death has therefore now become 'a phenomenon which belongs to God', since God has used death to define his own being.[79] He did this in choosing to define himself as God in the dead Jesus; by identifying his being with a crucified man he defines himself as a God of sacrificial love, and at the same time opens himself to the death which befalls Christ. In maintaining his life in the face of this death, it is now the death 'of' God, possessed by him as part of his being.

In the event of the death of Jesus, the being of God and the being of death so strike against each other, that the being of the one puts into question the being of the other. This is the meaning of the Lutheran hymn, 'O Great need, God himself lies dead!' This reciprocal putting of each into question ends with the rising of Jesus from the dead.[80]

To make sense of this rather mythological language we must understand that Jüngel perceives death to be a simile for non-being, and the chief instance of it. The validity of this talk of the 'death of the living God' therefore finally depends upon whether meaning can be given to the idea of an assault of non-being upon the being of God. That will be the subject of the next two chapters. Our concern here is with asking how closely we can compare the divine experience which we call

Seinsfrage: Die Natur des Menschen und die Welt der Natur', *Aufsätze und Vorträge* 1930–1970 (Kolhammer Verlag, Stuttgart, 1971), pp. 195–6. Moltmann has in fact appealed to Löwith's argument verbally, in his unpublished lecture series 'Glauben und Wissen', Tübingen, 1977.

[78] See Jüngel's earlier articles 'Vom Tod des lebendigen Gottes' (ch. 1 n. 36 above) and 'Das dunkle Wort vom "Tode Gottes" ' (n. 1 above); now also see extensively *God as the Mystery of the World*, chs. 2 and 3 *passim*.

[79] Jüngel, 'Vom Tod des lebendigen Gottes' (ch. 1 n. 36 above), pp. 120, 123. See *God as the Mystery of the World*, p. 364.

[80] Jüngel, 'Vom Tod des lebendigen Gottes', p. 121.

'suffering death' with our human experience of death, so that the God who suffers like this is relevant to our world. We have seen that our experience of death is actually an experience of perishing, since only the living (and the dying) experience death. Here Jüngel helpfully insists that we *can* think of God as 'perishing', for he points out that perishing has a positive, even creative, side to it. Our experience of perishing is not only the negative one of 'directedness towards death' or a tendency to non-being; it is also positively the basis for new possibilities. It is negative, for instance, as the experience of time running out to which we have referred. But the passing of time also makes possible new steps in relationship with others. Perishing is a process of becoming; 'that which is ontologically positive about perishing is the possibility'.[81] We only usually think of perishing in a predominantly negative way because of the triumph of non-being over it. However, in essence perishability is the 'struggle between being and non-being', and does not have to end in nothingness. So we think of God as involved in our typical human experience of death, that is as the momentum towards nothingness. As Creator *ex nihilo* God is always relating himself creatively to nothingness in costly love.[82] If we compare this insight to that of Moltmann, we might say that far from being exempt from 'dying', God does experience 'dying'—at least in the sense of perishing; but he is certainly not dead.

This account does have an ambiguity, however. Jüngel does not think that God first becomes this kind of God at the cross; rather, this particular event reveals what the nature of God has been all the time.[83] However, Jüngel also speaks of God as finally defining himself in this particular dead man. The particular and the universal might be brought together better if we were able to think of God as involved in different intensities of perishing, as we have frequently thought of his experiencing different intensities of suffering. Though this might sound absurd, in fact the concept of death is exactly suited for it as we are used nowadays to thinking of death not as a single point but as a process. In our own experience it is hard to say when dying begins, and through advances of medical technology we are all used to the idea that dying can be survived and reversed, though the actual state of being dead cannot. There are, as it were, grades of dying, some more serious than others. The Old Testament notion of death as a power which reaches

[81] Jüngel, *God as the Mystery of the World*, p. 213.
[82] Ibid., pp. 217–23.
[83] Ibid., pp. 218, 218 n. 64.

into life expresses this process very well; the Psalmists could think of themselves as descending into Sheol and yet recovering because death is the weakest form of life, when all vitality has ebbed away.[84] Any assault upon vitality is already dying, an entrance into the valley of the shadow of death, a plunging beneath great waters.

To speak then of God's suffering death is to speak of his exposure to the negation we feel in the experience of 'perishing', and while God suffers this universally in sympathy with all mankind, we can conceive of his going furthest at one point. In identification with one dead man, Jesus Christ, who was most intimately bound up in relationship with him, he reaches the point of greatest weakness and most extreme negation, putting his being most at risk. He goes furthest into the valley of the shadow of death and yet is not consumed. Such a complete identifying of himself, in act and being, with a human son is possible because there is an eternal Sonship within the relationships of God's Triune being. Jesus suffers dying and death, and has died. The Triune God suffers dying and death also, but is not dead; this is the victory that is witnessed to in the resurrection of Jesus from among the dead.

7. THE DEATH OF GOD AS A BREAKING OF RELATIONSHIPS

Before we go on to enquire into the notion of an aggressive 'non-being', we should consider one aspect of the power of death which further illuminates the views mentioned above, as well as the difference between them. In our human experience the destructive power of death consists to a large degree in its relationlessness. If we wilfully fragment our relationships with our own selves, with others, and with God, then death takes on the threatening aspect of acute loss of relationship. The millionaire who lives in an island suite on the top floor of first-class hotels, breaking off all links because he does not trust anyone, dies a death of isolation and loneliness. The finality of death puts the seal on self-sufficiency; we are left only with ourselves. Indeed, the impact which death has upon us, the living, bears witness to the basic nature of life as consisting in relationships. It is in the face of death that we perceive that our life is not fully under our control and so not totally our own; we discover that we stand at a distance from ourselves and need to be related to ourselves. Not fully to possess the ground of our being means that we can live only in relationships, and our relatedness to our own self is part of a nexus of relationships which include our neighbours

---

[84] See Psalms 18: 5 ff., 30: 3, 23: 4, 32: 6, 40: 2, 55: 4 ff., 88: 4 ff.

and God.[85] Our aim, then, living in the face of death is to maintain the relationships in which we stand, and to which death itself bears witness. When we dissolve and distort these relationships, then death becomes the most extreme point of relationlessness.

Now God, by his own sovereign will, holds himself in possession *through* relating himself to his creation. That has been the argument of our study. To claim that God experienced the most intense kind of human death in the cross of Jesus is to suggest therefore that he reached the furthest pitch of relationlessness. We have already considered the element of forsakenness in the experience of the crucified Jesus, its extremity arising from contrast with the uniqueness of communion which Jesus enjoyed with the Father in his life and ministry.[86] Into this desolation the Father enters in an identification of feeling. Now, the doctrine of the Trinity seems to offer a way in which we might think of this experience of relationlessness, and thus death, as entering into the being of God. 'Trinity' expresses the idea that God is complex Being, happening as a communion of relationships, or movements of being which are characterized by their relationships to each other. This leads to the thought that we might think of death (or 'perishing') as separation entering into the heart of God's relationships with himself. The way in which exponents of 'Kreuzestheologie' today have put it is this: in the cross of Jesus God is most differentiated and yet most at one.[87] There is 'identity in difference'. These theologians find signficance here in the New Testament witness to the various modes of 'giving' by the Father and the Son.[88] On the one hand, God cannot be more acutely differentiated, and even 'divided' from himself,[89] in that the Father gives up the Son to death while the Son gives up *himself*; there is one who forsakes and another who is forsaken. On the other hand,

---

[85] This link between our relationships to self and to others is argued above, pp. 171–3.

[86] See above, ch. 6, pp. 162, 168.

[87] e.g. Mühlen, *Die Veränderlichkeit Gottes*, pp. 32–3, Moltmann, *The Crucified God*, p. 244, Jüngel, *God as the Mystery of the World*, pp. 372, 375 n. 3.

[88] The key New Testament term is *paradidonai*; see Rom. 8: 32, Gal. 2: 20, cf. Rom. 4: 25, John 3: 16. Reference is frequently made to the study by Wiard Popkes, *Christus traditus: Eine Untersuchung zum Begriff der Dahingabe im Neuen Testament* (Zürich, 1967), esp. pp. 286 ff.

[89] Moltmann, *The Crucified God*, p. 244 and Jüngel, *God as the Mystery of the World*, p. 374 both use the language of 'division' or 'separation' within the Trinity; Mühlen, op. cit. p. 32 (to whom both the others are indebted for this thought), keeps to the more cautious term 'differentiation', though he does speak of the Father's 'dismissing' the Son.

Father and Son cannot be more deeply united than in their common spirit of giving-up, or loving surrender and this unity of nature is the Holy Spirit of love. The cry of forsakenness at the cross unveils the Trinitarian being of God; the traditional unity of substance means being one in love, and the threeness of person means being differentiated through experience of death.

But while for some theologians the doctrine of the Trinity offers a conceptualizing of God's experience of relationlessness, for others the notion of a cleft within the inner being of God presents insuperable problems. Karl Barth resisted any view of a division within God himself; he was willing to speak of God's enduring his own contradiction (i.e. judgement) of sinful humanity on the stage of human history, but not of God as contradicting himself within his own inner life.[90] The God who enjoys a harmony of relationships within his being can certainly suffer a history of contradiction when he takes on human experience. God can do this if he chooses. But Barth did not want to speak of an eternal division within the very being of God because this would not adequately preserve the unity of God as the one Lord. Strict followers of Barth have thus been critical of the way that theologians such as Moltmann have taken the cry of forsakenness from the cross as the point of departure for building a total doctrine of God.[91] They make an important point when they complain that a stressing of division within God runs the danger of stating a nonsensical disruption of the wholeness of God. Indeed, I have already suggested that Moltmann exacerbates the danger by making a wide division between Father and Son in terms of one who suffers death and another who suffers dying. Moltmann himself seems a little uneasy that in his thought the being of God might be broken up eternally, and so offers a contrast between what God is now and what he will be. While the division between Father and Son in the cross is the very nature of God at present, in the future all contradictions will become analogies.[92] Suffering will be replaced by doxology; God has a future wholeness. The problem with this kind of contrast, however, is that it makes the future too static;

---

[90] Barth, *CD* IV/1, pp. 185–6, cf. IV/2, p. 401. According to Barth, the history of the covenant is prior to God's involvement in the history of contradiction.

[91] See e.g. Bertold Klappert, 'Tendenzen der Gotteslehre in der Gegenwart', *Evangelische Theologie*, 35 (1975), pp. 203–5, and 'Die Gottverlassenheit Jesu und der gekreuzigte Gott' (ch. 6 n. 32 above), pp. 50–1.

[92] Moltmann, 'The Revelation of God and the Question of Truth', in *Hope and Planning*, trans. M. Clarkson (SCM Press, London, 1971), p. 16.

all the features of an unmoving God that Moltmann rightly criticizes are postponed into the eschaton, rather than there being, in the words of J. Macquarrie, a 'continuing consummation'.[93] Moltmann, however, must be listened to in reminding us that the inner being of God cannot be sealed off from the vast desolation and the breaking of relationships that are visible at the cross of Jesus, and at many other crosses in our world.

A valuable attempt to think of the relationlessness of death entering into the very heart of the Trinity, but in a way that also conceives a convincing amount of unity in God, has been made by Heribert Mühlen. He presents what he calls 'the personological basic law', observing that in human relationships we only become really close to someone when we experience the other person as different from us.[94] As our encounter with someone deepens, we become more and more aware of the uniqueness of the other, and only from this awareness of his difference from ourselves can the relationship take on a new depth of nearness. Nearness leads to a sense of difference, and only this can lead to an even closer nearness. So by analogy in God, who is an event of relationships, we may say that:

The distinction of the divine persons, in so far as they are distinct modes of being, is so great that it could not be conceived of as greater, while their unity is so intensive that it could not be conceived of as more intensive.[95]

That is, the modes of God's being are so closely united with each other that they must be infinitely different from each other. This is a rather contrasting opinion to the view that the love of Father for Son can be simply described as 'love of like for like'.[96] Mühlen appeals to Basil among the Cappadocian Fathers, who spoke of God's unity as being an indivisible community, and yet thought that the divine persons had such particularity as persons that each had 'no commonness whatever' with the others.[97] Mühlen also recalls Aquinas' verdict that the non-identity of each person with the other meant that the idea of a 'person' of the Trinity could not be a universal; admitting there is no 'real common-

---

[93] Macquarrie, *Principles of Christian Theology*, p. 356.

[94] Mühlen, *Die Veränderlichkeit Gottes*, pp. 25 ff., *Die abendländische Seinsfrage*, pp. 53 ff.

[95] Mühlen, *Die Veränderlichkeit Gottes*, p. 26. Cf. A. Von Speyr, op. cit. (ch. 6 n. 16), pp. 60–1: 'Their estrangement [i.e. of the Father and Son] is a form of their supreme intimacy.'

[96] Moltmann: see my critique of his view, ch. 5. above, pp. 138–9.

[97] Mühlen, *Die Veränderlichkeit Gottes*, p. 26.

ness', Aquinas strains hard to find what he calls a 'conceptual
commonness'.[98] We might conclude from this, with one modern
adaptor of Aquinas, that the single word 'person' is only a stopgap, as it
were; one really needs the three different words Father, Son, and Spirit
to do justice to the difference between the distinct modes of being in
God.[99] Now Mühlen is suggesting that one can take this differentiation
between the modes of God's being as a basis for the relationlessness that
enters into God's being as he experiences death. There is a backcloth, or
groundbass of differentiation in the being of God which can allow for a
new kind of differentiation. There is room to experience death without
breaking up the unity of the divine being. In exposing himself to death
in the cross of Jesus, the Father now experiences the distinction of the
Son from himself in a new and unexpected way:

... The Father and the Son, in so far as they are persons, have absolutely
nothing in common. From this fact the cry of forsakenness of Jesus on the cross
gains its inconceivable depth. This cry of Jesus shows in the first place that the
Father's delivering up the Son to sin in the history of salvation dismisses the Son
into a differentiation that is so great it could not be conceived to be greater,
namely into a full God-forsakenness. At the same time, however,—and this is
important for an understanding of the divine sameness of being—there is
shown in this absolute differentiation the absolute nearness between the Father
and the Son, which is equally so great that it cannot be thought to be
greater.[100]

  Mühlen is in effect suggesting that the 'otherness' of the Father from
the Son makes possible the 'alienation' of one from the other, while they
remain one in the spirit of loving surrender. We ought frankly to admit
that this runs quite counter to Aquinas, who was very careful to allow
'other' (*alius*) as proper to the persons, but not 'alien' (*alienus*), to allow
'distinction' (*distinctio*) of persons but not 'difference' (*differentia*).[101] It
may be true, as Mühlen suggests, that the Fathers would have allowed
more difference between the persons of the Godhead if they had not
defined unity of being as indivisible essence rather than as relationship.
But the fundamental reason for extending 'other' into 'alien' within the
being of God can surely be only the free choice of God; by this own

[98] Aquinas S.Th. 1a 30. 4; terms translated as in Blackfriars Edition, Vol. 6 (1965),
pp. 79–81.
  [99] Rahner, *The Trinity*, pp. 104 ff.
  [100] Mühlen, *Die Veränderlichkeit Gottes*, p. 32.
  [101] Aquinas S.Th. 1a. 31. 2.

desire, his relationship with himself ('otherness') is inseparable from his relationship to his creatures in all their estranged state ('alienation'). This comes to an intensity in the person of Christ, so that we can speak in a Trinitarian way of a willing identification of God's eternal mode of Sonship with the man Jesus, who belongs within the sphere of alienated humanity. Thus the 'other' in God is felt as the 'alien'. This is an idea we shall later be working out more carefully, with the aid of reflection upon the symbol of non-being. We must take care, then, not to fall into imagining that the experience of alienation within God can be simply and logically extrapolated from the abstract notion of the uniqueness of a 'person' of the Trinity; at the heart of the link between 'other' and 'alien' is the free desire of God and the scandal of the cross.[102]

However, the dialectic between difference and nearness to which Mühlen alerts us might well lead us to question the language of 'God casting out God', or 'God abandoning God'. The point is not that God expels one mode of being out of himself, but that in the face of death, God willingly defines his relationship to himself anew. The complexity of his being makes it *possible* to receive the experience of death—in the sense of perishing—into himself. He enters with feeling into the human situation of relationlessness, and can identify with that situation because he himself exists in relationships which have 'otherness', requiring (in the words of Aquinas) 'relative contrast' in order to be distinct.[103] God thus experiences his own being in a new way by entering into human desolation and estrangement. In fact, we might even dare to say that for God this is a movement into the unknown. Here we begin to see something of what it might mean to say, as we did above, that God's being is put into question in the conflict with death. It surely cannot mean that there is any possibility of God's ceasing to exist; to speak of God's *becoming* non-being would be to use the word 'God' in a way that ceased to have any useful meaning. There is, nevertheless, a risk for God in the way he experiences his own being in encounter with death, since what this might mean cannot be exactly predicted ahead of time, any more than can the agony of forgiveness of which this exposure to death forms a part. The cross of Jesus cannot be a 'new' experience for God in

---

[102] Mühlen sees the scandal (op. cit., p. 30), but tends towards an extrapolation of the cross from the being of God, in seeing the contrast between Father and Son in terms of an I–Thou relationship, with the Spirit as 'we-being'. This particular concept of 'persons' in God as an I and a Thou can veer towards tritheism, or at least ditheism. See above, p. 140 and n. 108 there.

[103] Aquinas *S.Th.* 1a. 30. 2; cf. 1a. 28. 3.

the sense that God for the first time experiences an alienation within his own life, though talk of God's 'casting out God' implies just this. Rather, the cross is 'new' in the extreme to which God goes in experiencing alienation within his own relationships. It shows he is the living God, vital in his own victory over death, and relevant to an adult and yet broken world. Because he experiences death, God is not dead.

8

The Alienation of the Creator

'No one really believes in his own death.' This observation by Freud[1] points to our experience of death as something alien to our existence, indeed so alien that it seems altogether apt to call it 'nothingness' or 'non-being'. Freud's epithet rings true; while we know intellectually that all men die, we often do not feel it emotionally as something that will happen to us. In war the soldier believes that somebody else's name is on the bullet; in peace the motorist thinks of accidents as happening to nameless 'victims'. We should beware of dismissing this phenomenon as mere self-deception or a refusal to face facts. The feeling, irrational as it is, is a sign that death is utterly strange to us, since we cannot relate to it or find ourselves in it.[2] It is the nature of man to try to find his way out of every situation, and in thinking through possible routes out of a problem he 'finds himself' or establishes his identity. But we cannot escape death; we cannot master it and so we cannot recognize ourselves within it. It is alien to us, as an offensive opposite to life. But, as E. Jüngel points out, because we cannot escape death it is equally true that death belongs intimately to us. 'No one can rob us of our death', for it belongs to our life from the beginning, and (as we have already seen) we orientate our sense of passing time by its boundary. Thus we experience death as something, in Jüngel's fine phrase, 'most alien and yet most our own'.[3] It is strange to us, and yet also reaches back into our life with an estranging power.

A second piece of human experience that makes it apt to speak of death as 'non-being' is the one made familiar to us by such existentialist novelists and philosophers as Sartre and Camus.[4] They vividly portray the feeling of meaninglessness which can beset us in life, and which

---

[1] Sigmund Freud, 'Thoughts on War and Death' in *Complete Psychological Works*, Vol. 14 (Hogarth Press, London, 1957), p. 289.
[2] Further on this, see Jüngel, *Death*, pp. 6–7.   [3] Ibid., pp. 6, 9.
[4] See Helmut Kuhn, *Encounter with Nothingness: An Essay on Existentialism* (Methuen, London, 1951), pp. 9–12, 24 ff.

seems to be summed up by the brute fact of death. Death is a ceasing to be, and in its horizon we can see the tendency of all of life to slip away from a meaningful 'something' to 'nothing'. These writers expose our sense of human finitude as being something which we find threatening and disturbing; they suggest that we suffer from a general anxiety, a feeling of not being at home in the world, and death stands as the epitome of this loss of meaning. 'Death removes all meaning from life', claims Sartre.[5] Death brings us the shock of non-being, the unimaginable state of not being 'I'.

Such experiences as these, which may come and go as fleeting moods, seem to make it suitable to speak of death as the simile and chief example of a non-being which is woven into our living. From these phenomena, some theologians have extrapolated an ontological scheme in which existence is understood as a conflict between being and non-being, where being is constantly threatened by an aggressive power of non-being.[6] This idea of a hostile *nihil* has seemed to fit in neatly to the long philosophical tradition of *mē on*, or relative non-being, as distinct from *ouk on*, or absolute nothing.[7] The former, which was originally understood in Greek philosophy as the unrealized potential to be a particular thing, has come to be regarded as an active opponent of being, resisting it and so operating as a kind of negative influence in life. More particularly to our purpose now, it has seemed to some theologians that there is scope here for talk of God's redeeming activity in the world, together with the suffering it costs him, as an encounter with non-being. Theologically, this may be urged as being the true meaning of 'the death of God'—a confrontation of God as Being with an alienating power of non-being for which our best simile is 'death'. The suffering and victory of God over non-being is seen as coming to sharpest focus in the event of the cross of Jesus Christ, making a modern version of the *Christus Victor*

[5] Jean-Paul Sarte, *Being and Nothingness* (English trans., Methuen, London, 1957), p. 539.

[6] Theologians employing this scheme of thought who are surveyed in this and the next chapter include Barth, Tillich, Berdyaev, Macquarrie, Jüngel, and Altizer. Moltmann unfortunately fails to make clear how the 'nihil' which comes into being through God's self-limitation becomes a hostile and annihilating nothingness: see his study *God in Creation*, pp. 86–93.

[7] The classical expression of this idea is in Plotinus, *The Enneads* 1. 8. 3: 'By this Non-being, of course, we are not to understand something that simply does not exist, but only something of an utterly different order from Authentic-Being': trans. S. MacKenna, Revised B. S. Page (Faber and Faber, London, [4]1969), p. 68. The precursor is Plato, *Parmenides* 160c–162a.

theory of the early Fathers, with the enemy of non-being replacing the devil.

Some critics have suspected, however, that this alliance of the meontic tradition with existentialism is simply a careless use of language. Phenomena of experience (a feeling of meaninglessness, a sense of the strangeness of death) have been translated into ontology without any metaphysical justification. John Hick, for example, protests that a valid poetic metaphor of experience ('non-being') has been mistakenly reified into a hypostasis: 'such language becomes deprived of its symbolic power . . . if it is understood literally'.[8] I believe, nevertheless, that talk about God's exposure of his being to non-being *is* a coherent way of talking about God's experience of suffering, and in particular the acute suffering which can be called in simile 'the death of God', though we must take Hick's challenge about reification seriously. We must ask searching questions about the various nuances of the term 'non-being', and guard against sliding carelessly from one meaning to another. The topic is notoriously difficult to discuss, as 'nothingness' appears to be 'the night in which all cats are grey'. We are inclined to say with Shakespeare's King Lear that 'nothing can come of nothing', until we recall that the play proves him wrong.[9]

There are two main routes which theologians have taken to arrive at the idea of a hostile non-being which we, and God himself, confront. Both routes begin from the concept of mere or absolute non-being (*ouk on*), and move towards the nothingness of an aggressive and alienating kind (*mē on*). By commenting upon them we should, I hope, be able to see the indispensable value of the symbol of non-being for expressing the suffering of God, when used with due care. In this chapter we shall be considering the first argument, from the nature of creaturely existence, and in the next chapter we shall consider the second, from the differentiation of the divine being. These directions of thought are often intertwined, and need to be separated out for analysis, but they basically represent ways from below and from above.

[8] Hick, *Evil and the God of Love*, p. 191. Similarly, Adrian Thatcher has shown up inconsistencies in Tillich's dialectic of Being and Non-Being: see *The Ontology of Paul Tillich* (Oxford University Press, 1978), ch. 3 *passim*.

[9] Reduced to nothingness at the end of the play, stripped of his royal robes and with Cordelia dead in his arms, Lear understands more about himself than he did at the beginning. See the comments of George I. Duthie on the suffering of Lear, *The New Shakespeare* edition of the play, ed. G. I. Duthie and J. Dover Wilson (Cambridge Unversity Press, 1960), pp. xxxiii–xxxviii.

I.   HOSTILE NON-BEING AND CREATURELY EXISTENCE

When thinkers begin on the road to non-being from the notion of existence itself, they usually define 'existence' as a 'standing out' (*ek sistere*) from nothing, where nothing is understood in the first place as absolute non-being.[10] This is so far only a way of stating the traditional doctrine of *creatio ex nihilo* and the nature of creatures as finite, limited by non-being. There is nothing hostile about this kind of non-being, and when death is taken as the epitome of nothingness in this sense, it is a neutral boundary to life. Though it cannot strictly be said to be a created thing, as it is nothing, it is a limit which God ordains as part of his good order. Yet this recognition of non-being and death as harmless negation must pass over into an admission of their alien nature, and our route of thought to such an aggressive non-being might travel by either a shorter or a longer path.

The short cut of thought makes a very quick leap from the fact of absolute non-being to the fact of hostile non-being. Tillich, for example, inherits the tradition from Plotinus that non-being as potential being resists actualization. It is not yet, and resists coming to be. Now, since an existent thing which stands out of non-being stands in it at the same time (one's mind is drawn irresistibly to the picture of a paddler wading in a black sea of nothingness), Tillich argues that it is also standing in a non-being which all the while opposes being. This is relative non-being, or non-being characterized by its dialectic with being.

An actual thing . . . remains not only in absolute non-being, as its finitude shows, but also in relative non-being, as the changing character of its existence shows . . . Existing can mean standing out of relative non-being, while remaining in it; it can mean actuality, the unity of actual being and the resistance against it.[11]

Thus we quickly arrive at the proposition that just to exist is to be threatened by alienating non-being, typified by death.[12] E. Jüngel seems to start from quite a different point when he defines non-being as

10 See Macquarrie, *Principles of Christian Theology*, p. 60; Tillich, *Systematic Theology*, Vol. 2, p. 22; Jüngel, *God as the Mystery of the World*, pp. 223–4, cf. p. 121. Note that this appeal to *creatio ex nihilo* need not imply a temporal beginning to creation: see above, ch. 3, pp. 75–6.

11 Tillich, *Systematic Theology*, Vol. 2, p. 23.

12 To be fair, Tillich has other routes to this destination as well, which we shall be examining below.

a total *lack* of potential, since 'nothing can come of nothing'. But then he concludes that all existent things, with a potential for becoming, must always be being sucked into the annihilating whirlpool of loss of potential in which they stand. Standing in non-being they are always being swept by a destructive undercurrent of non-being, so that life is a struggle between possibility and impossibility, being and non-being.[13]

We ought, I suggest, to resist this temptation to take a short cut from existence to alienating nothingness (*mē on*). Hick's general objection to the whole meontic tradition seems valid at this point at least. A poetic description of the anxieties of life and our situation of perishing (which we have already seen to have an existential truth[14]) has been reified into a conflict with an objective power. This drama seems to offer an easy transition to the life of a suffering God; once non-being is established as an objective force it can be suggested that as Creator from nothing God too is exposed to this hostile nothingness in which existence stands; in moving out from himself to make existent things, he confronts non-being. However, the experience of non-being in this sense is so bound to being a creature that it is hard to see how God could experience it in anything but an imaginative leap of sympathy.

There is a longer path from the situation of creaturely existence, created *ex nihilo*, to an encounter with nothingness, and this does provide scope for the belief that God exposes himself to alienation and even perishing (though, as we have stressed above, God has not *perished*). This is the path to non-being which goes by way of the tradition of evil as *privatio boni*, or deprivation of the good.[15] The argument goes that since man is created from nothing (absolute non-being, *ouk on*) he is changeable; raised to communion with something— the good—he can slip back towards nothing by simply turning away from the good. Evil is thus loss of the good, a sliding from being, and can be described as 'nothing' since it is merely parasitic upon the created good. In the words of Augustine, 'Nothing evil exists in itself, but only as an evil aspect of some actual entity.'[16] There is hence a relative or dialectical non-being, akin to the Platonist *mē on*, which prevails when anything defects from the mode of being proper to it in God's creation.

[13] Jüngel, *God as the Mystery of the World*, pp. 216–19.

[14] See my account of death as the experience of perishing, ch. 7 above, pp. 197–9.

[15] Tillich appeals to this move in support of his argument, but he does not travel the whole way patiently, resorting to the short cut of thought I mention above: see *Systematic Theology*, Vol. 1, p. 209.

[16] Augustine, *Enchiridion* 4. 13–14.

We ought to be clear, if we follow this scheme of thought pioneered by Origen, Athanasius, and Augustine,[17] that the nothing from which the creature is raised is not itself *mē on*, but is simply absolute non-being (*ouk on*); it is the *slipping back* towards this non-being which may be called *mē on*, or hostile non-being.

Such a turning from God by the creature means that the natural negative of death is now felt in a different, more threatening way. Allied to the alienating force of non-being (*mē on*), it has become another kind of death. 'The sting of death is sin.' One kind of nothing has become another. In the terminology of Karl Barth, death as a boundary of *das Nichts* (nothingness) has become 'the ultimate irruption and triumph' of *das Nichtige*—'that alien power which annihilates creaturely existence and thus discredits and disclaims the Creator'.[18] An example of the way this alienating power reaches back into life is its effect upon our experience of work. If a man makes the works of his hands the final value in his life, and thereby declines from the good, or turns away from God as his true ultimate concern, then he is bound to find that death makes a mockery of all his achievements in bringing them to an end. The story of the judgement of Adam and Eve as told by the Yahwist in Genesis 3 expresses this insight; the narrator does not say that the couple would never have known death if they had continued to obey, but he does make clear that after their disobedience they now felt death as a destructive force, making all their work into thorns and thistles.[19] Death takes on its hue from non-being. On the other hand, death is a conditioning factor for the arousal of relative non-being; the limit of death makes us anxious as it reminds us of our finitude, and this forms the temptation (not in itself a sin) to escape our anxiety by trusting in ourselves and our works rather than in God. In this way, neutral non-being and its focus in death is the departure point for aggressive non-being.

Now, our concern here is not directly with framing a theodicy built on the 'free-will defence' of God's goodness. Our purpose is to ask whether this path to a hostile non-being in human life also maps out the

---

[17] e.g. Origen, *De Principiis* 2. 9. 2; Athanasius, *De Incarnatione* 4–5; Augustine, *De Civitate Dei* 11. 9.

[18] Barth, *CD* III/3, p. 310. For Barth, *Das Nichtige* takes form in sin and death but cannot be exhausted by them. It is distinguished from *Das Nichts* by its universal scope of negation, in opposing the totality of the created world (ibid., p. 302).

[19] My comment follows the exegesis by Gerhard Von Rad, *Genesis: A Commentary*, Old Testament Library, trans. J. Marks (SCM Press, London, [2]1962), p. 92, cf. p. 98.

suffering of God in a coherent way. First, does it make sense of the notion that God himself encounters non-being as an objective enemy when he participates in the experience of the world? Second, does it allow us to speak of God's suffering the kind of alienation that can as aptly be called 'death' as the nothingness we experience? I believe that the idea of the emergence of non-being as *privatio boni* satisfies both these criteria, if we accept that it means God encounters something 'new' in his creation. Something has been introduced into creation by the creature with its slipping away from the divine purpose, and so God encounters something strange to his life. Non-being is thus objectively real, not as a personality or hypostasis of any kind, but as something which arises in interaction between God and his world, and which therefore befalls God as he enters empathetically into creaturely experience. We have seen that suffering cannot be simply something one does, though active suffering is one way of dealing with suffering when it occurs; genuine suffering befalls the victim like a fate. Suffering is endured as well as performed. So we may say that God suffers in falling victim to a strange and alienating experience that meets him as he enters human experience. Non-being is objectively real in that it happens. Thus God confronts non-being, and the simile of death is most apt because—like our human awareness of death—he encounters that which is 'most alien and yet most his own'. It is his own, as springing from his creation; it is most alien, in that it arises from the side of the creation itself. As we discovered in our earlier discussion of the transforming power of suffering, the tragedy of human sin is central to the suffering of God, and it is curious how much debate goes on about God, suffering, and non-being without reference to it.

For all this to be coherent as talk about God, two further things must be the case. First, we must be able to accommodate the notion of God's meeting what is 'strange' to him, with his being God and having perfect knowledge. Our previous discussion about the true meaning of the omniscience of God should have made clear that talk of God's having new experiences is by no means incongruous, and there is no need to repeat the argument here.[20] Second, the slipping of creation away from the good cannot be a logically necessary consequence of God's creative activity if it is to be felt as strange by the creator. Though a logical inevitability would make the experience 'most his own', it would hardly be 'most alien'. For the rest of this chapter we shall therefore be

---

[20] See above, ch. 4, pp. 93–8.

exploring and justifying the claim that the creation introduces something distorting into the situation from its autonomy, and that this act of the creature is felt by the Creator as a real struggle with non-being.

2. THE ALIENATION OF THE CREATOR BY MORAL EVIL

If God is really estranged by something in his creation then the breakdown of creation towards non-being cannot be a logically necessary consequence of his creative act. This applies in the first place to the slippage of human moral decline. As Tillich claims, 'Creation and fall coincide . . . but it is not a logical coincidence . . . the leap from essence to [estranged] existence is the original fact . . . it has the character of a leap and not a structural necessity.'[21] In his talk of a 'leap' here Tillich is appealing to what we must identify as a basic paradox in human life, though he himself rejects the term 'paradox' in this context, referring instead to the 'riddle' of existence.[22] One side of the riddle is the pressure of finitude upon man, with all its conditioning factors, making him anxious and tempting him to sin, so that failure to trust God seems in practice inevitable. For this universal human predicament the creator must be held responsible. On the other side there is man's moral responsibility which makes him a person, and which makes it possible to respond to the divine lure towards living with a courage to break all false securities and to trust God. Again, Reinhold Niebuhr puts the paradox succinctly when he says that sin is 'inevitable, but not in such a way as to fit into the category of natural necessity', and that 'sin is natural for man in the sense that it is universal, but not in the sense that it is necessary'.[23]

This paradox arises when Christian theology wants to do equal justice to various features that it sees as givens in the human situation, among them the feeling of man's moral freedom, the observation that mankind has an inherent tendency to decline from the good, and an underlying belief in the goodness of God. This paradox cannot be evaded, either by a belief in a single-point historical fall which denies any responsibility to God (Augustine's solution), or by a view that sin is necessary for human moral development, which cuts the Gordian knot in the opposite way. Theology must meet the challenge of trying to

---

21 Tillich, *Systematic Theology*, Vol. 2, p. 50.   22 Ibid., pp. 45, 107.
23 Niebuhr, *The Nature and Destiny of Man* (ch. 6 n. 71 above) Vol. 1, pp. 279, 257.

make this paradox at least reasonable (since it cannot admittedly be reduced to complete rationality); but our concern here is the more limited one of establishing that there can be no concept of God's encountering non-being unless the paradox is held to.

The 'riddle' of the fall makes clear that God experiences the negation of life that arises from human sinfulness in the same manner as we experience death, as something 'most alien and yet most our own'. The human decline from the good is most alien to God because it is not a necessary result of creation, yet it is in a sense his own in so far as the conditions of finite creation makes the possibility a very strong one. Only a creator who gives his world real freedom, so that the breakdown towards non-being is inevitable in practice but not necessary in logic, can experience a death which is 'most alien and yet most his own'. Another way of stating this paradox is to speak of creation as a 'risk' for God, which is a constant theme in recent theology. John Macquarrie, for example, makes the idea of a risk central to his theology of God as Being going out of himself to let other beings be:

God risks himself, so to speak, with the nothing; he opens himself and pours himself out into nothing . . . in giving himself in this way, he places himself in jeopardy, for he takes the risk that Being may be dissolved in nothing.[24]

Macquarrie is thinking here of creation as a movement from unity of Being to glorious diversity, a loving overflow of Being into a fecundity of differentiation, as God lets many beings be.[25] It is the quality of finite beings to have a boundary of non-being, and so Macquarrie deftly combines the danger of their slipping towards this non-being with God's own exposure of himself to non-being as he goes out of himself into creation. This latter sort of idea (which has Hegelian undertones) will be examined in greater detail in our next chapter, but for the moment we could notice the implications of the language of 'risk'. A risk logically excludes necessity; things *can* in theory go the other way. However, the nature of finite creation is such that the risk is not an even-handed one. Macquarrie admits the tragic element in creation, that 'natural evil and human sin are alike unavoidable possibilities in a creation the end of which is good'.[26] The phrase 'unavoidable possibility' nicely catches the paradox of which we have been speaking, though Macquarrie himself seems to shift the weight towards a logical necessity by using the terms 'inevitable' and 'necessary' as synonyms,

[24] Macquarrie, *Principles of Christian Theology*, p. 256.
[25] Ibid., pp. 215–17.   [26] Ibid., p. 267.

particularly in regard to natural evil.[27] It helps to keep the risk a real one if we distinguish, as Niebuhr does, between the practical 'inevitability' that free and finite beings will plunge towards non-being, and a logical 'necessity' that creation obliges them to do so. If we are to keep hold of the creature's responsibility before God, and indeed God's own suffering of the alien in his creation, we must keep in play both risk and inevitability. In Macquarrie's own words about natural evil, this is

an *inevitable* accompaniment in the creation of a universe of particular beings. It is not a fate chosen, but a *risk* taken [my italics].[28]

A further dimension of non-being, of great significance for the suffering of God, arises from the riddle of creation and fall. We have seen that when the creature takes the leap into estrangement this brings self-destructive consequences, as the limits of his environment, including death, are felt as distorting and alienating forces. Boundaries become enemies; neutral non-being (*ouk on*) is experienced as hostile non-being (*mē on*). But this experience of alien non-being can also be understood as judgement, or God's wrath, in so far as God is confirming the structure of justice in which sin brings its own inherent rewards. 'The wages of sin are death.' Broken relationships run out remorselessly into a death which is sheer isolation, and God consents to this process. The judgement of God is not a penalty inflicted from outside, but his underlining of the reaction of life itself, as 'the injured life appears as a hostile power against the trespasser' (Hegel).[29] Karl Barth usefully describes this process as God's speaking his 'no' to man's life; when the creature says no to God, he experiences the negatives of life as threats, and these are thus carriers of God's 'no' to him.[30] The Old Testament prophets spoke of the wrath of God as his turning away his face, and a giving up of men to the results of their own works.[31] Karl Barth aptly sums up the tragedy like this: 'My turning from God is followed by God's annihilating turning from me.'[32] Now, this process of judgement bears directly upon God's own exposure to non-being. When he participates in the world he experiences non-being not only as the alien action of his creatures, but also as coordinate with his own verdict upon life. If God experiences the effects of his own 'no' as he participates in

[27] Ibid., pp. 257–8.   [28] Ibid., p. 258.
[29] Hegel, *Early Theological Writings*, p. 230.
[30] Barth, *CD* II/2, p. 13; III/1, pp. 257 ff. 330 ff.
[31] See my discussion in ch. 2 above, pp. 23–5.
[32] Barth, *CD* IV/1, p. 253, cf. p. 173.

our estrangement, this exactly matches our experience of death as something 'most alien and yet most our own'. These consequences of human sin are God's own in so far as they accord with his justice, but they are most alien in that they are the outworking of an act of his creation which is strange to him. Thus Tillich writes:

He cannot remove these consequences; they are implied in his justice. But he can take them upon himself by participating in them.[33]

Similarly, Barth speaks of God's suffering the assault of *das Nichtige* in terms of suffering his own judgement. The cross of Jesus discloses that

in Him God has entered in . . . not merely affirming the divine sentence on man, but allowing it to be fulfilled on Himself. He, the electing eternal God, willed Himself to be rejected and therefore perishing man . . . The One who lives for ever has fallen a prey to death. The Creator is subjected to and overcome by the onslaught of that which is not (*das Nichtige*).[34]

Barth stresses that there is no question here of Christ's offering satisfaction to the wrath of God the Father. He judges that such presentations of the doctrine of the Atonement are 'quite foreign to the New Testament.'[35] His point is that by facing *das Nichtige*, 'The nothingness to which man has fallen victim as a sinner', Christ has nullified it. By 'treading the way of sinners to its bitter end in death', Christ has 'broken, judged, refuted and destroyed' *das Nichtige*.[36] God has negated the negative, saying no to nothingness by taking it in himself, so that there is always a 'yes' to man hidden under his no. Indeed, the malignant nature of nothingness can only be seen in retrospect of the fact that it has been negated in Christ; *das Nichtige* 'has its reality and character as the adversary whom God has routed as His own enemy'.[37] This last phrase ('His own enemy') indicates Barth's concern to think of *das Nichtige* as a phenomenon which I have characterized as presenting an experience to God which is 'most alien and most his own'. Ironically, however, when Barth considers the origin of *das Nichtige* he defuses it of real alienation, despite his definition of it as 'this most dreadful of all foreign spheres' to which God gives himself.[38] If the suffering of God is to be a coherent idea, we must take the alien nature of this nothingness with utter seriousness.

An enquiry into Barth's view of the origin of *das Nichtige* shows up

---

[33] Tillich, *Systematic Theology*, Vol. 2, p. 201.   [34] Barth, *CD* IV/1, pp. 175–6.
[35] Barth, *CD* IV/1, p. 253.   [36] Barth, *CD* III/3, p. 367.
[37] Barth, *CD* III/3, p. 366.   [38] Barth, *CD* IV/1, p. 175.

some of the issues involved in trying to think of this kind of non-being as really alien, but not dualistic. Barth does not want to say that *das Nichtige* exists by the will of God, as this would seem to question God's goodness. On the other hand, he refuses to conceive of it as a pre-existent reality and power, as in Platonic dualism.[39] The obvious alternative, to which I have been subscribing, is to think of its existing solely because of the free will of the creature, arising from his free lapsing from the good. However, Barth fears that this would endow man with an inherent power against God, putting evil 'more or less outwith the providence of God', which he damns as Pelagian.[40] Barth's solution is to declare that *das Nichtige* exists as that which God does not will; God's rejection of it gives it reality, as 'his own enemy'. It has 'the existence of that which does not exist', and this is why it is called nothing.[41] What this amounts to is that God's will is indirectly the basis for that which is hostile to God; destructive nothingness is God's alien work (*opus alienum*) and it results from God's negative willing, or non-willing, rather than from his positive will. This nothingness came to be as that which God rejected when he elected his good creation; by saying 'no' to it he has given it objective reality.[42] Though it is an alien element in the creation, Barth claims that 'it cannot be envisaged and apprehended as outside the jurisdiction of the fatherly rule of God'.[43]

This is a fascinating re-running of the meontic tradition, along the route of deriving hostile non-being from the very notion of existence, but in the special Barthian vehicle of insisting upon the sovereign will of God. *Das Nichtige* exists because God does *not* want it to exist. Thus it is 'the impossible possibility'.[44] Barth's scheme has been criticized by others as an inadequate theodicy,[45] but our concern is with the reality of the suffering of God, which requires a genuinely alien enemy whom God confronts. In Barth's own splendid metaphor, there needs to be a truly 'far country' into which God makes his journey in the person of the Son. But this notion of hostile non-being as the *opus alienum* of God comes down heavily on the side of the *opus* of God. It is too much 'his own' and not enough 'most alien'. D. R. Griffin finds an apt comparison when he says, 'Like Midas, who could not touch things without their

---

[39] Cf. Barth, *CD* III/1, pp. 100–3. [40] Barth, *CD* III/3, p. 292.
[41] Barth, *CD* III/3, pp. 77, 108.
[42] Barth, *CD* III/3, pp. 351, 361–5; cf. IV/1, p. 409.
[43] Barth, *CD* III/3, p. 365. [44] Barth, *CD* III/3, p. 351.
[45] There are critiques in Griffin, *God, Power and Evil*, pp. 150–73, and Hick, *Evil and the God of Love*, pp. 136–50.

turning to gold, God is cursed with the fate of not being able to reject the actual existence of something without giving it thereby a kind of actuality.'[46] Since Barth repudiates the Leibnizian view that God is limited by an eternal realm of logical possibilities outside himself,[47] the Midas curse can only be something within his own nature, and so non-being is not really alien to God at all. It is simply his own, though hapless, work. Moreover, God is not really free over his own being, which obliges him to give non-being actuality. He must have this freedom if, as Barth has well argued and I have have already accepted, God's ability to suffer and die is rooted in his freedom to be the kind of God he desires to be.

Further still, if *das Nichtige* holds all its reality from the providence of God, and God has now overcome this nothingness in the cross of Jesus, it can no longer exist even in the 'impossible' form it did before. Barth admits, in fact rejoices in, the conclusion that God simply permits *das Nichtige* to have henceforth an appearance of reality to our blinded eyes, so it should serve as an instrument for God, reminding us of what evil used to be.[48] This leaves us no way of articulating the exposure of God's being to suffering here and now, after the event of the cross of Jesus, as there is now no genuine enemy left even if there were one before. Barth rightly reminds us of the decisive victory of the suffering God over evil at the cross, but we have seen that this is best understood as the ongoing power of the cross to transform us in the present,[49] rather than suggesting that the power of evil is now only illusory.

Much of this criticism would, of course, equally apply against the adequacy of Barth's ideas as a theodicy. D. R. Griffin, for example, has argued (from a process point of view) that that the origins of aggressive non-being in the world are much less problematic when the creature is allowed to have some power to determine its own state of being against God.[50] From our perspective on the suffering of God, it is clear that unless the creature is allowed to introduce something new into creation on its own account, there is bound to be a softening of the claim that God suffers in exposing his being to alien nothingness. Fear of a Pelagian

---

[46] Griffin, op. cit., p. 166.   [47] Barth, *CD* III/3, pp. 316 ff.

[48] Barth, *CD* III/3, p. 367. See the critique by Griffin, *God, Power and Evil*, p. 170, who thinks this claim throws doubt upon whether *das Nichtige* was ever genuinely evil.

[49] See above, ch. 6, p. 164 and below, ch. 10, p. 267.

[50] Griffin, *God, Power and Evil*, pp. 172–3. Hick, *Evil and the God of Love*, (p. 150) observes that all attempts to speak of the creation as lapsing into nothing must end with a qualification of divine power.

endowment of mankind with power over against God should be dispelled if we base the suffering of God, and so his allowance of the entrance of the strange into his creation, upon his own self-limitation, with his desire for the growth of free personalities. It is this allowing of something strange to occur in creation, however, which scandalizes one writer who is otherwise thoroughly committed to the idea of a suffering God. Andrew Elphinstone, in his posthumous book *Freedom, Suffering and Love*,[51] therefore takes a much more radical view of the instrumentality of evil than Barth does, who is after all deliberately offering a 'broken utterance' about evil rather than a tidy system.[52] For Elphinstone, it is frankly incredible that the creation should come up with anything which might surprise God, and to which God should have to adjust or react. With a sense of outrage Elphinstone protests that such a view

. . . implies that the Creator's plan was not (for want of a better word) watertight . . . This means that God made a miscalculation about the consequences of the freedom he has bestowed upon humanity. To be absurdly anthropomorphic, the Creator must have been disagreeably taken by surprise at this untoward turn of events.[53]

This is a healthy piece of polemic, forcing us to come to a decision about the event of man's moral decline from the good, and so the emergence of evil. Either it was something strange to God, or it was an instrument for the good, necessary for man's moral growth and development, part (as Elphinstone argues)[54] of God's providential 'plan'. I have been opting for the first alternative; the word 'surprise' is a highly symbolic form of language when applied to God, but it indicates something true about God's knowledge of his creation. We recall that the process theologians usefully point out that there is all the difference in the world between God's knowing something as a possibility (even a likely possibility) and as an actuality.[55] The element of the alien and the surprising resides in the gap between the potential and the actual, in which there is room for the free response of God's creatures.

I have been critical of Barth's explanation of the origin of *das Nichtige*, but with the notion of *das Nichtige* itself Barth has certainly clarified different kinds of negation in the relationship between God and the world. There is the harmless negative of finitude (*das Nichts*), the

[51] Andrew Elphinstone, *Freedom, Suffering and Love* (SCM Press, London, 1976).
[52] Barth *CD* III/3, p. 293.   [53] Elphinstone, op. cit., p. 50.
[54] Ibid., pp. 18–21, 54–7, 93–5.   [55] See above, pp. 93–6.

aggressive non-being of rebellion against God's purpose (*das Nichtige*), and the negative which God speaks to man (*das Nein*). Finally there is the nothingness to which God has brought non-being through the cross, though we shall need to ask later what it actually means to claim that non-being has been nullified. We must take care then not to confuse these different kinds of negation, and we should learn from Barth that it is the overlap of *das Nichtige* and God's 'no' to man which makes God's experience of non-being such a deathly affair. If we are to make sense of the desolation within God to which the cross of Jesus witnesses, then we must incorporate the fact of human sinfulness at the centre. It is this strange rebellion and God's underlining of its consequences that makes God's participation in human life an event of such pain to him that it can be called 'death'—a negation which is most alien and yet most his own.

3. THE ALIENATION OF THE CREATOR BY NATURAL EVIL

Many theologians would accept the alienation of God as far as human moral choice is concerned, within the paradox of a virtually inevitable though not necessary fallenness. But they find it far more difficult to conceive of a slippage or dislocation in the natural order along the same lines, once they have rightly dispensed with the belief in a historical fall of nature caused by a historic fall of Adam. They are inclined to view 'natural evil', of which man is a merely helpless victim, as something logically necessary within creation. They work hard at accommodating untimely and cruel death, disease, natural disasters, and other frustrations inflicted upon humankind within a fully instrumental view of evil. If only we had keener vision, they propose, we would see that these are a natural kind of non-being (*ouk on*), not hostile non-being (*mē on*).

This might be urged from the viewpoint of man's moral development. Recently, for example, Andrew Elphinstone, to whom reference has already been made, has tried to cut the Gordian knot of theodicy by roundly asserting that suffering is necessary for man's growth in personality. In a manner reminiscent of Unanumo he finds that love needs pain, or else there is no tragedy for love to deal with, and for verification of this he points to the actual facts of evolutionary struggle. Whereas evolution, he suggests, is driven onward by the instinct to survive by avoiding pain, love transforms evolution by meeting and bearing pain.[56] Thus physical evolution is the foundation for the next

---

[56] Elphinstone, *Freedom, Suffering and Love*, pp. 10, 28–31. Unanumo similarly argued that man attains to moral personality, and to a knowledge of God as the

stage of love or spiritual transcendence, and the pain of 'natural evil' is built into the whole process by God. At the same time, Elphinstone affirms the suffering of God, for the groaning of creation in travail 'must be part-shared, part-borne by the one who has fashioned it'.[57] It is hard, however, to conceive how a God who has planned this educational scheme of pain could really 'groan' with the same sense of frustration and futility that creation suffers (Rom. 8: 20–2). If the pains of existence are in fact God's hidden work, they can hardly be alien to him, as the enduring of non-being would have to be.

Moreover, if we are to appeal to phenomena of experience, we can equally point to the sense of protest against natural evil which is inherent in human consciousness. The prime example of 'natural' or 'metaphysical' evil is once again the experience of death, which is often felt as the tragedy of untimely death. 'Ripeness is all', says Edgar to his suicidal father in Shakespeare's King Lear,[58] but as a matter of fact much (perhaps most) death in our world is not in the ripeness of old age or fulfilled achievement. Even in the rare cases where death is timely, it is still felt as an offence against love; far from allowing us the opportunity to meet pain with love, it takes away from us the opportunity of spending love on another. While death can in the abstract be defined as 'natural' or 'neutral', in reality we always experience it as a mixture—in varying proportions—of natural limit and hostile force. Karl Rahner describes death as having a 'natural element' within it, but concludes that:

The death which is actually experienced by all men individually cannot be identified in some naïve and unreflective manner with that natural essence of death.[59]

The biblical symbols of the resurrection of the dead and the eschaton when 'death will be swallowed up for ever'[60] bear witness to a basic religious feeling that the phenomenon of death has a provisional place at

supremely suffering Personality, only through suffering. See Miguel de Unanumo, The Tragic Sense of Life, trans. J. E. Crawford Flitch (Macmillan, London, 1921), pp. 138–42, 167, 210–14: e.g. 'the evolution of organic beings is simply a struggle to realize fullness of consciousness through suffering' (p. 141); 'Pain, which is a kind of dissolution, makes us discover our internal core' (p. 212).

[57] Elphinstone, op. cit., p. 52.

[58] Shakespeare, King Lear, Act V, Scene ii, 11.

[59] Karl Rahner, On the Theology of Death, trans. C. H. Henkey (Herder, Freiburg–Burns & Oates, London, 1961), p. 45.

[60] Isa. 25: 8, cf. 1 Cor. 15: 26, Rev. 21: 4.

best within God's creative purpose. J. Moltmann perceptively remarks that the feeling of sorrow for suffering is in fact a protest against it, and so to believe that God participates in the sorrow of the world is to say that God himself is in protest against the conditions of natural evil.[61] Thus the sorrow of the cross, no less than the glory of the resurrection is God's contradiction of the suffering and death of the present world. With regard to pain, God is a protestor rather than an educator.

To take this view does not imply that the bare fact of death itself stands outside God's creative intention, and that it must have occurred as a punishment for sin.[62] It does not even imply that every *experience* of death as something threatening is the consequence of sin, though as we have seen, a slipping towards non-being can give death an aggressive countenance. Rather, we can regard natural death as a provisional stage within God's purpose for the maturing of mankind, a boundary which is finally to be abolished.[63] Even natural death, considered in the abstract, is provisional. But death as we actually know it is interfused with frustrations, untimeliness and regrets of which man is simply a victim (whatever his own sin might contribute as well), and this is a tragedy which God himself actively opposes.

A sorrowing God is in protest against natural evil, of which death as we know it now is the paradigm. If natural evil were a necessary consequence of creation, God could hardly protest against it or feel it as something 'most alien' to his being; he would have planned it as an educational enterprise and it would be altogether 'most his own'. Such a view of the instrumentality of natural evil tends to underplay the disproportionate amount of natural evil suffered by mankind, its excessive and wasteful character. John Macquarrie, whom we have seen to take a rather cautious (and ambiguous) view of the logical necessity of natural evil, recognizes the 'dysteleological' elements in creation, and regrets them deeply as mysterious 'loose ends'.[64] Karl Barth is less embarrassed, and his account of the 'shadow-side' of creation (*das Schattenseite*) is a good example of the tendency to smooth away the

---

[61] Moltmann, *The Crucified God*, pp. 225–6. Cf. J. Moltmann, 'Die Auferstehung des Gekreuzigten und die Zukunft Christi', in B. Klappert (ed.), *Diskussion um Kreuz und Auferstehung*, (Aussaat und Schriftenmissions–Verlag, Neukirchen-Vluyn, 1971), p. 251: 'As long as the dead are dead . . . God is still not God'.

[62] Shaw, op. cit. (ch. 7 n. 18 above), pp. 280–1, finds the view of physical death as punishment for sin to be an unhealthy motivation for Christian behaviour, though in my opinion he wrongly finds it to be central to Pauline theology.

[63] Cf. Irenaeus, *Adversus Haereses* 4. 38.

[64] Macquarrie, *Principles of Christian Theology*, pp. 257–9.

offensive shock of natural evil—which he alludes to with such euphemisms as 'bad days and dark hours'. Determined to clear creation from 'slander' he insists that it is good and perfect in both its light and its shadow, its inclination 'not only to the right hand but also to the left', its Yes and its No. In its abysses as well as its heights, he declares, it sings the praises of God—especially through the harmony of light and darkness in the music of Mozart.[65] He only wishes that those whose faith was disturbed by the Lisbon earthquake had been listening to the theodicy in Mozart's music, composed in the same period.

Barth is concerned lest our protest against the 'shadow-side' of creation will obscure what ought to be our proper reaction against the utter Nothingness, *das Nichtige*, which opposes itself to the totality of God's creation.[66] But in his concern for us to recognize the malignant enemy of *das Nichtige*, he seems to trivialize the impact of natural evils. Of special significance to our present theme is his presentation of these as part of a world in which God appears to be thoroughly at home. Barth does not attempt to defend the ultimate goodness of the shadow-side by a philosophical argument,[67] but bases his argument upon the presence of God in Christ:

We cannot ignore the fact that in Jesus Christ God has again and expressly claimed the whole of creation as His work, adopting it and as it were taking it to heart in both its positive and negative aspects.[68]

Barth's point is that because Christ has taken on existence in which the shadow side was present, this is sufficient reason to make us ashamed to protest against it: 'It is for us to acquiesce without thinking that we know better.' What was good enough for God is good enough for us. Barth is surely right to keep directing our attention to God's experience of the world as being the key issue, but how does he know that God's participation in the shadow-side of creation was an approving one, in which he found that it 'sang the praise of God just as it was'? He admits

---

[65] Barth, *CD* III/3, pp. 297–301.   [66] Ibid., pp. 302–3.

[67] Barth does appeal to the philosophical idea of the distinctiveness of created things in order to explain the presence of natural evil: 'The diversities and frontiers of the creaturely world contain many "nots" ' (*CD* III/3, pp. 349–50). However, he does not employ a philosophical argument for the goodness of natural evil, such as the argument that all *prima facie* evils, such as suffering, are only apparently evil. The modern versions of this argument are more modest, claiming only that it is *possible* that reasons exist which would justify all apparent evils, even though they are not available to us: see e.g. M. B. Ahern, *The Problem of Evil* (Routledge & Kegan Paul, London, 1971), p. 50.

[68] Barth, *CD* III/3, p. 301.

that 'we did not see it'.[69] Barth does, of course, insist that in the cross of Jesus there was a conflict between Christ and *das Nichtige*; how does Barth know that God was not also there protesting against and challenging the natural evils of disease and death?

The more appalled we are by the excessive nature of natural evils, the less possible it is to suppose that God feels at home with them, or that 'the real or supposed antithesis between the negative and the positive side . . . is basically not only innocuous but even salutary, in view of the orientation of creation on Jesus Christ' (Barth).[70] Of course, we must recognize, with both Barth and Macquarrie, that finite beings exist within a boundary of non-being; to *be* something means that one is *not* something else.[71] The question is whether it is a logical necessity for the natural creation to slide towards this non-being in such a way that mass distortion arises, and pain is inflicted upon its sentient members to the excessive degree that appears characteristic of our world. Our feeling of protest is not against pain as such, for some pain is obviously necessary to the condition of physical existence; unless we had such a warning system we should continually be getting ourselves burned, drowned, or damaged by using our bodies (or minds) in a way which they are not in a fit condition to bear. We would also surely not feel a deep sense of protest against a limited amount of pain caused by the random processes of nature, if they really were only a few 'loose ends'. But we speak of 'natural evil' in order to draw attention to the wide-ranging and intensive nature of pain which is felt as offensive to life and love, and the point is whether *this* kind of pain is necessary. My argument is that if God experiences hostile non-being when he shares the life of the world, then we must speak of the fall of nature, like that of man, as being a strange factor to God; this means being practically inevitable but not logically necessary.

We cannot evade the implications of this view; it is only possible to say such a thing if the whole of creation and not just mankind is envisaged as having some kind of free response to its creator, and is capable in some way of turning aside from the creative purpose. We shall not be able to speak of the fall of nature as strictly unnecessary if we define the unique status of man as the level of being at which freedom emerges for the first time. This is precisely why many theologians see no alternative to affirming the logical necessity of natural evil, as we began

---

[69] Ibid., p. 297.   [70] Ibid., p. 299.
[71] Barth, *CD* III/3, pp. 349–50 (see above, n. 67); Macquarrie, *Principles of Christian Theology*, p. 215.

this section by remarking.[72] Perhaps this is why John Macquarrie appears to make the slipping of nature towards non-being more of an automatic process than the fall of man, although he affirms that both are inevitably involved in falling. While, he suggests all levels of being have some capacity to imitate Being, only mankind can copy Being freely, and so only mankind can forget Being through his own wrong decisions.[73] Yet if we do not speak of the free will of all creation we surely cannot speak of the alien within creation, and we cannot therefore speak of a suffering God. The idea that God suffers is not an easy one: it has implications for the whole nature of God and the cosmos. Also, as Schubert Ogden argues, without ascribing freedom and self-creativity to all levels of creation we cannot sustain a theodicy; he points out that the 'free-will defence' of evil will not work if it only covers human life, as this by no means copes with the extent of the problems of evil in the world.[74]

How then might freedom be allowed to the natural world as well as to humanity? One appeal might be to the randomness of the world as a form of freedom. A. R. Peacocke, for example, speaks of suffering as 'the cost of the existence of self-conscious, aware persons', and therefore as 'the consequence of allowing that free play of randomness which generates the new emergent realities of the cosmos and enables all its potentialities to be explored'.[75] This feature of randomness apparently leads Peacocke himself to side with those who affirm the necessity of suffering for conscious beings:

In exercising their freedom they are bound to encounter the opposition of the random elements in the world process, which come to man as 'natural evil'— those same elements of chance whose creative interplay with law have been the means of their own emergence in the universe.[76]

But Peacocke also expresses some doubts about whether the amount of pain which is produced through this process can be justified morally, even if it can be accounted for intellectually.[77] Surely, we might suggest, the consequences of random processes cannot themselves be strictly necessary. Peacocke has in fact already spoken of human

---

[72] See, e.g. Elphinstone, *Freedom, Suffering and Love*, pp. 100–1, cf. pp. 56–8.

[73] Macquarrie, op. cit., pp. 267, 232–3.

[74] Schubert M. Ogden, *Faith and Freedom: Toward a Theology of Liberation* (Christian Journals Ltd., Belfast, 1979), p. 79.

[75] A. R. Peacocke, *Creation and the World of Science* (Clarendon Press, Oxford, 1979), p. 246.   [76] Ibid., p. 166.   [77] Ibid., p. 182.

evolution as an 'inevitable process' with an 'indeterminate course', in a subtle interplay of chance and law. He envisages God as Creator giving the material of this world one set of potentialities rather than another, but then the potentialities are 'unveiled by chance exploring their gamut'.[78] If we apply this insight to the presence of pain in the universe, we might judge that while some pain is inescapable, the excessive amount of pain that we usually identify as 'natural evil' is a risk or hazard due to random processes rather than a necessity. We might then speak of God's experience of that excessiveness as hostile non-being, a slipping of nature away from his purpose, due to the autonomy he has given it.

However, a fuller sense of freedom than mere randomness could be ascribed to the natural world if we were to follow the view of process theology that all actual entities are self-creative and therefore free. According to this account, as we have already seen, the smallest particles of reality are organic, capable of some level of response to God and others. While each is influenced by God in that it receives an initial aim which would make for its fullest satisfaction, it is free to reject or modify this aim. Evil therefore arises from the capacity to refuse to conform to the divine persuasion; as Whitehead states, 'So far as the conformity is incomplete, there is evil in the world.'[79] The whole universe is thus capable of exercising the freedom which God has to an eminent degree, though there is 'a finite difference between emergent levels of value corresponding to different emergent levels of freedom' (S. Ogden).[80] Lest we descend into absurdity, we must not forget that the 'actual entities', or smallest building blocks of reality, should not be confused with their organization into everyday 'things' (or 'enduring individuals'). There is no question, for example, of a stone's deciding to do anything, as it is an aggregate without any co-ordinated response; there has been no buildup of each entity's mentality into an overall 'mind'. But the claim is nevertheless being made that all levels of actuality can enjoy some experience of feeling and some freedom.

Following this pan–cosmic scheme, resistance to the aim of God at the lowest levels takes the form of the evil of remaining unnecessarily trivial, while at higher levels there is the greater evil of discord. God in his creative persuasiveness takes the risk of discord, and so the danger of excessive suffering, in order to avoid the evil of the creation's remaining

---

[78] Ibid., pp. 103–5.
[79] Whitehead, *Religion in the Making*, p. 60.
[80] Ogden, op. cit. (n. 74 above), pp. 111–12.

trivial.[81] The destructive effect of microbes and earthquakes alike upon mankind can therefore be understood as discord in nature arising from freedom, which God himself experiences as alien. Of course, the criticism is often made that there is little scope for lack of response to God at the lower levels of creation according to this scheme;[82] a stone cannot refuse to be a stone since it is not an integrated organism. But such a criticism misses the point that even the lowest levels of being interact with other entities of higher capacities for response; they play a role in the total ecosystem, and we have to admit, as Cobb and Griffin remind us, that 'we still understand relatively little about the mutual interdependencies of the various types of enduring individuals'.[83]

I believe that we do not have to accept the whole metaphysic of process theology in order to entertain the thought that there is some consistency and family relationship throughout the cosmos. In dealing with the problem of suffering, process thought begins the opposite way round from the traditional approach which deals first with 'natural evil' and then works up to 'moral evil'. Rather it begins with what we know most about, human experience, and then argues by analogy with this to other levels of being in nature; since man has emerged from the natural world, process thinkers argue that something akin to the basic features of human experience—feeling and enjoyment—must be present everywhere. However hard it is to express the term of the analogy at lower levels of creation, and I have already argued that the notion of pan-mentality has problems for the doctrine of God as well as for a natural theology, nevertheless I believe that process thought is on to something here. Some overall vision of the 'responsiveness' and 'resistance' of creation to the Spirit of God is needed for a doctrine of creative evolution, for a proper theodicy, and certainly for the claim with which we have been most concerned—that God suffers conflict with a non-being which is alien to him. It may be that process thought is pointing in a direction whose destination we do not yet have the conceptual tools to map; if we cannot yet define the mystery we may need 'mythologies' such as universal mentality to recognize it. Perhaps the truth lies somewhere between mere randomness and universal

---

[81] Whitehead, *Adventures of Ideas*, p. 355. See also Cobb and Griffin, *Process Theology*, pp. 70–1.

[82] See the critique, for example, by Ian G. Barbour, *Issues in Science and Religion* (SCM Press, London, 1966), p. 452.

[83] Cobb and Griffin, *Process Theology*, pp. 79–80.

responsiveness, but somehow we must think of nature as generating something strange to God if we are to say that he suffers within it.

In this chapter we have inevitably touched upon aspects of theodicy, but our basic concern has been with the coherence of saying that God suffers death, in the sense that he suffers an experience of non-being which is 'most alien and yet most his own'. In tracing the route from creaturely existence to hostile non-being, we have seen that creation from an absolute non-being (*ouk on*) can be conceived as the basis for the emergence of an aggressive non-being, as long as this kind of non-being is understood to be a convenient term for something that happens in relationship between God and his world. Both natural evil and moral evil offer an experience of something strange to God, and cannot therefore be understood as logical consequences of creation. The objectivity of hostile 'non-being' lies in the strangeness of the situation to God, disrupting the harmony of his life with himself and the life he shares with the world, offending his love. We must not forget these conclusions as we move on to consider the second major route of thought to an encounter with the enemy of non-being.

9

The Alienation of the Living God

So far we have been exploring one route taken by God on his way to an encounter with non-being. The path is one of empathy with his creatures, who suffer a non-being which makes its base in their finite existence. As he identifies with the lives of his creatures he is met by something strange in their experience which also becomes his. But some theologians who find the category of non-being a valuable one also point to a parallel route which God treads, depicting him as suffering a non-being more directly developed from his own being.[1] The argument here is not in the first place from the nature of creaturely existence but from the nature of the divine life, though the two paths are bound to meet finally in the suffering of God. Whether expressed as an aspect of his vitality, creativity or sacrificiality, there is believed to be a movement of God's being into a negation which springs intimately from his own life. There is, to use an ancient word, a 'kenosis' of the divine being, an emptying which is inseparable from fullness, a negative bound up with the positive.

If we are to describe God as taking this second path, accepting that the symbols correspond in some way to the reality of God, we must go on to ask whether the kind of negation which God encounters here can be understood as the basis for an experience of *hostile* non-being. We have seen that simple creaturely non-being or finiteness can be the area in which a more hostile non-being takes hold; can the same be said of the negativity which is proposed to be part of the divine life? There is another way of putting the same question: is there any real link between God's inner experience of self-negation and his outer act of empathy with the human tragedy of non-being, or is the term 'non-being' simply being used in a slippery manner for different realities? Does the notion

---

[1] In this chapter we shall be mainly concerned with Hegel, Altizer, and Tillich, but we notice that there are also elements of this method in Macquarrie (*Principles of Christian Theology*, pp. 215–17), Jüngel (*God as the Mystery of the World*, pp. 222–3), and Moltmann (*The Trinity and the Kingdom of God*, pp. 109–10; *God in Creation*, pp. 86–93).

that the life of God consists in facing its own negative help to illuminate the claim that God suffers death?

The chief architect of the road from the life of God to alienation was
Hegel, and he begins it by appealing once more to the feeling of non-
being as we know it in our experience. We have already seen that to be a
determinate creature means having a boundary of non-being; in the
homely illustration offered by J.-P. Sartre, if Jacques *is* somewhere he is
not in another place, and so if I go looking for him in a café and do not
find him there, the atmosphere is full of his non-being.[2] But if, observed
Hegel in his *Logic*,[3] instead of beginning with a determinate being we
try to think of pure being, then we find we are thinking of nothing at all,
since the concept of wholly indeterminate being is indistinguishable
from nothing. So our thought passes from being to non-being and back
again, unable restlessly to remain in either, each concept disappearing
into the other. This movement is 'becoming', a synthesis which is the
truth of both being and non-being. Although 'being' is the poorest
category of reality, and in itself far from the concept of Spirit, yet it
must apply to anything that can be a reality to us; thus (by a sequence of
argument which need not concern us here)[4] Hegel claims that this
dialectic of becoming applies not only to the next category, determinate
being, but to all categories of reality. Each category generates its own
contradiction, or negates itself, and this conceptual phenomenon is
finally true for Absolute Spirit (*Geist*) itself or, in religious language,
God.[5] The reality of the Absolute is in a process of self-development,

---

[2] Sartre, *Being and Nothingness*, cit. Mary Warnock, *The Philosophy of Sartre*
(Hutchinson, London, 1965), pp. 46–8.

[3] Hegel, *The Science of Logic*, pp. 85–6, 94–102; *The Encyclopaedia of the Philosophical
Sciences: Part* 1, 87–91 (pp. 127–35); cf. *The Philosophy of Religion* 3 (ed. Hodgson), pp.
89–90.

[4] Further, see Charles Taylor, *Hegel* (Cambridge Unversity Press, 1975), pp. 227–9,
and Walter Kaufmann, *Hegel: A Reinterpretation*, Vol. 1 (University of Notre Dame
Press Indiana, 1978), pp. 188–9. Taylor argues for a successive chain of contradictions
moving from category to category, while Kaufmann argues that Hegel is simply
presenting a list of categories and their contradictions. They both stress, however, that
Hegel intends the dialectic to apply pre-eminently to *Geist* itself (Kaufmann, op. cit., p.
184; Taylor, op. cit., p.231). Taylor judges that we ought to regard the argument from
our experience of non-being less as a proof, than a hint towards Hegel's vision of
embodied Spirit (ibid., p. 231).

[5] In the following discussion I am assuming that Hegel's philosophy is panentheism
and not pantheism, Absolute Spirit being finally something more than the relative forms
of Spirit that make up the whole; for argument in support of this, see Quentin Lauer, SJ,
Hegel's Concept of God (State University of New York Press, Albany, 1982), pp. 243 ff.

going out of itself into its opposite, or exposing itself to negation, and thence coming back to itself in a synthesis of becoming. There is a kenosis of the Spirit, in a movement of 'sacrifice',[6] and this is the archetype for the facing of negation by all finite realities.

In Hegel's own world-view, the justification for leaping from an observation about words and concepts to an argument about realities is twofold. First, the life of Absolute Spirit *is* self-thinking Thought (or Concept, *Das Begriff*)[7] and so the dialectical movement of our human minds is a relative expression of the movement of absolute Mind. Second, it is a mark of vitality to go out beyond oneself to face opposition and contradiction. This second rationale has an appeal to many who are not Hegelians in the strict sense of affirming an Absolute Idea. We can well agree that if the divine Spirit is a living God and not an empty, lifeless thing, he will affirm his positive being in exposing himself to the power of the negative and overcoming it. We might then regard the argument from 'logic' (thinking the concept of being) as an analogy or even a mere illustration of the adventurous movement of the divine life. Paul Tillich, for example, appears to do so when he claims that without negation God could not be God, or the power and ground of being.[8] Though Hegel would have been outraged by the suggestion that he had not after all produced the ultimate philosophy, it seems clear that variations can be played upon his theme of God's self-differentiation and self-negation, and contemporary thought about the suffering of God has not been slow to compose them. In this chapter we shall be reviewing some aspects of Hegel's basic theme, and then two modern variations upon it, all the time asking whether there is any non-being spoken about which is a really challenging opponent to the divine life, and so whether terms like 'kenosis', 'self-sacrifice', 'alienation', and 'death' are either justified or illuminated.

---

    [6] Hegel, *Phenomenology of Mind*, pp. 536, 755; cf. p. 722, 'the absolute Being must have from the start implicitly sacrificed itself'.

    [7] The meaning of *Begriff* in Hegel's scheme includes such elements as (a) God's inner intellectual life, (b) a purposive organizing principle immanent in nature akin to Aristotle's 'entelechy', and (c) self-mediation or knowing oneself as object as well as subject. It can formally be distinguished from Spirit, with Spirit as the ultimate principle of becoming and Concept as the pattern or structure of becoming, but in the last resort it is hardly possible to distinguish them, any more than Mind can be distinguished from Thought.

    [8] Tillich, *Systematic Theology*, Vol. 3, p. 302.

1. THE DIVINE LIFE GENERATES THE NEGATIVE: HEGEL

In Hegel's own system, divine Being understood as Absolute Spirit generates its own opposite by distinguishing itself from itself. The forward movement of the Spirit is a process of self-negation. By negating itself, Spirit in itself (*an sich*) becomes Spirit for itself (*für sich*); then, by negating that negation Spirit once more becomes in itself, yet in a fuller and richer way. The return of Spirit (or Mind) to itself through its opposite is its self-consciousness, and the opposite through which Universal Spirit finally comes to knowledge of itself is the minds of conscious finite beings, which as determinate subjects are bounded by non-being. The divine Spirit therefore apparently exposes itself to a double negativity, first by movement within its own essence, positing its own opposite, and secondly by going out into the estranged life of finite creatures. The second kind of negativity is linked logically to the first, indeed it is a manifestation of it,[9] and the relationship between them is what we have already identified as our particular concern at the moment. It is in that nexus that the reality of divine alienation, if anywhere, must lie.

In Hegel's account of divine life, the first movement of the Spirit is within its own essential being. Already, 'before'[10] any creation of the world, Spirit differentiates itself and passes over into its opposite. There is a 'play of love' within the Absolute itself, which corresponds to the Christian doctrine of the Trinity. The Universal goes out of itself and engenders the particular 'for itself', which in terms of Christian imagery (*Vorstellung*) is the eternal generation of the Son by the Father. Then the particular returns to the universal in a common life (*bei sich*), which in Christian imagery is the bond of unity of the Holy Spirit.[11] We recall that Barth later speaks of the Father's reflective movement out of himself to generate his 'Other' in the Son, eternally 'positing' and 'repeating' himself in another mode of being;[12] Hegel's distinctive stress

---

[9] See Taylor, op. cit. (n. 4 above), p. 110.

[10] Of course, this is not a temporal 'before'. See Hegel's *Science of Logic* 1, p. 60: Logic 'shows forth God as he is in his eternal essence before the creation of Nature and of a Finite Spirit'; cf. *Philosophy of Religion* 3, p. 37.

[11] Hegel, *Phenomenology of Mind*, pp. 81 ('love disporting with itself'), 579, 766–77; *Philosophy of Religion* 3, pp. 38–9, 86–7. There is a good discussion of Hegel's notion of the essential Trinity by Bernard M. G. Reardon, *Hegel's Philosophy of Religion* (Macmillan, London, 1977), pp. 68–9.

[12] Barth refers to the Father–Son relationship as 'God's self-positing in which He is also and through Himself alone indissolubly distinct' (*CD* I/1, p. 432), 'an intradivine

is to understand this movement as a process of negativity. The movement from infinite universal to infinite particular is the emerging of a negative, since all 'opposition' and 'self positing of the other' is negation.[13] But it is clear that this 'opposite' in God is not a *hostile* negative; it is a negation without division, separation, or alienation.

In a second movement, eternal Spirit goes out of itself into external existence, coming to exist as an object over against itself. Absolute Spirit expresses itself in relative spirit, which is the creation of the world; this is exposure now not just to a negative but to an *alien* negative.[14] As Spirit which thinks itself, the Absolute comes to self-awareness through finite particulars, and this must be an experience of alienation since the finite is cut off from the infinite. 'God is not God without the world.'[15] At its furthest throw, Spirit comes to consciousness through finite beings who themselves have consciousness, viz. human beings; Spirit thinks itself through beings who can think. Thus Absolute Spirit exposes itself to the negative of minds which are estranged from Spirit itself, and which show this by being limited by each other; determinate beings are what they are because they are not something else. In Christian imagery, the immersion of Absolute Spirit into negation in all its forms is the event of the cross of Jesus. The meaning of the incarnation is that infinite Spirit has become finite, individual man, and in the cross has endured the utter non-being that belongs to this existence. In one moment Spirit encounters all dimensions of negation—its own opposite ('the Son'), finitude, death, and evil since the Son dies the death of a criminal:

> It is the lot of human finitude to die. Death is the most complete proof of humanity, of absolute finitude; and indeed Christ has died the aggravated death of the evil-doer: not merely a natural death, but rather a death of shame and humiliation on the cross. In him, humanity was carried to its furthest point.[16]

relation or movement, as *repetitio aeternitatis in aeternitate*—the copy of an original . . .' (ibid., p. 394, cf. p. 350: 'One God in threefold repetition'), and 'the original, source . . . in God from which proceeds the second thing, the copy, issue . . .' (ibid., p. 394).

  [13] Hegel, *Phenomenology of Mind*, p. 80, and *Philosophy of Religion* 3, p. 180. See further *Philosophy of Religion* 3, pp. 69–73. Hegel was much influenced here by Spinoza's dictum, 'all determination is negation'.

  [14] Hegel, *Phenomenology of Mind*, p. 81, 'the seriousness, the suffering, the patience and the labour of the negative'; ibid., pp. 769–70, and *Philosophy of Religion* 3, pp. 89, 109, 119. See Taylor, op. cit. (n. 4 above), pp. 490–1.

  [15] Hegel, *Lectures on the Philosophy of Religion: Part 1, The Concept of Religion*, trans. E. B. Speirs and J. B. Sanderson (Routledge & Kegan Paul, London, 1895), p. 200.

  [16] Hegel, *Philosophy of Religion* 3 (ed. Hodgson) p. 210, cf. p. 205.

In a third movement Spirit returns to itself, negating the negation of finitude and death, and this is expressed in the Christian symbol of the resurrection. 'The third moment, accordingly, is that Christ has risen. Negation is thereby overcome.'[17] This death is 'the focal point of reconciliation',[18] the means of the return of the Spirit, because here the Absolute Spirit has identified itself with a dead being who is both finite and individual. In the first place, identification with a dead *finite* being has an effect upon our consciousness. If man is to return from his separateness to union with the universal then he must develop a form of life in which he recognizes his painful plight of separation from the infinite, and then recognizes that in himself (*an sich*) he is already united with infinite Spirit, hence shaping his life so that this reality becomes real for himself (*für sich*). As we recognize the horror of death in God portrayed in the cross we realize our situation of separation from the infinite, and yet our participation in it:

God has died, God is dead: this is the most frightful of all thoughts, that everything eternal and true does not exist, that negation itself is found in God . . . 'God himself is dead' it says in a Lutheran hymn, expressing an awareness that the human, the finite, the fragile, the weak, the negative, are moments of the divine.[19]

Another reason that Hegel gives for the salvific effect of the immersion of the Spirit into the death of the cross is its identification with a dead *individual* being. Through the death of Christ as an individual comes the founding of the Christian community (at Pentecost) to which we can relate ourselves, and so there is a movement of the Spirit from individual to community, from particular to universal.[20] In this decisive point of history of the divine Spirit, God cancels his inherence in a particular place and time, so that his incarnation passes on to the community of mankind in general. In Hegel's view, unity between God and man cannot be consummated in single individuals, since there is opposition between Universal Spirit and any particular embodiment of it. Spirit ultimately comes to self-understanding in a community which is conscious of itself as the vehicle of the Spirit.

These features of the reconciling return of the Spirit to itself are ones

[17] Ibid., p. 211.   [18] Ibid., p. 217.
[19] Ibid., pp. 212, 217; cf. *Phenomenology of Mind*, pp. 776–8, 780.
[20] Hegel, *Philosophy of Religion* 3, pp. 233, 256–7. Cf. Taylor, op. cit. (n. 4 above), p. 207.

we shall be taking up again shortly in considering the particularity of the death of Christ. Overall, Hegel's scheme is a magisterial working out of the pattern of the positive generating the negative as the dynamism of divine life, but it must be questioned whether we can accept his claim that the negativity or non-being which God encounters is an alien one. It is hard to see how Hegel's portrayal of self-negating Spirit can be the basis for the story of a suffering and self-sacrificing God, as Hegel wanted it to be and as it has often casually been assumed to be by later theologians. Hegel certainly insists that the negative inhering in finitude is something alien to God, and he rightly perceives that for this to be the case it must be something brought into creation by man's own decisions and actions:

It is shown that finitude is something alien to [God] and has been adopted from an other; this other is the human beings who stand over against the divine process. It is their finitude that Christ has taken upon himself, this finitude in all its forms, which at its furthest extreme is evil. This humanity, which is itself a moment in the divine life, is now characterized as something alien, not belonging to God. This finitude, however, in its being-for-self against God, is evil, something alien to God. But he has taken it upon himself in order to put it to death by his death.[21]

Yet, despite Hegel's insistence that God is alienated, he hardly seems to be so. The pattern of self-negating spirit means that finitude as spoilt by man's rebellion is in the end only a part of a higher reality, the process of becoming. As Tillich judges, 'the negative is not the continuous threat against the positive but is overcome in the fulfilled synthesis'.[22] In the scheme of a God who negates himself, the negative can never really be strange to God, and so God cannot suffer the kind of experience of death which human beings undergo. This is made clear in the case of human evil, which Hegel describes as 'the furthest extreme' of the alien. However, while evil is the assertion of the will against God, finite beings need to assert their wills in order to become truly self-conscious, aware of their particularity over against nature. Their wilful assertion of their finitude cuts them off from the Universal, but at the very same time it makes them spiritual beings and so vehicles for God's self-knowledge. As the critic Charles Taylor puts it, 'the antidote for the evil of concentration in self is more of the same', and 'the Universal which is

21 Hegel, op. cit., p. 213.
22 Tillich, *Perspectives on Nineteenth and Twentieth Century Protestant Theology*, p. 133.

sinned against cannot exist except at this price'.[23] Hegel's version of the forgiveness of sins is a matter of coming to terms with the necessity of sin as the betrayal of the Universal by particular beings.[24] This hardly represents sin as something most alien to God.

The absence of real alienation in God's experience of negativity is due to two features of the relationship between God's own self-negation within his essence, and his exposure to creaturely non-being in the world. Both features are highly significant for our enquiry. In the first place, the pattern of God's encounter with hostile negativity is set by the reflexive movement of his own being. Whatever Hegel is going on to say about alienation as Spirit goes out beyond itself into nature, the basic sense of negation is established by Spirit's generating of its own opposite; it is a negation which is swallowed up in the coming of Spirit to be 'at home with itself' (*bei sich*).[25] Although the exposure of Spirit to its own 'infinite particular' (the Son) is not an experience of hostility, it sets the pattern for exposure to the 'finite particulars' in creation which *are* supposedly hostile. The second kind of negation is a smooth progression from the 'true opposite' within the divine being, as Spirit unfolds itself into the finite world.

Some contemporary theologians who affirm the suffering of God are critical altogether of the Hegelian notion of the self-differentiation of the divine Being; Moltmann for example believes that there can be no real Trinitarian diversity within God when he is conceived as a sovereign subject who repeats himself reflectively.[26] He accuses Barth, who speaks similarly of God's positing himself as Another over against himself in the Son,[27] of an 'idealist heritage' which implies a monarchianism contradictory to suffering. I have already defended the idea of God's self-repetition as a way of ascribing complex personality to God, and it certainly seems preferable to speaking about three consciousnesses.[28] The point at which Hegel is really open to criticism about 'otherness' in God is his definition of it as, already in itself, a

---

[23] Taylor, op. cit. (n. 4 above), p. 212, cf. pp. 490–1. See Hegel, *Philosophy of Religion* 3, pp. 153–61, *Phenomenology of Mind*, pp. 770 ff., 579.

[24] See Hegel's account of 'The Dialogue of the Two Consciousnesses' in *Phenomenology of Mind*, pp. 675 ff.

[25] Hegel, *Phenomenology of Mind*, pp. 766–77.

[26] Moltmann, *The Trinity and the Kingdom of God*, pp. 139–40, 142–3. Also see Mackey, *The Christian Experience of God as Trinity*, pp. 203 f.; Mühlen, *Die Veränderlichkeit Gottes*, pp. 34–5.

[27] e.g. Barth, *CD* I/1, p. 433 ('God posits His own reality'); ibid., pp. 316–20, 392 ff.

[28] See above, ch. 5, pp. 138, 140–2.

negation of the Father's being. This is bound to weaken the notion of the non-being which God meets when he enters finite creation, and it is this that undermines the suffering of God.

Nevertheless, it seems to me that Hegel is on to something when he brings 'otherness' or 'opposition' within God so closely together with negation. He is attempting to express an intimate binding together of God's own dynamic life with his experience of worldly negativity. God's awareness of himself, as an object to his own knowing, is inseparable from his awareness of objects in the world, and those objects are estranging to the purpose of the Spirit.[29] When Spirit knows itself as opposite, it is at least trembling on the borders of finding itself a stranger to itself. Now Karl Barth, for all his professed antagonism to Hegel, has been powerfully influenced by these ideas. After all, according to Barth we only know God as object of our thinking and praying because we share in God's own objective knowledge of himself.[30] But Barth finds another way of bringing together the movement of God's inner being in self-reflection with his immersion into suffering and death in the world. Barth's way is his doctrine of the election of the Son. That is, while God eternally differentiates himself, willing himself to be God in the mode of Son as well as Father, he also decrees eternally that the Son should become one person with the man Jesus Christ.[31] In one movement of will, freely determining himself, he brings forth the eternal Son and chooses mankind for fellowship with himself, electing Jesus who is its representative. Thus as God wills to live a complex life which we call in symbol the relation between the Father and the Son in the fellowship of the Spirit, he chooses man, his finitude, the real risk of his decline from the divine purpose, and finally the passion of the cross. We might say, following Barth's insight, that God takes what is strange upon himself as he begets the Son. This is because there is a simultaneity between the generation of the Son and submission to passion in the

---

[29] For Hegel, self-consciousness is knowing oneself as object as well as subject, or self-mediation. See the exegesis by George R. Lucas, *Two Views of Freedom in Process Thought: A Study of Hegel and Whitehead*, American Academy of Religion Dissertation Series 28 (Scholars Press, Missoula, 1979), pp. 71–2, 74–6.

[30] Barth, *CD* II/1, p. 51, cf. II/1, pp. 45 ff., 9–10. The converse, that God only knows himself through us, is not of course true for Barth.

[31] More exactly, Barth's view is that the Father appoints the Son to elect himself to become one with the man Jesus Christ, and the Son is obedient to the decree of the Father. Thus Jesus Christ is both 'the electing God' and 'the elected man'. (*CD* II/2, pp. 95 ff., 115 ff., cf. II/2, pp. 9–10, III/1, p. 97, IV/2, p. 32.) See further above, ch. 5, p. 117 nn. 22, 23.

world, not because the Son is in himself a negation of the Father's being. God encounters the strangeness of non-being in relating himself to himself, but the Son and negation are not identical.

We can in this way approve an indirect version of Hegel's scheme of a self-negating God. God indeed shows his vitality in going out of himself to face contradiction and negation, and this is bound up with his own movement into diversity, or being other than himself. In willing to be God in the mode of Son as well as Father he brings a strangeness upon himself because he includes man in his circle of relationships. This description of his opening himself to non-being in the very act of his becoming himself exactly corresponds to our experience of death as 'most alien and yet most our own'. Barth's doctrine of God makes the useful correction of Hegel that the generation of the Son is not in itself a negation of the Father, but there is also something here which must be learnt from both Hegel and process thought; the exposure to negativity in the world is not an optional extra which God need not have undertaken. It is impossible to conceive God except in terms of creativity, though I have also been arguing throughout the present study that this is due to the given fact of God's own desire and not to the process of either concrescence (as in process thought) or the dialectical movement of the Spirit (as in Hegel). There is a parallel, as G. Lucas has shown, between the urge of Creativity in a process view and the Hegelian *Geist*, as there is also between the immanent teleological principle of concrescence in process thought and the Hegelian notion of the indwelling concept.[32] But the comparison only throws into sharper relief the alternative motivation which we can perceive as lying behind creation, that God has a personal desire for his world.

A second feature of the relationship between the essential self-negation of God and his encounter with negativity in the world, as Hegel depicts it, is the necessity of the process. This too detracts from the reality of the suffering of God. The verdict of the Hegel scholar Charles Taylor is that:

In Hegel's system, God cannot *give* to man—neither in creation, nor in revelation, nor in salvation through sending his Son. To see [these] acts aright is to see them as emanations of a necessity which is no more God's than it is man's.[33]

Taylor's objection is that the movements of Spirit are a matter of

[32] Lucas, op. cit. (n. 29 above), p. 123.
[33] Taylor, op. cit. (n. 4 above), p. 493.

necessity, and only appear to be acts of God in the narrative form of the *Vorstellung*. A complementary objection is that of the existentialists (beginning with Kierkegaard),[34] that reconciliation is achieved in too easy and automatic a manner in Hegel's presentation of the world process. It was all very well for the philosopher in his study to propose that the negative was always necessarily being negated in the movement of the Spirit, but in real life things did not look very reconciled. Alienation was a constant aspect of existence, and death remained a threat. Hegel was convinced that there was a secret work of the Spirit through history, actualizing the eternal essences in space and time. Providence reigned in the unfolding of history; the fact that people did not appear to be as happy as they should just showed that history was not the place for the happiness of the individual, but that Spirit was engaged in forming reconciled communities. There is, we notice, another parallel here with the organicism of process thought. Hegel adds that the path of the Spirit could take diversionary routes, accommodating itself to the obstacles which objective institutions placed in its way; this is the 'cunning of the idea',[35] and may mean that at any one point the progress of Spirit may be veiled. An example of such a piece of 'cunning' is the experience of the 'speculative Good Friday' which we have already considered. The existentialist thinkers certainly learned from Hegel that there is a negative element in every life process, that the positive lives from the negative it negates. Life is the negating of the threat of non-being. But they did not agree with the optimism of Hegel that everything was thus being reconciled; for them there was no synthesis in which the negative was overcome. It remained a permanent threat and source of anxiety.

The necessity of the process of reconciliation is thus put into question by the sheer absence of reconciliation. Necessity also means that non-being is not really alien to God, but an extrapolation of his own life. However, the argument has recently been advanced by G. Lucas that the 'cunning of the idea' in Hegel is not so much a way of expressing necessity, as a way of affirming freedom. He claims that Absolute Spirit has to take account of the choices of finite spirits and is conditioned by them, since as bearers of the guiding Concept they can develop and

---

[34] Kirkegaard, *Concluding Unscientific Postscript*, pp. 270 ff.

[35] Hegel, *Lectures on the Philosophy of World History. Introduction: Reason in History*, trans. H. B. Nisbet (Cambridge University Press, 1975), p. 89; *Encyclopaedia: Part 1*, n. to 147 (p. 209).

modify it for themselves to some degree.[36] But this bringing of Hegel into closer parallel with process thought only leaves us with the same problems about the suffering of God that we noticed before. There is a higher necessity of creativity. Freedom resides only in the concept of creativity,[37] and it is the principle of creativity that requires Spirit to take finite spirits into account, rather than freely chosen suffering love. While free in the way it knows itself, and so in the development of creativity, Spirit is not free to be *other than* creative. In line with this, Lucas plays down the element of negation in Hegel, suggesting that this is merely a way of speaking of the freedom of Spirit to develop itself along the path of creativity, sublating (*aufheben*) elements alien to it.[38] Yet without a real alienation there can be no suffering.

However, we must certainly recognize that history matters for Hegel. Despite the criticism often levelled against Hegel that he evaporates history into a cosmic process, he does in fact counter the de-historicization of the Liberal Protestantism of his time. History is the solid stuff in which timeless truths must inescapably take shape for us. 'Hegel insists that the incarnation must be seen as a real historical event, and one which has played a decisive role in the history of Spirit.'[39] We have criticized Hegel's view of the divine history as being a necessary process, but it is still a historical process. While for Hegel God is always 'incarnate' in finite beings (coming to self-consciousness), he still asserts that in Christ God is really present in a particular subject in a sense that is without precedent.[40] We have already seen that only in the death of Jesus has Universal Spirit passed from incarnation in the individual to the community. Again, in the cross of Christ the Spirit has faced nothingness and estrangement in an unprecedented way. Hegel declares that 'this infinite suffering' of God must appear 'in sensible immediacy, in sensible presence' in Christ.[41] The Absolute Idea must 'become certain for men' in the form of 'something seen and experienced in the world'.[42]

Taylor, in discussing Hegel's proposal of a unique incarnation in Christ, professes himself somewhat perplexed as to how the concept can fit into Hegel's overall scheme, since according to Hegel, 'ultimately

---

[36] Lucas, op. cit. (n. 29 above), p. 125, cf. pp. 62, 88–9, 121–2, 128.
[37] Hegel, *Encyclopaedia: Part 1*, p. 160.
[38] Lucas, op. cit., p. 72.
[39] Taylor, op. cit. (n. 4 above), p. 483; cf. p. 209.
[40] Hegel, *Phenomenology of Mind*, pp. 757–8.
[41] Hegel, *Philosophy of Religion* 3, p. 177.   [42] Ibid., p. 181.

Jesus is not God in any sense in which all other men are not'.[43] What can
Hegel mean by saying that the substance itself of the Spirit 'became self-
consciousness'?[44] It is not difficult to discern a part of what Hegel
means; in the event of Jesus, people *perceive* for the first time that God
does not just appear in the form of flesh (as other religions preached) but
that divine essence actually becomes self-consciousness in humanity.
There had to be a historical development of human consciousness to a
point of maturity where people could see the truth of the universal
incarnation, and so feel the horror of death in God. That moment of
realization, under the guidance of Spirit, came with the cross of Jesus.
But Taylor admits this explanation is not enough, and suggests that
Hegel must be affirming something more objective about the
unprecedented unity between God and man in Christ; it appears that the
essential factor in the birth of this new religious consciousness was the
actual emergence, as Taylor puts it, of an 'exceptional, trail-blazing
individual who really did live in unity with the universal in a way that
none other could in his time'.[45] Taylor suggests that this idea is a
leftover in Hegel's thought from his earlier work, when he represented
Jesus as someone who responded to the Spirit in a unique way,[46] in
contrast to his developed system where all the emphasis lies upon the
agency of the Spirit. But it seems to me highly significant that Hegel
brings together a decisive presence of God in the flesh, and so an extreme
facing of death and negation by God, with a unique human response to
the Spirit, even though it does not fit tidily into his system.

Hegel has been highly influential in recent discussion of the suffering
of God, which has drawn constantly upon his insights that God from his
sheer vitality differentiates himself into complex life, and in the same
mood of vitality faces negation and contradiction in the diversity of the
world. Hegel himself makes the shift between the dual dimensions of
inner reflection and outer negation too progressive and too necessary for
God to be a truly suffering God. But despite this he does usefully insist
that negation must be implicated in some way in God's reflective life,
and that God expresses the most extreme depth of that negation at one
point in history. For man's growth in spiritual maturity there needs to

---

[43] Taylor, op. cit. (n. 4 above), p. 209.
[44] Hegel, *Phenomenology of Mind*, p. 757; cf. pp. 486–7. 'Substance' is the process by
which Spirit becomes what it is in itself. See also *Philosophy of Religion* 3, pp. 180–2.
[45] Taylor, op. cit., p. 410.
[46] Hegel, 'The Spirit of Christianity and Its Fate', trans. T. M. Knox, in *Early
Theological Writings*, pp. 299–31.

be a place in history where the death of God becomes evident, and this means where it happens, for it can only become evident through the particular consciousness of one person. Hegel just stops short of saying that God faces the most alienating experience in the cross of Jesus *because* he has been drawn most deeply there into humanity through human response and obedience to him, but it is a natural conclusion from what he does say.

2. THE DIVINE LIFE ANNIHILATES ITSELF: THOMAS ALTIZER

In the light of our conclusion that Hegel's system portrays a negativity that is finally not alien to God at all, but which is continually being 'sublated' in the triumphant progress of the Spirit, it might seem extraordinary for a theologian of the 'death of God' movement to base his proposals upon an exposition of Hegel's self-negating Spirit. T. J. Altizer finds his inspiration for a self-sacrificing God in Hegel, but only by modifying Hegel's scheme in at least two major respects, which he either does not notice or neglects to draw attention to. It is worth choosing to take a second look at Altizer's thought from among the other 'death of God' theologians in our earlier survey, since his approach represents an attempt to deepen the element of kenosis within Hegel's framework, and also makes a further exploration of the possibilities of 'non-being' as a symbol for the suffering of God.

In the first major modification of Hegel's thought, Altizer depicts the self-giving movement of God as a total evacuation of divine being into the human person of Jesus Christ. Altizer takes his text from William Blake—'God is Jesus'[47]—and his exposition is that 'God himself has become incarnate and is fully and totally identical with Christ'.[48] By this act God negates himself in the sense of completely cancelling his primordial essence or selfhood. He 'negates his transcendent epiphany' so that henceforth any concept of God's having objective, transcendent reality is an 'alien and oppressive nothingness'.[49] God has annihilated his own being in becoming a man and suffering death, undertaking a 'kenotic metamorphosis'. Though Altizer hails Hegel's view of God's

---

[47] Blake, 'The Laocoön' (engraved about 1820), in *Blake: Complete Writings*, ed. Geoffrey Keynes (Oxford University Press, London, 1966), p. 777. Cf. *Jerusalem* 4: 18–21 (ed. Keynes, p. 622). According to Blake, Jesus is both the Human Imagination and Universal Humanity. (see e.g. *Jerusalem* 38: 16–21, ed. Keynes, p. 664). Altizer's debt to Blake is marked especially in his study *The New Apocalypse*; see pp. 143 ff.

[48] Altizer, *The Gospel of Christian Atheism*, p. 91.   [49] Ibid., p. 113.

self-negation as the basis for his thought, this is not quite what Hegel means by the term. For Hegel, as we have seen, God in his essence would remain an empty and lifeless thing unless he exposed his being to negation; for Altizer, emptiness of essence is the result of God's act of self-negation. For Hegel, God's being is taken up into a higher synthesis through the contradiction of the finite, returning to itself in a new way; for Altizer, it has been metamorphosed into something else—a finite being. For Hegel, death is the means of cancelling finitude; for Altizer, God's death cancels his essential nature. At root, for Hegel Absolute Spirit is not simply identical with the man Jesus; since man is finite spirit, God must be both identical *and* yet non-identical with all men in general and Jesus in particular.[50]

When Altizer echoes Hegel in saying that 'it is crucial to maintain that God remains God . . . while in a state of self-estrangement', he immediately interprets this as meaning that what is involved in the process of 'absolute negation' is the whole of God.[51] The differences between Altizer and his avowed mentor Hegel might be summed up in two images. For Altizer, God metamorphoses from one historical form to another, for which an apt image might be a caterpillar changing into a butterfly and then evolving on into other colourful forms unknown to any lepidopterist at present. For Hegel, the forward movement of the Spirit is like a flame, 'which passes from mortal candle to mortal candle, each destined to light and go out, but the flame to be eternal' (Taylor).[52] For Hegel, the flame remains in itself and the candle changes; for Altizer, God remains only in the sense that the metamorphosis goes on, and there is hope for a future epiphany of the Spiritual in some as yet undetectable form.

By this shift of meaning, Altizer has certainly converted the movement of the Spirit in Hegel into a moment of real self-sacrifice; within the Hegelian dialectic of a self-negating God this is perhaps the only way to take kenosis with utter seriousness. Altizer understands Hegel's view of the divine sacrifice of self in terms of Blake's annihilation of self.[53] But this does not allow God to remain God in the process as he does in Hegel's scheme. Nor does it seem possible to speak of a God who goes on suffering with mankind, though (as I observed

---

[50] See Taylor, op. cit. (n. 4 above), pp. 210, 491.

[51] Altizer, *The Gospel of Christian Atheism*, p. 88.   [52] Taylor, op. cit., p. 495.

[53] Altizer, *The New Apocalypse*, pp. 71–2. But note that according to Hegel the divine self is replaced by the self-making-the-sacrifice, not annihilated altogether; e.g. *Phenomenology of Mind*, p. 722.

before) he suffers a moment of loving suicide in the moment of metamorphosis. Moreover, the result of the total immersion of God into the finite world is that Altizer encourages us to embrace all life as it is.[54] There is no sense of protest against suffering, but an injunction to say yes to the world in all its pain. This indiscriminate acceptance of things as they are is underlined by Altizer's understanding of the incarnation of God beyond the death of Christ. This is not, as in Hegel, the passing of the flame from its concentrated brightness in one man to burn in the life of the community of the church. Rather, the incarnation today is the contemporary presence of the crucified Christ, which Altizer identifies as the modern sense that God is dead. The contemporary consciousness of the death of God is the form that Christ takes among us today, or at least faith takes a wager on the fact that it is. In totally loving the world, we 'can embrace even its pain and darkness as an epiphany of the body of Christ'.[55] This kind of affirmation of all suffering runs the danger of sanctioning pain in the name of faith; in Altizer it owes much to Nietzsche's myth of the Eternal Recurrence, with the need to say yes to chaos and meaninglessness in the present in order to bring about the turn of the age. In contrast, the idea of an objectively existing God who suffers with us has room for protest against the causes of suffering.

The second way in which Altizer deepens the *kenosis* of God in Hegel's thought is to describe an alien 'nothingness' which seems at first sight to have a genuine strangeness over against God. This nothing can be pictured as the 'shell' of the old primordial essence of God which he has cast off in his kenotic metamorphosis, or as the 'dead body' of God; so it is alien to God's present form of incarnation.[56] It is the concept of the absolute Sovereign to which Christianity regresses after the event of the death of God, or his self-evacuation into the person of Christ and his self-annihilation in the death of Christ. In a kind of reversal of the incarnation, religious belief wants to revive the idea of a transcendent world ruler, and it makes this the principle of negative judgement against life, upon which we project all our noes to life. As the embodiment of an absolute no-saying, it is an alien and oppressive nothingness, the Satan of Blake's visions.[57] The crucifixion of Jesus has

[54] Altizer, *The Gospel of Christian Atheism*, pp. 147–57.   [55] Ibid., p. 156.
[56] Ibid., pp. 101, 109–10; *The New Apocalypse*, pp. 74–5.
[57] Altizer, *The Gospel of Christian Atheism*, p. 109; *The New Apocalypse*, pp. 133–4. Further on the figure of Satan, see Katherine Raine, *The Human Face of God: William Blake and the Book of Job* (Thames and Hudson, London, 1982), pp. 193–201, 303–5.

reversed the primordial, detached sacrality of God, so that henceforth it is simply 'nothing', but a nothing that still oppresses humanity with the threats of legalism and absolute demands.

If this 'nothingness' is understood as a creation of man's religious desires, keeping alive what God himself has declared to be dead, then it is indeed something alien to God. We might say (though Altizer himself would not) that God suffers from having a strange role thrust upon him by mankind, and so encounters an alien phantom which his creatures have brought into creation and called by his name. Though I have been opposing the view that *any* kind of objectively existing God would be an oppressor, Altizer makes the important point that the *dominating* kind of God is strictly 'nothing', in the light of the cross; the Apostle Paul had of course said something similar (1 Cor. 1: 28). This is a nothing which can be felt as hostile, laying upon us the laws of rationalism and moralism which Blake called 'mind-forg'd manacles'.[58] Indeed, Blake (who is Altizer's second major mentor) dubbed such a God 'Nobodaddy'; he appears in Blake's *Songs of Experience* as 'selfish Father of men' and takes final shape in his mythological illuminated books as Urizen, a deity who is portrayed as using Newton's compass to measure the deeps in his capacity as the presiding genius of scientific mechanization and deism.[59] Urizen is simply the faculty of human reason which has supplanted the imagination and has been allowed to construct a world under the dominion of law, whether the laws of Newton, Locke, or Moses. Reason has entered the 'state' of Satan, and become Nobodaddy. Blake is concerned with the false God created by human consciousness, and with the true divinity of the human imagination, represented by Jesus. He is not concerned either to affirm or deny the existence of a transcendent God, but he does deny that any real Father Almighty can be known *directly*; the true Almighty can only be known in his image, the Man Jesus, or the 'human face' of God.[60]

---

[58] Blake, 'London', v. 2, in *Songs of Experience*; cf. the 'Satanic Mills' of *Milton*, Preface.

[59] Blake, 'To Nobodaddy' (ed. Keynes (see n. 47 above), p. 171); 'Earth's Answer', v. 2, in *Songs of Experience*. See also 'The Ancient of Days', Frontispiece to *Europe: A Prophecy*, and with this picture compare *The First book of Urizen*, ch. 7. 8, 'He formed golden compasses' (ed. Keynes, p. 234) and Milton, 4. 11, 'Art thou not Newton's Pantocrator?' (ed. Keynes, p. 483). It is ironic that the picture of the Ancient of Days, who is Blake's false 'God of this world' appears on the dust-jacket of the recent book by Keith Ward, *Rational Theology and the Creativity of God*.

[60] See Blake, 'The Divine Image', in *Songs of Innocence*; also *Annotations to Swedenborg's Divine Love*, 11, 'God is a man . . . because he is the creator of man' (ed. Keynes, p. 90). Cf. Raine, op. cit. (n. 57 above), pp. 47–8, 216, 310–11.

Altizer, however, does not restrict the 'Satanic' kind of creator-God to the sphere of human illusions. He takes up Blake's imagery within the Hegelian framework of Absolute spirit which negates itself. The erstwhile transcendent God has sacrificed himself, and so produced the 'Satan' as his dead body. This dead body, the notion of an objective world ruler whom God once was, has gone on decaying in Christendom, becoming more and more tyrannical as it has drawn human denials of life to itself.[61] Christian faith has paid it the dubious compliment of trembling before it in guilt and dread. But the time will come when it reaches such a peak of nothingness that it will stand revealed for what it is, an empty and lifeless thing; there will be 'an epiphany of the Antichrist', and being stripped bare its power will be broken.[62] In the face of that epiphany, we too will be able to annihilate our Selfhood, or our self-righteousness. Like Blake's figure of Milton, we shall address the Satan within the deadly 'shadow' of our own Selfhood:

> '. . . Know thou, I come to Self Annihilation.
> Such are the Laws of Eternity, that each shall mutually
> Annihilate himself for others' good, as I for thee.'[63]

So, according to Altizer, the present consciousness that 'God is dead' is in fact the darkness before the dawn; it is the first glimmering of perception that the cosmic ruler is really Nothing, an alien emptiness which is the antithesis of all life and energy, and it heralds the coming apocalypse. We must have the courage to name the darkness as Antichrist, to detect the 'smell' of the decomposing dead body of God.[64] In Altizer's scheme of history, the alien 'nothing' is the necessary consequence of God's kenotic sacrifice, and the negation of this Satan in a universal self-annihilation will therefore complete the self-annihilation of God. Altizer in a burst of mysticism conflates into one reality the negation of Satan, the crucifixion of Jesus, and the self-sacrifice of the Father. The alien 'dead body of God' is revealed as 'the atoning body of Christ' and one can even speak of 'the atoning work of Satan':

We cannot dissociate the alien body of the Antichrist from the Christ who is the embodiment of the self-negation of God.[65]

---

[61] Altizer, *The Gospel of Christian Atheism*, pp. 94–8.
[62] Ibid., pp. 120–1; cf. *The New Apocalypse*, pp. 211–13.
[63] Blake, *Milton*, 38. 29–36; cf. Altizer, *The New Apocalypse*, pp. 197 ff.
[64] Altizer, *The Gospel of Christian Atheism*, p. 96.
[65] Ibid., p. 122; also pp. 115–17 and *The New Apocalypse*, pp. 81–2, 206–7.

Dressed in the borrowed robes of Blake's symbols, Altizer is arguing for a universal process of loss of Selfhood (or self-righteousness), in which God and man equally participate. 'Only when the crucifixion is accepted as the innermost reality of the "Human Imagination" will the Kingdom of God appear in its universal form as the God who is becoming all in all.'[66] Altizer looks beyond the present age to an apocalypse, an unveiling of a new spirituality in which the human passions and imagination will flower in a new Jerusalem. In Blake's terms, the annihilation of the Selfhood, and so the transforming of the 'state' of Satan, is the human reason returning its stolen sovereignty to the imagination. In a new version of Hegel, it is the infinite spirit becoming fully immanent in humanity.

Altizer's mystical vision presents a 'Nothingness' which breaks out of Hegel's dialectic in so far as it is properly alien to God as the phantom of human Selfhood. But Altizer draws the 'dead body of God' back into the Hegelian orbit of necessity, by seeing the epiphany of the Satan as a necessary unfolding of the kenosis of absolute Spirit. Altizer's version of apocalypse requires us to accept all manifestations of darkness in the present as a necessary herald to the dawn; they are the necessary preparation for the forming of the imagination, the 'human form divine'. All things will dance when we greet them with affirmation, and so release ourselves from a life of no-saying which goes with obeisance to a transcendent deity. But to this apocalyptic scenario we must surely repeat our objection, that there are horrors to which we cannot say yes, some darknesses which we cannot name as the frontier to light. There are some against which we must simply protest, as a fundamental part of sharing in God's sacrifice.

Yet Altizer has an important insight into the nature of Nothing as the phantom of Selfhood, which we must take up into a theology of a suffering God. He envisages the emergence of the Satan as a reaction of the human religious spirit to the self-sacrifice of God. It is a human regression to an empty and alien form of Spirit in response to divine kenosis. Though Altizer regards any belief in a transcendent personal God as such a regression, we may at least agree with him that the images of cosmic law giver and oppressive judge are such a reaction. The building-up of the Satanic Nothing is then, if not a necessary part of the kenosis of God, at least a by-product of it, by way of human reaction.

---

[66] Altizer, *The New Apocalypse*, p. 205.

The human spirit cannot bear too much humility from God, and to bolster its own Selfhood retreats into worship of a self-preserving God. This kind of emergence of the Antichrist fits well into the pattern we have been exploring of a Nothing which is 'most alien and yet most his own' for God. It is most alien in that it comes from the side of the creature, yet it is most his own because it is the consequence of his own sacrifice as the living God. Indeed, following our previous exposition of God's generation of his own Other in the Son, we may say that it is the consequence of his own self-differentiation. In choosing to be God again a second time, he begets the Son who is to be identified with mankind in humility and suffering, yet this movement of self-sacrifice provokes a reaction from his creatures who, as Barth puts it, object in their 'small and perverted thinking' that God ought to be the 'Wholly Other'.[67] God suffers this reaction, this creation of a phantom God, as the pain of rejection. Altizer himself, however, can only think of God's self-sacrifice as self-annihilation since he has renounced the concept of the Trinity; the 'Son' is simply the new form which the whole of God takes in history.[68]

3.   NON-BEING ACTIVATES THE DIVINE LIFE: PAUL TILLICH

In trying to make sense of the notion that God suffers by confronting an alien 'non-being', we have been examining the way in which some theologians have envisaged the confrontation as arising within the vital movement of God's own being. The living God generates the negative, whether in terms of Hegelian self-negation or Altizer's self-annihilation. Now, Paul Tillich (with other existential thinkers) has learned from Hegel that there is no life without negativity, but he is highly critical of the smooth way in which the negative is synthesized with positive life in the Hegelian system, and protests that estrangement in existence is not conquered as easily as that.[69] He therefore proposes a notion of God as Being in whom there is no synthesis into a higher reality, but a continual dialectic of opposites, each side of the dialectic remaining in creative tension with the other. Thus God as 'Being as such' or 'being-itself' eternally includes and overcomes non-being, but non-being is infinitely

---

[67] Barth, *CD* IV/1, p. 186.
[68] Altizer, op. cit., pp. 105–6.
[69] See above, n. 22. Also see Tillich, *Systematic Theology*, 2, pp. 26–8, 34, *Theology of Culture*, pp. 82–4.

resistant to being. Since the negative is always there to be coped with by being, it is in effect the activating element in the divine life:

Non-being drives being out of seclusion, it forces it to affirm itself dynamically. . . . Non-being (that in God which makes his self-affirmation dynamic) opens up the divine self-seclusion and reveals him as power and love. Non-being makes God a living God. Without the No he has to overcome in himself and in his creature, the divine Yes to himself would be lifeless.[70]

We might say that while in Hegel the positive generates the negative, here the negative generates the positive. The conquest of the negative is like the making of a pearl in the oyster; the grit is the source of the treasure. In a study of the ontology of Tillich, Adrian Thatcher has usefully drawn attention to the manner in which Tillich pairs the terms 'ground of being' and 'abyss of being' as a reflection of the interplay between being and non-being in God. Thatcher claims convincingly that the 'abysmal element in the ground of being' or 'the negative side of the mystery', is modelled firmly on the *Ungrund* of Jacob Boehme and the *Potenz* of Schelling's thought.[71] In both these previous statements about divine Being, non-being is the basic creative force which generates life and goodness. We notice that Berdyaev is similarly indebted to Boehme when he speaks of Freedom as the not-created will ('non-being') which 'precedes being', so that he defines *Ungrund* as 'the primal pre-existential freedom'.[72]

If we ask why Tillich develops such a speculative scheme, the answer to be gleaned from his *Systematic Theology* is his concern to speak of a God who 'participates in the negativities of our lives'. It is not enough to speak of ourselves as beings participating in ultimate being. That which is of ultimate concern to us must be meaningful to those who are in 'the boundary situations of life', and so we must try to speak of being-itself as participating in the existential situation of beings.[73] Despite the fact that only a few pages of the *Systematic Theology* explicitly comment on the idea of the passibility of God, the concerns of theodicy underly the whole sweep of the system. Although Tillich refers to traditional patripassianism as an 'error', he finds that the truth behind it is the

[70] Tillich, *The Courage to Be*, p. 174; cf. Tillich, *Systematic Theology*, 1, pp. 210, 258–60, 280.

[71] Thatcher, op. cit. (ch. 8 n. 8 above), pp. 57–9. Tillich himself of course draws attention to non-being in the thought of Boehme, Schelling, and Berdyaev: *Systematic Theology*, 1, pp. 198–201, 210.

[72] Berdyaev, *Spirit and Reality*, p. 130. Cf. Calian, op. cit. (ch. 3 n. 78), pp. 15–17.

[73] Tillich, *Systematic Theology*, 1, p. 300; 3, pp. 430–2.

eternal conquest of the negative by God.[74] In our human existence we experience the 'shock of non-being', for instance in the mystical 'dark night of the soul' and universally in the threat of death; this shock awakens us to the presence of being, which offers us the 'courage to be' in the face of non-being and estrangement. Since God is being-itself in which all beings participate, he must include the same polar elements within himself, namely the ground (the positive) and the abyss (the negative) of being.[75]

Thus Tillich's method is to move from the existential to the ontological, from our experience of being and non-being to the very structure of being. In a further move he gives the symbolic name 'God' to being-itself (though it is never clear in Tillich's presentation whether he admits that 'being-itself' as well as 'God' is only a symbol for ultimate reality).[76] He has certainly been criticized for failing adequately to defend this movement from the existential to the ontological, from thought to reality. However, though he hints at the Hegelian defence that there is an identity of being and thinking,[77] it seems clear that the pervasive motive within his method is theodicy; our encounter with non-being is only tolerable, and we can only draw the courage-to-be from the ground of being, if that which is our ultimate concern is also meeting and conquering non-being.

So we must ask whether the confrontation between God and non-being, in the form that Tillich describes it, can in fact be called an exposure to real alienation or, in other words, suffering. Does the sequence of a negative power activating positive life in God support and illuminate the claim that God participates in the negativities of our creaturely existence?[78] Does Tillich's way of thinking present a God whose experience is sufficiently analogous to our experience of facing death, even given his reservation that we should be aware of the symbolic character of all religious language? These are questions which Tillich himself echoes when he asks: 'What does it mean that God takes the suffering of the world upon himself by participating in existential estrangement?'[79] To answer these questions we must (as with Hegel) look first to what Tillich has to say about negation within God himself,

---

[74] Ibid., 1, p. 300.   [75] Ibid., p. 122.

[76] Thatcher, op. cit. (ch. 8 n. 8 above), pp. 33–40, has an excellent discussion of this point. See also Tillich, *The Courage To Be*, pp. 173–5, and *Systematic Theology*, 2, pp. 10–11.   [77] Cf. Paul Tillich, *Theology of Culture*, p. 81.

[78] I argue for this linkage at the beginning of this chapter: see pp. 230–1.

[79] Tillich, *Systematic Theology*, 2, pp. 201–2; cf. 1., p. 300.

and then to what he says about God's participation in the estrangement of human life.

In considering Tillich's vision of the divine life, we become immediately aware that he is sliding between two sorts of aggression in describing a non-being that is dialectical with being. On the one hand, non-being is aggressive in the sense of the Platonic-Augustinian tradition of *mē on*—the resisting of being. For us, in a state of creaturely existence, this is bound to mean an experience of threat and anxiety, and it is to our lives that Tillich applies this impact of hostile non-being. On the other hand, non-being in the divine life is aggressive in the sense of the *Ungrund* of Boehme, a vitality which drives being out into action and manifestation. While this certainly applies to God in Tillich's scheme, it hardly seems the same kind of shock that we have to endure. Though Tillich uses the language of aggression about God's engagement with his non-being, such as 'serious fight' and 'risk',[80] it is an aggression of healthy vitality. In his earlier writings Tillich spoke of the 'depth and abyss of being' as 'demonic', but he made it clear that it had only a creative power in the being of God.[81]

Our doubts about the alien and hostile nature of the non-being God conquers in himself are underlined by what Tillich has to say about the place of the finite in the divine life. Tillich explains that God must include the finite, arguing in a manner reminiscent of Hegel that if finitude remained outside the infinite then the infinite would be limited by it. Tillich adds that since God includes the finite, he also contains 'the element of non-being which belongs to finitude'.[82] Finitude cannot be conceived without non-being, since we know the finite as 'being, limited by non-being'.[83] For instance, as we have seen before, to be here and now is *not* to be something or somewhere else. Now, in its essential character, the finitude of the creature is conditioned by a non-being which is a mere boundary and not a destructive force; in traditional terms, this non-being is simply *ouk on*, or neutral nothingness. But creatures do not in fact experience finitude in its essential form, since they have their being in a state of existence. In Tillich's language, existence is estranged from essence;[84] this, as we shall see in a moment, is

---

[80] Ibid., 3, p. 431.
[81] Paul Tillich, *The Interpretation of History*, trans. N. Rasetzki and E. Tabney (Charles Scribner's Sons, New York, 1936), p. 93, cf. pp. 80–4. For discussion, see R. A. Killen, *The Ontological Theology of Paul Tillich* (Kampen, Kok, 1956), pp. 173 ff.
[82] Tillich, *Systematic Theology*, 1, p. 279.   [83] Ibid., pp. 210–11.
[84] For this whole paragraph, see Tillich, ibid., 2, pp. 78–86.

the given fact of creation. So they experience the limits of non-being and death as hostile negatives (*mē on*), which threaten and distort life. However, as being-itself, God is beyond the contrast between essence and existence,[85] transcending even essence, and so the non-being he apparently takes into himself along with finitude must be, to say the least, of the most neutral and harmless kind. Nor can the infinite be limited by non-being anyway, but continually negates it. All this has scarce similarity to our situation as finite creatures.[86]

Thus, the fact that the vital non-being which 'drives out' being presents no real 'risk' to God is underlined by its equation with the weakly non-being which finitude brings into his infinite life. The non-being which God faces in himself seems to have merely a verbal link with the non-being we encounter, and it is hard to see how Tillich can claim that it gives the basis for God's 'sharing the negativities of our lives'. We are not surprised that Tillich is highly critical of patripassianism in its full sense, and judges that the Early Church was correct to reject the doctrine that 'God the Father suffered in Christ', for 'God as being-itself transcends non-being absolutely'.[87] At first sight the thrustful non-being which activates the positive within God seems to have more of a potential for alienation than the negative in Hegel's view of God, which is simply a 'play of love'. But on closer examination, it turns out to be no threat at all.

This does not mean, I suggest, that the symbol of non-being as 'driving out' being can make no contribution to the idea of the suffering of God. It expresses a hunger and thirst of God for fellowship with his creation, evoking the sense of a hollow (an 'abyss') in the heart of God which craves satisfaction. This is the permanent validity of the baroque speculations of Boehme, and their inheritance in Tillich. Curiously, however, Tillich himself undercuts this aspect of the symbol by his conception of God as being-itself, which 'transcends the fulfilment and

[85] Although Tillich also defines 'being-itself' as beyond both the finite and the infinite (ibid., I, pp. 263, 212: 'being-itself precedes the infinite negation of the finite), this does not apparently prevent his speaking of God or being-itself as 'infinite' in his power of being (ibid., p. 72), and as uniting the finite with the infinite in the way described above. The difficulty here in using the language of Being for transcendence and immanence is not solved by the occasional notion of 'God above God' (e.g. in *The Courage to Be*, pp. 176–83, and *Systematic Theology*, 2, pp. 13–14), as we then have the problem of relating grades of God to being-itself.

[86] I have already made this point when considering the development of the notion of hostile non-being from creaturely existence: see Ch. 8, section 1, p. 211.

[87] Tillich, *Systematic Theology*, I, p. 300; cf. 3, p. 431.

non-fulfilment of reality' and so makes it difficult to speak of desire in God. He judges cautiously that the divine urge towards the fulfilment of the eschaton can only be 'compared, but not equated with eros';[88] the eternal conquest of the negative in God is such a constant state of blessedness that it can be nothing less than the blessedness of the fulfilment of the Kingdom of God.

If, in this respect, we give fuller force to the symbol of an abyss in the heart of God than Tillich himself does, we must however recall our earlier conclusion that we can go no further in our thought about the self-sacrifice of God than his willing desire to be this kind of God. The hollow of non-being in God is not the cause of his desire for fellowship with his world, but a consequence and a symbol of it. With this crucial modification, it is a valuable symbol, making the link between God's primordial choice for suffering and his actual exposure to the hostile non-being which he encounters in his creation. This choice of God, I have been suggesting, is inseparable from his primal choice to be himself as One Lord in self-repetition, living a complex personal life which we can only call Father, Son and Spirit. In the very act of loving the eternal Son, he freely chooses covenant with man and all the suffering that entails; suffering then is implicit in the very desire of God for fellowship, and this is well expressed by using the symbol of non-being both for the hollow of God's desire and its outworking in empathy with his creatures. A genuinely alien non-being can only enter the life of God from the life of the creature, and neither directly from God's positing his opposite (Hegel) nor as a negative life force which God 'overcomes' within himself (Tillich). Neither of these kinds of negative can be really hostile to God. There *is* a basis in God's character as the living God for exposure to alienation, but it can only be his own desire for fellowship and sympathy with finite creatures, which is inseparable from his personal diversification as Father, Son and the Spirit of unity.

Tillich, of course, admits the validity of personal language as an analogy for being-itself. Indeed, he appeals to Trinity as effectively symbolizing the dynamic life of God in its dialectic of being overcoming non-being, with non-being providing the continual element of 'otherness' in God.[89] But something is odd in this equation.

---

[88] Ibid., 1, p. 312; cf. 3, pp. 340–2.

[89] Ibid., 3, pp. 301–2. Thatcher, op. cit. (ch. 8 n. 8 above), pp. 92–3, is surely not correct in regarding as a Hegelian remnant the equation that Tillich makes between Trinity and the dialectic of being and non-being. In Hegel, the basic pattern is that the positive generates the negative, and so negation within the essence of Spirit is the 'true opposite' of the Father, not an opposition to be conquered.

Taken exactly, it would mean that 'non-being' must be identified with one person of the Trinity, and so we would have the absurd symbol of the Father's demonstrating his vitality in overcoming the Son, or the Son's provoking the Father into exerting himself. Tillich is clearly not at ease with the personal symbol of Trinity. Though he affirms that God is not less than personal, as the ground of everything personal,[90] he is claiming that the most adequate language for ultimate reality which we have is 'being-itself' rather than Personal Being. This he believes best articulates the transcendence and immanence of that which is our 'ultimate concern'. Yet we have already seen some of the problems that the notion of Being (or 'being-itself') as beyond existence and essence has for the claim that God encounters a non-being and estrangement anything like ours.

As we move from Tillich's thought about the divine life in itself to God's atoning activity in the world, we find further problems stemming from his preference for making 'Being', rather than Personality, the final definition for God. we must certainly admire his perceptive unveiling of the heart of atonement as a matter of participation:

God participates in the suffering of existential estrangement, but his suffering is not a substitute for the suffering of the creature. Neither is the suffering of the Christ a substitute for the suffering of man. But the suffering of God, universally and in the Christ, is the power which overcomes creaturely self-destruction by participation and transformation.[91]

This is a magnificent short statement of the Christian doctrine of atonement, yet we are bound to ask what content can be given to participation by God in creaturely suffering. There is undoubtedly *scope* for a real divine suffering in Tillich's account of human life, since the non-being which is present to be encountered in human experience is genuinely alien, both to God and to man's essential being. The riddle of the Fall, as we have previously seen,[92] is that all beings who exist have actualized their freedom in a way that means falling into estrangement, but this has the 'character of a leap and not of a structural necessity'.[93] Tillich affirms that while the Fall is not a logical necessity of creation, as a matter of fact it coincides with creation. According to his profound analysis of human existence, we live in the tension between our freedom

---

[90] Tillich, op. cit., 1, p. 271; cf. 2, pp. 12–14.
[91] Ibid., 2, p. 203.
[92] Ibid., p. 45. (See above, p. 214, for a discussion of the 'riddle' of the Fall.)
[93] Ibid., p. 50.

and our limitations, or in 'the polarity of freedom and destiny'.[94] In this situation of finite freedom we become anxious, and try to cope with our anxiety in inauthentic ways; instead of trusting in the power of being we make our ultimate concern of things that are not ultimate, and the result is that we are estranged from our essential selfhood. The things within the world which we make our final security, or our 'idols', acquire power over us, for if we must have them they have become our masters. They have become 'demonic', or instruments of destructive non-being. The limit of finitude (non-being) is felt as threat; Death itself which ought to be a neutral non-being becomes a force of non-being that distorts our existence: 'the essential anxiety about non-being is transformed into the horror of death'.[95]

Tillich, then, graphically depicts the Fall as a riddle which has scope within it for a divine suffering of something truly alien. We may, however, doubt whether Tillich has found the right ontological framework for the riddle. Tillich certainly aims to avoid making hostile non-being a necessity of creation. In his ontology, the Fall is a movement from essence to existence which needs to be told as a story and not a dialectical step because, in spite of its tragic universality, this estranged existence 'cannot be derived from essence'.[96] If it were so derived, then there could be no possibility of salvation; while 'essence' is not a literal realm in time or space which creatures ever did or will occupy, it is possible to live by the *power* of essence in the midst of existence.[97] But since, in this system of thought existence is estranged from essence by its very definition, the notion of 'a transition from essence to existence' perhaps tips the balance towards necessity. What concerns us even more here, however, is that the scheme makes it difficult to see how God can participate in the self-destructive consequences of our estranged existence. While we are estranged from essence, God as being-itself transcends both essence and existence. We thus have the curious situation that on the one hand Tillich succeeds in describing a genuinely alien non-being which could give cogency to the idea of God's suffering, but on the other hand effectively excludes God from encountering it. Tillich himself explains that 'God's taking the suffering of the world upon himself' is a highly symbolic kind of

[94] For this and the following account, see Tillich, ibid., 1, pp. 212–14; 2, pp. 39–41, 78–80.
[95] Ibid., 2, p. 78.
[96] Ibid., p. 50, cf. pp. 34–5.   [97] Ibid., p. 50, cf. pp. 38–9.

speaking, and refers us instead to the eternal conquest of non-being in the living God:

This element of non-being, seen from the inside, *is* the suffering which God takes upon himself by participating in existential estrangement or the state of unconquered negativity. Here the doctrine of the living God and the doctrine of Atonement coincide.[98]

But do they? The conquering of non-being within being-itself cannot be an equivalent experience to an actual participation in existential estrangement, so that the one can simply stand for the other. Tillich thus has a further proposal; God participates in estranged existence only in a certain mode—that is, in the manner of conquest, overcoming estrangement. What his inner conquest of non-being actually corresponds to is not *any* kind of participation in worldly existence, but a very special kind—a victorious participation which takes the form of the 'creation of the New Being'. According to Tillich, 'New Being is essential being under the conditions of existence, conquering the gap between essence and existence'.[99] Essential being comes into existence but resists the forces of estrangement that normally distort existence. This New Being has appeared in a 'personal life', the life of Jesus of Nazareth, for the power of the New Being cannot have become actualized except in the sphere where the transition from essence to existence is most radical, that is in an individual finite person. The fact that a being who has finite freedom under the conditions of time and space is nevertheless not estranged from the ground of his being is, admits Tillich, a paradox; but it is not irrational, and is the one basic paradox in the Christian gospel.[100]

Tillich finds Jesus to be the final revelation of the mystery of being, because he negates the non-being which distorts existence, while sharing in the negativities of existence. That is, unlike our response to the anxieties of human life, Jesus refuses to make an idol (a 'demon') of anything finite; he even refuses to allow his fellowship with the Father to become an authority to be imposed on other people, and in his death he surrenders the last idol of his own self. We should certainly acknowledge that this is an illuminating way of explaining the uniqueness of Jesus, as consisting in his obedient relationship to the Father. However, because of Tillich's ontological framework, we have the curious result that Jesus is presented as not only negating the *demons* of the finite (the idols) but finitude itself. We have already seen that

[98] Ibid., p. 202. [99] Ibid., p. 136. [100] Ibid., pp. 138–9, 145.

Tillich equates that non-being which God eternally overcomes in himself with the non-being which is the natural, negative element in finitude, or its limits. In line with this equation, the full manifestation within existence of the ground of being must similarly mean the negating of the boundaries of the finite. In his theory of the symbol, Tillich in fact declares that the infinite can only reveal itself through the negation of the finite.[101] Jesus therefore has to subjugate the finite because it is idolatry not only for anything finite to replace the infinite, but even to claim to represent it. In giving himself up to death, he prevents his finite being from becoming something ultimate for his followers. Jesus as 'Jesus of Nazareth' sacrifices himself to Jesus as 'The Christ', or the power of the New Being. This, according to Tillich, is essential manhood under the conditions of existence, or God-manhood.[102]

The result of this ontological scheme is that Tillich tries to depict Jesus as both engaging in finite existence, experiencing all the anxieties which belong to it, and yet also negating it. So he pictures Jesus as suffering such anxieties as having to die, the insecurity of homelessness, the loneliness and frustrations of his mission, the desires of temptation, and doubts about his own work.[103] But at the same time, Jesus apparently has 'the character of the one whose communion with God is unbroken' and he has 'the serenity and majesty of him who preserves this unity against all the attacks coming from estranged existence'. In a way reminiscent of Schleiermacher, Tillich asserts that even in facing utter non-being in the cross, his blessedness of communion with the father remains undisrupted: 'There are no traces of unbelief . . . even in the extreme situation of despair about his messianic work, he cries out to his God who has forsaken him.'[104] Tillich is drawing a close analogy ('and more than an analogy') between the eternal blessedness of God in overcoming non-being, and the certainty of communion with God which Jesus had in the midst of temptation.[105] Tillich claims that both

---

[101] Ibid., 1, p. 148; cf. Tillich, *Dynamics of Faith* (Harper Torchbooks, New York, 1958), pp. 44–5.

[102] Tillich, *Systematic Theology*, 1, pp. 148–53; 2, pp. 137–8.

[103] Ibid., 2, pp. 150–4.

[104] Ibid., pp. 145, 157, 159, 172–3. Cf. F. Schleiermacher, *The Christian Faith*, H. R. Mackintosh and J. S. Stewart (T. & T. Clark, Edinburgh, ²1928), pp. 435–6. Despite Tillich's criticism of Schleiermacher (op. cit., p. 173) on the grounds that his view of the God-consciousness of Jesus is too anthropological, their ideas of unbroken communion are very similar.   [105] Tillich, *Systematic Theology*, 3, pp. 431–2.

the temptations of Jesus and the eternal victory of being over non-being are a matter of 'serious fight, risk, and uncertainty', but it is difficult to credit this in the light of Tillich's view (which, amazingly, he ascribes to the Synoptic Gospels) that Jesus cannot be described as 'identifying' himself with the estranged condition of humanity:

He enters it and takes the tragic and self-destructive consequences upon himself, but he does not identify himself with it.[106]

Such a subtle distinction between participation and identification has its origin in the prior ontological scheme of a dynamic non-being which generates the positive life of God. Given such a definition of non-being, victory over it easily takes on the form of undisturbed blessedness, and the proper insistence that God 'does not *lose* his identity in his self-alteration' (my italics)[107] becomes an inability of God to identify himself with finite creatures, despite Tillich's insight that being-itself participates in the consequences of estrangement.

We ought not to assume, of course, that Tillich has in mind a historic Jesus of Nazareth at all, when he affirms that the New Being is fully manifest in a person. Some commentators take his reference to 'the picture of Jesus' to mean that he is concerned not with a literal person but a portrait of essential manhood; others take it to mean that this is an admittedly 'expressionist' painting but that there must have been an original historical figure who was at least a 'sitter' for it.[108] Whichever exegesis we adopt (and I incline to the latter view of what Tillich intends), there is a diminishing of the notion of the suffering of God. Whether in a particular historical person, or simply in an ever present principle of essential manhood which is on offer to us, essential being surely cannot appear under the conditions of existence without estrangement, and yet still be said to suffer risks.

---

[106] Ibid., 2, p. 157.

[107] Ibid., 3, p. 432; Cf. 1, p. 148; 2, p. 173.

[108] See John P. Clayton, 'Is Jesus necessary for Christology? An antinomy in Tillich's theological method', in S. W. Sykes and J. P. Clayton (eds.), *Christ, Faith and History* (Cambridge University Press, 1972), pp. 147–64; John Knox, *The Humanity and Divinity of Christ* (Cambridge University Press, 1967). Clayton takes the view (op. cit., p. 132) that there is a historical basis for the portrait, quoting Tillich's statement that there is some *analogia imaginis* 'between the picture and the actual personal life from which it has arisen'. (Tillich, op. cit., 2, p. 132). Knox, however, argues (op. cit., p. 86) that Tillich cannot mean that essential manhood was made fully existential in Jesus of Nazareth, since this would be docetic. Our present argument agrees with Clayton about Tillich's meaning, and with Knox about its docetic result.

Once more, I suggest, we see by contrast the strength of personal language as the final analogy for the being of God. A God who opens himself to suffering through his own desires can willingly identify himself with estranged humanity, and feel the impact of hostile non-being in a more real way than he would by merely overcoming a vital non-being within himself. A human being who uniquely responds to God in trusting obedience gives God the greatest opportunity for entrance into the human condition in empathy and activity. What matters is what Jesus makes of estrangement, growing in trustful obedience through moments of broken communion, not his exemption from it. God can indeed be said to experience alien non-being through his relationship with Jesus, if in death Christ undergoes utter despair, disruption of fellowship, shattering of blessedness, and total desolation.

Tillich's account of non-being rightly directs our attention to the relation of God to the finite. But instead of finding that God negates the finite when he participates in it, we may say that God is humble enough to hide his glory within it. This is part of his suffering, that he conceals himself within flesh, that he manifests his glory in the unlikely and hidden form of mortal life and death. He transcends the finite through his commitment to it; he is manifest precisely in his hiddenness. He takes on the strange form of the finite with its limits of non-being, and thus exposes himself to the yet stranger encounter with the non-being of estrangement. He is free to do this and not to lose himself, as the one who is supremely Personal, for it is the mark of being personal to give oneself away to the uttermost and thereby to reach fullness of life.

10

Overcoming Nothingness

E're time and place were, time and place were not
When Primitive *Nothing* something strait begot,
Then all proceeded from the great united—What?

So, in the seventeenth century, the Earl of Rochester gleefully satirized the widespread appeal in the theology of his time to the idea of 'non-being'.[1] He certainly has his successors today who suspect that 'non-being' has become a blanket term covering a careless confusion between a feeling in experience and a description of reality. Yet we cannot dismiss the fact that very different religious thinkers such as Hegel and, in recent times, Barth, Tillich, Macquarrie, Altizer, and Jüngel are on to something important when they find the notion of 'non-being' or 'negativity' an indispensable accompaniment to the notion of God as Being.[2] I have been suggesting that its chief validity lies in being a way of speaking about the sacrifice or the suffering of God, although we have also seen how easy it is to slip from one sense of the term to another, and to defuse it of its hostility and power of alienation. 'Non-being' is a rich symbol for the suffering of God, evoking as it does something alien that befalls God in relationship with his creation. The encounter of God with an alienating 'nothingness' can only be a symbol for the reality of the suffering of God, but it does provide a focus for much of what we have discovered in this study about the suffering of the God who lives and yet experiences death.

'Non-being' is objectively real, not as a hypostasis, but because it *happens* in relationship between God and the world, underlining the fact that suffering must befall God as well as being something he actively

---

[1] 'Upon Nothing', v. 2, in *Poems* by John Wilmot, Earl of Rochester, ed. V. de Sola Pinto (Routledge and Kegan Paul, London, [2]1964), pp. 77–9.

[2] While these theologians agree that God ought to be conceived as 'Being' in contradistinction from 'an individual being', Barth and Jüngel differ from the others in holding (as I have also been arguing) to the equal primacy of language of personality; See Jüngel, *God as the Mystery of the World*, pp. 289–90; Barth, *CD* II/1, pp. 297–8.

undertakes, if it is to be a suffering recognizably like ours. Much of my earlier discussion was concerned to show that God's suffering must be not only a feeling and an act, but also an injury and a constraint upon him. Hostile 'non-being' aptly symbolizes the alien nature of this suffering, arising from the freedom of God's creation. Moreover, the standing of non-being in a dialectic with Being also points to the ambiguous relationship of suffering to God, as something hostile, and yet intimate to him and inseparable from him. In the first place this dialectic expresses, in its own symbolism, the point made by the process theologians about the relationship between God and the world; the fact that the world has a painful impact upon God is not something that could have been otherwise. When we speak of God, we cannot but speak of someone on an adventure to reap tragic beauty, in this or some other world; according to the symbolism explored in the last two chapters, we can only conceive of Being in dialectic with non-being. But throughout this study we have found the reason for this in the *desire* of God and the response of creation rather than in any ultimate process of creativity. There can be no 'otherwise' in the suffering of God, because we cannot go back further in thought about God than his free choice to be a God who is vulnerable to hurt from his world. As supreme Personality, God determines his being as God 'for us', and it is not our place to protest in an excess of metaphysical politeness that he need not have done so.

Thinking about the suffering of God in the context of a dialectic of being and non-being gives expression, in the second place, to the claim that God endures something analogous to our experience of death. The human experience of 'perishing' is characterized by being 'most alien and yet most our own', and this is precisely what several religious thinkers have perceived (though in admittedly diverse ways) about the encounter of God with hostile non-being; it is strange to him and yet somehow belongs to him. If we trace the path to 'non-being' from creaturely existence,[3] then alien non-being arises from the freedom which God himself has granted to creation, together with his own gift of an environment in which a lapsing towards non-being is practically inevitable. We learn, nevertheless, from Barth to recognize the sting of man's 'no' to God within the divine and human experience of death, and from the process theologians we learn to ascribe to the whole of nature a freedom to resist God.

---

[3] This is the theme of ch. 8 above.

If we trace the path to hostile non-being from the movement of God's own being,[4] as do Hegel and Tillich, then we find that God's self-differentiation as Father, Son, and Spirit in his inner life is bound up with an experience of negativity. Once again, however, I have wanted to make clear that God's sovereign desire is at the centre of this suffering of non-being, as he chooses eternally to open the fellowship of his self-related Being to include a world which produces alienation. Truly, God's suffering is something most alien and most his own, and (as Altizer, following Blake, suggests) this is underlined by a further ironic tragedy about God's relation to non-being; his very humility gives birth, by process of human reaction against it, to the spectre of a dictatorial God, a Nothing, a shadow, who nevertheless represses life for mankind and causes God himself pain. It is as if the tragedy of Judas, whose betrayal was actually prompted by the humble path taken by Jesus, were writ large in the whole of human history.

However, the Christian story is not just that God encounters non-being in his suffering love, but that he conquers it; he negates the negation. E. Jüngel, for example, claims that:

In the death of Jesus Christ God's 'Yes', which constitutes all being, exposed itself to the 'No' of the nothing. In the resurrection of Jesus Christ this 'Yes' prevailed over the 'No' of the nothing. And precisely with this victory it was graciously settled why there is being at all, and not rather nothing.[5]

What kind of sense can we make of this affirmation? Here especially, in thinking of the victory of God over non-being, it seems that we are in danger of remythologizing, or reifying, non-being as a hypostasis which can literally be defeated. In his little book about death, the author of the above quotation rightly insists that we must demythologize 'non-being':

As alien to God, death is aggressive. This is not to be understood mythologically . . . it implies that man poses a threat to himself.[6]

This agrees with our conclusion that non-being has objective reality as something strange that happens in interaction between God and the world. Yet, a little later, Jüngel speaks of a cosmic drama between God

---

[4] This is the theme of ch. 9 above.
[5] Jüngel, *The Doctrine of the Trinity*, p. 108.
[6] Jüngel, *Death*, p. 79, cf. p. 73.

and a personified Death or non-being, which has an effect upon our particular lives:

In God's endurance of death, the being of God and the being of Death encounter one another. It is in and through this encounter that our own being is put in question.[7]

It may be, of course, that as with Aulen's claim for the drama between God and Satan in the Christus Victor theory of the Atonement, there is a power in this poetic symbol which cannot be rationalized.[8] Yet I think we must press on to make it at least a little more reasonable. Karl Barth, we notice, has a similar concern to demythologize, and yet also seems to fall into the making of non-being into a hypostasis when he considers the victory of God over non-being and death in the cross. He argues that the end-point of sinning is non-being (*das Nichtige*), and because only Christ is fully identified with human sinfulness only he goes right to the end of the dark pathway of sin and encounters total non-being there. Non-being takes its prey by engulfing the sinner, so that sin is killed. Thus God uses *das Nichtige* to serve him, wiping out the sin which is an obstacle between man and God.[9] In an ingenious move therefore, God employs the punishment for sin as the means to abolish sin. Then Christ in his resurrection overcomes death and destroys *das Nichtige* since it has no power left now that sin has been eliminated. In killing sin, *das Nichtige* has unwittingly disarmed itself.

Though this is highly satisfying as a drama, with non-being playing the part of the Marlovian anti-hero who overreaches himself, or of the devil as the greedy fish who is caught by the bait of Christ's human nature,[10] it is hard to make rational sense of it. Barth slips too easily from the notion of death's cancelling out a *sinner* to the cancelling out of *sin* altogether. How can our sin be killed in another person? Sin, as a description of our attitudes and responses can only be dealt with in us and in the present. Moreover, non-being itself is not an agent who can

---

[7] Jüngel, op. cit., p. 111.

[8] See Gustav Aulen, *Christus Victor*, trans. A. G. Hebert (SPCK, London, 1931), pp. 174–5.

[9] Barth, *CD* IV/1, pp. 252–5.

[10] Marlowe's theme of 'the betrayer betrayed' is expounded by Harry Levin in *The Overreacher: A Study of Christopher Marlowe* (Faber & Faber, London, 1954); see esp. pp. 41–6, 97–8. The image of the devil's fish-hook is found, for example, in Gregory of Nyssa, *Oratio Catechetica Magna* 24, 26. J. A. T. Robinson suggests that Paul also had the idea that the evil powers defeated themselves in the killing of Christ; see his study *The Body*, pp. 40, 42.

'kill' or be killed. Donne's exultant cry, 'Death thou shalt die'[11] remains a poetic image.

Barth is, nevertheless, surely right to find the centre of the atonement in the cancelling of sin rather than the placating of God's wrath. How then can we talk of God's negating the negative in the act of suffering it? There are perhaps two main answers, and they recall and expand our earlier conclusions about the power of the suffering of God. Because non-being has its objective reality in the interaction between God and the world, its negation can only happen there also. Our answers are bound to be 'subjective' in that they will be a matter of changing human response to God, though this must have an objective basis in the suffering nature of God.

First, to claim that God conquers non-being, or the death which has become an alien power through the fall of creation away from the good, means that God is not destroyed by it when he exposes his being to it. Instead, he uses it to define his own being, and in *this* way makes death serve him. He takes it into himself in the sense that he makes the experience of it a continuing event within his own life. E. Jüngel offers the illustration of certain animals who die when they have emitted all their poison; as a man disables a wasp by taking the sting into his flesh, so God takes the sting of death into himself.[12] We must not be carried away by this picture, however, into forgetting that when we talk about the dying of death, this is not really a statement about death itself but about God and human beings who have to face death. The point is not what has happened to alien death, but what has happened to God in confronting it, in terms of alienation and relationlessness. Such death now belongs to God as 'the death of the living God' (Jüngel's phrase), in the sense that the experience of it leaves a permanent impression upon his life. This means that we cannot think of God except as the one who has experienced death, and we cannot think of death except as the power which could not shatter God. So God uses death to define his being.

Above all God uses the death of Jesus Christ to define himself. As Pannenberg declares, 'If God is revealed through Jesus Christ, then who or what God is becomes defined only through the Christ event',[13] and God reveals himself fully as self-giving love in the cross. This is a

---

[11] 'Death be not proud', Holy Sonnets 6, John Donne, *The Divine Poems*, ed. Helen Gardner, (Clarendon Press, Oxford, 1952), p. 9.

[12] Jüngel, *Death*, p. 112. Cf. 1 Cor. 15: 55.

[13] Pannenberg, *Jesus—God and Man*, p. 140. Also see Jüngel, *God as the Mystery of the World*, pp. 363–4: 'God has defined himself in this dead man.'

definition of God which continues eternally; the words of the Apostle Paul, that 'Christ being raised from the dead will never die again' (Rom. 6: 9) imply, beyond the triumph over death, that the resurrected Jesus is always the Jesus who was crucified. He does not need to die again, because the resurrection of Jesus does not simply cancel the cross, wiping it out as if it were a mistake. If it did, the cross of Jesus would have nothing to say to suffering and dying people; we could not identify ourselves with it, and there would be no Christian tragedy for a tragic world. The resurrection makes the cross of Jesus eternal in the life of God; that is, the particular experience of death which God endured in the death of Jesus is preserved in the life of God just as all experience of the world enriches his being. This is a conquest of death and non-being because the resurrection of Jesus, which is God's vindication and exaltation of his representative, also assures us that the absorption of the effects of death into God has not distorted his being. In the Christian story the risen one remains the crucified one; in the words of the Seer of the Book of Revelation, the lamb in the midst of the throne has the marks of slaughter upon him (Rev. 5: 6).

To say that God overcomes non-being by using it to define his own being does not mean that this definition happens solely in the cross of Jesus. Throughout human history, indeed from the beginning of creation, God has been encountering death and making it serve him. But the depth of alienation God experiences in the death of Jesus, due to the depth of relationship between the Father and this Son, means a corresponding clarity of definition. The most dreadful assault of non-being has become the most articulate word about God. We can speak therefore of a transcendent suffering of God in Christ, which is witnessed to by the way our own language about death has been transformed in the light of the death of Jesus. Our human talk about death has been burst open, or as Barth puts it, 'Revelation has grasped the language'.[14] Jüngel perceptively points to the way that the story of Jesus makes us talk of death in an odd manner, saying for example that we have already 'died with Christ' or that we 'die daily'.[15]

This verbal phenomenon brings us to a second aspect of God's negation of non-being. It means that the permanent impression of death upon God contributes to the life-giving quality of the being of God for his world. As we have seen, we encounter God as the one who

[14] Barth, *CD* I/1, p. 340.
[15] Jüngel, *Death*, p. 85.

participates in our estrangement, and this has a persuasive power, moving us to trust him. In our trust of God, non-being loses its aggressive power over us; death becomes the place where we trust God to preserve our relationships with him and others, rather than being the place of the curse where all relationships are broken. Death is changed in the sense that our perception of it is changed and because we ourselves are changed. The sign of the resurrection of Jesus affirms that God does something new for his creation in the face of the finality of death. He creates new possibilities of life and relationships where, from a human point of view, life has come to an end.

There is, then, no mechanically causal link between God's experience of death and the offering of resurrection life, as if God had literally met and killed an enemy being called 'death'. That would be to remythologize death and non-being. Yet, from another angle, it is true that resurrection happens, overcoming death, *because* death has entered into the being of God. It is true in a compressed sense. If we unpack this affirmation it will be something like this: by responding to the self-giving love displayed in God's encounter with death, we are enabled to co-operate with God in new possibilities for life which he eternally offers to human personalities, in this life and the life to come. So God wins our response to him, the response that nullifies non-being where our lack of response had given it power over us.

Again, we cannot and must not suppose that death only enters into the being of God in the cross of Jesus or that God only overcomes death there. Wherever trust in God is created, death ceases to be the instrument of hostile non-being. But in the cross of Jesus the encounter of God with death reaches its uttermost pitch, and so his suffering becomes most creative and persuasive. Here God goes furthest in speaking his word of acceptance to us, so that his offer can truly be named a 'new covenant', and through the cross he calls out a new word from us to him. In his humility, this is the conversation of the Spirit that God desires and suffers to create.

Bibliography of Works Frequently Cited

Altizer, Thomas J. J., *The Gospel of Christian Atheism* (Collins, London, 1967).
—— *The New Apocalypse: The Radical Christian Vision of William Blake* (Michigan State University Press, 1967).
Aquinas, Thomas, *Summa Theologiae*, Blackfriars Edition (Eyre & Spottiswoode, London, 1964–).
Barth, Karl, *Church Dogmatics*, English Translation, ed. G. W. Bromiley and T. F. Torrance (T. & T. Clark, Edinburgh, 1936–77).
Berdyaev, Nicolas, *Freedom and the Spirit*, trans. O. F. Clarke (Geoffrey Bles, London. ²1935).
—— *Spirit and Reality*, trans. G. Reavey (Geoffrey Bles, London, 1946).
Bonhoeffer, Dietrich, *Letters and Papers from Prison: The Enlarged Edition*, ed. E. Bethge, trans. R. Fuller *et al.* (SCM Press, London, 1967).
Burrell, David B., *Aquinas: God and Action* (Routledge & Kegan Paul, London, 1979).
Cobb, John B., *A Christian Natural Theology: Based on the Thought of Alfred North Whitehead* (Lutterworth Press, London, 1966).
Cobb, J. B., and Griffin, D. R., *Process Theology: An Introductory Exposition* (Christian Journals, Belfast, 1976).
Creel, Richard E., *Divine Impassibility: An Essay in Philosophical Theology* (Cambridge University Press, Cambridge, 1986).
Cupitt, Don, *Taking Leave of God* (SCM Press, London, 1980).
Elphinstone, Andrew, *Freedom, Suffering and Love* (SCM Press, London, 1976).
Ford, Lewis, S. *The Lure of God: A Biblical Background for Process Theism* (Fortress Press, Philadelphia, 1978).
—— (ed.), *Two Process Philosophers* (American Academy of Religion, Tallahassee, Florida, 1973).
Fretheim, Terence E., *The Suffering of God: An Old Testament Perspective* (Fortress Press, Philadelphia, 1984).
Griffin, David R., *God, Power, and Evil: A Process Theodicy* (The Westminster Press, Philadelphia, 1976).
Hamilton, William, *The New Essence of Christianity* (Association Press, New York, 1961).
Hamilton, William and Altizer, Thomas J. J., *Radical Theology and the Death of God* (Penguin Books, Harmondsworth, 1968).
Hartshorne, Charles, *Creative Synthesis and Philosophic Method* (SCM Press, London, 1970).

—— *The Divine Relativity: A Social Conception of God* (Yale University Press, New Haven, 1948, repr. 1976).

—— *The Logic of Perfection* (Open Court, La Salle, Illinois, 1962).

—— *Man's Vision of God, and the Logic of Theism* (1941, repr. Archon Books, Hamden, 1964).

—— *A Natural Theology for our Time* (Open Court, La Salle, Illinois, 1967, repr. 1973).

Hartshorne, Charles, and Reese, William L., *Philosophers Speak of God* (The University of Chicago Press, 1953).

Hegel, G. W. F., *The Christian Religion: Lectures on the Philosophy of Religion. Part 3: The Revelatory, Consummate, Absolute Religion*, ed. and trans. P. Hodgson, based on the edition by George Lasson, American Academy of Religion, Texts and Translations, 2 (Scholars Press, Missoula, 1979).

—— *Early Theological Writings*, trans. T. M. Knox and R. Kroner (University of Pennsylvania Press, Philadelphia, 1948).

—— *The Encyclopaedia of the Philosophical Sciences: Part 1* (The Science of Logic), trans. W. Wallace (Clarendon Press, Oxford, ³1975).

—— *The Phenomenology of Mind*, trans. J. Baillie (George Allen & Unwin, London, 2nd ed. revised, 1949).

—— *The Science of Logic*, Vol. 1, trans. W. H. Johnston and L. G. Struthers (George Allen & Unwin, London, 1929).

Heidegger, Martin, *Being and Time*, trans. J. Macquarrie and E. Robinson (Basil Blackwell, Oxford, 1962).

Heschel, Abraham, J., *The Prophets* (Harper & Row, New York, 1962).

Hick, John, *Evil and the God of Love* (repr. Fontana Library, Collins, London, 1958).

Jüngel, Eberhard, *Death: The Riddle and the Mystery*, trans. I. and U. Nicol (Saint Andrew Press, Edinburgh, 1975).

—— *The Doctrine of the Trinity: God's Being is in Becoming*, trans. H. Harris (Scottish Academic Press, Edinburgh, 1976).

—— *God as the Mystery of the World: On the Foundation of the Theology of the Crucified One in the Dispute Between Theism and Atheism*, trans. D. L. Guder (T. & T. Clark, Edinburgh, 1983).

Kee, Alistair, *The Way of Transcendence: Christian Faith without Belief in God* (Penguin Books, Harmondsworth, 1971).

Kierkegaard, S., *Concluding Unscientific Postscript*, trans. D. F. Swenson and W. Lowrie (Princeton University Press, 1941).

Kitamori, Kazoh, *Theology of the Pain of God*, trans. M. E. Bratcher (SCM Press, London, 1966).

Küng, Hans, *Menschwerdung Gottes: Eine Einführung in Hegels theologisches Denken als Prolegomena zu einer künftigen Christologie* (Herder, Freiburg, 1970).

Lee, Jung Young, *God Suffers for Us: A Systematic Inquiry into a Concept of Divine Passibility* (Martinus Nijhoff, the Hague, 1974).

Mackey, James P, *The Christian Experience of God as Trinity* (SCM Press, London, 1983).

Macquarrie, John, *Christian Hope* (Mowbrays, London and Oxford, 1978).

—— *Principles of Christian Theology*, Revised Edition (SCM Press, London, 1977).

Mascall, E. L., *Existence and Analogy* (Longmans, Green, & Co., London, 1949).

—— *He Who Is: A Study in Traditional Theism* (Longmans, Green, & Co., London, 1945, repr. 1958).

Moltmann, Jürgen, *The Church in the Power of the Spirit: A Contribution to Messianic Ecclesiology*, Trans. M. Kohl (SCM Press, London, 1977).

—— *The Crucified God: The Cross of Christ as the Foundation and Criticism of Christian Theology*, trans. R. A. Wilson and J. Bowden (SCM Press, London, 1974).

—— *The Future of Creation*, trans. M. Kohl (SCM Press, London, 1979).

—— *God in Creation: An Ecological Doctrine of Creation*, the Gifford Lectures 1984–5 (SCM, Press, London, 1985).

—— *Theology and Joy*, trans. R. Ulrich, with an Extended Introduction by David E. Jenkins (SCM Press, London, 1973).

—— *Theology of Hope: on the Ground and Implications of a Christian Eschatology*, trans. J. W. Leitch (SCM Press, London, 1967).

—— *The Trinity and the Kingdom of God: The Doctrine of God*, trans. M. Kohl (SCM, Press, London, 1981).

Mozley, J. K., *The Impassibility of God: A Survey of Christian Thought* (Cambridge University Press, London 1926).

Mühlen, Heribert, *Die abendländische Seinsfrage als der Tod Gottes und der Aufgang einer neuen Gotteserfahrung* (Paderborn, 1968).

—— *Die Veränderlichkeit Gottes als Horizont einer zukünftigen Christologie: Auf dem Wege zu einer Kreuzestheologie in Auseinandersetzung mit der altkirchlichen Christologie* (Aschendorf, Münster, 1969).

Owen, H. P., *Concepts of Deity* (Macmillan, London, 1971).

Pannenberg, Wolfhart, *Jesus—God and Man*, trans. L. L. Wilkins and D. A. Priebe (SCM Press, London, 1968).

Pittenger, Norman, *The Lure of Divine Love: Human Experience and Christian Faith in a Process Perspective* (Pilgrim Press–T. & T. Clark, New York–Edinburgh, 1979).

—— *Process Thought and Christian Faith* (James Nisbet, Welwyn, 1968).

—— *The Word Incarnate: A Study of the Doctrine of the Person of Christ* (Library of Constructive Theology, James Nisbet, Welwyn, 1959).

Rahner, Karl, *The Trinity*, trans. J. Donceel (Burns & Oates, London, 1970).

Robinson, H. Wheeler, *Suffering Human and Divine* (SCM Press, London, 1940).

Robinson, J. A. T., *The Body: A Study in Pauline Theology*, Studies in Biblical Theology, 1 (SCM Press, London, 1952).

Smith, R. Gregor, *The Doctrine of God* (Collins, London, 1970).

Sölle, Dorothee, *Christ the Representative: An Essay in Theology after the 'Death of God'*, trans. D. Lewis (SCM Press, London, 1967).
—— *Suffering*, trans. E. R. Kalin (Darton, Longman & Todd, London, 1975).
Tillich, Paul, *The Courage to Be* (Fontana Library, Collins, London, 1962).
—— *Perspectives on Nineteenth and Twentieth Century Protestant Theology*, ed. C. E. Braaten (SCM Press, London, 1967).
—— *Systematic Theology*, Combined Volume (James Nisbet, London, 1968).
—— *Theology of Culture*, ed. R. C. Kimball (Oxford University Press, New York, 1959).
Von Hügel, Friedrich, *Essays and Addresses on the Philosophy of Religion, Second Series* (J. M. Dent, London, [2]1930).
Ward, Keith, *Holding Fast to God: A Reply to Don Cupitt* (SPCK, London, 1982).
—— *Rational Theology and the Creativity of God* (Basil Blackwell, Oxford, 1982).
Whitehead, A. N., *Adventures of Ideas* (Cambridge University Press, London, 1933, repr. 1939).
—— *Process and Reality: An Essay in Cosmology* (Macmillan, New York, 1929, repr. 1967).
—— *Religion in the Making* (Cambridge University Press, London, 1926).
—— *Science and the Modern World* (The University Press, Cambridge, repr. 1938).
Williams, Daniel Day, *The Spirit and the Forms of Love* (Library of Constructive Theology, James Nisbet, Welwyn, 1968).

Index of Names

Subject Index

260

Printed in the United Kingdom by
Lightning Source UK Ltd., Milton Keynes
140073UK00001B/13/A